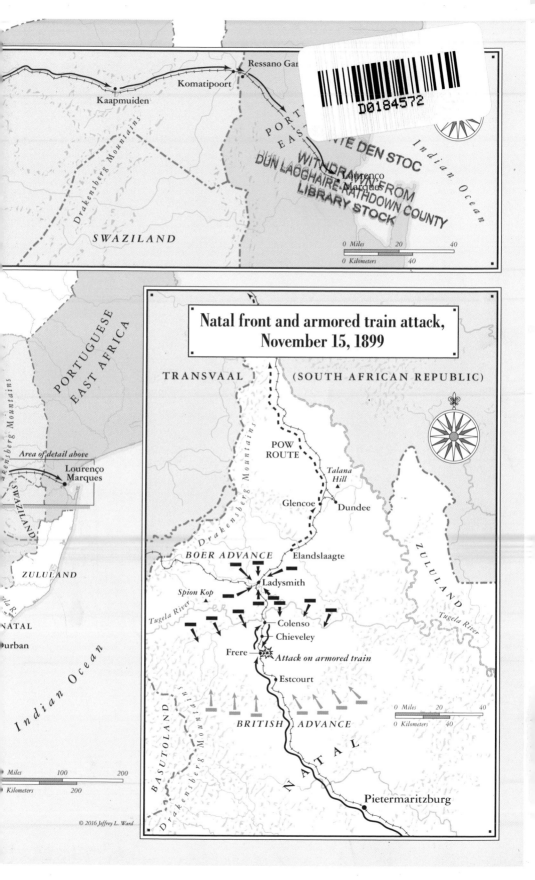

Natal front and armored train attack, November 15, 1899

HERO OF THE EMPIRE

Hero of the Empire

THE MAKING OF WINSTON CHURCHILL

Candice Millard

ALLEN LANE
an imprint of
PENGUIN BOOKS

ALLEN LANE

UK | USA | Canada | Ireland | Australia
India | New Zealand | South Africa

Penguin Books is part of the Penguin Random House group of companies
whose addresses can be found at global.penguinrandomhouse.com.

First published in the United States of America by Doubleday,
a division of Penguin Random House LLC 2016
First published in Great Britain by Allen Lane 2016

002

Text copyright © Candice Millard, 2016

Title page and part opener photograph © SZ Photo/Scherl/Bridgeman Images
Maps designed by Jeffrey L. Ward

The moral right of the author has been asserted

Printed in Great Britain by Clays Ltd, St Ives plc

A CIP catalogue record for this book is available from the British Library

ISBN: 978–0–241–28097–3

For Kelly

CONTENTS

PART THREE

CHANCE

PART FOUR

PRISONERS OF WAR

PART FIVE

IN THE HEART OF THE ENEMY'S COUNTRY

HERO OF THE EMPIRE

◄◄─►►

PROLOGUE

Crouching in darkness outside the prison fence in wartime southern Africa, Winston Churchill could still hear the voices of the guards on the other side. Seizing his chance an hour earlier, the twenty-five-year-old had scaled the high, corrugated-iron paling that enclosed the prison yard. But now he was trapped in a new dilemma. He could not remain where he was. At any moment, he could be discovered and shot by the guards or by the soldiers who patrolled the dark, surrounding streets of Pretoria, the capital of the enemy Boer republic. Yet neither could he run. His hopes for survival depended on two other prisoners, who were still inside the wall. In the long minutes since he had dropped down into the darkness, they had not appeared.

From the moment he had been taken as a prisoner of war, Churchill had dreamed of reclaiming his freedom, hatching scheme after scheme, each more elaborate than the last. In the end, however, the plan that had actually brought him over the fence was not his own. The two other English prisoners had plotted the escape, and agreed only with great reluctance to bring him along. They also carried the provisions that were supposed to sustain all three of them as they tried to cross nearly three hundred miles of enemy territory. Unable even to climb back into his hated captivity, Churchill found himself alone, hiding in the low, ragged shrubs that lined the fence, with no idea what to do next.

→→

Although he was still a very young man, Churchill was no stranger to situations of great personal peril. He had already taken part in four wars on three different continents, and had come close to death in each one. He had felt bullets whistling by his head in Cuba, seen friends hacked to death in British India, been separated from his regiment in the deserts of the Sudan and, just a month earlier, in November 1899, at the start of the Boer War, led the resistance against a devastating attack on an armored train. Several men had died in that attack, blown to pieces by shells and a deafening barrage of bullets, many more had been horribly wounded, and Churchill had barely escaped with his life. To his fury and deep frustration, however, he had not eluded capture. He, along with dozens of British officers and soldiers, had been taken prisoner by the Boers—the tough, largely Dutch-speaking settlers who had been living in southern Africa for centuries and were not about to let the British Empire take their land without a fight.

When the Boers had realized that they had captured the son of Lord Randolph Churchill, a former Chancellor of the Exchequer and a member of the highest ranks of the British aristocracy, they had been thrilled. Churchill had been quickly transported to a POW camp in Pretoria, the Boer capital, where he had been imprisoned with about a hundred other men. Since that day, he had been able to think of nothing but escape, and returning to the war.

The Boer War had turned out to be far more difficult and more devastating than the amusing colonial war the British had expected. Their army, one of the most admired and feared fighting forces in the world, was astonished to find itself struggling to hold its own against a little-known republic on a continent that most Europeans considered to be theirs for the taking. Already, the British had learned more from this war than almost any other. Slowly, they were realizing that they had entered a new age of warfare. The days of gallant young soldiers wearing bright red coats had suddenly disappeared, leaving the vaunted British army to face an invisible enemy with weapons so powerful they could wreak carnage without ever getting close enough to look their victims in the eye.

Long before it was over, the war would also change the empire in another, equally indelible way: It would bring to the attention of a rapt British public a young man named Winston Churchill. Although he had tried again and again, in war after war, to win glory, Churchill had returned home every time without the medals that mattered, no more distinguished or famous than he had been when he set out. The Boer War, he believed, was his best chance to change that, to prove that he was not just the son of a famous man. He was special, even extraordinary, and he was meant not just to fight for his country but one day lead it. Although he believed this without question, he still had to convince everyone else, something he would never be able to do from a POW camp in Pretoria.

→→

When Churchill had scrambled over the prison fence, seizing his chance after a nearby guard had turned his back, he felt elated. Now, as he kneeled in the shrubs just outside, waiting helplessly for the other men, his desperation mounted with each passing minute. Finally, he heard a British voice. Churchill realized with a surge of relief that it was one of his co-conspirators. "It's all up," the man whispered. The guard was suspicious, watching their every move. They could not get out. "Can you get back in?" the other prisoner asked.

Both men knew the answer. As they stood on opposite sides of the fence, one still in captivity, the other achingly close to freedom, it was painfully apparent that Churchill could not undo what had already been done. It would have been impossible for him to climb back into the prison enclosure without being caught, and the punishment for his escape would have been immediate and possibly fatal.

In all the time he had spent thinking about his escape since arriving in Pretoria, the one scenario that Churchill had not envisioned was crossing enemy territory alone without companions or provisions of any kind. He didn't have a weapon, a map, a compass, or, aside from a few bars of chocolate in his pocket, any food. He didn't speak the language, either that of the Boers or that of the Africans. Beyond the vaguest of outlines, he didn't even have a plan—just the unshakable conviction that he was destined for greatness.

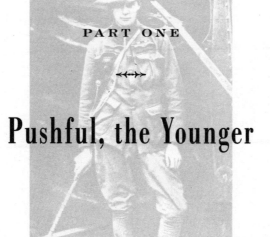

PART ONE

❮❮—❯❯

Pushful, the Younger

CHAPTER 1

DEATH BY INCHES

From earliest childhood, Churchill had been fascinated by war, and dreamed of gallantry in battle. "There is no ambition I cherish so keenly," he had confided to his younger brother, Jack, "as to gain a reputation for personal courage."

As a boy, he had collected a miniature army of fifteen hundred toy soldiers and spent hours sending them into combat. "From very early youth I had brooded about soldiers and war, and often I had imagined in dreams and day-dreams the sensations attendant upon being for the first time under fire," he wrote. "It seemed to my youthful mind that it must be a thrilling and immense experience to hear the whistle of bullets all around and to play at hazard from moment to moment with death and wounds." At Sandhurst, the Royal Military College, from which he had graduated in 1894, Churchill had loved nothing more than to participate in war games, regretting only "that it all had to be make-believe."

To be an aristocratic Englishman in the late nineteenth century meant being surrounded not merely by the lavish benefits of imperial power but by its equally vast responsibilities. Covering more than a fifth of the world's land surface, the British Empire had come to rule about a quarter of the human race—more than 450 million people living on every continent and on the islands of every ocean. It was the largest empire ever known, easily outranking the once mighty Spanish Empire, which had been the original object of the awe-filled description "the empire on which the sun never sets." It was five times the size of the Roman Empire at its zenith, and its influence—over people, language, money, even time, for the clocks in every time zone were set to Greenwich mean time—was unrivaled.

By the time Churchill reached adulthood, the greatest threat to the empire no longer came from the other major powers—Spain, Portugal, Germany or France—but from the ever-expanding burden of ruling its own colonies. Although long the object of admiration, envy and fear, the British army had been stretched impossibly thin as it struggled to keep the empire intact, crisscrossing continents and oceans to put down revolts everywhere from Egypt to Ireland.

To Churchill, such far-flung conflicts offered an irresistible opportunity for personal glory and advancement. When he entered the British army and finally became a soldier, with the real possibility of dying in combat, Churchill's enthusiasm for war did not waver. On the contrary, he had written to his mother that he looked forward to battle "not so much *in spite* of as *because* of the risks I run." What he wanted most from his life as a soldier was not adventure or even battlefield experience but a chance to prove himself. He wanted not simply to fight but to be noticed while fighting.

For a member of Churchill's high social class, such bold, unabashed ambition was a novelty, if not an outright scandal. He had been born a British aristocrat, a direct descendant of John Churchill, the 1st Duke of Marlborough, his parents personal friends of the Prince of Wales, Queen Victoria's oldest son and heir. Yet in his open pursuit of fame and popular favor, Churchill seemed far less Victorian than Rooseveltian. "The immortal Barnum himself had not a greater gift for making himself and his affairs the talk of the world," his first biographer, Alexander MacCallum Scott, would write just a few years later. "Winston advertises himself as simply and unconsciously as he breathes."

In a world in which men were praised not just for their stiff upper lip but for extreme modesty when it came to their own achievements, Churchill was widely criticized for being that most offensive of creatures, the medal hunter. He was called a "self-advertiser," a "young whippersnapper," even, by a reporter for the *Daily Chronicle,* "Pushful, the Younger." He was not unaware of these criticisms and even years later, bewildered by the viciousness with which he was attacked, would admit that it was "melancholy to be forced to record these less amiable aspects of human nature, which by a most curious and indeed unaccountable coincidence have always seemed to present themselves in the wake of my innocent footsteps." He was not, however, about to let them slow him down.

Churchill knew that the surest and quickest route to recognition, success and perhaps, if he was lucky, fame was a military medal. It was "the swift road to promotion and advancement in every arm," he wrote, "the glittering gateway to distinction." Distinction, in turn, could be parlayed into political clout, opening a door onto the kind of public life that he longed for, and which he believed was his destiny. So while the military was not, for Churchill, an end in itself, it was certainly a very useful means to an end. What he needed was a battle, a serious battle, one that would be talked about, would be remembered, and, with a good dose of courage and a little showmanship on his part, might propel him to the forefront of the military stage. For that, he was willing to risk anything, even his life.

➤➤

Churchill had seen real fighting for the first time in 1895. Instead of spending his leave playing polo or foxhunting like most young officers, he had gone to Cuba as a military observer, joining a fighting column of the Spanish army during an uprising that was a prelude to the Spanish-American War. It was here that he began smoking cigars, giving birth to a lifelong habit and a distinct preference for Cubanos. It was also here that on his twenty-first birthday he heard for the first time "bullets strike flesh." In fact, he had very nearly been killed by a bullet that, by the capriciousness of fate, had

sailed just a foot past his head, striking and killing the horse standing next to him. In Cuba, however, he had been only an observer, not
an active participant, and for Churchill that would never be enough.

Churchill's true education in the harsh realities of Britain's colonial wars began the next year, in the remote mountains of British
India's North-West Frontier, modern-day Pakistan, whose sweeping
vistas, unforgiving beauty and lethal conflicts would later suggest
powerful parallels to those of southern Africa. For the British army,
few territories had been as difficult to subdue as India, the jewel in
the empire's crown, and no part of India had proved more deadly for
British soldiers than the tribal lands of the Pashtun, an ethnic group
renowned for their military skill and unyielding resistance to outside
control.

It was, in fact, the Pashtun's unmatched ferocity in battle that
drew Churchill to India, and to the Pashtun heartland known as
Malakand. In October 1896, Churchill had arrived in India with
his regiment, the Fourth Queen's Own Hussars. He had come hoping to find himself quickly at the center of action. Instead, he had
spent month after frustrating month in Bangalore, which he irritably
described to his mother as a "3rd rate watering place."

The incredible luxury in which he lived had made little difference. Left to find their own lodgings, Churchill and two fellow
officers had chosen what Churchill described to his mother as "a
magnificent pink and white stucco palace in the middle of a large
and beautiful garden." They paid for this lavish abode by combining
their salaries, given to them in silver rupees poured into a string net
bag "as big as a prize turnip," with any allowance they managed to
pry from dwindling family fortunes.

Like some of his fellow officers, Churchill came from a family
that was rich in titles and grand estates, but little else. The Churchill
family palace, Blenheim, was, like most great houses in England
at the end of the nineteenth century, hovering on the brink of collapse. The 5th and 6th Dukes of Marlborough had lived lives of
such extravagance that when Churchill's grandfather inherited the
title and the palace, he had been forced to sell not just land but

some of the treasures that the family held most dear. In 1875, when Churchill was not yet a year old, the 7th Duke sold the Marlborough Gems, a stunning assortment of more than 730 carved gemstones, for more than £36,000. A few years later, despite the protestations of his family, he sold the Sunderland Library, a vast and historically significant collection.

The most effective means the Churchills had found of keeping the palace from going under, however, had been to marry the successive dukes off to "dollar princesses," enormously wealthy heiresses whose families longed for an old British title to burnish their new American money. Soon after becoming the 8th Duke, Churchill's uncle George Spencer-Churchill, whose first wife divorced him in the wake of an affair, married a wealthy New York widow named Lillian Warren Hamersley. His son, now the 9th Duke, dutifully followed in his footsteps, marrying a dollar princess of his own, the American railroad heiress Consuelo Vanderbilt, in 1895.

Despite his family's financial failings, Churchill was accustomed to a lavish lifestyle, and he hired a veritable army of servants while in India. "We each have a 'Butler' whose duties are to wait at table—to manage the household and to supervise the stables: A First Dressing Boy or valet who is assisted by a second DB: and a sais [syce] to every horse or pony," Churchill had coolly explained to his mother. "Besides this we share the services of 2 gardeners—3 Bhistis or water carriers—4 Dhobies or washermen & 1 watchman. Such is our ménage."

When a Pashtun revolt began in the mountains of Malakand the next year, Churchill, bored and restless, had been on leave in London, at the world-famous Goodwood Racecourse. It was a perfect day, the racecourse was so beautiful that the Prince of Wales referred to it as a "garden party with racing tacked on," and Churchill was "winning my money." As soon as he learned of the revolt, however, Churchill knew that this was the opportunity he had been waiting for, and he was not about to waste a moment or wait for an invitation.

Quickly scouring the newspapers, Churchill had learned that the military had formed a field force of three brigades to send to

the front, and as luck would have it, its commander was a friend of
his mother: the Dickensian-named Sir Bindon Blood. Having anticipated just such a turn of events, Churchill had, a year earlier, cul-
tivated a friendship with Blood himself and had extracted from the
major general a promise to take him along if he were ever in command of a regiment on the Indian frontier.

Churchill had never had any qualms about pulling every string
he had. "I am certainly not one of those who need to be prodded," he
would admit years later in a speech to the House of Commons. "In
fact, if anything, I am a prod." Over the years, he would often turn to
his American mother, a renowned beauty who had many admirers in
high-ranking positions, to help him get appointments. "In my interest she left no wire unpulled," Churchill wrote, "no stone unturned,
no cutlet uncooked."

Racing to the nearest telegraph, Churchill had sent Blood a telegram, reminding him of his promise, and then, without waiting to
hear back, set sail for India. "Having realized, that if a British cavalry
officer waits till he is ordered on active service, he is likely to wait
a considerable time," he later wrote, "I obtained six weeks' leave of
absence from my regiment . . . in the hope of being sooner or later
attached to the force in a military capacity."

Churchill had not heard back from Blood until he reached
Bombay, where he found waiting for him a less than encouraging
telegram. "Very difficult; no vacancies," Blood had written hastily.
"Come up as a correspondent; will try to fit you in." Churchill, however, did not need encouragement. He only needed a chance. After
swiftly securing assignments as a journalist with the *Pioneer* newspaper and the *Daily Telegraph,* he had made his way by rail across the
two thousand miles that stretched between Bangalore and Malakand
in just five days.

➤➤

On September 15, 1897, as the mountain sky darkened and the
cold night fell, Churchill lowered himself into a makeshift trench

he had dug in the rocky soil of Malakand. The trench was a critical defense against enemy snipers in the surrounding mountainsides, but as the dry gray dust sifted onto Churchill's khaki uniform, leather boots and pale hands, it seemed as though he were not settling in for the night but fitting himself for his own shallow grave. The fact that he was wrapped in a dead man's blanket—bought just weeks earlier from the possessions of a British soldier killed in these same mountains—only seemed to complete the ominous tableau.

Everywhere Churchill looked, death, or the imminent threat of it, pressed in on him from the frigid, dark peaks of the Hindu Kush. Malakand, he would later write, was like an enormous cup, with his camp, Inayat Kila, at the bottom and a jagged rim of rocks looming above. The giant black walls of the mountains closed around him, glittering with the menacing campfires of hundreds of enemy Pashtun tribesmen—the "hell fiends" he had come to fight.

Crouching silently in their twisted turbans and pale, loose shirts, with heavy bandoliers of ammunition across their shoulders, the Pashtun themselves were invisible in the dark. The largest and most feared tribal group in Afghanistan, they had for centuries dominated not just Malakand but the entire Hindu Kush, a massive, five-hundred-mile-long mountain system that separated central and south Asia. They knew every jagged, rain-carved crevice, every barren hillock, every bullet-pocked boulder. This was their land, and ever since it had been divided by the separation of Afghanistan and British India four years earlier, they had held a particular hatred for the British Empire and its soldiers. As a Pashtun proverb put it, "You should always kill an Englishman."

Now, in the midst of their rebellion, the Pashtun warriors prepared to do just that, gripping their long, elaborately decorated rifles, training their sights on anyone brave or foolish enough to light a match or lift his head above the sanctuary of a trench. Even before the percussion of the Pashtun weapons reached them across the thin night air, the British could hear the bullets striking around them, ringing against rocks, kicking up geysers of dust and, too often, drawing a shriek of agony. The night before, the Pashtun had killed forty men in a nearby camp with astonishing accuracy, shooting one man through the heart and another through the head, dropping him like a stone as the bullet shattered his skull.

Even more frightening than the Pashtun's long-range marksmanship was the ferocity with which they fought hand to hand, face-to-face. To British soldiers, who were themselves renowned for their courage, the Pashtun seemed terrifyingly heedless of their own safety, or even survival. They fought when they had no chance of winning, when they were alone on the battlefield, when they had been shot and speared and bayoneted. "Careless of what injury they may receive," Churchill observed in awe, "they devote themselves to the destruction of their opponent."

Unflinching in the face of their own suffering, the Pashtun were merciless when it came to the enemy's. They did not just kill but slaughtered, slicing men's bodies to ribbons with their long, curved swords. "Death by inches and hideous mutilation," Churchill wrote, "are the invariable measure meted out to all who fall in battle into the hands of the Pathan tribesmen." Just a few days later, he would watch, shocked and sickened, as the body of one of his friends was carried away after it had been "literally cut to pieces" by the Pashtun.

Long after night had descended completely, obscuring everything before him but watch fires and the occasional dull gleam of a bayonet, Churchill, unable to sleep, peered intently at the stars overhead. As he listened to nearby soldiers tensely coughing and shifting in their trenches, yearning for the night to end, he contemplated "those impartial stars, which shine as calmly on Piccadilly Circus as on Inayat Kila." Bindon Blood had ordered the men to march into the mountains the next morning, burning homes and crops and destroying water reservoirs. Reveille would sound at 5:30, and the Pashtun, they knew, would be waiting.

→→

When the soldiers and officers of Blood's brigade climbed out of their trenches on the morning of September 16, not one of them could be sure he would live to nightfall. Whatever unspoken thoughts they might have harbored of home or even the relative safety of their trenches, however, they had little choice but to face the Pashtun. Among them, only Churchill could have turned around and left at any moment, and he had no intention of going anywhere but into battle.

Buttoning a padded cloth onto the back of his uniform to protect his spine, straightening the chain-mail epaulets on his jacket, meant to shield him against the slash of a sword, and adjusting his khaki-covered cork pith helmet, Churchill knew that many of the young men surrounding him would perform acts of striking heroism on the battlefield that day. He also knew that very few of them would be seen or, if seen, remembered. Where his own future was at stake, he was determined to even the odds.

As Blood divided his thousand men into three columns, Churchill quickly attached himself to the center column, a squadron of Bengal Lancers that was headed deep into the valley on a mission of destruction guaranteed to provoke the Pashtun, and to give Churchill plenty of opportunity for conspicuous bravery. The squadron, however, also appealed to him for another reason: It was part of a cavalry regiment, which allowed him to do something that, although it stunned every man in the brigade, would guarantee that he, at least, would not be forgotten. Gripping the side of his saddle, he swung a leg, wrapped in leather from his riding breeches to his boot, over the back of a gray pony.

Churchill had acquired the pony on his way to Malakand, at the same auction in which he had bought his blanket from the effects of a young soldier killed in battle. His plan, he would later tell his brother, was to ride "about trying to attract attention when things looked a little dangerous," hoping that his "good grey pony" would catch someone's eye. Although it was much more likely to catch the eye of a Pashtun tribesman who would kill him before anyone had an opportunity to admire his courage, Churchill was willing to take that chance. "The boy seemed to look out for danger," an article in *Harper's* magazine would later marvel. "He rode on a white pony, the most conspicuous of all marks, and all the prayers of his friends could not make him give it up for a safer beast."

Churchill understood that he could very easily be killed in the battle that lay before him, but he did not for a moment believe that he would be. "I have faith in my star," he had written to his mother just days earlier. "That I am intended to do something in the world." In fact, soon after arriving in India, he had told a fellow officer that not only did he plan to leave the military soon for a seat in Parliament but he expected to be prime minister one day.

As he rode out with the cavalry on his gray charger, like a bright fish in a sea of khaki and brown, Churchill took great satisfaction in the knowledge that, if nothing else, he would be impossible to miss.

→→

What struck Churchill most forcefully that morning as he entered the valley, cloaked in the mountains' deep shadows, was the pervading silence. Every village the cavalry passed was deserted, all the plains empty. The men knew that thousands of Pashtun were watching as they rode farther and farther from camp, but they could neither see nor hear them. It was not until Churchill pulled out his telescope and scanned the mountains where the watch fires had burned the night before that he could see, covering the terraced sides, long white rows of Pashtun.

As the cavalry came closer, the tribesmen silently turned and began to scale the mountainside. Stopping at a small cemetery, the British dismounted and, unable to bear the tension any longer, opened fire. The response was immediate. Puffs of white smoke erupted on the mountain, and the sound of bullets whistling through the air filled the cemetery. While the rest of the men dived behind trees and rough tombstones, however, Churchill, sensing an opportunity and the eyes of the other officers, refused even to dismount. "I rode on my grey pony all along the front of the skirmish line where everyone else was lying down in cover," he would later confess. "Foolish perhaps, but given an audience there is no act too daring or too noble. Without the gallery things are different."

The skirmish, which was relatively brief and bloodless, seemed to make the men in Churchill's unit forget who they were fighting. Before climbing deeper into the mountains, on the trail of the Pashtun, therefore, they divided again. Reluctantly leaving his pony behind, Churchill joined a group of just ninety men who were headed toward an isolated village, which, when they reached its small collection of mud houses, they found, like all the others, completely deserted.

On the way up, Churchill had stopped to squint through his telescope, scanning the mountains and plains for the rest of the army. Memories of his days at Sandhurst and the repeated warnings of his professors about the danger of "dispersion of forces" slipped through his mind as he searched without luck for the thousand men with whom he had left camp that morning. "Mud villages and castles here and there, the deep-cut water-courses, the gleam of reservoirs, occasional belts of cultivation, isolated groves of trees," he wrote, "but of a British-Indian brigade, no sign." The entire region, in fact, was unnaturally, almost eerily still, with neither friend nor enemy in sight.

Although Churchill had spent much of his young life thinking about war, until this moment it had all been supposition. He had never been the intended target of a sword or bayonet, and he did not know what it felt like to try to kill another man. Young, eager and desperate for adventure and opportunity, it all seemed to him little more than a game. "This kind of war was full of fascinating thrills," he would later admit. "Nobody expected to be killed." This, at last, was a real battle, and he wanted nothing more than to charge into it, launching his own thin body, fresh from childhood, into the knives and swords, rocks and bullets of the enemies of the empire.

As Churchill stared intently at the silent, apparently empty hills around him, it seemed as though the chance he had been waiting for might not come after all. The captain of his small unit, however, sensed something different. Realizing that he and his men were "rather in the air here," and as such extraordinarily vulnerable, he ordered them to withdraw. Before they could even begin to retrace their steps, the mountainside, in Churchill's words, "sprang to life."

"Now suddenly," Churchill wrote, "black tragedy burst upon the scene." Seemingly materializing from the stones of the mountain, Pashtun tribesmen descended on the tiny village from all directions. Everywhere the stunned British soldiers looked, Pashtun were leaping from cover, letting out sharp, shrill cries as they raced in a terrifying frenzy toward their enemy. "From high up on the crag, one thousand, two thousand, three thousand feet above us," Churchill would later recall, "white or blue figures appeared, dropping down the mountainside from ledge to ledge."

Before Churchill could fully understand what was happening, young men, friends and fellow soldiers, were dying all around him. It was a scene that, even after a long and war-strewn life, he would never forget. "One man was shot through the breast and pouring with blood, another lay on his back kicking and twisting," he would write years later. "The British officer was spinning round just behind me, his face a mass of blood, his right eye cut out." The war cries of the Pashtun were punctuated by the high-pitched screams of even the bravest young soldiers as they were butchered beyond recognition.

Turning, Churchill watched in outrage and fury as a dozen Pashtun fell upon a wounded British soldier when the men who had been desperately trying to rescue him dropped him in their frantic race to cover. The man who Churchill believed was the leader of the tribesmen stood over the fallen soldier and repeatedly slashed at him with his sword. "I forgot everything else at this moment," Churchill would write, "except a desire to kill this man." Pulling out his revolver, he fired into the melee—again and again and again. "It was a horrible business. For there was no help for the man that went down. I felt no excitement and very little fear," he would later write home. "I cannot be certain, but I think I hit 4 men. At any rate they fell."

Churchill would never know how many men he killed that day before help came in the form of a relief column, or if any had fallen by his hand, but even as he looked down on the mutilated bodies all around him, the bodies of men he knew, men very much like him, he knew that he would not share their fate. He was meant to live, of that he was certain. More than that, he was meant to do something great with his life, and he was eager to take the next step in what he was confident would be a remarkable and dizzyingly fast ascension. "Bullets—to a philosopher my dear Mamma—are not worth considering," he would assure his mother in a pencil-written letter from Bangalore two months later, after the siege of Malakand had been lifted and the Pashtun forced to retreat. "I do not believe the Gods would create so potent a being as myself for so prosaic an ending."

CHAPTER 2

THE GRAVEN PALM

For Churchill, it was not enough to believe that power and fame would come eventually. As soon as the New Year, 1898, began, he set his sights on realizing not one daunting ambition but three, daring the world to ignore him. He published his first book, *The Story of the Malakand Field Force*, began agitating for an assignment to fight in the Sudan, and made it clear to anyone who would listen that despite his youth he was not only eager to begin his political career but eminently qualified to do so. "I am somewhat impatient of advice as to my beginning in politics," he complained to his mother soon after returning from Malakand. "If I am not good enough—others are welcome to take my place. . . . Of course—as you have known for some time—I believe in myself. If I did not I might perhaps take other views."

Convinced that another war, and another opportunity for heroism, would be of use in his political life, Churchill recruited no less than the prime minister of Great Britain to help him win an assignment in the Sudan, where the British were trying to wrest power from the Mahdists, followers of the Muslim leader Al-Mahdī. He set sail for Africa before the Indian army had even granted his leave. What he witnessed there would leave a lasting mark. He described the campaign in *The River War,* the book he would publish the following year. Even years later he described a nightmarish scene of death and dismemberment, with "horses spouting blood, struggling on three legs, men staggering on foot . . . fish-hook spears stuck right through them, arms and faces cut to pieces, bowels protruding, men gasping, crying, collapsing, expiring." Churchill himself shot and likely killed half a dozen men, one of whom was so close to him that the pistol itself struck the man as Churchill galloped by. In fact, although the British ultimately prevailed, so horrific was the campaign that even for Churchill war was finally beginning to lose a little of its gallant gleam. "You cannot gild it," he wrote to his mother from Khartoum. "The raw comes through."

As sobering as Churchill had found the carnage he witnessed in the Sudan, his faith in himself and his future had not for a moment been shaken. On the contrary, he was acutely aware of the fact that once again he had forced his way into the deadliest colonial battle the British Empire had to offer, watched as men all around him were killed and horribly wounded, and emerged not just alive but whole. "Nothing touched me," he calmly wrote just two days after the Battle of Omdurman, in which the British had lost five hundred men to death and injury and the Mahdists twenty thousand. "I destroyed those who molested me and so passed out without any disturbance of body or mind."

Churchill believed that, whatever had kept him alive on the battlefield, whether divine intervention or simply good fortune, his luck had been "set fair," and he was eager to test its indulgence. "On what do these things depend," he mused as a train carried him home. "Chance-Providence-God-the-Devil—call it what you will. . . . Whatever it may be—I do not complain."

Nor did he hesitate. As 1898 came to an end, so did Churchill's career as a soldier. Although he was in considerable debt, had not been trained for any other occupation and had been warned against leaving the army by everyone from his formidable grandmother, the Duchess of Marlborough, to the Prince of Wales, he resigned his commission in the British army early in the New Year. "I have sent my papers in and in three months more I shall not be a soldier," he wrote to his cousin Sunny Marlborough in the first weeks of 1899, confessing, in a rare admission of uncertainty, that he knew he was taking a very great risk. "It is not without some misgivings that I let go of my tow rope," he wrote, "and commit myself unaided to the waves of life's oceans, propelled only by my own machinery." He would not have to tread water for long.

→→

In early April, when the spring rains lashing London's cobble-stoned streets still had the bite of winter, Churchill approached the entrance to the House of Commons, a wide, Gothic archway cut into the imposing stone face of the Palace of Westminster. Looming hundreds of feet above him, its reflection wavering in the ruffled surface of the river Thames, was the Clock Tower, one of the most immediately recognizable architectural structures in the world. The tower, which was only fifteen years older than Churchill himself, was famous not just for its Great Clock but for its nearly fourteen-ton bell, nicknamed Big Ben, most likely in honor of Ben Caunt, a six-foot-two-inch, two-hundred-pound bare-knuckle boxer who had been the heavyweight champion of England in 1841.

As Churchill stepped into the shadow of Big Ben, he knew that waiting for him in the cool, hushed interior of the House of Commons was a man who could open the doors to this iconic seat of political power. One of two members of Parliament for the town of Oldham in the northwest of England, Robert Ascroft, with his graying hair, full, dark mustache, and fine features, not only looked more substantial and respectable than his young visitor but seemed to be the embodiment of old-world dignity. As he led Churchill through the dimly lit halls and down the narrow stairs to the members-only smoking room, Ascroft had a gravitas that Churchill, with his feverish ambition and blatant self-promotion, did not yet have, but that they both hoped he could do without.

Despite Churchill's youthful energy and awkwardness, when he stepped through the heavy doors that led into the smoking room, he easily slipped into a world that most Britons not only would never see but could not even fully imagine. Although this was the House of Commons, more than half its members came from the British aristocracy. To most young men, the room alone, with its soaring ceilings, paneled walls, casually scattered chess tables and curved wooden chairs upholstered in rich leather and tarnished brass tacks, would be imposing, even awe inspiring. For Churchill, it was, in reputation at least, as familiar as his own childhood. Although this was not yet his world, it had long been his father's.

→→

Lord Randolph Churchill, the brilliant, talented and arrogant third son of the 7th Duke of Marlborough, had had an extraordinary political career, made even more remarkable by the fact that he had lived to be only forty-five years old. He had won his first seat in Parliament in 1874, the same year in which he had married an American beauty named Jennie Jerome and his first child, Winston, had been born. By the time he was thirty-six, he was secretary of state for India. A year later, the prime minister, Lord Salisbury, appointed him leader of the House of Commons and Chancellor of the Exchequer, just one position below Salisbury himself.

Although Churchill had never had the close relationship with his father that he longed for, he had been fiercely proud of Lord Randolph's public position and had dreamed of one day becoming, if not a trusted adviser, at least a help to him in his meteoric career. "To me," Churchill would write years later, "he seemed to own the key to everything or almost everything worth having." He would never forget walking down the street as a child and watching as men doffed their hats in respect as his father passed by. He scanned the papers, hungrily reading every mention of Lord Randolph's name, every quotation from his speeches, every word of criticism or admiration. "Everything he said even at the tiniest bazaar was reported verbatim in all the newspapers," Churchill would proudly recall, "every phrase

being scrutinized and weighed." When at Harrow, the public school
he attended as a boy, Churchill had repeatedly begged his mother to
send him not just his father's autographs but even her own so that he
could give, or perhaps sell, them to his classmates.

Lord Randolph's career, however, had been as brief as it was blazing. "The darling of democracy," one contemporary writer called him,
"a wayward genius who flashed across the political firmament like a
dazzling meteor burning himself out too soon." Famously outspo-
ken and sharp-tongued, he had, from the beginning of his tenure as
Chancellor of the Exchequer, publicly and unapologetically disagreed
with many of the other members of Lord Salisbury's administration.
When his first budget was rejected, Randolph, in a cold rage, had
written Salisbury a letter of resignation, confident that it would not
be accepted. It was.

Years later, Churchill's mother could still vividly recall her own
horror and that of Randolph's private secretary, A. W. Moore, when
they realized what he had done. "Mr. Moore, who was devoted to
Randolph, rushed in, pale and anxious," she wrote, "and with a falter-
ing voice said to me, 'He has thrown himself from the top of the ladder.'" Not only would Randolph never rise again, he would die eight
years later following a long, frightening and excruciatingly public
mental decline.

Although the memory of Lord Randolph still haunted the
House of Commons, lingering in every spiral of smoke, scribbled
note and murmured comment, it was his son who now had Ascroft's
full attention. He had invited Churchill there to ask him a question
that could greatly affect both of their political careers. The city of
Oldham would be holding a by-election that summer, and Ascroft's
counterpart, James Oswald, who was sixty years old and had long
been chronically ill and conspicuously absent, had made it clear that
he would not be seeking reelection. Ascroft was, he told Churchill,
"on the look-out for someone to run in double harness with him."
Would he like to join the race?

➤➤

The only barrier now between Churchill and his place on the Conservative ticket was a trial speech, which Ascroft suggested he give in Oldham before the campaign began in earnest. Then a final decision would be made. It was a reasonable and customary formality, but for Churchill the uncertainty was almost unbearable.

It went against every instinct Churchill had to sit still and wait to be called to the test. Desperate to do something, he decided that although he had faith in his star, it couldn't hurt to peer into the misty future to make sure it was still shining. He was not without connections in this unusual area of expertise. The year before, his American aunt Leonie Jerome had taken him to a mysterious little house on Wimpole Street in the West End of London, just one block from the lushly green and stubbornly round Cavendish Square. This was home, at least temporarily, to Mrs. Charlotte Robinson, arguably the most famous palm reader of her day.

Although the Victorian era is most often associated with scientific progress—the establishment of scientific principles, the advancement of medicine, the development of railroads, steamships, telephones and radios, even the publication of Charles Darwin's *On the Origin of Species*—it was also a time of growing interest and belief in mysticism. Attempting to look into the future and to make contact with the spiritual world was considered a serious pursuit by everyone from Sir Arthur Conan Doyle to the editors of the prestigious magazine *Scientific American,* who sponsored a contest among mediums to see who could show "conclusive psychic manifestations." Even Queen Victoria and her husband, Prince Albert, had taken part in séances, and when Albert died in 1861 of typhoid fever, the queen had invited to Windsor Castle a thirteen-year-old boy who claimed the prince had sent her a message through him during a family séance.

Churchill's chosen palmist, Mrs. Robinson, had risen to fame largely because one of her most devoted clients also happened to be one of England's best-known and most infamous authors: Oscar Wilde. Robinson had told Wilde, who was already famous for his controversial and only novel, *The Picture of Dorian Gray,* that he would "write four plays, and then you will disappear. I cannot see you at all after that." After this prophecy, between the years 1892 and 1895, Wilde wrote *Lady Windermere's Fan, A Woman of No Importance, An Ideal Husband* and *The Importance of Being Earnest,* all of which were enormous theatrical successes. In April 1895, just two months after his last play debuted at the St. James's Theatre in London, Wilde was arrested and later convicted of "gross indecency" for his affair with Lord Alfred Douglas and sentenced to two years' hard labor. He died three years after leaving prison, having written, as Mrs. Robinson foretold, no other plays.

In the wake of Wilde's conviction, Robinson gained a power and prestige that set her apart from even the most celebrated palmists. She charged exorbitant rates, "expecting four guineas for the first visit, two for the second, and ten if she writes down her prognostication," one contemporary newspaper marveled, and refused to appear at parties or private homes, demanding that even her most exalted clients come to her. She had even begun to write a book, *The Graven Palm,* which would become the standard for palmistry in its day.

Unlike her predictions for Oscar Wilde, Mrs. Robinson saw in Winston Churchill's pale young palm so extraordinary a future that she wanted to describe it in her book. In early May 1899, soon after taking leave of Robert Ascroft in the House of Commons smoking room, Churchill sent Mrs. Robinson a check for £2 2s., presumably in payment for a second, more recent session, and wrote in a letter labeled "Private" that he wished to take the opportunity to compliment her on her "strange skill in Palmistry." Three days later, he wrote to her again, turning down her request to tell his story in her book, explaining that he "would rather not have my hand published to the world," but confessing that he was impressed by what she had told him. "I trust," he wrote cheerfully, "you may be right in your forecast."

➤➤

Churchill's rise to prominence was to begin even sooner than he, and perhaps Mrs. Robinson, had predicted. Just a few weeks after

Churchill dropped his letter in the mail, the town of Oldham, in a stunning turn of events, lost one of its representatives to sudden death. It was not, however, the aged and feeble James Oswald, who had long appeared to be at death's door, but his robust and charismatic partner, Robert Ascroft. Stricken with pneumonia on June 12, Ascroft quickly fell into a semiconscious state. By the eighteenth, his doctors acknowledged that there was "very little hope," and by the nineteenth he was dead.

There was less than a month before the election, and the Conservative Party now needed not one candidate but two. The trial speech was forgotten, and Churchill was on the ticket, whether he was ready or not. In his own mind, of course, he was more than ready. He was chomping at the bit. "There is no doubt," he wrote to his mother, "that if anyone can win this seat I can."

CHAPTER 3

THE SCION

A few days after Robert Ascroft's death, Churchill arrived in Oldham for the first time in his life. Although the town held none of
the glitter of London or the mystery of Bangalore, it was gritty and
real, and, in its own way, powerful. Founded in the Middle Ages,
Oldham had transformed during the Industrial Revolution from
a tiny, thin-soiled hamlet good for little more than grazing sheep
to a powerhouse of the textile industry, widely recognized as the
cotton-spinning capital of the world. "If ever the Industrial Revolution placed a town firmly and squarely on the map of the world," a
local historian would declare some seventy years later, "that town is
Oldham."

Churchill, however, was in Oldham for only one reason: to win
an election. His first speech there was to be given at the most impressive building in town, the Theatre Royal. Rebuilt after a fire had
burned it to the ground twenty years earlier, the theater, a four-
story redbrick building, was now perched somewhat awkwardly on
Horsedge, a precariously steep cobblestoned street in the middle of
town. Its massive front doors, however, flanked by two ornate pillars,
its keystone inset with a carved bust of William Shakespeare, opened
onto a lavish, Italianate hall.

Inside, three horseshoe-shaped galleries faced the curtained stage, stacked one on top of another and held up by ten Corinthian columns. Although the lower galleries were ostentatiously decorated, the third was noticeably more modest, and the fourth, just visible beneath a large chandelier that hung from the arched ceiling, did not even have seats, only wooden steps on which the audience stood. Every row, from the first to the fourth, was completely filled for the night's event. In fact, so great was the interest that even in this cavernous hall there was not enough room to accommodate everyone, and hundreds of people had to be turned away.

→→

Churchill's life on the public stage had begun just a few months earlier, when he gave his first political speech before he had even become a politician. While visiting the Conservative Party headquarters in London, he had spotted a book with a white label that read, in words that had filled him with the thrill of possibility, "SPEAKERS WANTED." Scanning the pages "with the eye of an urchin looking through a pastrycook's window," he had alighted upon an opportunity in Bath, speaking to the Primrose League. Although he had given that speech on a platform made of four boards precariously balanced over a row of barrels, he had immediately been hooked. For Churchill, few things in life could compete with the thrill of climbing onto a stage, stepping behind a podium and commanding the attention of every man in the room.

As much as he loved public speaking, it did not come naturally to him. To begin with, he had a speech impediment that had plagued him since childhood. Unable to pronounce the letter *s*, he had practiced over and over the sibilant sentence "The Spanish ships I cannot see for they are not in sight." Before leaving for India, he had turned for help to a family friend, Sir Felix Semon, who was a renowned throat specialist. Semon had assured him that he did not have a physical deformation and should be able to overcome the problem with "practice and perseverance."

Instead, Churchill slowly came not only to accept but even value his distinctive way of speaking. A number of men whom he admired, from the Prince of Wales to the prince's close friend Colonel John Palmer Brabazon, could not pronounce the letter *r,* a defect that, because of the Prince of Wales, was considered fashionable in many circles. Churchill would admiringly recall Brabazon shouting, "Where is the London twain?" and, when told that it had already left, demanding haughtily, "Gone! Bwing another."

Although he would become famous for his sharp wit, Churchill was also uncomfortable addressing an audience unless he had carefully written and exhaustively rehearsed every line of his speech. Unlike his father, who was famous for his long, witheringly eloquent extemporaneous speeches, Winston spent hours preparing for every formal lecture or even brief remarks, and would do so throughout his life. His close friend Frederick Edwin Smith, 1st Earl of Birkenhead, would later joke that "Winston has spent the best years of his life composing his impromptu speeches."

Neither his speech impediment, however, nor the long nights spent writing and rehearsing had dimmed Churchill's delight in campaigning, or his confidence that he could captivate any crowd. "Personally I am very popular here," he wrote unselfconsciously to his cousin Sunny early in the campaign. "I am always received with the greatest enthusiasm."

Nor did it take Churchill long to realize that he had something more than just personal charm at the podium. Not only was he a uniquely talented orator, but even at just twenty-three years of age it was clear to him that he had the potential to become a great one, perhaps one of the greatest. "I improve every time," he would write to a friend just before the election, strikingly aware of what the future might hold. "At each meeting I am conscious of growing powers."

On the night of Churchill's first speech in Oldham, among the many faces in the crowded, darkened theater was one that he had only begun to recognize—that of his running mate, James Mawdsley. Mawdsley, bearded, balding and fifty-one years old, was as different from Winston Churchill as it was possible to be. The father of seven children, he had been born a cotton spinner's son and had worked in a cotton mill himself from the time he was nine years old. Mawdsley knew firsthand what it meant to be a member of the working class in Victorian England and had been politically active for decades, serving as chairman of the Trades Union Congress and holding the position of general secretary of the Amalgamated Association of Operative Cotton Spinners since 1878, when Churchill was four years old.

The press, thrilled with this odd pairing, had christened Churchill and Mawdsley "the Scion and the Socialist," a nickname that embarrassed Churchill not at all. Although, of the two, Mawdsley was the only one with any actual political experience, Churchill was not shy about what he believed to be his own contributions to their candidacy. Mawdsley, he would later write, "was proud to stand upon the platform with a 'scion' of the ancient British aristocracy." Not surprisingly, the newspapers often saw things differently. "We shall see throughout the contest," predicted the *Manchester Evening News,* "Mr. Churchill, who as a politician is hardly out of his swaddling clothes, pushed to the fore in order that Mr. Mawdsley may be able to carry him into Parliament."

The audience at the Theatre Royal, however, which was made up almost entirely of cotton spinners and textile workers, did not seem to mind that they had in their midst a young man whose life had been nothing like their own. When Churchill, who was the first to speak, took the stage, it was to the sound of raucous cheers. As he began to speak, his carefully prepared notes before him, his hands either placed confidently on both hips or raised in the air to emphasize a point, he found that the audience was not just willing to listen but was an enthusiastic and active participant in his speech. "Throughout he was listened to with the closest attention," a reporter from the *Morning Post* would write, "the only interruptions being those of hearty spontaneous applause, or the interjections of the delighted auditors. . . . 'That's plain speaking,' shouted a stentorian voice, 'we understand that, and we like it.'"

Although Churchill's speech lasted nearly an hour and covered everything from workingmen's compensation to the future of imperialism, making the argument that England without a navy "would be like Oldham with all its tall chimneys broken, all its furnaces cold, all its factories deserted," the audience's interest never waned. Nor did its enthusiasm for this young patrician, this scion of the British aristocracy. He has "a touch of mysticism that attracts the mob," a writer for *Harper's New Monthly Magazine* would write the following year. "A born orator, with power to move people as he wills, Winston Spencer Churchill must go far."

The men and women of Oldham heartily agreed. By the end of the night, the town's alderman would invite the audience to "recognize in Mr. Winston Spencer Churchill a Statesman of the future." An audience member, perhaps seeing in Churchill's speech what Mrs. Robinson saw in his palm, went even further. "We have, I do believe, if God should spare his life," he predicted, "the future Premier of England."

➤➤

Although Churchill was quick to believe every good thing ever said about his potential, he wasn't willing to leave anything to chance. On Election Day, therefore, he used his most powerful political weapon: his mother.

Unlike his opponents, the middle-aged Alfred Emmott and Walter Runciman, Churchill did not have a wife to help him campaign. He had something better—a highly unusual, uniquely powerful mother; and he did not hesitate to use guilt, flattery or any power at his disposal to persuade her to help him. "Mrs. Runciman goes everywhere with her husband and it is thought that this is of value to him," he had written to her on July 2, just four days before the election. "How much more!—but you will complete the sentence for yourself."

Churchill's mother, Jennie, was many things, each of them more appealing or shocking, depending on the point of view, than the last, but she was never boring. Blindingly beautiful, with thick black hair and porcelain skin, she was said to be part Native American, the great-granddaughter of a woman who had been raped by an Iroquois. She moved with an assurance and sensuality that made her an irresistible force to nearly every man she met, and a threat to every woman. Lord D'Abernon, the British ambassador to Berlin, would write years later that Jennie had "more of the panther than of the woman in her look." Recalling her as she looked the first time he saw her, in Dublin not long after her marriage to Randolph Churchill, he described her in almost reverent tones as "a dark, lithe figure, standing somewhat apart and appearing to be of another texture to those around her, radiant, translucent, intense."

The daughter of the American financier and speculator Leonard Jerome, Jennie had spent a privileged childhood in Brooklyn until the age of fifteen, when her mother, who had had enough of her husband's serial infidelities, had moved to France, taking her three daughters with her. Even though Jerome, who had founded the American Jockey Club and briefly co-owned the *New York Times,* was famous for his flamboyant and conspicuous consumption, he had lost as many fortunes as he had made and could offer his daughters very little in the way of a dowry. He had, moreover, the type of reputation that made Americans take notice and Britons take flight.

None of that had mattered to Randolph Churchill, however, the first time he laid eyes on Jennie. He had been in the middle of a conversation with the Prince of Wales during a ball aboard the royal yacht HMS *Ariadne* when Jennie, nineteen years old and wearing a white tulle dress with fresh flowers, her hair shining like a dark jewel, appeared at the door. Before she had even said a word, she had Randolph's undivided attention, as well as that of every other person in the room.

Jennie was well aware not only of her beauty, but of the power it gave her. She used it as both a weapon and a wand, breaking hearts and enthralling anyone who caught her eye. Even when Randolph was still alive, there had been rumors of flirtations, possibly even affairs, but after his death she was openly surrounded by a legion of powerful older men and, to her sons' dismay, handsome younger ones.

She had had a friendship with the Prince of Wales that was so lasting and intimate that many believed her to be not just one of his many mistresses but his favorite. Because the prince was himself married, and had such a wandering eye that he was nicknamed Edward the Caresser, he did not much complain about Jennie's dalliances. In fact, he had scolded her only twice: The first time was just a year earlier, when she had had an affair with Major Caryl Ramsden, a man who was so strikingly handsome he was nicknamed Beauty and who was fourteen years her junior. "You had better have stuck to your old friends," the prince had chided her after her very passionate and public breakup with Ramsden on a trip to Egypt. "Old friends are best!"

Now, however, the prince's reprimand was more severe because Jennie's latest love affair was more serious, and more dangerous. Apparently determined to risk everything—the prince's displeasure, her reputation, her sons' happiness—she had fallen in love with a dashing young officer who was not only well known to Winston but only two weeks older than he was.

Like Randolph, George Frederick Myddleton Cornwallis-West came from an aristocratic family and traveled in the same social circles as the Prince of Wales. In fact, one of Jennie's few real rivals for the prince's affection over the years had been Patsy Cornwallis-West, George's mother. There had even been rumors that George could be the prince's son. None of which had added to the prince's enthusiasm for Jennie's choice of companion. "You are evidently up to your old game again," he had written archly to her after finding out about her affair with George. "It is a pity that you have got yourself so talked about—& remember you are not 25!"

Jennie, however, had never been interested in other people's opinions about her life, even the prince's, and she continued to do exactly as she liked. "I suppose you think I'm very foolish," she had written to a friend. "But I don't care. I'm having such *fun*." At forty-five years of age, she was as beautiful as she had been the day Randolph first saw her, and Winston, like every young man in her orbit, could not help but adore her. "She shone for me like the Evening Star," he wrote. "I loved her dearly—but at a distance."

Over the years, Churchill's mother had, on occasion, made life difficult for him, but she had also been extremely useful. At his insistence, she had charmed and coaxed everyone from the Duke of Cambridge to the prime minister to the Prince of Wales in a blatant attempt to help her son win military appointments. Now he needed her more than ever. "This is a pushing age," he had written to her. "We must push with the best."

Despite Jennie's rebellious nature and shocking social life, or perhaps because of them, Winston knew that she would be an irresistible draw to any public event, even the campaign of a young politician in a cotton mill town. As Election Day drew near, he wanted nothing more than to have his mother by his side.

→►

Jennie arrived in Oldham as she did any place she deigned to appear, with high style and supreme confidence. Dressed all in blue, the Conservative Party color, and carrying a parasol of the same hue, she galloped into town riding in a highly decorated horse-drawn carriage, a postilion sitting stiffly up front, his uniform covered in blue ribbons and rosettes. Turning heads wherever she went, Jennie seemed less like the mother of a political candidate than an American stage star, shipped over for the day to scatter fairy dust on a dreary campaign. "Lady Randolph Churchill was, naturally enough, the observed of all observers," a local reporter panted. "Indeed she created quite a sensation in these grimy old streets."

Neither his mother's bright glamour, however, nor his own magnetism at the podium could change Churchill's fate on Election Day. On July 6, the men of Oldham, who filled the city's polling centers by the tens of thousands—a voter turnout that was "as big as was

known in England"—gave the Liberal candidates nearly 53 percent
of the vote, leaving Churchill thirteen hundred votes short of victory
and Mawdsley even more. Churchill left Oldham feeling, he would
later write, like "a bottle of champagne . . . left uncorked for the
night."

The high-ranking members of his party were not inclined to
offer words of comfort and encouragement to a young man who had
failed, even if he was Randolph Churchill's son. On the contrary,
Churchill arrived in London in time to learn that Arthur Balfour,
Lord Salisbury's nephew who would himself become prime minister
just three years later, had been talking about him in the lobby of the
House of Commons. "I thought he was a young man of promise,"
Balfour had sneered, "but it appears he is a young man of promises."

Balfour's searing assessment only hardened Churchill's resolve.
He had no money, no occupation and, it appeared, no one who
believed in him quite as much as he believed in himself. The only
thing he knew with any certainty was that in the end, whatever it
took, he would succeed or, quite literally, die trying. "What an awful
thing it will be if I don't come off," he had written to his mother just
months before. "It will break my heart for I have nothing else but
ambition to cling to."

CHAPTER 4

BLOWING THE TRUMPET

If Churchill was looking for a refuge where he might, for a time, forget his failure, even escape the relentless demands of his own ambition, he should not have returned to the place of his birth: Blenheim Palace. Soon after the election, with no home of his own and no real plan, he traveled to the small town of Woodstock, in Oxfordshire, where his family's estate sprawled in ornate splendor across seven acres of a vast, two-thousand-acre park. As his carriage passed the massive stone pillars flanking the entrance to the grounds and rattled down the Grand Avenue, he could see from his window the house itself as it came into view: a massive, stunningly beautiful Baroque palace built of a local cream-colored limestone that over the span of time had turned a radiant golden hue.

It was a sight that had astonished nearly two centuries of visitors, from Alexander Pope, who had written an arch letter about the extreme lavishness of Blenheim after touring it in the early eighteenth century, to Churchill's own Brooklyn-born mother, who saw it for the first time after her wedding more than 150 years later. "Looking at the lake, the bridge, the miles of magnificent park studded with old oaks, I found no adequate words to express my admiration," she would later recall, "and when we reached the huge and stately palace . . . I confess that I felt awed. But my American pride forbade the admission."

Churchill had been born in a relatively modest room on the first floor. Although he had never lived at Blenheim, he had spent much of his childhood there, hunting in the open countryside, fishing in the lake, racing through the grand corridors, and alternately charming and exhausting his famously stern grandmother, the duchess. "Winston is going back to school today," she had written to Randolph after one particularly taxing visit from her spirited grandson. "*Entre nous* I do not feel very sorry for he certainly is a handful."

Churchill had always believed that Blenheim—its history, its grandeur, its power to awe—had molded him, creating the foundation for the great man he was destined to become. "We shape our buildings," he would later write, "and then our buildings shape us." Now, however, as he wandered around the palace in the wake of his defeat, trying to finish the manuscript for his second book and playing endless rounds of chess with his cousin Sunny, the current Duke of Marlborough, the magnificence of Blenheim seemed less a proud symbol of his exalted lineage than a painful reminder of his inability thus far to live up to it.

-->-

Everything Churchill saw as he walked the broad, seemingly endless corridors of Blenheim, everything he admired, everything he was determined to become, was inescapably linked to his illustrious ancestor John Churchill, the 1st Duke of Marlborough. John Churchill, whose own father had been a man of much more modest means, had won his grand estate through his own courage and hard-edged intelligence. Although he had fallen into and out of favor with every ruler of England from King James II, whom he had at first supported and then helped to depose, to William of Orange to Queen Anne, and had even been imprisoned in the Tower of London, he had one skill that had made him indispensable: He never lost on the battlefield. "Amid all the chances and baffling accidents of war he produced victory with almost mechanical certainty," Winston would write in his biography of John Churchill more than thirty years later. "He never rode off any field except as a victor. He quitted war invincible; and no sooner was his guiding hand withdrawn than disaster overtook the armies he had left."

It had been during the War of the Spanish Succession, in fact, following Churchill's extraordinary defeat of the French in the Battle of Blenheim in 1704, that Queen Anne had given him, as a token of gratitude, the royal manor of Woodstock, on which he had built Blenheim Palace. He had also been made a sovereign prince of the Holy Roman Empire by the emperor Leopold and given a gift of land—the principality of Mindelheim in Bavaria, Germany—for his accomplishments as commander in chief of the Grand Alliance's armies. Even those who hated and envied him believed him to be the greatest general in England and perhaps, before Napoleon, even the world.

Nearly two hundred years later, the weight of John Churchill's legacy followed his ambitious young descendant wherever he went. If Winston entered the Great Hall, his shoes echoing on the marble floors, an elaborate mural depicting the 1st Duke kneeling before Britannia, unfurling his grand plan for the Battle of Blenheim, loomed above him from the room's breathtaking sixty-seven-foot-high ceiling. If he wandered into the Green Writing Room, whose walls were covered in a rich green silk damask, he was confronted by an enormous, incredibly detailed tapestry depicting John Churchill's triumph at Blenheim. If he escaped the palace to stroll across the enormous park with its arboretum, vast lake and elaborate, themed gardens—the Italian and the Rose—he could see, from almost any direction, the Column of Victory, a soaring Doric column that loomed over the grounds and lifted 134 feet into the sky a statue of the 1st Duke clothed as a Roman general, two proud eagles at his feet and a Winged Victory held aloft in his hand.

John Churchill had been fifty-four years old during the Battle of Blenheim, but Winston refused to accept his own youth as an excuse for inaction. His father had been a member of Parliament at twenty-five, barely a year older than Churchill was now. Earlier in the year, before Winston had even been asked to run for Parliament, Lord Salisbury had appointed Sunny, who was just three years older than Winston, paymaster general. Sunny, in fact, had had a political career for seven years, after inheriting his title and accompanying seat in the House of Lords from his father, who, like Winston's, had died an early death. "You are young to be in the ministry," Churchill had congratulated Sunny after his appointment, "but this is an age of youth, so accept my tribute not only as coming from a friend but from one of the generation that has yet to divide the world."

Although Churchill believed that his youth was an advantage that it would be foolish to squander, the constant reminders at Blenheim of the 1st Duke's extraordinary achievements could not help but serve as a stark lesson: He had leaped too soon. By running for Parliament on the strength of his father's name rather than his own, Churchill had made a serious miscalculation. "It is a fine game to play—the game of politics," he had written to his mother from India, "and it is well worth waiting for a good hand—before really plunging." This time, as desperate as he was to dive back in, he was determined to take his own advice and distinguish himself first. All he needed was an opportunity. All he needed was another war.

→→

Before the summer was out, Churchill would not only find the spark he needed to begin again, he would fan the flames himself. The idea would come to him not in the hallowed halls of Parliament or the stately rooms of Blenheim Palace but on a boat adrift in the slow-moving waters of the Thames.

In late July, Churchill received an invitation to a dinner party at the riverside home of his friend Lady Jeune. It was an invitation that no one, not even those in Churchill's rarefied social sphere, would ever refuse. Although the widow of a colonel and the wife of a barrister, Lady Jeune owed her fame not to her husbands' titles or achievements but to her own sparkling intellect. Known for her sharp mind and quick wit, she wrote for some of the most prestigious society journals of the day and was one of the most formidable hostesses in London, drawing to her the greatest minds in the empire. Her gatherings were famous and frequent, and a place on her guest list, which included everyone from Thomas Hardy to Robert Browning to even Mrs. Robinson's devoted client Oscar Wilde, was nearly as coveted as an invitation to Buckingham Palace. "An introduction to her became a passport to many social privileges," a contemporary American writer would recall. "Her intellectual and political influence was as great as the charm which made her salon so brilliant."

Churchill knew that by attending one of Lady Jeune's gatherings, he was certain to meet someone interesting, and quite possibly useful. He might not have been surprised, therefore, but he was certainly thrilled when, soon after arriving at her home, he stepped onto a launch for an afternoon cruise on the Thames and found none other than Joseph Chamberlain, secretary of state for the colonies and one of Britain's most powerful politicians. Churchill quickly took a seat next to him, and the two men were soon lost in conversation.

Had he been delivering a lecture to a crowded amphitheater, Chamberlain could not have had a more eager audience than he had in Churchill alone. "His conversation was a practical political education in itself," Churchill would later recall. "He knew every detail, every turn and twist of the game." Chamberlain also knew how to fight, although apparently not when to lay down arms. A radical politician and a fierce competitor who had worked his way up through the narrow British hierarchy from his father's shoe factory to mayor of Birmingham to Parliament, he kept careful track of his grudges, even those that had long since ceased to be a threat. When Lady Jeune pointed out in surprise an old political enemy of Chamberlain's who happened to be sitting in a chair near the river as they glided by, Churchill was astonished by Chamberlain's reaction. The famously dignified man, often caricatured for his carefully combed hair, long, patrician face and glinting monocle that trailed a silky ribbon down his cheek, glared at his now elderly and harmless rival and spat, "A bundle of old rags!" before turning away in disgust.

What was foremost on the minds of both Chamberlain and Churchill that afternoon, however, was not old disputes but the shadow of a new one. There had been whispers of war, a war unlike anything the empire had seen since the Crimean War nearly half a century earlier, perhaps even the American Revolution more than a hundred years in the past. This war, however, was brewing not in eastern Europe or North America but in southern Africa, thousands of miles away in a part of the world that was difficult to reach and almost impossible to fully understand. Nor was it simply the threat of another colonial war, to add to the scores of others taking place at that moment around the globe. This would be a European war on African soil, a prospect that seemed to most Britons to be far less terrifying than tantalizing, and few hoped it could be averted, least of all Winston Churchill.

→→

Although southern Africa had been an object of great interest to the British Empire for centuries, more recently the allure had turned to lust. Perfectly positioned as it was, the region had long been a critical link in the trade route to India, which led British ships down the jutting western coast of Africa, around the Cape of Good Hope, where they would stop for supplies before heading back north, up the eastern coast, past the Horn of Africa and into the Indian Ocean. The British had colonized the southern tip of the continent, Cape Colony, as well as Senegal in the west, parts of northern Africa—Algiers and Tripoli—and a swath of Egypt that dipped down into the Abyssinian Empire, now Ethiopia. For many years, that had been enough.

Just seven years before Churchill was born, however, everything had changed. In 1867, Erasmus Jacobs, the fifteen-year-old son of a South African farmer, is said to have sat down to rest beneath a tree on his father's farm and found an extremely large and shiny stone lying at his feet. The stone turned out to be a 21.25-carat diamond, later known as the Eureka Diamond, the first diamond ever discovered in South Africa. Four years later, more diamonds were found not far from the Jacobses' home, on the farm of two brothers named Johannes Nicolaas and Diederick Arnoldus de Beer, a discovery that would lead to the formation of De Beers S.A., the largest diamond company in the world.

Then came the gold. About two decades after the Eureka Diamond was discovered, the world's largest known gold reserve was found in the Witwatersrand mountain ridge. The tiny, filthy camp that sprouted up around the mine quickly became flooded with fortune seekers and eventually grew to become one of South Africa's largest and most important cities: Johannesburg. Together, these discoveries transformed the region from one of the poorest in the world to one of the wealthiest.

As is often true, with great wealth came great trouble. As Churchill put it, "The discovery of an El Dorado had attracted . . . a vast and various swarm of humanity." Tens of thousands of prospectors descended on the region, the great majority of whom were British. The problem was that neither the gold nor the diamonds had been discovered in British territory. They had been found in the South African Republic, also known as the Transvaal, an independent country that belonged to a group of Dutch, German and Huguenot descendants known as the Boers.

A deeply religious, stubbornly independent people, the Boers wanted, above all else, to be left alone. Many of them could trace their ancestry back to the members of a Dutch East India Company expedition who had sailed to the Cape of Good Hope in 1652 to establish a shipping station and decided to stay. When Cape Colony became a British possession in 1806, they had grudgingly submitted to British rule, but not for long. After centuries of devastating entire populations of native Africans and taking over vast swaths of their land, much like the Pilgrims and pioneers in North America, the Boers were furious when the British Empire abolished slavery in 1833. Just two years later, in what would become known as the Great

Trek, large groups of Boers, called *Voortrekkers,* or pioneers, left Cape
Colony and began pushing their way hundreds of miles into the Afri-
can interior, eventually establishing three Boer republics: the Orange
Free State; the Republic of Natalia, later Natal; and the Transvaal.

The Boers' independence, however, had lasted only as long as
their poverty. "This gold," Paul Kruger, who would become president
of the Transvaal, had predicted, "will cause our country to be soaked
in blood." He was right, and he knew well the dangers it posed. Ten
years after the discovery of diamonds, Britain had annexed the Transvaal, a move that infuriated the Boers and quickly led to the Transvaal War—later known as the First Boer War. Although the war had
lasted only a few months, from the end of 1880 to the early spring
of 1881, it held a prominent place in the collective memories of both
countries for one reason: The British Empire did not win.

The turning point of the Transvaal War had been the Battle of
Majuba Hill, which ended not with the Union Jack triumphantly
planted on Boer soil but with the shocking, sickening sight of British
soldiers fleeing in humiliating retreat. For the Boers, the day of that
battle, February 27, had become a national holiday. For the British, it
was a searing memory, one that they vowed to repay. Even Churchill,
who had been only six years old at the time, hungered for revenge. "I
longed for the day," he wrote, "on which we should 'avenge Majuba.'"

➤➤

That day, Churchill now believed, had not only come, it was long
overdue. He fiercely defended the importance, even the benevolence,
of British imperialism, and he had been brooding over the problem
of South Africa for years. The more he thought about it, the more
certain he was that war was the only answer. "It is not yet too late to
recover our vanished prestige in South Africa," he had written two
years earlier in a treatise titled "Our Account with the Boers." "Imperial troops must curb the insolence of the Boers. There must be no
half measures."

As he continued his conversation with Chamberlain over dinner at Lady Jeune's home following their cruise on the Thames, Churchill did not try to hide or even temper his belief that the empire should take a hard line with the Boers. Chamberlain, he knew, had a long history with the Transvaal, and none of it was good. He had been Prime Minister William Gladstone's lieutenant in the House of Commons during the Transvaal War, an experience that had left him with an undisguised loathing of the Boers. Then, at the end of 1895, in the first year of his tenure as secretary of state for the colonies, he had been tied to an ill-conceived and spectacularly failed raid on the Transvaal. Concocted by the mining magnate Cecil Rhodes and led by his closest friend, Leander Starr Jameson, what became known as the Jameson Raid had ended with Jameson's capture and Rhodes's forced resignation as prime minister of Cape Colony. Rhodes had narrowly escaped imprisonment, and the raid, as well as Chamberlain's involvement in it, had been splashed across the front pages of every newspaper in England and South Africa and had led to a parliamentary investigation of Chamberlain himself.

Even Chamberlain, though, who could not forgive an old political slight much less a humiliating scandal that could have destroyed his career, was taken aback by Churchill's fervor for war. "A war in South Africa would be one of the most serious wars that could possibly be waged," Chamberlain had warned the House of Commons after the raid on the Transvaal three years earlier. "It would be a long war, a bitter war and a costly war . . . it would leave behind it the embers of a strife which I believe generations would hardly be long enough to extinguish." After listening to Churchill's passionate argument for war with the Boers, Chamberlain advised him to resist the urge to call for arms. "It is no use blowing the trumpet for the charge," he warned, "and then looking around to find nobody following you."

The last thing that Churchill was worried about, however, was finding followers. Although he was only twenty-four years old, he was already confident of his ability to stir the hearts of men, and where the Boers were concerned, he was not about to back down, not when there was so much to be gained. "Sooner or later," he had written in "Our Account with the Boers," "in a righteous cause or a picked quarrel, with the approval of Europe, or in the teeth of Germany, for the sake of our Empire, for the sake of our honour, for the sake of the race, we must fight the Boers."

>>

Within just a few weeks of Lady Jeune's dinner party, Churchill stood at the imposing, pillared entrance of Blenheim Palace, surrounded this time not just by tributes to the 1st Duke of Marlborough but by an eager audience of hundreds, and, heedless of Chamberlain's advice, made his case for war. His opportunity had come at the annual meeting of the Woodstock Conservative Association, following a day of festivities that had included everything from a ladies' bicycle race over the palace grounds to a potato-picking race in one of the gardens to an obstacle course that had ended with the exhausted challengers shakily trying to thread a needle. At 6:00 p.m., long before the summer sun had begun to set, the association's members gathered at the foot of the palace's broad stone steps to hear remarks by the 9th Duke of Marlborough as well as two of his cousins: the calm, dark-haired Ivor Guest, who was the son of Lady Cornelia, Randolph Churchill's older sister, and Guest's polar opposite, the fair-haired and forceful Winston Churchill.

As soon as Sunny had finished his perfunctory welcome, but before Ivor Guest, with his thick black mustache, sharply twisted at the ends, could deliver his brief remarks, Winston took the stage. As his audience stood patiently in the blazing August heat, he wasted little time getting to the subject that he believed had the greatest power to affect the empire's future, not to mention his own: South Africa. Nor did he temper his remarks with even a single note of caution. On the contrary, as the reporters attending the event noted with growing alarm, he was unabashedly beating the drums of war.

"Inspired possibly by memories of that great warrior the founder of his house, he was in a warlike vein," a reporter for the *Manchester Evening News* wrote of Churchill. "The present condition of things could not go on indefinitely without war breaking out, he said, and he was not sure that the prospect of war was very terrible or one to be trembled at." England, after all, was a "very great power," Churchill reminded his rapt audience, and the Boers were "a very small and miserable people."

While Churchill's audience was swept up in his speech, laughing at his jokes and cheering at his energetic declarations, many of the reporters in the crowd were astonished by the force of his argument, and deeply concerned by his powers of persuasion. "If he would encourage the political supporters of Mr. Chamberlain to enter upon war in a cavalier fashion, careless of the amount of suffering and misery it causes because they know that we are strong and the Boers are weak," one reporter railed, "he commits himself to a course of action which is highly reprehensible." He also guessed that Churchill's motives, like those of his most famous ancestor, were not entirely pure. "The first Duke of Marlborough was more than suspected of bringing about a great battle in the hope that the victory he was pretty sure to obtain would restore his popularity," the reporter charged. Fortunately, he wrote, "in a more enlightened age," Churchill's radical point of view "finds no advocates outside the ranks of the young aristocracy."

In this last pronouncement, however, the reporter could not have been more mistaken. Churchill was far from alone in his desire to take on the Boers. Nor, on this issue at least, was there any class divide. In fact, the British people seemed to be not following the charge to war but leading it. Not only did they still feel sharply the sting of Majuba, but most had never experienced what they considered to be a real war—a "civilized war" between men of European descent—and the idea was electric. As the summer began to fade, England's interest in South Africa and its excitement over the possibility of war only grew in strength. "The atmosphere," Churchill would still remember years later, "gradually but steadily became tense, charged with electricity, laden with the presage of storm."

➤➤

The coming storm was also felt thousands of miles away in South Africa. The atmosphere there, however, was one not of exhilaration but of grim determination. The thousands of Britons who had flooded the Transvaal were now demanding not just a share in the country's riches but an equal vote and a voice in its government. The British Empire, meanwhile, had begun amassing troops at the Transvaal borders and claiming large swaths of new territory in southern Africa. As well as Cape Colony, which it had taken in 1806, during the Napoleonic Wars, and the former Boer republic of Natalia, which it had annexed in 1843, it began surrounding the country to the west, north and southeast, effectively cutting it off from the sea.

Finally, on October 9, driven by fear and fury, the Boers issued an ultimatum to the British Empire: Stand down or prepare for war. "The Government must press for an immediate and affirmative answer before or upon Wednesday, October 11, 1899, not later than 5 o'clock p.m.," read the ultimatum, which had been telegraphed to London from the Transvaal capital of Pretoria. "It desires further to add, that in the event of unexpectedly no satisfactory answer being received by it within that interval, it will, with great regret, be compelled to regard the action of Her Majesty's Government as a formal declaration of war."

The British allowed the deadline for the ultimatum to pass with little more than a sneer. At 3:00 p.m. on October 11, just two hours before the deadline, William Conyngham Greene, Her Majesty's agent at Pretoria, received a telegram from London, which he brought immediately to the president of the Transvaal, Paul Kruger, and his secretary of state for war, Louis de Souza. After reading the telegram, which dismissed his government's claims out of hand and refused to abide by its terms, Kruger, a large man with a wide, solemn face ringed by a graying chin-curtain beard, sat for a long time without saying a word, filling the nearly empty room with a heavy silence. Finally, bowing his head, he said simply, "So must it be." "We have crossed the Rubicon," de Souza's wife, Marie, wrote in her diary that night, "and God alone knows the end of it all."

Churchill had gotten his wish. England was going to war, and the bloody, war-torn twentieth century was about to begin. "The age of Peace had ended," Churchill would write years later, looking back on this moment from the vantage of a man who had witnessed the horrors of one world war and was about to endure those of another. "There was to be no lack of war. There was to be enough for all. Aye, enough and to spare."

PART TWO

❮❮←→❯❯

Into Africa

CHAPTER 5

"SEND HER VICTORIOUS"

Three days after war was declared, Churchill, now a journalist, was at the port of Southampton on England's southern coast, fighting his way through a massive crowd toward his ship, the *Dunottar Castle*. Known as the Gateway to the Empire, Southampton had been used as a port since the Middle Ages. The *Mayflower* and its sister ship, the *Speedwell,* had set sail from there for the New World in 1620, and in just a few years the RMS *Titanic* would do the same. Southampton, however, was best known as the port from which England had sent its young men into battle since 1415, when Henry V had left to fight the French at the Battle of Agincourt.

Although England had been engaged in countless conflicts in the nearly five hundred years since Agincourt, it had been a long time since Southampton had seen such frenzied excitement accompany the commencement of war. Since early that morning, the port had been choked with thousands of people breathlessly awaiting the arrival of Sir Redvers Buller, the newly appointed commander in chief of Her Majesty's army in South Africa. In fact, they had arrived at the port well before Buller had even reached Waterloo Station, where he had been given a grand send-off from London earlier that afternoon by the Prince of Wales. While Southampton continued to fill with eager revelers, men's silk hats glistening in the damp, salty air, women's long, layered dresses sweeping the ground, their hems already stained a stubborn black, the corpulent prince had been clapping Buller on the back, muttering, "Good bye; good-bye! Wish you jolly good luck!"

When Buller's special five-car train, its interior upholstered in a rich yellow silk, finally reached the port at 3:47 p.m., the long, low steam whistle announcing his arrival was immediately swallowed by the deafening roar of the crowd. Those who had resorted to sitting on everything from packing crates and cast-aside boxes to the port's filthy ground during their long wait leaped to their feet, cheering wildly. A rope that had been strung the fifty yards between the customs house and the ship in an effort to separate passengers from onlookers was straining to its snapping point. Harried policemen, their belted tunics by now wrinkled and stained and their helmets barely hanging on by the chin straps, fought to maintain order.

Even the most desperate attempts to control the crowd proved useless when Buller himself appeared. Although dressed for the chill, early autumn air, a felt bowler hat covering his strikingly large head and a dark gray overcoat that was, as one reporter disdainfully noted, "not quite new" thrown over his bearlike shoulders, he was absolutely unmistakable. If, as he looked over the crowd with a benign smile beneath his heavy mustache, he seemed more like a gentleman farmer than the commander of one of the most feared armies in the world, he was loved none the less for it. As he navigated the narrow passageway carved between the pressing crowds and ascended the steep ramp to the *Dunottar Castle,* the cheering rose with him, filling the port with the voices of thousands.

The ship itself had arrived from the Thames three days earlier, 420 feet long and displacing about 5,500 tons. Although it was ten years old, it had recently been renovated, the ladies' waiting room transformed into a sprawling stateroom for Buller. More important, it was fast. The *Dunottar Castle* could sail at sixteen knots per hour, a pace that had dramatically reduced the average travel time between

Southampton and Cape Town from a month and a half to just over two weeks.

Even that was too long for Churchill. To nearly everyone who gazed up at it, the *Dunottar Castle*, with its straight, strong masts, slanting lines of rigging and elegantly curving bow, was a thing of beauty. To Churchill, it was a sight that made his stomach churn. He had already crossed the ocean many times in his young life, traveling between England, India, Africa and North America before the invention of the airplane, and he had hated every moment he was forced to spend on a ship. Not once had he avoided becoming violently ill. Even crossing the English Channel was "worse than a flogging," he had written to his mother after returning to India from London, and it made him "wretched."

Churchill would never lose his hatred of traveling by sea. Later in life, quoting Samuel Johnson, he would compare being on a ship to being in prison, only "with the chance of being drowned." As much as he dreaded the two weeks that stretched before him now, however, he resolutely took his place in line and solemnly boarded the ship, knowing that whatever misery he was about to endure aboard the *Dunottar Castle*, war lay on the other side.

→→

At 6:00 p.m., with the final cry of "Any more for the shore!" hanging in the air, Churchill watched from the ship as reporters and photographers frantically dashed down the gangplank and the throng that swarmed the long pier shouted their last good-byes. As Buller stood on the captain's deck, waving to the upturned faces, the *Dunottar Castle* slipped its moorings, and the shouts slowly began to die away. In their place rose the soft, swelling sound of women's voices, singing "God Save the Queen." As men joined in the chorus, the words, solemn and strong—"Send her victorious, happy and glorious, long to reign over us"—followed the ship out to sea, and the passengers, looking "back towards the shores swiftly fading in the distance and the twilight," Churchill wrote, "wondered whether, and if so when, they would come safe home again."

Even Churchill, who had never been particularly nostalgic and now wanted nothing more than to leave England and the dashed dreams of the past year behind him, had brought along a few items of purely sentimental value. Inside his stitched brown leather wallet, a small bird tooled in gold on the front, four pencil sketches had been slipped in next to the silky dark green lining. One of the portraits was of Churchill's mother, looking proud and youthful with her long neck and perfect, bow-shaped lips, but the other three were of a much younger woman. She had delicate features, wide, heavily lidded eyes and a serene, thoughtful expression. Her name was Pamela Plowden, and she was the first great love of Churchill's life.

He had met her three years earlier in India, soon after arriving in Bangalore. "I was introduced yesterday to Miss Pamela Plowden," he had written breathlessly to his mother. "I must say that she is the most beautiful girl I have ever seen." Although Pamela had been born in India, the daughter of Sir Trevor John Chichele Chichele-Plowden, who was in the Indian civil service, she had only recently returned to the subcontinent. Five years before, following her mother's death from a poisonous snakebite, her father had remarried, and Pamela had moved for a short time to London, where her beauty and intelligence had attracted a great deal of attention. Even the acerbic Arthur Balfour, the future prime minister who had been so dismissive of Churchill after his defeat, referred to her as "the brightest star in London's social firmament." Winston could not agree more.

While in India, he had taken every opportunity to see Pamela. He had dined several times with her family and had even toured Hyderabad with her, on the back of an elephant. "You dare not walk," he had explained in a letter to his mother. "The natives spit at Europeans—which provokes retaliation leading to riots."

Once back in England, Pamela and Winston's relationship had deepened. He had invited her to Blenheim, where they had strolled the estate's expansive grounds, and while he worked on his second book, *The River War,* he had let her read the first two chapters, taking

great satisfaction in the fact that she had been "very much impressed."
He had even hoped that Pamela would help his mother campaign for
him in Oldham. "I quite understand your not coming," he had written to her after learning that she could not, or would not, travel to
the gritty mill town. "It would perhaps have been a mistake—but I
shall be sorry nevertheless." In an attempt to make up for Pamela's
absence, Churchill had worn a charm she had given him, which he
had hoped would bring him luck.

It had not taken him long to fall hopelessly in love. Everyone
could see the signs except, perhaps, Pamela herself, who had so many
admirers she was used to being more vigorously pursued. "Why
do you say I am incapable of affection," Churchill, offended, had
demanded in a letter to her the previous year. "Perish the thought. I
love one above all others. And I shall be constant. I am no fickle gallant capriciously following the fancy of the hour. My love is deep and
strong. Nothing will ever change it." The month before war had been
declared, Pamela had gone to Germany, leaving Winston bereft. "I
am lonely without her," he had admitted to his mother. "The more I
know of her, the more she astonishes me. No one would understand
her as I do."

Jennie, however, believed she did understand Pamela, all too
well. In late August, she had shared with Winston a conversation
she had had with Baron Revelstoke, who had told her that Pamela
had broken his brother's heart and ruined his career. Churchill had
quickly leaped to her defense, insisting that "while not madly in
love" with the baron's brother, Pamela "respected his devotion" and
would even have married him. "Now," he shrugged, "she loves me."

Two days later, Jennie received another troubling report about
Pamela, this time from a much closer source: the young man with
whom she was romantically involved, George Cornwallis-West.
"Jack [Winston's brother] dined with me last night, and opened his
heart to me about Miss Pamela," George wrote to her late that summer. "He doesn't often talk so I was pleased with his confidence. He
doesn't think much of her, in fact he dislikes her, he says she is
such an awful humbug, and is the same to three other men as she

is to Winston. He tells me they went about at Blenheim as if they were engaged, in fact several people asked if it was so. I am sorry for Winston, as I don't think he would be happy with her. I can't make her out. She is certain[ly] very clever, in a doubtful sense of the word."

When it came to taking advice, however, especially from George, Churchill was his mother's son. He was defiantly determined to decide for himself where he would go, what he would do and whom he would love. The question, anyway, like everything else in his life, had temporarily been cast aside. Nothing, not even Pamela, had been able to compete for his attention since war had been declared.

->-

Churchill was no longer a soldier, but he was still a writer, and a very good one. It had been that skill alone that had earned him a ticket to South Africa and an excuse to be near the fighting. As war had grown increasingly more likely, the most powerful publishers in London had begun rounding up their best foreign correspondents and scouring the city for new ones. Again and again, among the country's most cutthroat newspapermen, one name in particular had risen to the fore: Winston Churchill.

In fact, a bidding war for Churchill had begun before the Boers had even sent their ultimatum. On September 18, nearly a month before war had seemed inevitable, Churchill had received a telegram from Sir Alfred Harmsworth. Harmsworth had built Amalgamated Press, then the world's largest periodicals empire, and was the publisher of two of the most popular newspapers in the country—the *Daily Mail* and the *Daily Mirror*. He wanted Churchill to work for him as a correspondent in South Africa, and he was willing to pay him handsomely to do it.

Churchill, however, being Churchill, believed he could do better and was not shy about taking matters into his own hands. As soon as he received Harmsworth's telegram, he had turned around and wired it to a man named Oliver Borthwick, who was the editor of the *Morning Post*. A highly respected newspaper known for its coverage of foreign affairs, the *Morning Post* prided itself on having the best correspondents, regardless of their background, or even their sex. Nearly twenty years earlier, Borthwick's father, Algernon, who looked much like Father Christmas in a three-piece suit, had famously hired the first female war correspondent, Lady Florence Dixie, to cover the First Boer War. Responding immediately to Churchill's telegram, Borthwick had promised him £1,000 (approximately $150,000 today) for just four months' work, "shore to shore," and another £200 per month after that. It was an offer that not only eclipsed Harmsworth's but would make Churchill the best-paid war correspondent in England.

The fact that newspaper publishers had been fighting over Churchill was all the more impressive considering the competition. Not only would more journalists cover this war than any before it, but among them would be some of the most famous names in literature. Edgar Wallace, who would get the last scoop of the war for the *Daily Mail,* would go on to write hundreds of short stories, more than a dozen plays and 175 books, many of which were so popular his publisher claimed that a quarter of all books read in England at the time were written by him.

Rudyard Kipling, who would be covering the war for the *Friend,* a newspaper based in South Africa, was already a household name. He had published *The Jungle Book* five years earlier and, soon after, had written one of his most famous poems—"If," which was inspired by events leading up to the Boer War and offers some of the best-known advice in the English language: "If you can keep your head when all about you / Are losing theirs and blaming it on you, / . . . you'll be a Man, my son." Kipling would also raise £250,000 (more than $30 million today) for the British troops with his poem "The Absent-Minded Beggar," which Harmsworth, always looking for an opportunity, had commissioned. After naming a medal after the poem, and hiring Sir Arthur Sullivan to set it to music, Harmsworth sold copies for a shilling each, two pence of which went to the *Daily Mail*'s Kipling Poem War Fund.

The war had also attracted to it a rather pompous-looking physician turned writer who had created one of the most famous detectives—arguably *the* most famous—in literary history. Arthur Conan Doyle had published his first Sherlock Holmes story, "A Study in Scarlet," in *Beeton's Christmas Annual* twelve years earlier. The popularity of this story, along with the series of Sherlock Holmes mysteries that followed in the *Strand* magazine, had allowed him to give up his medical practice and begin writing full-time. He planned to go to South Africa in the capacity of a doctor, volunteering at Langman Hospital in Bloemfontein, but he would end up writing one of the best-known histories of the war: *The Great Boer War.*

Although the field was crowded with not just good writers but legendary ones, Borthwick knew what he was doing in choosing Churchill. He had hired him to cover the war in the Sudan, the dispatches for which had been turned into *The River War,* and he knew that in his reporting Churchill was not just relentless but fearless, even to the point of recklessness. His writing, moreover, had already been hailed as "exceedingly brilliant," and praised by everyone from the prime minister to Arthur Conan Doyle. Conan Doyle, in fact, would later refer to Churchill as "the greatest living master of English prose."

Churchill could not, in all modesty, disagree. He had long had, as he told his mother, "faith in my pen." The success of his books—the most recent of which the *Daily Mail* had called "an astonishing triumph"—had only strengthened his already substantial confidence. Churchill was no hack, and he knew it. "My literary talents," he wrote soberly, "do not exist in my imagination alone."

Churchill understood that the work of a war correspondent was among the most dangerous he could find, but although he was willing to risk his life in South Africa, he could not see any point in being uncomfortable while he was there. He had gone shopping for his wartime equipment not in army supply stores or back-alley bargain bins but on Bond Street, the most famous and expensive shopping district in London. Churchill had purchased what seemed to him to be the necessities for war. At the famous optical shop W. Callaghan & Co., he had chosen a compass set in bronze and a carefully crafted saddleback leather case with a pigskin lining, spending, or pledging to spend—because it was a transaction between gentlemen, payment was to be delivered at some unspecified time in the future—£3.15.6, approximately $500 in today's money. That bill, however, paled in comparison to his tally at Randolph Payne & Sons, where he had ordered a dizzying array of fine wines, spirits and liqueurs: six bottles each of an 1889 Vin d'Ay Sec, a light port, French vermouth and very old eau-de-vie landed 1866; eighteen bottles of St.-Émilion; another eighteen of ten-year-old scotch whiskey and a dozen of Rose's cordial lime juice. The final order, which cost more than £27 (roughly $4,000 today), had been packed and delivered directly to the *Dunottar Castle.*

Although he had little money to spare, Churchill would not even have considered traveling without his valet, Thomas Walden. Walden, who had once worked for Randolph Churchill and had enlisted in the army as a private, was to be Winston's soldier-servant, or batman, a term that derived from the French *bât,* or packsaddle. Most officers had their own batman to press their uniforms and deliver their orders to subordinates, but few had highly trained professional valets who had traveled the world with a single aristocratic family, as Walden had.

No one aboard the *Dunottar Castle,* however, from the cook to the commander in chief, was more serious than Churchill about the work he was there to do. Neither was he about to let rolling seas, which, just a few days into the trip, had already made him "grievously sick," keep him from it. As soon as he was able to stagger onto deck, Churchill set out in search of General Buller.

→→

Buller could usually be found on the deck, wearing a dark suit and a flat cap and sitting on a fragile-looking wicker chair. The general seemed to him to be "v[er]y amiable" and, naturally, "well disposed towards me," Churchill wrote. At the same time, Buller was famously difficult to get to know. Taciturn to a fault, he spent more time grunting and nodding during a conversation than actually talking. He was, Churchill wrote, "a characteristic British personality. He looked stolid. He said little, and what he said was obscure."

Fortunately, Churchill had enough to say for both of them and, on any subject, including the war, was more willing to share his opinions than the general and all of his advisers combined. Despite the fact that they were sailing to a war that had already begun, there seemed to be no sense of urgency among Buller and his men. "The idea that time played any vital part in such a business seemed to be entirely absent," Churchill marveled. "Absolute tranquillity lapped the peaceful ship. . . . Buller trod the deck each day with a sphinx-like calm."

Churchill had encountered this remarkably unhurried attitude toward the war well before he had climbed aboard the *Dunottar Castle,* and it was most conspicuous within the highest ranks of the British government. A few days before setting sail, he had called on Joseph Chamberlain, the secretary of state for the colonies, at his home in Prince's Gardens. Remembering Churchill fondly after their long talk on the Thames that summer, Chamberlain had agreed to write a letter of introduction for him to use in South Africa and, offering him a cigar, had strolled through the garden with him, smoking and discussing the coming war with the Boers. Finally, he had invited his young friend to ride with him to the War Office. During their fifteen-minute cab ride, Chamberlain had confided to Churchill that he believed that, by waiting until now to leave for South Africa, Buller was taking a serious risk and might miss the war altogether. He "may well be too late," Chamberlain warned. "He would have been wiser to have gone out earlier."

Chamberlain was far from alone in his belief that the war would be short-lived. Most Britons were confident that it would be over before the end of the year, in time for them to savor their victory over their Christmas pudding. The only surprise was that the Boers, weak and insignificant as they were, had dared to challenge the British Empire at all. When they had sent their ultimatum, it had immediately been dismissed among the British press as an "infatuated step," an "extravagant farce."

The men aboard the *Dunottar Castle* seemed to Churchill to be almost blasé about the war that lay before them. Their only concern as they lazily watched a shoal of flying fish race the ship, or debated the merits of throwing a fancy dress ball—some arguing that it would be "healthy and amusing," while others growled that it would be "tiresome"—was that they might miss their chance to fight. "Some of our best officers were on board," Churchill wrote, "and they simply could not conceive how 'irregular amateur' forces like the Boers could make any impression against disciplined professional soldiers." So certain were they that Buller would flatten the Boers they had nicknamed him the Steamroller. Even now, their enemy faced an entire infantry brigade, a cavalry regiment and two batteries of artillery in one region alone, not to mention the man in charge in Buller's absence: Brigadier General William Penn Symons, one of the most decorated and experienced officers in the British army.

Churchill was torn between fear that he would miss the war, which represented his best hope of regaining his political footing, and concern that the Boers might be more prepared, and far more capable, than the British gave them credit for. "Evidently the General expects that nothing of importance will happen until he gets there," he wrote to his mother from the ship. "But I rather think events will have taken the bit between their teeth."

While the rest of the passengers of the *Dunottar Castle* lounged in deck chairs or competed in athletic contests, racing "violently to and fro," Churchill often seemed to be urging the ship to go faster through sheer force of will. He was either pacing the deck in frustration, "plunging . . . 'with neck out-thrust,' as Browning fancied Napoleon," John Black Atkins, a fellow journalist who was working for the *Manchester Guardian,* noted with amusement, or sitting completely still, as if meditating. Only his hands moved, "folding and unfolding," Atkins wrote, "not nervously but as though he were helping himself to untie mental knots."

Whatever Churchill might have believed about the commander in chief, however, Buller was under no illusions when it came to the Boers. Although he hoped that he would arrive before the fighting began, he was certain that when it did begin in earnest, England would find itself in a war unlike anything it had ever seen. Buller knew South Africa, and, more than any other general in the British army, he knew the Boers. In fact, when the members of the War Office's Intelligence Branch had rushed to gather everything they had on the Boer republics, bind it into two volumes and send it to him, he had dismissively sent it back, attaching a note wearily reminding them that he already "knew everything about South Africa."

Twenty years earlier, during the Anglo-Zulu War, Buller had fought with the Boers rather than against them. He had won his Victoria Cross, the highest award given by the British military, for his gallant conduct during that war, and he knew that he owed much of his success to the Boers who had ridden next to him time and again, untiring and unafraid. As the British secretary of state for war, Henry Lansdowne, had disdainfully remarked, Buller "talked Boer," and, in stark contrast to nearly any other man in the British military, he openly admired their courage and skill.

Buller, however, like Churchill, was trapped on the sea, while other men were running the war. Worse, those in charge, Penn Symons and General George White, were quite possibly the last men who should have been chosen for the job. White, who had won his Victoria Cross in Afghanistan, had never before fought in South Africa. "The Army at large was quite as much astonished as the civilian world at the appointment of Sir George White to the command in Natal," a reporter for the *Daily Telegraph* wrote. "In the clubs and messes it had been taken for granted that the head of the force sent to the Cape would be men having experience of South African warfare." Penn Symons knew South Africa, but had no respect for or interest in the Boers. "Whatever the estimate formed of the fighting quality of the Boers," Leo Amery, a journalist for the London *Times,* wrote, "no one rated it lower than Sir W. Penn Symons."

Although Penn Symons and White had only twelve thousand men between them, and were surrounded by more than four times that number of fighting Boers, they did not for a moment worry that they would have any difficulty holding the enemy at bay until Buller arrived. "Personally," White had nonchalantly told a friend the day before he set sail from Southampton, "I don't believe there will be fighting of a serious kind."

CHAPTER 6

"WE HAVE NOW

GONE FAR ENOUGH"

Whatever waves of panic the British army might have imagined rippling through the Transvaal as news of war spread to its farthest reaches, the reality was starkly different. In the days leading up to the ultimatum, the Boers were not frantically preparing for war, rushing to gather maps and men, supplies and ammunition. They didn't have to. There had never been a time, either in their own lives or in those of their forebears, when they had not been ready to fight. For the great majority of Boers, as soon as war seemed imminent, there was little to do but leave for the front.

In isolated farms across hundreds of miles of southern Africa, from the Drakensberg Mountains to the vast plateaus of the Highveld, every Boer man and boy between the ages of sixteen and sixty, and many much older or younger than that, set out for war. There was no need to enlist in the army because there was no standing army, and there was no need to find a uniform because there were no uniforms. Uniforms were something soldiers wore, and Boers were fiercely adamant that they were not soldiers, a term they found deeply offensive. They referred to themselves only as burghers, or citizens.

When he left for war, a Boer pulled on the same clothes he wore every day—homemade shoes, a pair of stiff moleskin trousers and a wide-brimmed hat to keep the sun and rain out of his eyes, all of it in the same drab grays and browns. The only flourishes he might allow himself were affixed to his hat, either a small flag of the Transvaal sewn into the fabric or, as a nod to the customs of the past, a meerkat tail, dark tipped and slightly bushy, tied to the upturned brim.

As he walked out the door, his wife or mother handed him a linen sack filled with enough food to allow him to survive on his own for several weeks. He was accustomed to living on just a handful of staples—coffee, brown bread and biltong, a dried meat made of anything from beef to zebra or giraffe and cured with a mixture of vinegar and spices. His native servant hooked a roll with a rough blanket and a raincoat onto the front of his saddle and a kettle to the back. Likely wearing a wide bandolier over his shoulder, and with a Bible tucked into his pocket, he climbed onto his horse and rode off with little more than a backward glance.

By early October, thousands of Boers had already flooded into Pretoria, the Transvaal capital. The town, which had been built in a warm, fertile valley north of Johannesburg, about three hundred and fifty miles from the eastern coast, seemed far less a bustling center of political power than a sleepy frontier outpost. Although the wide streets had large government buildings clustered at each end, most of them were made of dirt, with small streams running beside them. The home of the president, Paul Kruger, had two imposing stone lions standing guard at its entrance, a lavish gift from the British mining magnate Barney Barnato, but Kruger's wife, the First Lady of the Transvaal, could often be seen out front, milking their cow.

With the onset of war, the usually quiet town had been rapidly transformed. Trains arrived every day crowded with burghers from all corners of the republic; hundreds of heavily bearded men, clearly unused to, and uncomfortable with, being anywhere but their own farms, wandered the town; and a crush of horses kicked up the dirt streets until everything and everyone was coated with a fine red dust. On the day before the deadline for the ultimatum, which also happened to be Kruger's birthday, the town even did something very un-Boer-like: It had a military parade.

As their commandant general, Piet Joubert, the man who had led them to victory against the British twenty years earlier, stood in silent and awkward appraisal, his men rode past him one by one in their own makeshift version of a military review. Even Deneys Reitz, the seventeen-year-old son of Francis William Reitz, the Transvaal's secretary of state and the man who had written the ultimatum, could tell that there was a striking lack of uniformity among the men, or even any apparent plan to the military exercise. Although "it was magnificent to see commando after commando file past," he wrote, "each man brandish[ed] hat or rifle according to his individual idea of a military salute."

Had they been able to witness the scene, the British military would have mocked it as unworthy of any military tradition. The rifles the Boers were holding, however, would have gotten their attention, and stolen the smiles from their faces. Accustomed to fighting colonial wars against enemies who had little more than a few antiquated shotguns, the British War Office assumed that, at best, the Boers would be carrying the outdated Martini-Henry carbines they had used during the First Boer War. They could not have been more wrong.

For years, the Boers had been making one critical concession to war preparedness. They had been stockpiling weapons. Since the Jameson Raid, Cecil Rhodes's disastrously failed attempt to take over the Transvaal nearly four years earlier, Kruger had been sending men to Europe to buy the most effective and modern weapons available anywhere in the world. In particular, the Boers had been amassing German Mausers, a magazine rifle that was not only lighter but faster loading than the Lee-Enfield, the rifle the British army had been using since 1888. In 1895 alone, the Boers bought ten thousand rifles and roughly twelve million rounds of ammunition, which they stored in a fort in Pretoria. The following year, the secretary of state for war, Louis de Souza, had gone back to buy more.

As good as the guns were, the men using them were even better. Even the British had to begrudgingly admit that when it came to marksmanship, it was impossible to compete with the Boers.

Whether they were hunting lions, which raided their herds of cattle and flocks of sheep and posed a threat to their families, or fighting the native Africans whose land they now occupied, their lives depended every day on the speed and accuracy of their shooting. They were "the finest mass of rifle-armed horsemen ever seen," Churchill wrote, "and the most capable mounted warriors since the Mongols."

They were also determined to win. They felt that they had no other choice. Although southern Africa had been populated for millions of years before the Boers arrived, they believed that this land was their birthright, no less than a gift from God. They were certain that if they lost, the resulting tragedy would not only devastate them, it would, in Kruger's words, "stagger humanity."

↦

As the burghers filed past Joubert that day, brandishing their Mausers in a self-styled salute, one man stood out among the long gray beards and rough, heavily lined faces of the members of the Volksraad, the Transvaal parliament. Louis Botha, nearly six feet tall, broad-shouldered and sinewy with dark hair, a closely trimmed goatee and violet-blue eyes, looked as though he could have been carved out of the heavy clay soil of Natal, where he had been born. Although he was only thirty-seven years old, among a people who revered age, he was already a respected member of the Volksraad, a position he was about to abandon so that he could go to war.

No man in the crowd that surrounded him was more thoroughly Boer than Louis Botha, and the story of his ancestry was the story of Boer creation. He could trace his family back to some of the earliest days of European settlement in southern Africa, to the hundreds of Huguenots who left France for South Africa in 1685 after the revocation of the Edict of Nantes, which had made their religion, and any but Catholicism, illegal. On one of the ships sailing out of France was a man named Botés, or it might have been Bottes, or perhaps Bodes. No one knows with any certainty because he changed his name to Botha soon after reaching the Cape of Good Hope. So infuriated were the Huguenots at being cast out of France that when they arrived in Africa, they refused to speak the French language, a ban that extended even to their own names.

Botha and his fellow Huguenots quickly joined forces with the Dutch, and together they seized control of the region. Spreading from Table Bay to the foot of Table Mountain, they raised cattle and sheep and grew everything from grain to wine grapes in the fertile soil. Armed with guns and horses, neither of which the Cape's inhabitants—the San and KhoiKhoi peoples—had ever before seen, and bringing with them devastating European diseases, they quickly decimated the native population.

By the time the British began making their own claims on the Cape at the end of the century, the Dutch and the Huguenots, along with an infusion of German immigrants, had already transformed themselves from rogue splinter groups into an entirely new ethnic group—neither European nor African, but Boer. "In their manner of life, their habits . . . even in their character," a journalist for *The Times* would write, "they had undergone a profound change." The Boers even developed their own language, Afrikaans, which mixes Dutch with everything from French and Portuguese to KhoiKhoi. The word *boer* itself, which means "farmer," is Dutch, but the Boers quickly developed new words as they needed them, from *kopje* (hill) and *veld* (grassland) to *Voortrekker.*

Early in the nineteenth century, soon after the British had made the Cape of Good Hope a permanent possession of the empire, two new generations of Bothas—Philip Rudolph Botha and his two young sons—joined the Great Trek. As they struck out from Cape Colony in an attempt to escape British rule, their slow, rolling processions of covered wagons pulled by long, serried lines of oxen were almost indistinguishable from the westward movement that was taking place at the same time in North America. In fact, like the American pioneers, the Boer *Voortrekkers* crossed part of a vast continent that was not only unknown to the outside world but inhabited by large groups of native people with whom they would spend decades in brutal combat. Instead of the Cherokee and the Iroquois, however, the Boers faced the Zulu, one of the greatest warrior races in the world, and the Xhosa, the tribe into which Nelson Mandela would one day be born.

While many *Voortrekkers* settled in pockets of grassland scattered across an enormous, sweeping desert known to the Boers as the Great Karoo, the Bothas skirted the eastern coast, passing from the desert into the veld and winding their way toward the Republic of Natalia. It was here, about halfway between the port town of Durban and Pietermaritzburg, roughly fifty miles inland, that Philip Rudolph Botha and his sons finally stopped, establishing a farm and helping to build a railroad station in a town that would become known as Botha's Hill.

It did not take the Bothas long to lose any trace, or even memory, of the Frenchmen they had been only a few generations before. Although the Natal had already fallen into British hands by the time Louis, Philip Rudolph's grandson, was born in 1862, the family continued to lead a solitary, fiercely independent way of life that was stubbornly Boer. They had no interest in any land beyond Africa, no tolerance for any man or institution meddling in their lives, and no allegiance to any flag other than the thick, colorful stripes of the two remaining Boer republics—the Transvaal and the Orange Free State.

Although technically a British citizen by birth, Louis Botha had had the most traditional of Boer childhoods. He grew up in a family of thirteen children on an isolated farm in Greytown, about a hundred miles from Durban, and, between a German mission school and a traveling tutor, had received only a couple of years of formal education. He was, however, fluent in several languages, including Zulu and Sotho, both of which he knew better than English. He also learned how to shoot a rifle as soon as he was strong enough to hold one.

Like most Boers, Botha's family had spent the great majority of their lives at war, in one form or another. As a child, his mother had hidden with her grandmother, the two of them frantically making bullets, while her family desperately tried to repel a Zulu attack. Botha's father often clashed with nearby Zulu who, while fighting the Boer incursion onto their land, had on several occasions burned down their farmhouse. Louis himself had fought not only against the Zulu but with them. In 1884, when he was just twenty-two years old, he had formed and led a group of Boers who, in exchange for vast swaths of land, had helped Dinuzulu, crown prince of the Zulu nation, defeat his rival for the throne after his father's death.

In fact, Botha had nearly been killed during that war, not by Dinuzulu's rival, but by his own men. After a long day riding by himself through Dinuzulu's territory, setting up landmarks for the other men, Botha had come upon an abandoned shanty, where he decided to sleep. In the middle of the night, he was awoken by the sound of chanting. Peering through a window onto the moon-drenched veld, he saw to his horror that he was surrounded by Zulu, all armed with assegai, or throwing spears, and chanting in unison, "We have come to kill the white man." Leaning out the window, Botha shouted in Zulu, "Who are you?" "We are the warriors of Dinuzulu," came the reply. "But I have been fighting on *your* side!" Botha shouted back. The chanting immediately ceased, and the men lowered their weapons. As Botha walked out of the shanty and stood in the moonlight before the men who, moments earlier, had been about to slaughter him, he was hailed as a friend and fellow warrior.

Perhaps because of his long experience in battle, Botha did not like the idea of killing other men. When tensions with the British had begun to rise, he had hoped that war could be averted. He had even been among the handful of men in the Volksraad who had voted against sending the ultimatum to England. Finally, however, he had come to the conclusion that if his people wanted peace, they must first have war. "The Transvaal has done all it can in order to preserve peace," Botha had said in a somber speech to the Volksraad, "but I think that we have now gone far enough."

➤➤

On October 12, the day after the deadline for the ultimatum, the Boers burst southeastward out of Pretoria like the breaking of a dam, rushing toward Natal, the British colony on the Indian Ocean coast that had once been theirs. It was raining in heavy sheets, and a fierce, freezing wind was blowing off the mountains, but the men, most of whom had neither tents nor overcoats, took little notice. "As far as the eye could see the plain was alive with horsemen, guns and cattle, all steadily going forward to the frontier," Deneys Reitz would recall years later, when he was no longer a boy. "The scene was a stirring one, and I shall never forget riding to war with that great host."

The next day, the Boers crossed into Natal, and, with a suddenness that would leave the British military reeling, the war began. Although he had hoped for peace, Botha was among the first wave of horses and men surging out of the capital. Breaking away with a small group to capture the first British prisoners of the war, six frontier policemen who were so shocked and unprepared they were able to put up no resistance, he rejoined his commando, a Boer combat unit, just beyond the Buffalo River. By the time they merged with another commando, they were eight thousand men strong, all sweeping eastward with an irresistible force toward the little coal-mining town of Dundee, where the commanding British general, Sir William Penn Symons, had set up his camp at the base of Talana Hill.

In Natal, Penn Symons and his counterpart, General George White, were equally unconcerned about the tens of thousands of burghers surrounding them from nearly every direction, and had decided to divide their already woefully inadequate force. Of their roughly twelve thousand men, some eight thousand had gone northwestward to the British garrison town of Ladysmith with White and the other four thousand farther north with Penn Symons to Dundee. Both towns were beyond the curving Tugela River, which Buller had repeatedly warned them not to cross until he arrived.

By the time he reached Ladysmith, White, taking in the stark terrain and the tension that seethed in every town he passed, had quickly realized that he had made a serious mistake. "Goodbye dear old lady," he had written miserably to his wife. "We should have 20,000 more troops in South Africa than we have." Penn Symons, however, continued to insist that there was no cause for concern and confidently marched his small brigade even farther north than Ladysmith, to Dundee, where he planned to set up camp.

In Dundee, Penn Symons ran his brigade much as he had in India. He hosted guest nights in the regimental mess so that his officers might bring their wives, encouraged his men to wear their scarlet and green dress uniforms, and cheerfully discussed plans for Christmas dinner in Pretoria. Even as his scouts warned him that the Boers had begun to descend upon Dundee, Penn Symons scoffed that no Boer commando would dare to attack a British brigade, no matter its size. "I feel perfectly safe," he coolly told the agitated officers under his command. "I am dead against retreating."

At 5:00 on the morning of October 20, after a night of rain so heavy the British were certain it would deter any man, even the Boers, from scaling the hills surrounding their camp, a shell suddenly rent the quiet morning air. Penn Symons was just about to sit down to his breakfast when the second shell thundered down in the midst of his tents, missing his own by only a few yards. Outraged by the Boers' impudence, he smoked a cigarette as he began issuing orders, commanding his men to train their guns on Talana Hill.

For Botha and his commando, watching from the same hill on which Penn Symons had set his sights, the entire British brigade, racing from tent to tent, scrambling to respond to the attack, made a stunningly easy target. No man among them, however, was more conspicuous than Penn Symons himself, who insisted that his aide-de-camp ride by his side, holding a dashing scarlet pennant. Within minutes, nearly every inch of ground surrounding the camp was, in the words of one British soldier, "literally rising in dust from the bullets, and the din echoing between the hill and the wood below and among the rocks from the incessant fire of the Mausers seemed to blend with every other sound into a long drawn-out hideous roar."

In the midst of the onslaught, Penn Symons refused to find cover or take even the slightest precaution. Angrily climbing over a low wall that was impeding his force's progress, he disappeared from sight, making his way over ground that was littered with the bodies of his men. Minutes later, he returned to his aide-de-camp, his face strained and pale, and tersely informed him that he had been shot in the stomach and was "severely, mortally, wounded."

The Boers, who had only three artillery guns to Penn Symons's eighteen, could not sustain the attack and were finally forced to retreat. But they had accomplished what they had come to do—shatter their enemy's confidence. As Botha's commando disappeared in the distance, a veil of rain obscuring their tracks on the muddy veld, they left behind more than five hundred British casualties, among them Penn Symons, who lay dying in a hospital tent while his second-in-command, Brigadier General James Yule, hastily ordered his brigade to pack up what they could and flee southward to Ladysmith. Two days later, a Boer commander taking possession of Dundee would find Penn Symons dead and stand watching, hat in hand, as the fallen officer's body was sewn into a British flag and buried in the yard of a local English church.

On October 26, nearly a week after the Battle of Talana Hill, Yule and his five thousand men finally reached Ladysmith, following an exhausting and harrowing journey. They quickly learned, however, that they had hardly outmaneuvered the Boers. Not only had the British lost another three hundred men, wounded and dead, in the Battle of Elandslaagte, less than twenty miles away, but George White's regiment was also completely surrounded. Worse, the Boer force deploying around Ladysmith was not eight thousand strong but twenty thousand.

As he had been in Dundee, Louis Botha was situated on a prominent hill overlooking Ladysmith, ready for the battle to begin. This time, however, the order to fire would come not from the commando's leader, his old friend and mentor, Lucas Meyer, but from Botha himself. Soon after reaching Ladysmith, Meyer had fallen ill and Botha had quickly been chosen to take command, making him the youngest Boer commander in the war. "He had already won confidence all round by the clearness of his views and the intrepidity of his actions," the Irish journalist and activist Michael Davitt, who covered the Boers during the war, wrote of Botha, "and his promotion to the command in question became exceedingly popular, especially among the younger and more ardent Boers."

The Battle of Ladysmith lasted only a day, but it had devastating consequences for the British. It began on the morning of October 30, and by the time it ended that night, the British had lost twelve hundred men, a tenth of their troops in Ladysmith. Perhaps most stunning of all, the British army had been forced to retreat, and they now found themselves under siege, their water supply cut off, railroad links and telegraph lines severed, and their only hope Sir Redvers Buller, who had yet to even land in Cape Town.

After the battle, Botha did not stop to celebrate, or even rest. Leaving a few thousand burghers to guard Ladysmith, he and Joubert turned their attention to a small town named Estcourt, forty miles south, where a British force of some twenty thousand was rumored to be headed after landing in Cape Town. Now that Ladysmith was under siege, Estcourt was the new front for the war.

Botha knew the region well. He had been born nearby and had grown up herding cattle over hundreds of miles of its scrubby grassland. The British, on the other hand, knew almost nothing about Estcourt or its surroundings, and had no idea what tactical opportunities or dangers it held. By the time Buller's men reached Natal, they would be exhausted from a long journey, disoriented by their strange new surroundings and shocked by their recent losses to an enemy that, until only a few days before, they had believed to be hopelessly unequal to the task of fighting the British army. Most of them still refused to acknowledge that the war would not be over by Christmas, when in fact, the Boers were determined to prove, the new arrivals' bloodshed and hardships were just beginning.

CHAPTER 7

THE BLACKEST OF ALL DAYS

On October 29, the day before the Battle of Ladysmith, the passengers of the *Dunottar Castle,* their long journey nearly over, sighted another vessel on the horizon. It was a large steamship, the *Australasian,* heading away from South Africa with soldiers aboard and bearing, Churchill excitedly wrote, "who should say what tidings." Desperate for news of the war, the men rushed to the decks, hanging over the railings with their telescopes, binoculars and cameras trained on the ship as the distance between them quickly closed. Even Buller stepped onto the lower deck and peered at the ship through his field glasses.

When the two ships came within two hundred yards of each other, the men on the *Australasian* gave their fellow soldiers a raucous three-cheer salute. What happened next, however, sent an electric thrill of shock through the passengers of the *Dunottar Castle.* "It was," Atkins, the reporter for the *Manchester Guardian,* would later write, "the most dramatic encounter at sea that any of us could call to mind, or was likely to experience again."

As the ship passed by, the men on its decks, too far away to be heard, slid onto the ratlines a long black board with words written on it in bright white chalk:

BOERS DEFEATED
THREE BATTLES
PENN SYMONS KILLED

The men surrounding Churchill gasped and took a collective, reeling step back from the bulwark. The fighting had already begun, and it had been fierce. "Under Heaven," Churchill wrote, "we have held our own," but the shock of Penn Symons's death reverberated throughout the ship. If the general, who had had "no misfortunes" in India, whose men, even his rear guards, had always come "safely into camp," had fallen to the Boers, how many more had shared his fate?

As the ship swiftly disappeared from sight, taking with it the answers to their many, desperate questions, Churchill, never shy about making his opinion known, openly complained that "it would only have taken ten minutes to have stopped the ship and got proper information." Buller, with "characteristic phlegm," dryly replied that it was "the weakness of youth to be impatient. We should know everything that had happened quite soon enough." Churchill, however, although not even a soldier, let alone the commander in chief, remained "impenitent and unconvinced."

The next day, when the *Dunottar Castle* arrived at Cape Town's Table Bay, and waited to be pulled into the harbor, Churchill watched hungrily as a tugboat ran alongside the ship and a man stepped aboard. He was, in Churchill's words, not just any man, but a "Man Who Knew." It was the moment Churchill had been waiting for since leaving Southampton two weeks earlier, and he was determined to extract every last bit of information there was.

Churchill was not alone in his impatience. Surrounded by nearly three hundred soldiers and journalists, the man was practically chased across the oiled floorboards until he reached the ladder leading to the hurricane deck. Quickly climbing the rungs, he chose a step halfway up and took a seat. Only then, with an "odd quiver of excitement in his voice," did he finally tell his story.

While his audience stood transfixed, the man described one battle after another that had already been fought between the Boers and the

British, every major battle but Ladysmith, which was taking place as he spoke. Finally, after listening to tales of "stubborn, well-fought fights with honour for both sides, triumph for neither," one man in the audience asked the question that was on all of their minds. "Tell us about the losses," he said. "Who are killed and wounded."

It was a stunningly long list, Churchill would later remember, a list "of the best officers in the world." As the names of friends, mentors, fathers and brothers were read out loud, the men who had gathered eagerly at the foot of the ladder began to turn, one by one, and hurry away, overcome with emotion that they did not want their fellow soldiers to see. Churchill himself knew several of the men on the list—"all lying under the stony soil or filling the hospitals at Pietermaritzburg and Durban"—but one name in particular leaped out at him with a painful jolt of recognition: Aylmer Haldane.

Churchill had met Haldane the year before, when he was trying to persuade Sir William Lockhart, then commander in chief of Her Majesty's army in India, to let him fight on the northwest frontier. Haldane, who was Lockhart's aide-de-camp, had at first been "none too cordial," Churchill remembered, but for a reason that Churchill could not quite understand, his attitude had abruptly and completely changed. "I don't remember what I said nor how I stated my case," Churchill later wrote, "but I must have hit the bull's eye more than once. For after about half an hour's walking up and down on the gravel-path Captain Haldane said, 'Well, I'll go and ask the Commander-in-Chief and see what he says.'" Churchill had continued pacing back and forth by himself until Haldane returned with news that Lockhart had decided to add another orderly officer to his staff, and Churchill was to fill the position.

After that first meeting, Churchill had joined Haldane every day on his morning walk, and a friendship had quickly developed between the two young men. Although he thought Haldane a "clever, daring, conscientious & ambitious fellow," Churchill was baffled by his willingness not just to help him but to go out of his way to open doors and clear paths. "The success which has attended my coup is in some measure I feel, deserved," Churchill had written to his mother after winning the assignment with Lockhart, "but I have received a most remarkable assistance from Captain Haldane—the general's ADC. I have never met this man before and I am at a loss to know why he should have espoused my cause—with so strange an earnestness."

Despite his skepticism, Churchill had not hesitated to take advantage of the situation, and to ask Haldane for any favors he thought might be within his power to grant. "I am entitled to a medal and two clasps for my gallantry for the hardships & dangers I encountered {while in India}," he had written to Haldane soon after leaving for the Sudan. "I am possessed of a keen desire to mount the ribbon on my breast while I face the Dervishes here. It may induce them to pause. . . . If you will do me a favor and materially add to my joy as well as to my gratitude, please write me a letter to say exactly when I may consider my medal as issued & enclose in the envelope a little slip of the ribbon."

Although, in the intervening year, Churchill and Haldane had both moved quickly between countries and continents, and Churchill had left the army for his political campaign, they had somehow stayed in touch. Churchill had sent Haldane a copy of *The River War,* had made plans to see him again—"We shall meet anon. Piccadilly or the Pyramids"—and had even introduced him to his mother. But, having grown used to encountering people who were offended by his brash pride and obvious ambition and who wished to knock the rungs out of the ladder he was so determined to climb, he continued to wonder why Haldane would wish to help him, and ask for nothing in return. The only answer that made sense to him was that it must be the strength of his own résumé. "My idea is that my reputation— for whatever it may be worth—has interested him," Churchill had speculated to his mother. "Of course you will destroy this letter and show it to no one . . . or I may be found a fool as well as an ingrate."

Churchill had known that Haldane was already in Africa, but until that moment he had known nothing more. Even if his friend was not yet "lying under the stony soil," Churchill was not likely to see him, or be able to rely on his help, which he needed now more than ever. As a noncombatant, unattached to a regiment and with no official status beyond his assignment with the *Morning Post* and his letter of introduction from Chamberlain, he would have a difficult time getting anywhere near the front, which was exactly where he planned to be. This was quickly shaping up into a war that not only would sell newspapers but could make heroes out of men, and members of Parliament out of heroes.

➤➤

The next morning, however, when the ship finally docked in Cape Town, Churchill immediately realized that he was not going anywhere quickly with Buller. As he had learned early in his military career, although "the picture of war moves very swiftly," the British army does not. In the midst of the pomp and circumstance that surrounded Buller's arrival—a thundering salute from the harbor batteries, the streets lined with bunting-covered homes and cheering expatriates—the sluggish, overburdened machine that was the British military struggled to shake off the lethargy of the long voyage and shudder to life.

Even for England, used to dispersing its troops to the farthest reaches of its empire, it was no small undertaking to fight a war some seven thousand miles from home. In the month of October 1899 alone, including the men that Churchill was accompanying on the *Dunottar Castle,* the British Empire sent nearly 30,000 soldiers and officers to southern Africa. By March 1900, more than 160,000 men—an average of over 1,000 a day—would set sail from either Great Britain or Ireland. And that was just the troops.

In comparison to the astonishingly mobile Boers, who were able to wage war with little more than men, horses and Mausers, and to move from battlefield to battlefield at a moment's notice, the British army moved at a glacial pace, weighed down by the sheer number of its possessions. As, one after another, ships left Southampton, their cargo holds were filled with thousands of firearms—carbines, pistols and rifles with long bayonets—as well as huge pieces of artillery, everything from fifteen-pounders, which took their name from the fifteen-pound shrapnel shells they shot, to short-barreled howitzers, which lobbed gunpowder-filled cast-iron shells. There were hundreds of thousands of water bottles and bars of soap, thousands of tents and wagons and hundreds of camp kettles.

Even clothing its men was a complicated and time-consuming task for the British army. While the Boers were lucky to have any coat at all, Her Majesty's forces had the latest in rain gear to protect them from the South African summer downpours. The British clothier Thomas Burberry had developed a new fabric called gabardine, a chemically processed wool that could repel rain and was resistant to tears. The soldiers in the Boer War would be the first to wear jackets made from this fabric, which they called Burberrys. Fifteen years later, Burberry would design another coat for soldiers in World War I, with straps on the shoulders for their epaulets and brass D-rings on the belt for their swords and hand grenades. Because most of the men wearing it would be fighting in the trenches, it was called a trench coat.

British troops were no longer wearing their famous red coats, which had prudently been abandoned in favor of khaki. To the Boers, however, even the khaki uniforms seemed elaborate, if not ridiculous. British officers wore high, peaked pith helmets that shaded their eyes from the sun but were hot and uncomfortable and made easy targets for Boer sharpshooters. Their khaki jackets were crisscrossed with leather belts and straps—brown, white or black, depending on their regiment—that held everything from knapsacks to ammunition pouches to round, wooden water casks with pewter stoppers, the perfect breeding ground for disease. The Scottish Highland troops still wore kilts, but they were now required to wrap a khaki apron over them. They would also quickly learn to wear thick hose over their bare legs to protect them from the blistering South African sun.

When Deneys Reitz's commando had entered Dundee in the wake of Yule's frantic departure, he was stunned by the multitude of supplies that had been left behind, extravagant luxuries that he and his fellow burghers could not even imagine, much less expect to be issued. "Knowing the meagre way in which our men were fed and equipped I was astonished at the numberless things an English army carried with it in the field," he wrote. "There were mountains of luxurious foods, comfortable camp-stretchers and sleeping bags, and there was even a gymnasium, and a profusion of other things too numerous to mention."

To carry all these supplies, the British army had bought £645,000 worth of mules and oxen, ordered just weeks earlier. To carry their men, they had been forced to ship hundreds of thousands of horses to southern Africa, not just from England, but from Europe, North and South America and Australia. For the horses, the journey by sea was even more miserable than it was for Churchill. In an attempt to keep them calm and less inclined to kick as they were forced onto the ships, they were kept "rather low in flesh," deprived of food and water for hours before embarking. Their handlers kept the horses' shoes on so that they had a better chance of staying upright in rough seas as they slid and skidded in their wooden stalls, but also because it was assumed that they would be mounted as soon as the ship landed, which they always were. Those that survived the journey had little hope of returning home alive after the war. In fact, the average life expectancy of a horse in southern Africa during the Boer War was six weeks. Most were killed by bullets, disease, overwork or starvation, but occasionally, during sieges, they were eaten by soldiers who boiled their meat down to a paste and drank it like beef tea.

The crowd in Cape Town watched in excitement as Buller's own Irish chargers—Biffin, a six-year-old, white-faced chestnut, and Ironmonger, a dark bay with a white star on his forehead—were lifted off the *Dunottar Castle* one at a time, secured in wide leather harnesses, and lowered down into a scene of complete chaos. Buller himself, leaving in his wake a staggering amount of work to accomplish, was whisked away in an open carriage, chased by cheering crowds, to an urgent meeting with Sir Alfred Milner, the governor of Cape Colony.

→→

In sharp contrast to the unadorned practicality of Pretoria, Cape Town shimmered with modern life. As Buller's carriage rattled down broad brick roads flanked by ornate, many-storied buildings, he was surrounded by the hum of electric cars and the sharp gongs of rattling trolleys. To George Warrington Steevens, the journalist for the *Daily Mail* who had arrived there a few weeks earlier, Cape Town was less African or even British than a mix of continents and cultures. "It seemed half Western American with a faint smell of India," he wrote. "Denver with a dash of Delhi."

When Buller reached Milner's residence, however, the sheen of imperial calm in the face of war quickly evaporated. Shocked to life by the recent, stunning battlefield losses, Government House, a Georgian-style mansion with a brand-new ballroom, had become a center of tense, frantic action. Harried government workers scurried up and down the elaborate central staircase, their arms full of papers, tight frowns on their tired faces.

One night soon after arriving in Cape Town, Churchill, on the strength of Joseph Chamberlain's letter of introduction, was invited to dine at Government House. Confidently elbowing his way into a conversation between Milner and Buller, he critiqued the governor's colonial policy and then, turning his attention to the commander in chief, began to give him advice on how he should conduct his campaign. Buller, characteristically blunt, told Churchill "not to be a young ass."

Milner, however, was desperate, and willing to listen to just about anyone. He had done more than perhaps any man to bring about this war, arguing long and loudly that the Boers could easily be defeated. Now, sickened by the news coming out of Natal, he was terrified that Cape Colony would be next to fall to the Boers. "Sir Alfred Milner told me that the whole of Cape Colony was 'trembling on the verge of Rebellion,'" Churchill would write to his mother just days later. Milner himself took refuge in his diary, miserably confiding that "matters look extremely black . . . the blackest of all days."

Although he was urgently needed in Natal, Buller would have to wait until the ships that were now on the high seas, carrying additional men and supplies, caught up with him. Churchill, however, had no intention of cooling his heels in Cape Town. He had another plan.

Slipping into the city with Atkins, the correspondent for the *Manchester Guardian,* he learned that there was a rail line to East London, a harbor town on the east coast of Cape Colony, from where he could take a British mail boat into Natal, on the Indian Ocean coast. The journey by train alone would be seven hundred miles, all of it undefended and much of it bordering Boer territory. Once in the besieged colony, it would be a breakneck race to make it to Ladysmith before the Boers had surrounded it completely.

When the other journalists learned of this desperate and dangerous plan, they were determined to find their own way out of the Cape. Churchill and Atkins's train, however, would be the last to get through. Churchill was determined to travel faster and farther than any of them, and he would succeed. His carefully orchestrated life, however, was about to veer wildly off course.

CHAPTER 8

LAND OF STONE AND SCRUB

While Churchill slept, his train moved quickly eastward, slipping over smooth tracks as it carried him out of the Cape and toward a land that was starkly different from the incredibly green and diverse terrain he had first seen from the deck of the *Dunottar Castle*. He was leaving behind not just Table Mountain, which looms, broad-shouldered and flat-topped, behind Cape Town, but also the Cape Fold Belt, a series of low sandstone and shale mountain ranges that stretches along the sea like a curving fortress wall.

The jutting chin of southern Africa is rimmed with a low, narrow coastline. Not even a hundred miles inland, however, a jagged belt of mountain ranges rises up in dramatic peaks that in some areas reach more than ten thousand feet. Most of these ranges belong to the Great Escarpment, which was formed about 200 million years ago when Gondwanaland, the supercontinent that included South America, Africa, Madagascar, Arabia, India, Australia and Antarctica, was torn apart. The Cape Fold Belt, however, was created even earlier than that, 100 million years earlier.

Inside this framework of mountains lies a sprawling tableland that includes a vast semi-desert known as the Great Karoo. Much like the Andes mountain range in South America, which divides one of the richest, wettest regions on earth—the Amazon basin—from the driest—the Atacama Desert—the mountains of the Cape Fold Belt not only separate the sparkling Cape from the Great Karoo but are themselves the cause of their extreme contrast. When cold air coming off the Atlantic Ocean collides with the mountains, it is forced thousands of feet above sea level, where it meets the warm air of the Indian Ocean. This collision, which creates the famous "Table Cloth," the cottony cloud that often appears to be draped over the top of Table Mountain, sends the vast majority of the rainfall to the southern face, leaving very little precipitation for the northern side.

When Churchill awoke and peered out his train car window, the rising sun revealed mile after mile of seemingly endless, changeless desert. George Warrington Steevens, who had passed through the Great Karoo only a few weeks earlier, defended the brown and largely barren region in his dispatch for the *Daily Mail*. "It is only to the eye that cannot do without green that the Karroo is unbeautiful," he argued. "Every other colour meets others in harmony—tawny sand, silver-grey scrub, crimson-tufted flowers like heather, black ribs of rock, puce shoots of screes, violet mountains in the middle distance, blue fairy battlements guarding the horizon." The subtle colors and pleasures of the Karoo, however, were completely lost on Churchill. "The scenery would depress the most buoyant spirits," he scrawled in a dispatch from his train car. "Wherefore was this miserable land of stone and scrub created?"

Although he was relieved when, the next day, he finally escaped the Great Karoo, reaching East London and the mail boat that would take him northward to Natal, Churchill was not looking forward to another sea journey. He was right to worry. His ship, only 150 tons, was no match for the Indian Ocean, especially during the rainy season. In what Churchill would later describe as a "horrible Antarctic gale," the ocean churned and the little mail boat "bounded and reeled, and kicked and pitched, and fell and turned almost over and righted itself again . . . hour after hour through an endless afternoon, a still longer evening and an eternal night."

When morning finally came, and Churchill had somewhat recovered from the "most appalling paroxysms of sea-sickness which it has ever been my lot to survive," he gingerly ventured onto the deck to watch the coastline slide by. What he saw on the region's Indian Ocean coast brought on a surge of imperialistic fervor that was extreme even for Churchill, the kinds of emotions that a place like the Great Karoo could never have stirred within his British breast. "Here are wide tracts of fertile soil watered by abundant rains," he wrote in a gushing tribute to the rich, eastern coast of southern Africa. "The temperate sun warms the life within the soil. The cooling breeze refreshes the inhabitant. The delicious climate stimulates the vigour of the European. . . . All Nature smiles, and here at last is a land where white men may rule and prosper."

Although the white men Churchill had in mind for ruling and prospering in South Africa were certainly not the Boers, the Dutch descendants had had the same rush of desire and deep sense of entitlement when they first laid eyes on Natal. Since the earliest days of the war, both the Boers and the British had held an unshakable belief in the righteousness of their cause and the unworthiness of their enemy. Neither group, however, had given a moment's thought, or would have cared if they had, to the fact that the land over which they were fighting did not belong to either one of them.

→→

When the first Dutch ships landed on the Cape of Good Hope in the mid-seventeenth century, southern Africa had not been a forgotten land, any more than North America had been free for the taking when the Pilgrims had settled Plymouth just thirty years earlier. Unlike North America, however, Africa had already been inhabited not for thousands of years but for millions.

The first modern humans in southern Africa were the San, who lived there for tens of thousands of years before the KhoiKhoi arrived. After the KhoiKhoi, tens of thousands of years more passed before the Dutch made an appearance. It took the Dutch less than a hundred years, however, to so devastate both the San and the KhoiKhoi populations that by 1750 there was little sign of either tribe within 250 miles of Table Bay.

Because they had so quickly taken over the Cape, the Dutch believed that as they began to push deeper into the African interior, they would easily conquer any tribes they might meet. What they did not know was that, while they were moving north from the coast, seizing land, cattle and slaves along the way, another powerful group of immigrants had already made its way south, from the center of the continent. Known as the Bantu, which means "people" or "humans," they were a loosely knit linguistic family with hundreds of different ethnic groups, including two of Africa's largest, most powerful and most feared tribes—the Xhosa and the Zulu.

Tall, strong and nearly as brutal to the San and the KhoiKhoi as the Boers had been, the Bantu were not Stone Age Africans. They had large populations, grew their own crops and, perhaps most important from the standpoint of the Dutch, knew how to forge metal tools and weapons. It is widely believed that the Bantu came to southern Africa from the region that is today Nigeria and Cameroon. Five thousand years ago, they began what has become known as the Bantu expansion, a vast migration that moved steadily southward, ranging across thousands of miles of central Africa and covering stunningly diverse terrain, from the sprawling central African rain forest, second in size only to the Amazon, to the Kalahari Desert, the eastern Great Lakes and the southern savannas.

The steady and seemingly unassailable conquest of southern Africa by the Boers and the Bantu, one from below and the other from above, came to an abrupt halt by the 1770s, when they finally met face-to-face on the banks of the Great Fish River. The Bantu, who had seen few white men beyond the occasional desperate shipwrecked sailor, were as shocked as the Boers. At first, both sides had proceeded with caution, and, for a time, they had lived in relative peace. It took ten years for full-fledged war to break out, but when it did, it seemed as though it would never end. The Frontier Wars alone, a series of nine bloody battles between the Boers and the Xhosa, a large Bantu tribe, lasted nearly a century.

As fierce as they were, however, the Xhosa would not become the Boers', and later England's, bitterest rivals in Africa. That distinction belonged to the Zulu. An insignificant offshoot of the Nguni, a Bantu group that had migrated east while the Xhosa continued south, the tribe at first numbered no more than two hundred people. What transformed the Zulu into not just a powerful tribe but arguably the most storied group of people ever to live in southern Africa was the irresistible and terrifying rise of a single man—a young warrior named Shaka.

→>

In many ways, Shaka both created the Zulu Nation and nearly destroyed it. Although he rose to power as an effective and merciless warrior, it was Shaka's skill as a military tactician that would transform the Zulu tribe. He completely reorganized the army, instituting a regimental system that separated soldiers by age and assigned them kraals, or villages, in which they were forced to live celibate lives. He is credited with creating the famous "bull horn" battle formation, in which the enemy is trapped by the chest of the bull, the principal force; the horns, the secondary unit, circle in on them from both sides; and the loins, a reserve force stationed behind the chest, with their backs to the battle, ensure that no one escapes with his life.

Shaka also redesigned the most essential Zulu weapon, the assegai, turning the fragile throwing spear into a much heavier thrusting stick, with a broad blade and shortened haft. The new weapon quickly became known as an *iKlwa,* in imitation of the sucking sound it made as it was pulled from a body. After impaling his enemies on an *iKlwa,* Shaka, gorged with blood and victory, would shout, "Ngadla!"—"I have eaten!"

More than changing how the Zulu fought, Shaka changed who they were. Fear was his principal weapon, and he used it not just against his enemies, but against his own people. He trained his warriors in brutality, forcing them to dance barefoot over thorns, drill from dawn to dusk until they literally dropped from exhaustion, and walk more than fifty miles in a single day. On a whim, he would bury entire regiments alive or order them to march, one by one, over a cliff simply to prove their loyalty. He ordered men to be executed because they had sneezed in front of him or because he didn't like the way they looked.

So complete was Shaka's control over his people that, although the death he meted out was often lingering and always as excruciating as his imagination allowed, few of his victims tried to escape their horrible fate. "No fetters or cords are ever employed to bind the victim," recalled a Briton who, as a boy, had witnessed Zulu executions while on African hunting trips with his father. "He is left at liberty to run for his life or to stand and meet his doom. . . . Many stand and meet their fate with a degree of firmness that could hardly be imagined."

Shaka was finally assassinated in 1828, stabbed to death by his half brothers who used *iKlwas,* the weapon of his own creation, to put an end to his reign of terror. Although he had ruled the Zulu for only twelve years, the mark Shaka left on the tribe was as indelible as those of history's most legendary leaders, from Genghis Khan to Napoleon to, one day, Churchill himself. For the Boers, as for anyone who clashed with the Zulu, Shaka's impact on the tribe could be felt long after his death.

The British too had fought the Zulu, and had come so close to defeat that a stunned Queen Victoria had demanded to know, "Who are these Zulus?" But the Boers had lived beside them, fought with them and learned from them in a way that the British could not possibly understand. Through their bloody altercations with the Zulu, the Boers' military tactics had been forged in fire. They had learned how to fight like no other Europeans, and they were going to use everything Shaka had taught them to rid themselves of the British once and for all.

→→

Although the most famous battle between the Zulu and the Boers took place ten years after Shaka's assassination, it bore the unmistakable mark of his particular brand of military genius, and the widespread suffering that was also his legacy. It was a battle, moreover, that had begun where Churchill's journey into Natal in 1899 was about to end: a small, now largely abandoned town named Estcourt.

Situated on a broad expanse of green tufted veld and surrounded by low hills, Estcourt, just forty miles south of Ladysmith, was to the British nothing more than a convenient site from which to mount a defense of the besieged town. It could have been any rural village in any forgotten backwater of their sprawling empire. To the Boers, however, the town stood on hallowed ground.

Sixty years earlier, Estcourt and the surrounding area had been the scene of a brutal massacre of some five hundred *Voortrekkers* and KhoiKhoi laborers by Dingane, Shaka's half brother who had assumed the throne after murdering him. Not quite a year later, a group of Boers led by Andries Pretorius, a close friend of Louis Botha's grandfather, had retaliated, confronting the Zulu on the banks of the Ncome River. The Zulu had arrived for the battle in terrifying waves of as many as twelve thousand warriors, chanting and hissing as they brandished *iKlwas* and curled around the Boers in Shaka's own bull-horn battle formation. The Boers, however, although they had fewer than five hundred men, were armed with rifles and a cannon. By the end of the day, some three thousand Zulu lay dead. In fact, so great was the slaughter that the river was said to have run red with their blood, and the Boers changed its name from Ncome River to Blood River.

After the Battle of Blood River, the Boers had claimed much of southern Natal, including Estcourt. Families such as Botha's quickly moved in and established farms that stretched over thousands of acres. Just five years later, the British swept in, annexing the republic and forcing out most Boers, who refused to live under British rule.

As they had with the Zulu more than half a century before, the Boers had now returned to settle the score. This time, they had not hundreds of men in their ranks but thousands. They were encamped near Estcourt and Ladysmith, and were hiding in all the hills in between. They were heavily armed, flush with recent victory, fueled with moral outrage and impatient for the next battle to begin.

➤➤

After his ship landed at the Indian Ocean port of Durban, on the eastern coast of Natal, Churchill was torn from his daydreams about this golden land of opportunity, and harshly reminded of "the hideous fact that Natal is invaded and assailed by the Boers." As he and Atkins waited impatiently for the sun to rise, Churchill wanted only one thing, news of the war. When morning finally came, however, what he learned was exactly what he had feared: Ladysmith, just 125 miles to the northwest, had been cut off by the advancing Boers, and no one could get out, or in. He had crossed Africa's southern extremity at an incredible clip, easily outpacing Buller, his men and the other correspondents in the race to Natal, but he had not been fast enough. "I was too late," he wrote dismally. "The door was shut."

Angry and exhausted, Churchill was nonetheless determined to keep going. " 'As far as you can as quickly as you can' must be the motto of the war correspondent," he wrote. Finding a place on a mail train that was headed inland, he made his way through the mountains once again, northwestward this time, on a zigzagging railway that "contorts itself into curves that would horrify the domestic engineer." Finally, on November 6, his train pulled into the railway station at Estcourt, the new front for the war.

Most of the British troops in Estcourt knew little, and likely cared less, about the history of the blood-soaked land over which they had carelessly set up their tents and tossed their bags. They were very much aware, however, of the modern-day Boers watching them from the surrounding hills. Even the Boers themselves were stunned by the sheer number of burghers now scattered between Estcourt and Ladysmith. "As I approached I saw thousands of fires springing up on the hills," Deneys Reitz, the young man who had left Pretoria with

Botha, wrote after arriving in the region one night from Dundee. "The commandos were strung out over several miles."

In sharp contrast to the enemy, the British force in Estcourt was so small it had little hope of defending itself, much less charging into Ladysmith and freeing White and his men. Because Buller had yet to arrive, there were then only two battalions—the Royal Dublin Fusiliers, who had already fought one battle and had only just made it out of Ladysmith themselves, and a squadron of the Imperial Light Horse. A group of three hundred volunteers from Natal had also arrived, bringing with them twenty-five bicyclists and a battery of nine-pounder guns rolled in on enormous, spoked wheels. Even with this welcome addition, there were still only about twenty-three hundred men in Estcourt, fewer than three hundred of whom were mounted. "The enemy crouches at our door," Atkins wrote uneasily as he and Churchill took stock of their new home. "This place is scarcely defensible."

Every British soldier and officer knew that the question was not whether the Boers would attack Estcourt but when. What they couldn't understand was why the commandos hadn't already descended on their small force, which every day threatened to grow into a much larger one. "It was a period of strained waiting, when everyone wondered whether a Boer commando or a British brigade would be the first arrival," one of the soldiers would later write. "Reliable news was scarce, though rumours of every kind were rife." It was not difficult to picture the Boers streaming down the hills, or suddenly turning their massive guns from Ladysmith to Estcourt. "We live," Churchill wrote matter-of-factly, "in expectation of attack."

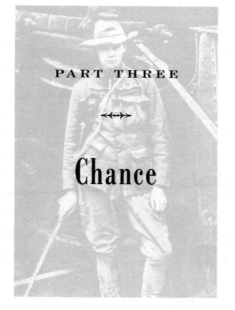

PART THREE

❬❬❬✦❭❭❭

Chance

CHAPTER 9

THE DEATH TRAP

Churchill cursed his luck for missing the chance to enter Ladysmith, but it was not the first time in war that he had arrived too late. Less than a year earlier, after talking his way into a military assignment in the Sudan, he had raced to Africa, only to find that the position that had been promised to him had already been given to another man. Churchill was particularly furious about that missed opportunity because his squadron was to lead the attack on the Dervishes. The man who had taken his place, Second Lieutenant Robert Grenfell, on the other hand, was thrilled. "Fancy how lucky I am," he had written to his family after hearing the news. "Here I have got the troop that would have been Winston's, and we are to be the first to start." Not long after he had written the letter, Grenfell rode triumphantly into battle, only to be slaughtered along with many of the men in his regiment. "Chance is unceasingly at work in our lives," Churchill would write years later, thinking back on Grenfell and the fate that might have been his, "but we cannot always see its workings sharply and clearly defined."

Churchill, now still too young to see the workings of chance in his life, certainly could not imagine that there might be any benefit or excitement to being trapped in Estcourt. Bitterly resigning himself to this "tiny tin township," he took in his new home with a weary eye. It was "of mean and insignificant aspect," he wrote gloomily. There were a few shops, but they were housed in "unpretentious shanties" and nearly all abandoned since the outset of war. A scattering of low stone and corrugated-iron houses lined Estcourt's only street, and Churchill could see a few more "straggling away towards the country." Beyond that toward the northwest and the Boer lines, there was nothing but the flat green veld and a few low hills. To the southwest, he could see the misty blue peaks of the Drakensberg, Afrikaans for "dragon mountains."

Hauling his bag from the train, Churchill looked for a place to stay near the railroad station, where most of the men had set up camp. He found an empty bell tent in the shunting triangle where train cars were coupled and uncoupled, and decided to make it his home for the time being. Because there were more men than tents, he was obliged to share his, choosing for his roommates two other journalists—Atkins, who had accompanied him as he had raced across the Great Karoo, and a young London *Times* correspondent named Leo Amery.

Although in theory Atkins was his competition, Churchill liked him. He admired his Cambridge education and the fact that, at just twenty-eight years of age, he had already covered several wars, including the Spanish-American War and the Greco-Turkish War two years earlier. Atkins was, Churchill wrote to his mother, "exceedingly clever & accomplished." Perhaps what he liked best about his new friend, however, was how interested Atkins seemed to be in him, and how willing he was to listen to him talk about himself.

For his part, Atkins found Churchill not just amusing but fascinating. He had seen his like only once before, in Cuba during the Spanish-American War, where Atkins had had lunch with Theodore Roosevelt. The young reporter had watched as the Rough Riders, the motley crew of cowboys, college athletes and law enforcement officials Roosevelt had brought together to fight in the war, gathered eagerly around him, hanging on his every word. "It was like a conference," Atkins later wrote, "with Roosevelt as both principal speaker and chairman." Before they parted ways, Roosevelt, who just three years later would become the youngest president in U.S. history, pulled Atkins aside to tell him that "so far as he knew, he was the only officer who had 'performed the feat' of shooting a Spaniard with his revolver in the charge up the slopes." Atkins, who was used to the almost extreme discretion and modesty of British military men, was startled by Roosevelt's blatant self-promotion, but he didn't hold it against him. In fact, he found his honesty refreshing. "I noted the simplicity with which he said this, in the manner of a man genuinely recording a fact of sufficient interest," he wrote. "Few British officers would have mentioned it, but Roosevelt was not boasting."

Nor did Atkins believe that Churchill was simply boasting when he reeled off his accomplishments and outlined his audacious plans. On the contrary, he thought that Churchill, like Roosevelt, was probably telling the truth. He struck him as a "most unusual young man," and as they lived and worked side by side, Atkins studied him with the eye not of a journalist but of a historian. "When the prospects of a career like that of his father, Lord Randolph, excited him, then such a gleam shot from him that he was almost transfigured," Atkins would later write. "I had not before encountered this sort of ambition, unabashed, frankly egotistical, communicating its excitement, and extorting sympathy."

Few people, however, shared Atkins's open admiration for Churchill. Although he was well known, and widely believed to be on his way to Parliament, if not 10 Downing Street, he was too brash and self-assertive to be generally well liked. Even Sir George White, then trapped in Ladysmith, would find Churchill annoying, although he had little doubt that the bold young man would rise quickly through the ranks of British politics. "I don't like the fellow," White would dryly tell another officer just a few months later, "but he'll be Prime Minister of England one day."

->-

Even within the confines of Churchill's own tent, there was a man who was hardly impressed by him. As highly as Atkins regarded Churchill, Leo Amery had formed a distinctly less favorable opinion of him. A thin, bespectacled Oxford graduate, Amery had known Churchill much longer than Atkins had. In fact, the two men had met eleven years earlier, at Harrow, when Churchill was just thirteen years old and Amery a year older. It had not been an auspicious beginning for a friendship.

Churchill had only been at the school for about a month when he saw Amery standing near the edge of a large outdoor swimming pool, which the students had nicknamed Ducker. Churchill, like many of the boys, spent most of his time around the pool pushing other kids into it, so when he spied Amery, who was small for his age, he assumed he was fair game. Sneaking up behind his victim, Churchill suddenly shoved him in the back with his foot, grabbing Amery's towel at the last minute "out of humanity, so that it should not get wet." The resulting effect, however, was not what Churchill had expected. "I was startled to see a furious face emerge from the foam, and a being evidently of enormous strength making its way by fierce strokes to the shore," he would recall years later. "I fled, but in vain. Swift as the wind my pursuer overtook me, seized me in a ferocious grip and hurled me into the deepest part of the pool." When Churchill climbed back out, he was quickly surrounded by the other boys, who gleefully explained the extent of his crime. "You're in for it," they said. "Do you know what you have done? It's Amery, he's in the Sixth Form. He is Head of the House; he is champion at Gym; he has got football colours."

Amery, too, had not forgotten the incident. He couldn't decide whether he was more infuriated by the "outrage on my dignity . . . [by] a red-haired freckled urchin" or the fact that, in a misguided attempt at an apology the next day, Churchill had explained to him that he had pushed him into the pool because he was small. "My father, too, is small," Churchill had said, awkwardly hoping to make amends, "though he also is a great man."

Churchill had been pleased to see Amery in Estcourt because

he felt that they could "for the first time meet on terms of equality and fraternity." To Amery, however, they were still far from equals. Although Churchill was the best-paid journalist, Amery believed himself to be the most senior newspaperman in South Africa. He was, first of all, working for *The Times* of London, one of the most admired newspapers in the world. Already more than a century old, it was the first newspaper to bear the name "Times," giving inspiration to every similarly named newspaper from the *Times of India*, which was started more than fifty years later, to the *New York Times*, thirteen years after that. Amery was not only a reporter for *The Times*, he was the chief of its war correspondent service. "I had an effective team of something like a score of representatives covering the whole field of action," he later boasted. "I found myself, in virtue of the status of *The Times*, at the age of twenty-five, chief representative of the Press in South Africa."

As much as Amery and Churchill were alike in their backgrounds, their early education, their ambition and their self-regard, there was one striking difference between the two young men: Churchill had a sense of humor, even about his own pretensions. He "could laugh at his dreams of glory," Atkins would later write. He had "an impish wit. It was as though a light was switched on inside him which suddenly shone out through his eyes. . . . The whole illuminated face grinned." Amery, on the other hand, was as thin-skinned as he was proud.

--+--

Although Amery, Churchill and Atkins were all desperate to be part of the war, in Estcourt they were far from alone in their frustration. Constantly on edge and in danger, the British soldiers they had come to report on felt not only helpless but useless as they stared impotently in the direction of Ladysmith. It was difficult enough just to find a place to sleep and, if they were very lucky, an occasional bath in a tiny canvas tub. Clean water was so scarce that obtaining it would become one of Buller's greatest challenges throughout the war. In just a few months, it would lead to a typhoid epidemic that would kill thousands of British soldiers in Bloemfontein, just three hundred miles west of Estcourt.

Food was in more plentiful supply, but until Buller and his wagons arrived, it was barely edible. The camp had a bleak tin building that the men used for a mess, but if they were marching from town to town or on reconnaissance, there was little more to eat than canned corned beef, known as bully beef, and rock-hard ration biscuits, which were themselves a danger to the soldiers who had bad teeth, as nearly all of them did. Occasionally, they were even forced to resort to something called Johnston's Fluid Beef, which they squeezed out of metal or waxed fiberboard tubes. So far removed was this processed paste from actual fresh beef that the leftovers would be given to British soldiers serving in World War I, twenty years later.

Dirty, tired and hungry as they were, the men in Estcourt knew that they were better off than their counterparts in Ladysmith, whom the Boers were hoping to starve out if they did not kill them first. From the hills surrounding the town, they could hear the Boer guns that were trained on Ladysmith, and they could see the bursts of light and billows of white smoke as they were fired. They could also see White's desperate attempts to communicate with the Estcourt relief force across the intervening Boer lines.

Although the trapped British general was in dangerously short supply of arms and rations, he did have an array of new battlefield technologies with which to signal his pleas for help to the outside world. From Estcourt, Churchill watched the flashes of Morse code White sent by sunlight and mirrors using a heliograph. White also had access to a pigeon post that had been established between Ladysmith and Durban by Colonel Hassard of the Royal Engineers, a man who had, an article in *Collier's Weekly* assured its readers, "spent years in pigeon culture for just this sort of an emergency."

Perhaps White's most inventive and elegant means of escaping Ladysmith, if only for one man and for a few hours, was a hydrogen-filled balloon. Used largely for reconnaissance, the balloon had a narrow basket with room for only one man, a set of binoculars, a telescope, a compass and signaling equipment. Occasionally, Churchill could see it, looking like a "brown speck floating above and beyond the distant hills . . . plainly visible." Unfortunately, the Boers could see it too and, whenever they did, tried their best to shoot it down. In fact, George Warrington Steevens, who was now trapped in Ladysmith with White, wrote that the "favourite diet" of the Boers' twelve-pounder field guns "appeared to be balloons."

→-

In Estcourt, the most the men could do until Buller arrived was monitor the Boers' movements, which in itself was an almost impossible task. Every day, they sent out the cavalry for ten to fifteen miles, searching for their elusive enemies. The British only had three hundred horses, though, and it was difficult to keep even that number fed and free from disease. The twenty-five bicycles the Natal volunteers had brought with them were slightly more useful, but they had their own problems. Bicycles, which had been used for military purposes since the Franco-Prussian War nearly thirty years before, were light, fast, easily taken apart, shipped and reassembled. They didn't have to be fed, and they didn't die. They could, however, and often did, blow a tire in the scrubby veld. In actual combat, they were worse than useless because they couldn't withstand the recoil of a rifle or offer their riders any balance while they tried to wield a sword.

Without question, however, the least popular means of reconnaissance the men in Estcourt had at their disposal was their armored train. In theory, the trains were useful. They could quickly transport men and supplies wherever they were most needed, and there were thousands of miles of railway line crisscrossing southern Africa, which the Boers had been loath to destroy. They were also cleverly designed, with the engine not at the front of the train but sandwiched between two armored cars. If the front was attacked or the rail line sabotaged, the engine could be quickly uncoupled from the damaged car, leaving it free to pull the rest of the train to safety. Later in the war, the British would cloak some of their armored engines in long coils of heavy rope. Nicknamed Hairy Marys, they looked like giant woolly mammoths lumbering down the tracks, but they were useful in protecting the engines from small arms fire.

The problem was that, confined as they were to conspicuous, unchanging rail lines, the trains were easy, slow-moving targets for Boer ambushes. "Nothing looks more formidable and impressive than an armoured train," Churchill wrote, "but nothing is in fact more vulnerable and helpless." The Boers needed to do little more than hide near the tracks and wait for a British train to come trundling by, filled with men and guns. At the outset of war, the British had thirteen armored trains in southern Africa. By the time Churchill had reached Cape Town, they had already lost two of them to the Boers. In fact, the first act of war, which, in Churchill's words, had given the Boers "the advantage of drawing first blood," had been the capture of an armored train near Mafeking, west of Johannesburg. The second was captured just a few weeks later. In that incident, only the engine driver, who lost four fingers in the attack, had escaped. The rest of the men had been taken prisoner, and the officer in charge was reported to have "seriously underrated the nature of the risk incurred."

If riding any armored train was a bad idea, then riding the train in Estcourt was madness. The men openly referred to it as "Wilson's death-trap," laying blame for the incredibly dangerous conveyance at the feet of Arthur Wilson, third naval lord and controller of the navy, who had famously improvised an armored train during the Anglo-Egyptian War seventeen years earlier. That train, however, had at least been a legitimate armored train. The one in Estcourt was hardly deserving of the name. "It was not really an armored train at all," Atkins wrote. "It was made up of an ordinary engine and ordinary iron trucks belonging to the Natal Government Railway protected by boiler plates; and through the boiler plates were cut loopholes for the rifles." It didn't have trapdoors or custom-built openings for gun muzzles. It didn't even have a roof. "To get in or out of the trucks one had to climb over the walls," Atkins marveled. "It was fun to see a small and clumsy climber pushed up from the inside by his comrades, then squirm preposterously on his stomach over the wall and drop or scramble down the seven feet on the outside." It wasn't hard to imagine the disaster that would occur if the train came under heavy fire, and the men inside were forced to perform their "slow and painful acrobatic feat to get out of their cage."

The train was also as regular as clockwork, an attribute that might have been admirable in a London commuter train but was disastrous in war. "Day after day, generally at the same hour, the armoured train . . . used to press forth unattended beyond the line of outposts," one officer in Estcourt wrote, "heralding, by agonized gasps and puffs, and clouds of smoke and steam, its advent to the far-sighted, long-hearing Boer." Although watching it leave the station every morning was, in Atkins's words, the "chief diversion of our life at Estcourt," waiting for it to come back was a source of widespread anxiety, not least of all for the men who had been forced to board it earlier in the day. "How relieved the occupants looked when they climbed over its plated sides," an officer would later recall, "and congratulated themselves that their turn to form the freight of this moribund engine of war would not come round again for at least some days!"

Although he was well aware of the dangers of riding in an armored train, so determined was Churchill to get out of Estcourt and get as close as he could to Ladysmith that a few days after arriving, he tucked his pistol in his belt and climbed aboard. Part of the impetus for his decision was doubtless the fact that Amery was going, and Churchill was not about to take the chance that the *Times* correspondent, his old nemesis turned tent mate, might see something of the war that he would not. Even had Amery not been there, however, Churchill almost certainly would have gone. It was not in his nature to pass up any opportunity, especially if it might give him an edge, and put his life in danger. A man "should get to the front at all costs," he wrote. "For every fifty men who will express a desire to go on service . . . there is only about one who really means business, and will take the trouble and run the risk of going to the front."

There was also something oddly romantic and exciting about an armored train, especially for a man like Churchill who loved nothing more than awe-inspiring displays of military might. It was a far cry from the glittering processions of soldiers and officers he used to admire marching through the streets of London on parade, the sun flashing on their bayonets, their gloves dazzlingly white, but it had an exotic aura that could only be found in a distant land. "An armoured train!" Churchill wrote from Estcourt. "The very name sounds strange. A locomotive disguised as a knight-errant; the agent of civilisation in the habiliments of chivalry. Mr. Morley attired as Sir Lancelot would seem scarcely more incongruous."

⇥

The train, with Churchill and Amery aboard, pulled out of Estcourt at 1:00 on the afternoon of November 8, rattling along the railway line that stretched toward Ladysmith. Although they made frequent stops to question locals and check in with their own scouts, the train moved relatively quickly through the empty veld until it reached the small town of Chieveley. From there, however, they were forced to slow down considerably. "Beyond Chieveley," Churchill wrote, "it was necessary to observe more caution." The train inched, yard by yard, along the tracks. The men scanned the horizon with their field glasses and telescopes, and if they came to a bridge or culvert, they stopped, climbed out and carefully inspected it before continuing on their excruciatingly slow journey.

When they finally reached Colenso, a village just thirteen miles south of Ladysmith, they were stunned by what they found. The town, which the British had been forced to evacuate, had been ransacked and then completely abandoned. Several houses had been burned down. The belongings of the former inhabitants were scattered all over the streets, and in the middle of one lay a horse that had clearly been dead for some time. It was on its back, belly swollen and legs sticking straight up in the air. On their way home, they passed broken telegraph wires trailing lazily over the ground, twisted posts and a cut in the rail line, where the tracks had been pulled up and thrown over the embankment. What they did not see was a single Boer.

When they pulled back in to Estcourt that night, the soldiers stretched out on the floor of the open truck, smoke from their cigarettes disappearing into the black plume of exhaust billowing out of the engine, they were all relieved simply to have gotten back alive. For Churchill and Amery, the trip had been not only a tremendous risk, but a colossal waste of time. The train "could see nothing, trundling along the valley bottoms," Amery wrote in disgust, "advertised its presence for miles by its puffing, and was at a hopeless disadvantage against any enemy who cared to tear up the rails behind it."

While his ride in the armored train had diminished Amery's respect for Estcourt's commanding officers, it had significantly improved his opinion of Churchill. Throughout the long, dangerous day, the "red-haired freckled urchin" had shown nothing but courage and pluck. As they climbed out of the car in which they had been riding, the two men vowed that, although there were many ways to die in this war, this was the last time they would risk their lives aboard the armored train.

CHAPTER 10

A PITY AND A BLUNDER

One night soon after arriving in Estcourt, Churchill, Amery and Atkins were walking along the town's only street when Churchill saw someone he had not expected to see there, or perhaps anywhere ever again. Because there was only starlight and the glow of camp-fires and the occasional lantern to illuminate the dirt road, it was at first difficult to tell who it was. As the man drew closer, however, his features began to come more clearly into view. There was the dark hair, there the thick, carefully combed mustache and the ramrod-straight back. Without question, the man standing before him was Aylmer Haldane.

The last time Churchill had heard any news of Haldane had been while he was still aboard the *Dunottar Castle,* and his friend's name had been read out among the list of the first known casualties of the war. Now here he was, nonchalantly walking down the street in Estcourt, alive and fairly, if not wholly, well. It also quickly became apparent that up to this point Haldane's time in South Africa had been far more interesting than Churchill's own.

Haldane had left for Africa about a month before Churchill and had soon found himself in the opening battles of the war. During the Battle of Elandslaagte, which had taken place midway between

Ladysmith and Dundee on October 21, the day after Penn Symons was fatally wounded, Haldane had been hit by rifle fire. Seventy percent of the British officers in that battle had been either killed or wounded, so he was lucky to have gotten away with his life. He had been injured in the leg, and there had been a hasty operation because he was eager to catch up with his battalion, the Gordon Highlanders, who had fallen back to Ladysmith. His leg had yet to completely heal, leaving Haldane with a pronounced if temporary limp and, like Churchill, stuck in Estcourt, in command of the Dublin Fusiliers until he could be reunited with his men.

Churchill was delighted to see his old friend, who seemed to have returned from the dead, but he could not help envying Haldane's battlefield experience and position in the war. Unlike in the past, when they had both been military men, Churchill was now just a journalist, a spectator forced to hover around the periphery, while Haldane was a real participant. "I can never doubt which is the right end [of the telegraph wire] to be at," Churchill had written a few years earlier, after returning from Malakand. "It is better to be making the news than taking it; to be an actor rather than a critic."

→→

Although Churchill had had little luck getting to the war, on November 14 the war seemed finally to come to him. At 11:00 that morning, less than a week after his ride aboard the armored train, the thunderous boom of an alarm gun suddenly shook Estcourt. The gun, which had been placed in front of the camp, a hundred paces from the artillery posts, was there to warn the men, not kill them, but the sudden, explosive sound was as jolting and sickening as that of the Boer field guns trained on Ladysmith. Even after weeks of tense waiting, and endless discussions about when and how the enemy would attack, it was hard to believe the Boers had finally arrived.

Despite the initial shock, the men did not lose a moment in leaping to their own defense. "Instantly the camp sprang to life," Atkins wrote. "In a moment belts were being buckled, straps thrown across shoulders, helmets jammed on heads, puttees wrapped feverishly round legs." Colonel Charles Long, who had been left in temporary command while his superior was sixty miles farther back in Pietermaritzburg, quickly strode to the center of the town's only street with his staff, anxiously peering through his field glasses while the wind and the rain picked up around him, darkening the skies and whipping the loose edges of the canvas tents. Long could see little more than shadowy figures in the low hills, slightly blurred by distance and mist, but they were there, dotting the horizon, threatening to sweep down upon them at any moment.

News of the Boer advance had been brought in by the cyclist scouts, pedaling as quickly as they could through the heavy mud on their thin metal bikes, rifles strapped to their backs or below their seats with wide strips of leather. The day before, a new battalion, the West Yorkshires, had arrived to bolster the town's defenses, and that morning Pietermaritzburg had sent three new guns, two long naval twelve-pounders and a seven-pounder. The men, however, had no illusions that they were suddenly a match for the tens of thousands of burghers who now faced them. They were desperate to do something in response to the threat, but no one, certainly not Long, seemed to know what that was. "A dense, paralyzing mist of uncertainty enveloped all things beyond a narrow radius from the village," Amery wrote. "The appearance of the Boer patrols . . . was the signal for a display of nervous irresolution, profoundly depressing to those who watched it, and full of portent for any one who reflected upon the future course of the campaign."

Seemingly incapable of making a decision and terrified of the potential consequences should he make a mistake, Long hardly projected an image of cool, confident command. One moment he was determined that his men would stand their ground, no matter how outnumbered they were, and the next he was frantically ordering everyone to pack up. "A moment of confidence and the tents were pitched again on ground which the pouring rain had meanwhile converted into a swamp," Amery wrote. "A passing cloud of despondency, and down once more fluttered the white walls and packing-up was resumed." All around them guy ropes were loosened, and the bell tents, which a minute earlier had stood in tight rows like starched white teepees, collapsed to the ground, their canvas sides flapping in the wet wind like sails.

Most of the men were sent to meet the Boers head-on—Haldane's Dublin Fusiliers, the Border Regiment, the West Yorkshires, the mounted troops. They stretched along the veld in silent firing lines while they waited for the enemy to arrive, rain dripping from their peaked pith helmets, the wet ground darkening their khaki jackets and seeming to seep into their very bones. Although tense and miserable, they were at least by then no strangers to drenching rains. Summer is the rainy season in the Highveld, and there had seldom been a day when the men hadn't been pummeled by a torrential afternoon thunderstorm, leaving them not just soaked but, more often than not, sick. "Lord, O poor Tommy!" George Warrington Steevens wrote of the wretched plight of the British soldier in South Africa. "He sops and sneezes, runs at the eyes and nose, half manful, half miserable."

The men were also terrifyingly vulnerable to lightning, which streaked across the sky like the finger of God that the deeply religious Boers had promised would vindicate them. "I saw the flash of lightning coming towards me rather high up," one British soldier would later recall, "it then seemed to me to come straight down over my head. The flash was rather circular in shape and pink in colour. I received a blow on the top of the head, just as if I had been struck by a mallet." On another occasion, four men were struck while sleeping in a tent. "The current seemed to have passed along the legs of the men," a report later noted, "and to have passed out about the buttocks, causing severe burning." In the end, eighty-six British servicemen would be struck by lightning during the war, many of whom would not survive the blow.

So frequent and violent were the rains that they had transformed the dry, dusty veld into a sea of mud, and the soldiers into something that seemed less man than monster. Mud caked the long strips of cloth called puttees, from the Hindi word *patti,* for "bandage," that wound from the tops of their shoes to their knees, weighing down

their legs or stiffening and cracking in the sun, either way making
it almost impossible for them to walk. "As for their boots, you could
only infer them from the huge balls of stratified mud men bore round
their feet. Red mud, yellow mud, black mud, brown mud," Steevens
wrote. "Rents in their khaki showed white skin; from their grimed
hands and heads you might have judged them half red men, half
soot-black. . . . Only the eye remained—the sky-blue, steel-keen,
hard, clear, unconquerable English eye."

After hours in the hills, however, the men returned with little
to show for their time and misery. Only the mounted infantry had
had any contact with the enemy, and even then it was only about two
hundred burghers with whom they had exchanged "perhaps thirty
harmless shots," Atkins wrote in disgust. When he returned to Estcourt, exhausted, frustrated and drenched, it was to find a camp full
of men who were neither excited nor relieved, but merely "jumpy."
"The camp wore an air of vacillation," he wrote, "and vacillation is
the blood-brother to demoralization."

That night, Churchill invited Long, who had been in the Sudan
with him, in command of the artillery during the Battle of Omdurman, to join him and Atkins for dinner. Even as the rain continued
to fall in torrents, Long ordered his men to sleep, tentless, on the
ground so they would be ready to retreat at a moment's notice. The
journalists, among the few who had been allowed to keep their tent,
sat with Long as he drank Churchill's wine and talked of nothing
but the Boer advance on Estcourt, wringing his hands in painful
and, for Churchill, maddening indecision. In the background, just
behind their tent, they could hear the heavy clang of metal and the
grunts of soldiers as they loaded the battalions' guns in preparation
for what they had been told would be the evacuation of the town the
following day.

Finally, unable to endure Long's nervous indecision any longer,
Churchill broke in. Addressing the colonel, Atkins would later write,
"with an unblushing assurance, which I partly envied and partly deprecated," he gave him the benefit of his opinion. The fact that he
was much younger and much less experienced than Long, and that

he was not even a member of the military, did not give Churchill a moment's hesitation. "He had small respect for authority," Atkins wrote. He had "no reverence for his seniors as such, and talked to them as though they were of his own age, or younger."

You should stay in Estcourt, Churchill told Long. Joubert, the Boer commandant general, was cautious, and unlikely to make a move just yet. Their position was fairly safe because it was south of the Tugela River, and as good a place as any to wait for Buller. Leaving Estcourt, and leading the Boers to Pietermaritzburg, would be "a pity and a blunder."

When Long finally said good night, neither Churchill nor Atkins knew if Churchill's words had had any effect on him. Just minutes after he had strode from sight, however, the clanging, which had ceased half an hour earlier, suddenly started up again. Dashing outside, the journalists watched with delight as the soldiers who had only just finished packing the trucks began the tedious and grueling process of unpacking them. "There could be only one explanation," Atkins wrote. "We were going to remain in Estcourt." Grinning at his friend, Churchill said triumphantly, "I did that!" Then, after a moment's reflection, he said, in a gesture of friendship so generous it surprised Atkins, "We did that."

->-

As Atkins would later write, "There was to be no retreat, no miserable night march, no military disgrace." Long realized, however, that there had already been one personal disgrace that day: his own. He had betrayed a weakness unseemly in a British military commander, and he was desperate to correct the impression, whatever the cost. Emphatically stating " 'what he'd be' before he would leave Estcourt," Long vowed that he was prepared to fight the following day, "if the Boers would have it so."

Later that night, not long before midnight, Churchill's old friend Aylmer Haldane was surprised when a young officer in his battalion named Tom Frankland appeared before him with a message from the

colonel. He was, Frankland told Haldane, to report immediately to
the brigade office for an assignment. Unlike Churchill, Haldane did
not know Long. In fact, he had never even met him, but he could
guess why the colonel had summoned him. It was his turn to take
command of the armored train.

Haldane walked to Long's tent "with a heart full of misgivings."
Although he was more than prepared to risk his own life, he was
reluctant to put the lives of his soldiers in the hands of a man who
clearly had no idea what he was doing. "Had he known anything of
the country in which the train was to operate," Haldane wrote, "one
where hostile guns could readily be concealed in places close to the
railway line, in positions from which to fire without warning—he
would surely have modified so inappropriate an order." As Haldane
had suspected, however, as soon as he stepped into Long's makeshift
office, the colonel informed him, "as if he were lavishing a favor," that
he would be leaving on the armored train at dawn the next morning.

As he ducked out of Long's tent, angry but resigned, Haldane
looked up to see Churchill standing with a group of journalists,
"hanging about to pick up some crumbs of information." When
he grimly told Churchill about his assignment, Haldane made no
effort to pretend that he agreed with his commanding officer. "I need
hardly point out that a single man on horseback would have sufficed
to accomplish what was required," he later wrote. "It was the height
of folly." Long had made a disastrous decision, and it would probably end in tragedy, but, Haldane told Churchill, ignoring the other
journalists, he was welcome to come along if he was willing to take
the chance.

After his first ride aboard the armored train, Churchill had tried
every other method he could think of to get news from Ladysmith.
He had even tried to hire a guide to take him into the besieged town.
When word got around that Churchill was offering to pay anyone
who was brave or crazy enough to test the Boers, a young trooper
in the Natal Carbineers named Park Gray, who had grown up game
hunting between Estcourt and Ladysmith and was widely considered
a crack shot, had decided to take the job. "When I approached him

he was sitting in the tent and gave me the impression that he was a lonely young, very young, Englishman," Gray would write years later. "He had a complexion that many a South African girl would envy and although four years older than I, looked to be about 17 or 18. He became very animated when I told him what I had come for." Gray's commanding officer, however, had put an end to the adventure before it could even begin. He "could not spare a single man," he had told Gray, let alone his best rifleman "to lead a bloody war correspondent into Ladysmith."

Churchill, Gray later recalled, was "more disappointed than I when I told him the news." He was bored, frustrated and, he would later admit, "eager for trouble." By the time he saw Haldane leaving Long's tent, even the armored train was starting to look appealing. If it was not a good idea, it was at least an interesting one. "I accepted the invitation," Churchill later wrote, "without demur."

→→

It was already raining when Thomas Walden, Churchill's long-suffering if well-traveled valet, woke him at 4:30 the next morning. Amery, who had decided against his best judgment to get back on the train with Churchill, took one look out the tent flap, the rain drumming against the canvas sides, and didn't stir from his sleeping bag. Although the train was scheduled to leave at 6:00 a.m., in all the trips it had made out of Estcourt, it had never actually departed before 8:00. "It was no possible use spending two hours getting wet at the siding only 300 yards away," Amery muttered to Churchill before closing his eyes and falling back asleep.

Churchill, already up and ready to go, decided to run over to the tracks to find out if the train would be leaving on time. Before he left, he woke Atkins and asked if he would like to join them. Although he was as eager as Churchill to get news from Ladysmith, Atkins refused the offer. His job was to tell the story of the war from the British point of view, he said, and if he ended up being captured by the Boers, his editor would hold him "very much to blame." After listening carefully, Churchill gravely replied that while he agreed with Atkins and knew that his own reasoning was far less logical, he had "a feeling, a sort of intuition, that if I go something will come of it."

When Churchill approached the train, which in the dim, early-morning light looked far more impressive and substantial than it was, he was surprised to find that it was already packed and ready to leave. Eager to get the trip over with, Haldane had insisted on starting early. There was no time to go back for Amery, or to change his mind.

Quickly assessing the situation, Churchill climbed into the front truck with Haldane, where he would have the best vantage point. Already inside were the seven-pounder that had arrived from Pietermaritzburg the day before and four sailors from the HMS *Tartar*, who would man the gun should it come to that. Behind them, stretching down the tracks, was a short line of cars and a large crowd of men. There were, in order, another armored car, the engine with its wide-mouthed black funnel and narrow tender, two more armored cars and finally an ordinary, low-sided car that held the tools and materials they would need if the line was damaged.

There was some confusion and difficulty while the soldiers tried to climb into the armored trucks, but as they knew themselves to be not just uniquely vulnerable but the object of great amusement as they scrambled over the tall, slate-colored sides, they moved quickly. Haldane's Dublin Fusiliers, their wool blankets rolled and hooked into suspenders that crisscrossed their backs, their arms straining as they gripped the sides, heaved themselves over the top of the first armored car. There were too many of them to fit, however, so one section had to move down the line and pile into an armored car behind the engine with a company of Durban Light Infantry and a small group of civilians. They were taking along a few platelayers and a telegraphist, who carried with him a small instrument that would allow Haldane to tap into the wires at the stations they passed and send messages back to Long.

As the train pulled out of the station a few minutes later, rain splashing on the peaked tops of the khaki pith helmets crowded into open cars, Colonel Walter Kitchener, a member of Buller's staff and the youngest brother of Lieutenant General Horatio Kitchener, stood nearby, watching in shock. He had not known until that morning that Long intended to send out the train after the Boers had been spotted so close to Estcourt just the day before. Turning to the colonel, Kitchener said bluntly that he did not expect to ever again see any of the men now disappearing in the distance. "In dispatching the train," he told Long, he had "sent the occupants to their death."

CHAPTER 11

INTO THE LION'S JAWS

For the first fourteen miles, Churchill could see nothing but the wide, seemingly empty veld that stretched before him. There wasn't "a sign of opposition or indeed of life or movement on the broad undulations of the Natal landscape," he wrote. To the European eye, used to moors and woodlands, fields and pastures, the land seemed to be an open expanse with little variety in its flat, scrubby topography. There were a few kopjes, or low hills, but rather than relieving the monotony, they seemed only to emphasize it. "If the veld can only be compared with the sea," one contemporary historian of the war wrote, "the kopjes . . . resemble in as marked a degree the isolated islands which rise abruptly from the waters of some tropic archipelago." Despite what seemed like an almost hypnotic, unwavering sameness, however, the veld was actually filled with thousands of places, small hills and valleys, folds and nooks, where the enemy could, and did, hide.

In stark contrast to the British, the Boers saw no shame in hiding. On the contrary, to them the shame would have been in risking the life God had given them simply in the pursuit of personal glory or, in their enemy's case, to gratify some inconceivable British vanity. For them, war was not an exciting adventure but the cold, cruel, inescapable business of life. The Boer "went out in a businesslike way to kill men," Amery wrote, "as he would to kill dangerous wild beasts, and he saw no more glory in dying at an enemy's hand than in being eaten by a lion."

The Boers knew the veld inside and out, every river and kopje, boulder and bush, and they used it all to get as close as possible to the enemy without being seen. Where there was no natural feature in the landscape to shield them, they made their own. They built sangars, or small shelters, out of piles of stones. They dug deep and incredibly long trenches, some stretching for as many as thirty miles, and covered them so expertly with grass and twigs that even to a British marksman within rifle range they blended seamlessly into the surrounding landscape.

They also had, in their simple leather kits, the one thing that could almost guarantee their invisibility, even after they had fired their guns: smokeless gunpowder. Alfred Nobel, the inventor of dynamite, had patented a form of smokeless gunpowder twelve years earlier, dramatically changing warfare and making it almost impossible to track down a sniper. The impact of these inventions was so profound that a year later, after seeing his own accidental obituary—to his horror titled "The Merchant of Death Is Dead"—the Swedish inventor would establish the Nobel Prize.

Unlike the Boers, who had been sharpshooters nearly all their lives, this was an entirely new world to the British. So alien was the concept of a man who shot from a distance and in hiding, rather than in a highly visible battlefield formation, that even the word "sniper" was new to them. It had originated in India, where riflemen skilled enough to shoot a snipe, a small bird with a notoriously erratic flight pattern, were referred to as snipers. Churchill himself had used the word in print for the first time just a few years earlier, in his book *The Story of the Malakand Field Force,* and so foreign did it seem to him that every time he wrote it, he put it in quotation marks.

Instead of admiring the effectiveness of the Boers' guerrilla tactics, however, the British derided them as ungallant and cowardly. The Boers were "a people whose only mode of warfare . . . has been that of crawling behind stones and picking off their enemy like springbok while themselves well protected," a British expatriate, or Uitlander, sneered in a letter to a Natal newspaper. "A wise mode of warfare no doubt, but not one that fills us with admiration." A soldier didn't hide in the brush like an animal. He stood in the open and faced his death like a man.

For the British, war was about romance and gallantry. They liked nothing more than a carefully pressed uniform, a parade ground and a razor-sharp fighting line. At most, British soldiers spent two months of the year actually training to fight. The other ten were devoted to parading, attending to their uniforms and waiting on their officers, for whom they were expected to serve as cook, valet, porter and gardener. "The actual conditions of warfare were studiously disregarded," Amery wrote. "Nowhere was there any definite preparation for war, nowhere any clear conception that war was the one end and object for which armies exist. In their place reigned a . . . hazy confidence that British good fortune and British courage would always come successfully out of any war that the inscrutable mysteries of foreign policy might bring about."

What took the place of actual training was an emphasis on character and courage so extreme it left room for little else. British officers in particular were expected not only to be brave, but to show a complete disregard for their own safety, an approach to warfare that often led to their untimely, if widely lauded, death. General Penn Symons was far from the only British officer killed in war because he refused to find cover. "These experienced soldiers never care how fast bullets may whizz about them," Solomon Plaatje, a native South African intellectual, journalist and statesman, wrote after observing the British army during the war. "They stroll about in a heavy volley far more recklessly than we walk through a shower of rain."

As the world had changed and warfare had changed with it, even the British army had been forced to make adjustments, but they had been bitter pills to swallow. The most painful change had been the loss of their dashing red jackets, which had earned them the often reviled nickname redcoats. Although they had originally been a practicality, allowing them to find one another quickly on smoky battlefields before the days of smokeless gunpowder, Britons had taken great pride in their traditional uniforms, and they hated the new ones. Not only were they forced to wear the dull, unromantic khaki, derived from the Urdu word for "dust," but they were prohibited from wearing their gleaming medals and ordered to cover their swords, hilts and scabbards in khaki paint. The new uniforms, they grumbled, left them looking less like military officers than bus drivers.

Whether they liked it or not, however, battle by battle the British were learning from the Boers. They were beginning to see the advantages of blending into their surroundings, being quiet and quick, and even ducking. "When this siege is over this force ought to be the best fighting men in the world," George Warrington Steevens wrote from Ladysmith. "We are learning lessons every day from the Boer. We are getting to know his game, and learning to play it ourselves. . . . Nothing but being shot at will ever teach men the art of using cover."

→→

Whatever their efforts with khaki uniforms and painted swords, the men on the armored train could not help but be painfully aware that they were not invisible to anyone, let alone the Boers. Standing out in bold relief against the flat landscape and rocky kopjes, the train, in Churchill's words, looked like a "long brown rattling serpent with the rifles bristling from its spotted sides." Loudly puffing and chuffing along the tracks, it sent a stream of smoke into the air so visible it must have seemed to the Boers that the British were signaling to them exactly where to strike. "It would be hard," Amery wrote, "to devise a better target than . . . that death trap."

In fact, not far away, standing on a hillside with about three thousand men and four field guns, was Louis Botha, listening as the train, a little early this morning, traced its well-known route to Colenso. While Churchill had spent the past two weeks trying to

find a way to get nearer to Ladysmith, Botha had been inching closer
to Estcourt. It seemed that they were destined to meet somewhere in
the middle.

Had Botha had his way, they would have met sooner, but he, and
all of the burghers, had been held back by Joubert. Although the
commandant general, a kindly, elderly man, was revered for his bravery and brilliance during the First Boer War, nearly twenty years earlier, he was also disparaged by many Boers for his longing for peace
and his insistence that, although they had been forced to fight, they
would conduct themselves with the utmost compassion and civility.

Joubert even went so far as to prohibit his men from attacking a
British force in retreat, believing that it was wrong to take advantage
of his enemy's misfortune. After one victory, Joubert had, to his officers' wild frustration, refused to allow them to follow the retreating
forces, which had proceeded to make their way to Ladysmith, and the
protection of White, largely unmolested. When asked why he would
not let them finish the job they had so successfully begun, Joubert
responded by quoting a famous Dutch saying: "When God holds out
a finger, do not take the whole hand."

Even Botha, whom Joubert trusted and admired, had difficulty
convincing him that, if the Boers were going to defeat the British,
they would have to do more than just defend their land. They would
have to go on the offensive. Finally, after weeks of persistent pressure from Botha, Joubert had agreed to allow him to go deeper into
Natal, and to take with him the men and arms he would need to
show the British what it meant to fight the Boers.

-->

Moving slowly, the armored train took about an hour to reach
the first station at Frere, a small settlement with an iron bridge that
crossed the Blaauwkrantz River. At this point, Haldane was ready to
turn back. Although they had yet to see any Boers, the closer they
got to the Tugela River, the more likely that was to change. Some-

how, however, he knew that he would keep going. Although Haldane was the commanding officer on the train, he had with him a man whose opinions about the objective of their journey, and the risks they should take, were stronger and more irresistible than his own. "Had I been alone and not had my impetuous young friend Churchill with me . . . I might have thought twice before throwing myself into the lion's jaws," Haldane would later write. "But I was carried away by his ardour and departed from an attitude of prudence."

Despite Haldane's reluctance, the train crept on, passing Frere and making its way to the next station, a tiny outpost named Chieveley that consisted of little more than a platform and a telegraph post. Just before they pulled into the station, Churchill and Haldane saw in the distance the one sight they had both feared and expected: the unmistakable form of Boers. "A long hill was lined with a row of black spots," Churchill wrote, "showing that our further advance would be disputed." The Boers were still about a mile away, but they could see perhaps a hundred of them, and they had with them teams of oxen pulling wagons that doubtless carried field guns. They were also, Churchill noted, moving south. "Certainly they were Boers," he wrote. "Certainly they were behind us. What would they be doing with the railway line?"

→→

Churchill and Haldane had no idea what the Boers were up to. They did know, however, that not only were the burghers almost invisible when in hiding, they could also move with enormous speed when they chose to. Every Boer had a horse, and that horse was as familiar with and comfortable in the veld as its master. Whenever they were forced to go on foot, British mounted troops had to leave a soldier behind to watch the horses, but Boer horses stayed where they had been left until their owners returned. Although they asked a lot of their horses, often riding them as many as sixty miles in a single day, the Boers always made sure their loads were light. While a British cavalryman and his equipment rarely weighed less than four hundred pounds, a Boer, who had with him only a saddle, rifle, blanket and food, was half that weight.

The Boer burghers themselves were often as different from their British counterparts as were their horses. In fact, most of the men Botha had brought with him were not at all what Britons would picture when they thought of a soldier. Many of them, despite their extraordinary skill with rifles and horses and their intimate knowledge of the region, would not even have been allowed to join the British army. "There were men in the Boer forces who had only one arm, some with only one leg, others with only one eye," Howard Hillegas, an American journalist who followed the Boers during the war, wrote. "Some were almost totally blind, while others would have felt happy if they could have heard the report of their rifles."

The Boers did not have the luxury of turning down men who wanted to fight, and it wouldn't have occurred to them to do it even if they had. They were free men—free to refuse orders, to make their own decisions in the heat of battle, and to fight whether they were well or ill, whole of body or severely maimed. Whatever their physical condition, they could still shoot, and they could kill a British soldier as well as any man.

As soon as the Boers passed Chieveley, heading south while the armored train continued north, they set their plan in motion. Their bush hats sagging and drooping in the rain, they worked quickly, careful to hide behind the kopjes that lay between them and the route to Chieveley. About a mile and a half from Frere, there was a long slope that was not only steep but curved sharply near the bottom. In fact, so steep was the gradient and so sharp the curve that a guide rail had been installed to prevent trains from running off the rails if they made the turn too quickly. It was Botha's plan to help this particular train do just that. Ordering his men to find as many stones as they could hold, he directed them to fill the space between the guide rail and the track so that when the train clattered down the hill, it would skid onto the stones as it made the sharp turn and, he hoped, jump the tracks.

The only factor not within their control was how fast the train would be going. Botha, however, was not the kind of man who left things to chance. As soon as the rocks had been piled along the guide rail, he ordered his men to push their guns up the hills that flanked the tracks. When the train crested the steep slope, they would greet it with such a barrage of bullets and shells that the driver would do everything in his power to escape, and there was only one way to go: down the hill as fast as he possibly could.

When their work was finished, rain was still falling, but the Boers ignored it. They stretched out on the wet ground, pulled down their hats and got out their pipes. Smoking in silence, they waited patiently for their prey to return.

CHAPTER 12

GRIM SULLEN DEATH

A s he pulled into Chieveley, his mind on the Boers he had seen only a mile away, Haldane was startled from his reverie by his telegraphist, who handed him a message from Long. "Remain at Frere in observation guarding your safe retreat," it read. "Remember that Chieveley station was last night occupied by the enemy." Haldane could not remember that the Boers had been at Chieveley the night before because Long, perhaps accidentally or perhaps because he was determined to send out the armored train, had not shared that particular piece of information with him before he left Estcourt. As soon as they reached Chieveley, however, Haldane could see for himself that the Boers had been there. "Everything about the station," he wrote, "showed signs of a hostile visitation."

Ordering the telegraphist to report to Long what they had just seen, and inform him that they were about to return to Frere, Haldane climbed back onto the train. Leaning forward, he pressed a button, which was his only means of communicating with the engine, to signal to the driver that they should begin their slow journey home. The engine reversed direction, and Haldane and Churchill felt their car lurch back toward Estcourt, now forming the final, rather than the first, car in the train.

Haldane knew that the Boers he had seen earlier were likely waiting for them up ahead, but beyond maintaining a constant vigilance,
he could do little about it now. When the train reached the crest
of a hill not far from Frere and he found that the land rising to his
left blocked his view of everything beyond it, Haldane pushed the
button to signal the driver to stop. Knowing that his wounded leg
would not allow him to easily climb over the tall sides of the truck,
he handed his binoculars to Churchill and asked him to scout ahead.
Without hesitating, Churchill scrambled out of the truck and scaled
the closest hill. He had only been gone a few minutes, the binoculars
pressed to his eyes as the rain blurred the lenses, when he heard the
sharp, piercing sound of Haldane's whistle, urgently signaling him
to return to the train.

Churchill had just dropped down into the open truck, his feet
landing heavily on the floor, when a shell flew overhead, narrowly
missing him. When it hit the ground just beyond them with a shud-
dering thud, there was no question in any of the men's minds that it
was a pom-pom. Designed by the American inventor Hiram Maxim
and nicknamed for the coughing sound they made when fired, pom-
poms were a new automatic cannon that used unusually small, one-
pound shells but shot them at the impressive rate of sixty rounds
per minute. Rejected by the British army as both unnecessary and
ineffective, pom-poms had quickly become a favorite weapon of the
Boers, who liked the fact that they were light and easy to move,
and so fit perfectly with their guerrilla style of warfare. "This noisome beast always lurks in thick bush," George Warrington Steevens
had warned his fellow Britons in a dispatch just a few weeks earlier,
"whence it barks chains of shell at the unsuspecting stranger." The
British soon came to regret their decision and, later in the war, would
ship fifty pom-poms to South Africa. At this moment, however, they
had none, and Botha had two, pointing directly at the armored
train.

Urgently pressing the button to signal the driver to start down
the hill, Haldane stood back and felt the reassuring tug as the train
began to pick up speed. He felt "rather elated," he would later write,

"as the pace grew faster and faster." Churchill, standing on a box in the back of the truck so that his head and shoulders were above the sides, giving him a good view of the surrounding land, suddenly saw a group of Boers at the top of a nearby hill. Seconds later, he saw something else. "Three wheeled things," undoubtedly field guns, appeared among the men. Moments later, blinding streaks of yellow light filled the sky, flashing ten or twelve times in rapid succession. Then there were two more flashes, larger this time, followed by an enormous ball of white smoke that "sprang into being and tore out into a cone like a comet." It was shrapnel, the first Churchill had ever seen, and, he would later write, "very nearly the last."

As the roar of the shells continued, whizzing and whirring overhead and then exploding in geysers of blue-white smoke, the Boer snipers joined the chorus. Having jumped down from his box, Churchill stood next to Haldane, listening to the rifle fire as it rattled the metal sides of the truck, bright pings like popcorn in a tin container. "When all is said, there is nothing to stir the blood like rifle-fire," a British journalist had written from Ladysmith. It "sends the heart galloping." Frantically, the sailors swung their heavy gun around to face the enemy. With a sinking heart, Churchill now saw, however, that this, their only secret weapon, which just minutes earlier he had believed would be a "nice surprise" for the Boers, was little more than "an antiquated toy."

As the train picked up speed, rushing down the hillside in a desperate attempt to outrace the Boers, a thought flashed through Churchill's mind with sudden, startling assurance: This was a trick. They were rushing toward a trap, and the only way to save themselves was to go not faster, but slower. Just as he was turning to Haldane to suggest that someone run, hunched and dodging, along the train to tell the driver to slow down, a tremendous jolt suddenly shook the car so violently that everyone in it was thrown to the floor.

→►

While Haldane was still lying on his back, dazed by the impact and trying to collect his thoughts, Churchill leaped to his feet, volunteering to find out what had happened. Hoisting himself over the side, he dropped to the ground and began to run in the direction of the engine, bullets whistling shrilly around him, punctuated by the deeper, jarring rasp of the shells that screamed overhead.

The first thing Churchill saw was that the train had not just been hit, it was in pieces. Botha's plan had worked even better than he had hoped. The moment the first car had struck the rocks, it had been catapulted into the air, flipping completely over and landing at the bottom of the hill, killing or horribly wounding the platelayers who had been riding in it. The armored car behind it had slid another twenty yards down the tracks before crashing onto its side and launching dozens of men onto the ground, where they lay, some wounded, some dead, all caught in a shower of Boer bullets. The third car, which was just in front of the engine, somehow remained upright, but its front half had twisted off the rails, leaving the other half on the tracks, blocking the rest of the train.

Just as Churchill passed the engine, another shell seemed to explode right over his head, spewing shrapnel everywhere. Terrified, the engine driver leaped from the cab, racing to the overturned truck in desperate search of protection. Fury contorting his face as it bled from a gash delivered by a shell splinter, he turned to Churchill and poured out his rage. "He was a civilian," Churchill would recall the man declaring. "What did they think he was paid for? To be killed by bombshells? Not he. He would not stay another minute."

Realizing that they were about to lose their driver, the only man who knew how to move what was left of the armored train, Churchill said the only thing he could think of that might persuade him to return to the engine. "No man," he assured the driver, "was ever hit twice on the same day." What was more, he said, if he climbed back into the cab and did his duty, he would be "rewarded for distinguished gallantry." This was a rare opportunity, one for which every Briton, soldier or civilian, hungered, and it might never come

again. Astonishingly, after listening carefully to Churchill, the man
reached a trembling hand to his face, wiped away the blood, and
pulled himself back into the cab. "Thereafter," Churchill wrote, he
"obeyed every order which I gave him."

Although it was painfully apparent that there was nothing they
could do to salvage the first three trucks, if they could use the engine
as a ram to shove the car in front of it off the tracks, they might
be able to escape. The third truck was wedged between the second
truck, which was on its side, and the engine, but the tracks themselves seemed to be intact, and there were enough men still alive and
unwounded to give them a glimmer of hope, however small. "This
arrangement gave us the best possible chance of safety," Churchill
wrote, although "the position appeared quite hopeless."

Turning on his heels, Churchill ran back to his own truck and,
shouting to Haldane through one of the narrow, vertical gun slots,
explained the situation and the plan he had devised. Although the
role Churchill was suggesting for himself was a military one, Haldane immediately agreed to it. "I knew him well enough," Haldane
wrote, "to realise that he was not the man to stand quietly by and
look on in a critical situation." He also knew that if anyone could
free the engine, Churchill could. In the meantime, Haldane told his
friend, he would do what he could to distract the Boers.

Even hunkered down inside their armored car, Haldane and his
men were in as much danger as Churchill. Although in theory the
metal sides would shield them from the Boer onslaught, the men
were well aware that the protection they offered was little more
than an illusion. "Any direct shell must pierce it like paper and kill
everyone," Churchill himself acknowledged. "It seemed almost safer
outside."

As if to prove that theory, soon after Churchill left, a shell struck
the car, passing clean through the side with little more than a hitch
in its trajectory. By an incredible stroke of luck, it did not explode
until it continued through to the other side, but it was to be only the
first of many. Three more shells tore through the armor, and several
more exploded just outside, each time landing with such a concussive

force that they slammed the men onto their backs. They were able to answer the Boer fire with three rounds from their field gun, but before they could fire a fourth, another shell struck the gun directly, and it, along with its smashed-to-splinters base, fell completely out of the truck. Shaken and terrified, the men struggled to maintain their positions. "It took more than verbal persuasion to keep the loopholes of the wagon continuously manned," Haldane admitted. "I felt that every moment must be our last."

→→

The enemy quickly surrounded the wrecked train on three sides, intensifying their barrage as the men frantically sought cover. For the next hour, as he ran the length of the train, trying to help free it, or stood in the open, instructing the terrified driver, Churchill was constantly in the line of fire. Had the platelayers not already been dead or running for their lives, and their tools scattered across the veld, caught in bushes or slipping down sandy holes, his job might have been easier. As it was, the work of clearing the line was one of the most difficult and, to Churchill's mind, thrilling moments of his young life, and he rose to the challenge as though he had been waiting for just such a disaster, which in many ways he had. "I know myself pretty well and am not blind to the tawdry and dismal side of my character," he had written to his mother from India two years earlier, "but if there is one situation in which I do not feel ashamed of myself it is in the field."

Although Churchill had been called many things—opportunist, braggart, blowhard—no one had ever questioned his bravery. "Winston is like a strong wire that, stretched, always springs back. He prospers under attack, enmity and disparagement," Atkins would later write of him. "He lives on excitement. . . . The more he scents frustration the more he has to fight for; the greater the obstacles, the greater the triumph."

Surrounded by screaming shells and deafening explosions, dead and dismembered men, desperation and almost certain failure,

Churchill, eyes flashing, cheeks flushed, began shouting orders. The first thing they had to do was uncouple the second and third trucks, and then drag the third car, which was half on and half off the rails, back until it could be pushed off the tracks altogether. Although the job seemed fairly straightforward, it was anything but. As useless as the armored trucks were when it came to repelling shells, they were unmanageably heavy, and it took several attempts, the engine's wheels spinning, skidding and squealing as it tried to pull the deadweight, before they had moved the car back far enough that Churchill could call for volunteers. He asked for twenty men and got nine, but they were enough. Together, with help from the engine, and under constant fire, they were finally able to push the car off the rails.

There was an exhilarating moment of triumph, followed, devastatingly fast, by utter disbelief. Although the tender could finally pass the derailed car, the engine, which was about six inches wider, could not. It was, Churchill would later write, "one of the bitterest disappointments of my life." It was a matter of only a few inches— the edge of the engine's footplate catching on the edge of the car— but each time they tried to nudge it farther, it became more and more tightly jammed against the second, overturned truck. They tried again to use men to push it, but despite the incredible risk they ran as they stood fully exposed to Boer fire, they were unable to make any progress.

Terrified that if they pushed too hard they would end up derailing the engine as well, thus destroying any hope they might have had, Churchill repeatedly cautioned the driver to proceed carefully. The Boers, however, who understood now what the British were trying to do, had intensified their fire, directing most of it at the engine. Suddenly one of the shells landed directly on the engine, causing it to burst into flames. In a spasm of reaction, the driver, already in a frenzy of excitement and terror, poured on the steam. "There was a grinding crash," Churchill wrote, "the engine staggered, checked, shore forward again until with a clanging, tearing sound it broke past the point of interception, and nothing but the smooth line lay between us and home."

Churchill would later remember this hour, fraught with danger of the most exceptional and immediate kind, with a fondness usually reserved for moments of the greatest joy and triumph. He would never forget "the expectation of destruction as a matter of course, the realization of powerlessness, and the alternations of hope and despair," he later wrote, "with only four inches of twisted iron work to make the difference between danger, captivity, and shame on the one hand—safety, freedom, and triumph on the other." Although, with the freeing of the engine, the latter outcome now seemed to be a possibility, however remote, they still faced almost insurmountable odds.

→→

The most immediate problem was that in the process of trying to clear the line, someone had uncoupled the engine from the last train car. After all they had endured to move it forward, it was too dangerous to risk moving the engine back again in an attempt to recouple it. Haldane and his men would have to abandon their posts.

Climbing out of his battered truck, Haldane was aghast when he saw the engine. The firebox was in flames, steam pouring out on all sides, but it was all they had. They would have to put the wounded men into and on top of the engine, and those who could still walk would have to try to run alongside it, using it as a shield until they could reach Frere, about half a mile away.

Shouting for Frankland, the young man who had summoned him to Long's tent the night before, Haldane instructed him to bring the other soldiers. Together they forced as many men onto the engine and tender as could possibly fit. The machine soon looked as though it had been quilted in khaki, with wounded soldiers shoved, stuffed and draped into and over every available space. They were "standing in the cab, lying on the tender, or clinging to the cowcatcher," Churchill wrote. "And all this time the shells fell into the wet earth throwing up white clouds, burst with terrifying detonations overhead, or actually struck the engine and the iron wreckage."

The sound was deafening, and the fire and bright flashes of the exploding shells seemed almost supernatural in the gray morning light. One shell struck the engine's footplate, which was only about a yard from Churchill's face, erupting in a flash of yellow so brilliant and blinding he was astonished he was still alive. A black plume of coal filled the air as another shell hit the tender, and then, to Churchill's horror, a third struck the arm of a young private from the Dublin Fusiliers who was standing next to him. "The whole arm was smashed to a horrid pulp—bones, muscle, blood, and uniform all mixed together," he would write years later, still unable to free himself from the sickening memory. "At the bottom hung the hand, unhurt, but swelled instantly to three times its ordinary size."

In the midst of the chaos, Haldane had climbed onto the engine's step, perched precariously on the edge to make room for more wounded inside. So tightly packed were they, however, that a man in front of him suddenly lurched back, stepping on Haldane's fingers. Reflexively jerking his hand away, he lost his grip and, before he could regain his hold, fell backward off the engine onto the wet ground. By the time he had scrambled to his feet, it was too late. The engine had already gone too far, and he could do nothing but watch it move farther and farther out of reach. "No shouting on my part would have caused the driver to stop," he wrote. "I prayed fervently that one of the bullets would come my way and put an end to the business."

➤➤

The Boers, determined to prevent the enemy from escaping, now directed all their firepower at the engine. As Churchill watched, help- less, the men who had been running alongside it, desperately trying to use it for protection, began to fall under the barrage, dropping suddenly to the ground like birds from the sky. "Several screamed— this is very rare in war," Churchill wrote, "and cried for help." As the wounded or just exhausted began to fall behind, leaving them com- pletely unprotected, Churchill shouted at the driver to slow down.

Even had they been able to creep along, however, he knew that there would have been little they could do to shield the men, and the slaughter continued unabated.

So untenable did the situation become that finally, to Churchill's outrage, one man, a wounded soldier, pulled his white handkerchief out of his pocket and began to wave it in an unmistakable sign of surrender. Although in the British army surrender was considered a fate worse than death, there had already been an unusually and, to the minds of the British public, appallingly high number in this war. "What a shame! What a bitter shame for all the camp!" Steevens had written two weeks earlier when he learned of the British surrender after the Battle of Nicholson's Nek, just outside Ladysmith. "All ashamed for England! Not of her—never that!—but for her."

Churchill himself had often complained bitterly about the rash of surrenders. In fact, just two days earlier he had written to a friend who was a high-ranking officer that "there has been a great deal too much surrendering in this war." He and Haldane had spent many nights in Estcourt, Atkins would later recall, "crying out about the number of prisoners taken in this campaign."

Churchill, however, was as helpless to prevent the surrender as he had been to protect the men being butchered before his eyes. As soon as they spotted the handkerchief, the Boers had ceased fire and were already descending on them in clouds of thundering hooves and billowing coats. Many of the soldiers, unaware that one of their own had raised the white flag, continued to fight, the Boers yelling at them to put down their weapons or be killed. Frankland in particular, Churchill noticed, was astonishingly brave, wearing a wide smile and encouraging the other men not to lose heart.

When the engine finally reached Frere, most of the men by this time dead, horribly wounded or captured, Churchill forced his way out of the cab and dropped to the ground, planning to run back to help Haldane and any men who had survived the journey by foot. As he got his bearings, however, he quickly realized that the others had already surrendered, and he was alone. Standing in a shallow cutting next to the train tracks, he looked up and saw two men coming toward him. Because they were not wearing uniforms, he at first thought that they were platelayers, but then, in a sudden rush of understanding, he realized that he was wrong. They were Boers. "Full of animated movement," Churchill would later write, they were tall, "clad in dark flapping clothes, with slouch, storm-driven hats," and only a hundred yards away.

Instinctively, Churchill turned and sprinted down the track, feeling the Boers' bullets whizzing by, each pass a small miracle as it narrowly missed him. He launched himself into the cutting, but quickly realized that it was too shallow to provide any protection. As he scrambled desperately up the bank, he felt more bullets fly by as "two soft kisses sucked in the air." Near the top, as a shower of dirt kicked up beside him, one of the bullets grazed his hand.

Crouching in a shallow depression, Churchill watched as a lone Boer galloped up to him. "With a rifle I could have killed him easily," he wrote. "I knew nothing of white flags, and the bullets had made me savage." Reaching for his pistol, the sight of the mangled bodies of young British soldiers and officers vivid in his mind, he looked at the grim, bearded man descending on him and thought to himself, "This one at least." As his fingers touched the belt where he kept his Mauser, however, a terrible realization swept over him. It wasn't there. He had left it behind on the engine.

Staring at the Boer as he moved closer, rifle at the ready, poised to shoot should he make the slightest move to escape, Churchill knew that he had run out of options. He could be killed, or he could be captured. "Death stood before me," he wrote, "grim sullen Death without his light-hearted companion, Chance." The thought of surrender sickened him, but in this moment of fury, frustration and despair, the words of Napoleon, whom he had long studied and admired, came to him: "When one is alone and unarmed, a surrender may be pardoned." Standing before the man who was now his captor, Churchill raised his hands in the air.

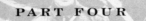

PART FOUR

❮❮❯❯

Prisoners of War

CHAPTER 13

TO SUBMIT,

TO OBEY, TO ENDURE

Still asleep in their tent at Estcourt, Amery and Atkins were suddenly wrenched awake by the sound of gunfire. Leaping up, they
struggled out of their sleeping bags and dived through the canvas
opening, racing toward the smoke and explosions. It was still raining
hard, and the ground had become a slippery, slimy mess, making it
almost impossible to get any purchase as they slid and skidded their
way across the nearly five miles that separated them from the battle.

Just two miles outside Estcourt, they were confronted with a
sickening sight. One look told them everything they needed to know
about the fate of the armored train. Limping its way toward them was
the battered and still-burning engine and tender, covered in bleed-
ing and shell-shocked men. Approaching what Atkins described as
"this emblem of calamity," they tried to find out what had happened. At a distance, the men aboard the engine could do little more
than gesticulate in dumb horror, desperately pointing back to the
charred remains of the train they had left broken and burning on
the tracks. When they were finally close enough to be heard, most
of what the returning soldiers said revolved around the man who
had cheerfully left Amery and Atkins asleep in their tent just a
few hours before. "They were full of praise of Winston's gallantry,"

Amery wrote. What the men could not tell them was whether their friend was still alive.

Hurrying on, crossing miles of barren veld, the two journalists finally passed a platelayer, staggering toward Estcourt on his own. The man, his blue eyes bloodshot, his words coming "shortly and stumblingly from his mouth," told them what he could. Stuttering about shells and bullets and Boers, he finally gasped that he had never seen "nor heard anything like it."

Peering into the distance, Amery and Atkins could now see the train wreckage for themselves and, just past it, a group of prisoners being led away by the Boers. They watched as the solemn procession disappeared over the skyline, not knowing who was among them and who lay dead on the veld. "Well, I devoutly hope Churchill is safe," Atkins wrote in his dispatch that night, hardly believing that the young man who had held so much promise could be so quickly lost. "But I half fear the gods love too much a man, only twenty-four years old, who . . . is that rare combination, the soldier, the reckless soldier even, and the bookman."

→►

As Churchill walked through the wet grass beside his mounted captor, the horse's steaming flank and the man's muddy boot rocking rhythmically next to his shoulder, he could think of nothing but the almost unbearable humiliation of his situation. "All military pride, all independence of spirit must be put aside," he would later write. "These may be carried to the grave, but not into captivity." Only a few minutes earlier he had been on equal terms with the Boers, all brave, determined men fighting for their country and their honor. Now he was their prisoner, and he would be forced to "submit, to obey, to endure."

Furious with himself, and ruminating over how differently things might have turned out had he not forgotten his gun, Churchill suddenly realized with a start that, although he had left his Mauser on the engine, he still had his ammunition. Two clips, each with ten rounds, were thumping, hard and heavy, in the breast pockets on each side of his khaki coat. Realizing that it would be very dangerous indeed for a newly captured man to be found carrying ammunition, he quietly reached into one pocket, slipped the clip into his hand and dropped it onto the saturated ground without a sound. Just as he had eased the second clip out, however, his captor looked down sharply from his horse and demanded to know what he was holding. Thinking fast, Churchill pretended that he himself did not know. "What is it?" he asked. "I picked it up." Taking the clip into his own hand, the man looked at it and, without saying another word, tossed it away.

The two men had not gone far when they reached the rest of Botha's commando, who had taken prisoners of their own. Among the nearly sixty men standing dismally in the rain, Churchill saw the faces of Haldane and Frankland, the ardent young lieutenant who had fought so hard against the Boers. They had been captured together on the iron bridge at Frere, where Haldane had been trying to prevent more men from surrendering. He was furious at having lost his field glasses to a "stalwart Boer," who, after seizing him, had tried to tear the glasses from his hands. Haldane had struggled to hold on to them until another Boer had warned him in English, "Better let him have them or he'll shoot you."

Utterly exhausted from the battle, the frantic efforts to free the engine and the race to elude capture, all of which had taken place in the span of just two hours, Churchill dropped to the ground. He quickly realized that he was surrounded not only by captors and fellow prisoners but by men who had been so severely wounded they would never make it to the "deep and dreary dungeon" that Haldane imagined awaited them. Although he could hear the gasps and moans of the dying men, a fate that he had only narrowly escaped himself, Churchill was filled not with gratitude but with frustration. He was about to be shut up in a prison while the war raged on without him, and it had all been, he felt, a useless sacrifice. "I had not helped anybody by attempting to return to the Company," he wrote, cursing his decision to jump off the engine. "I had only cut myself out of the whole of this exciting war with all its boundless possibilities of adventure and advancement."

Looking up, Churchill saw in the distance the severely damaged engine hobbling toward Estcourt with its load of wounded men. "Something at least was saved from the ruin," he thought. Perhaps "some little honour had been saved as well." Knowing that because of his actions other men had escaped his fate, however, was cold comfort. Sitting in the mud, surrounded by Boers, his future wrenched from his hands, he "meditated blankly upon the sour rewards of virtue."

As the prisoners were being rounded up—"like cattle!" Churchill would later write. "The greatest indignity of my life!"—hundreds of Boers streamed out of the hills in seemingly endless columns, two and three abreast. When they had all finally gathered on the veld, the Boers staring with open curiosity at their British counterparts, a voice called out, *"Voorwärts,"* Afrikaans for "forward." Forced to stand, the exhausted and disheartened men formed a ragged line and began their long march north, toward Pretoria.

As the Boers led them away, Churchill was struck by the civility of the men he had long thought of as backward, even barbaric. "You need not walk fast," one of them said, in perfect English. "Take your time." Noticing that Churchill had lost his hat and had no way to keep the still-falling rain out of his eyes, another Boer tossed him a cap that had once clearly belonged to a Dublin Fusilier. Whether the hat, like his own, had been lost during the battle or had been taken off the head of a dead soldier, Churchill did not know, but he was grateful for it either way.

Moving steadily deeper into the hills, Churchill could now see what the men of Estcourt had for weeks blindly but instinctively known—that they were surrounded by the enemy. Thousands of Boers, slowly revealed to him like apparitions, stared at the grim procession as it passed by. "Behind every hill, thinly veiled by the driving rain, masses of mounted men, arranged in an orderly disorder, were halted," Churchill wrote. "Certainly I did not see less than 3,000, and I did not see nearly all."

When they finally reached the commandant general's camp and the prisoners were ordered to wait in a line, Churchill spoke up. Confidently addressing the nearest Boers, he demanded to be taken directly to Joubert. "I am a newspaper correspondent," he said, "and you ought not to hold me prisoner." In his eagerness to escape imprisonment, however, Churchill had forgotten one critical detail: He had been in full view of the Boers during the attack, and they knew that, even if he was a civilian, he had acted as a combatant.

These men had watched as Churchill fought to free the engine, and his noisy protests over his capture were not only unhelpful, they placed him in immediate danger. "A civilian in a half uniform who has taken an active and prominent part in a fight, even if he has not fired a shot himself," Churchill later wrote, "is liable to be shot at once by drumhead court martial." In the Franco-Prussian War, thirty years earlier, any noncombatant who was caught carrying a gun was immediately executed, and the same code would be observed twenty years later, during World War I. "None of the armies in the Great War," Churchill would later admit, "would have wasted ten minutes upon the business." They would have shot him quickly and been done with it.

To his surprise, instead of being whisked off to Joubert's tent as he had expected, Churchill was suddenly removed from the line of prisoners and ordered to stand by himself. A field cornet took his credentials, which revealed a vital and, for Churchill, dangerous piece of information: his last name. It was, Churchill would later write, "a name better known than liked in the Transvaal."

In 1891, Churchill's father, Randolph, had traveled to South Africa at the invitation of Cecil Rhodes, then prime minister of Cape Colony. Already beginning to suffer from the mental degeneration that would lead to his death just four years later, Randolph had hoped that the trip might improve his health and perhaps even revive the political career he had wantonly destroyed. He had brought with him

Thomas Walden, the valet who now traveled with Winston, and, before setting sail, had also signed on as a correspondent with the *Daily Graphic,* the same newspaper for which Winston would cover the prelude to the Spanish-American War.

Randolph's dispatches, however, which were supposed to simply relate his adventures and describe this exotic land, were far more controversial than his son's had ever been. Never one to mince words, he had spent his three months in southern Africa insulting nearly everyone who had the misfortune to make an appearance in one of his articles. He even attacked the women of his own, exalted social class. After visiting a diamond mine and seeing how incredibly dangerous it was to extract "from the depths of the ground, solely for the wealthy classes, a tiny crystal to be used for the gratification of female vanity," Randolph had, to the horror and outrage of his British readership, come "coldly to the conclusion that, whatever may be the origin of man, the woman is descended from an ape."

The Boers themselves, who failed to meet Randolph's exacting standards in any respect, could not hope to escape his scathing critique. Although he was more than justified in his criticism of their treatment of native Africans, he did not confine his attacks to human rights abuses, lashing out at the Boers for what he perceived to be their lack of hygiene, innate laziness and complete and willful ignorance. "The Boer farmer . . . is perfectly uneducated," Randolph had sneered. "His simple ignorance is unfathomable, and this in stolid composure he shares with his wife, his sons, his daughters, being proud that his children should grow up as ignorant, as uncultivated, as hopelessly unprogressive as himself."

It had not taken long for news of the former Chancellor of the Exchequer's jaw-droppingly offensive articles to make its way into every parlor and pub in London. The response in the British press had been fast and unforgiving. "Lord Randolph Churchill in his time has played many parts, but not even in the famous somersault which terminated his career as leader of the House of Commons . . . has he afforded the public a more unseemly exhibition of irresponsibility than in his letters from South Africa," a journalist for the *Review of Reviews* spat. "They furnish the culminating evidence, if further evidence were necessary, as to the impossibility of Lord Randolph Churchill as the leader of men."

Randolph had been well aware of the offense he was giving, and the effect it was having both in South Africa and in England. Like his rebellious wife, however, he was uninterested in and unconcerned by others' opinions of him, no matter how damaging they might be to his political career and personal reputation, not to mention his country's relationship with the Transvaal. "I have composed here a sixth letter to the *Daily Graphic* in which I again come down on these Boers heavily," he wrote cheerfully to Jennie. "I imagine they will be furious when they see what I write of them."

Winston, however, who was then sixteen years old, did care what people said about his father, and he was outraged by the attacks in the newspapers. "You cannot imagine what vials of wrath you have uncorded [*sic*]," he had written to Randolph from Harrow. "All the papers simply rave. . . . The *Standard* quotes the *Speaker* & is particularly offensive. It states that—but oh I will not bore you with the yapping of these curs." A few months later, he again wrote to his father, still angrily defending him, but, because Randolph's articles had only grown more offensive and outrageous, now also concerned for his safety. "I hear the horrid Boers are incensed with you," he wrote. "It would have been much wiser, if you had waited till you came back before you 'slanged the beggars.'"

→–

Churchill could have had no doubt that most, if not all, of the men now staring at him had heard about his father's trip just eight years earlier and the defamatory things he had written about the Boers. As he stood alone, separated from the other prisoners and the object of intense interest by his captors, he began to fall "prey to gnawing anxiety." Struggling to come up with answers to any questions the Boers might ask him, he could not help but consider the possibility that he would be executed. "What sort of appearance," he wondered, could he "keep up if I were soon and suddenly told that my hour had come."

When the field cornet returned with Churchill's credentials fifteen minutes later, he said nothing beyond brusquely ordering him to rejoin the other prisoners. Churchill realized with a wave of relief that he would not be killed. Neither, however, would he be freed. Despite the fact that moments earlier he had feared for his life, Churchill could not resist again protesting his capture. A Scottish Boer standing nearby laughed at him. "Oh," he said, "we do not catch lords' sons every day." Joining in his laughter, the rest of the men assured Churchill that he would be allowed to play football in prison, but made it clear that they would keep an especially close eye on their young British aristocrat.

�»

After a ten-mile march, without food, water or relief from the rain, the men finally reached the ravaged town of Colenso. They were taken to a corrugated-iron shed near the station, a place that Churchill had seen on his first ride aboard the armored train, little thinking that he would soon be imprisoned there. As he tried to step deeper into the shed, he heard the dry, crackling sound of paper at his feet and looked down to find that the floor was covered with old railway forms and account books, ripped, stained and piled at least four inches deep. Above him, in the raftered ceiling, a skylight blurred as the rain fell on it in a dull, heavy tapping.

Outside, the Boers prepared dinner for their prisoners. Finally opening the shed door, they beckoned to the men to come out and eat. Before them burned two fires, near which lay an ox that had clearly been slain only minutes before. As the men, feeling slightly like cannibals but too hungry to care, tore bloody strips of meat from the carcass, speared them on sticks and cooked them over the fires, the Boers stood around them, watching quietly.

Churchill struck up a conversation with two of the men. They were, he would later write, "English by race, Afrikanders by birth, Boers by choice." Although they disagreed with him on why the war was being waged and who would win it, by the time the prisoners had finished eating, they regarded Churchill as a friend. One of the men even pulled off the blanket he had been wearing like a cloak, his head sticking out of a hole in the middle, and handed it to Churchill.

Even with a full stomach and wrapped in the Boer's blanket, Churchill had difficulty sleeping that night. He had fallen into a dark, brooding mood. With the loss of his freedom, he had, for the first time, also lost his ferocious grip on life. He was no longer master of his fate, in command of his own future. Robbed of his ability to make even the most basic decisions—where he went, how long he stayed, what he ate—he felt stripped of that part of his personality that had most defined him from his youth. "It seemed that love of life was gone," he would later write, "and I thought almost with envy of a soldier I had seen during the fight lying quite still on the embankment, secure in the calm philosophy of death."

Haldane too found himself so frustrated and discouraged that he was unable to summon the strength and determination he would need if he were to win back his freedom. For Haldane, searching for a means of escape was not only his best hope of regaining his pride and returning to the war, it was his sworn duty as a military officer. Nearly twenty years earlier, during the First Boer War, England had attempted to reform and modernize its military law by passing the Army Act. Haldane couldn't remember the exact clause that referred to the obligations of a prisoner of war, but he did remember that the implication was "if any officer, a prisoner, sees the opportunity of escaping, and does not take it, he can be punished."

The problem was that no one ever told these young men, in extraordinarily desperate and dangerous situations, exactly how they were supposed to pull off this feat. In the gloom of the metal shed, Haldane could feel the weight of the problem lying heavily on his shoulders. Tired and dispirited, he looked up at the raftered ceiling and studied its darkened skylight. He could, he thought, somehow shimmy up to the rafters, shatter the skylight, crawl out onto the roof and jump to the ground. There were guards, but not on all sides of the building, and in the dark and pouring rain escape was possible, although certainly at the risk of his life.

As much as Haldane longed for his freedom, in his exhaustion and sorrow he didn't have the heart to try that night. Unfortunately, that first night in captivity, he would later realize with deep regret, was his best chance. "I think that it is a cardinal fact that no time should be lost in effecting one's escape," he would later write, "for every mile one is removed deeper into the enemy's country it will be found that the precautions to prevent this become greater."

When Churchill woke early the next morning after a fitful night, he listened to the sharp sounds of the other men's snores and watched the first light of dawn filter into the shed from the skylight above him. As he lay on the cluttered floor, the memory of where he was and why he was there came back to him in a sudden, sickening rush, and the reality of his situation descended "with a slap." With it, however, returned his iron resolve. It was true that he was a prisoner, but prisoners, he thought, can escape.

While Haldane had looked above him for help, Churchill stared down at the trash covering his shoes. Maybe he didn't need to go anywhere. Maybe all he needed to do was to remain there, hidden, while the rest of the men were led away. "Why not lie buried underneath this litter until prisoners and escort had marched away together?" he thought. "Would they count? Would they notice?" Like Haldane's, however, Churchill's hesitation proved fatal to his plan. While he was still considering the strength of his strategy, the shed door opened, and a guard ordered them all outside.

Soon after a breakfast of last night's oxen, even less appealing on the second day, and a puddle of rainwater, they resumed their march. They were, Churchill wrote, a "sorry gang of dirty, tramping prisoners, but yesterday the soldiers of the Queen." The rains of the day before had gone, and the skies had cleared, but the gullies they had to wade through were now swollen into broad, fast-moving streams, and there was no shelter from the pitiless South African sun. What was more trying to Churchill than his wet feet and his sweltering body were the constant stares of the men guarding him, the "irritating disdain and still more irritating pity."

Later in the day, as they drew nearer to Ladysmith, the men looked up to see hanging above them a sight they had often seen from the hills surrounding Estcourt: General White's lonely balloon. Hovering over the besieged town, its goldbeater's skin—the outer membrane of a calf's intestine that's traditionally used in making gold leaf—catching the sun, it was a fresh reminder to the prisoners of the extent of the disaster that had befallen them. Only days earlier, they had pitied the men trapped in Ladysmith. Now the fate of those soldiers seemed far better than their own. "Beleaguered Ladysmith," Churchill wrote, "with its shells, its flies, its fever, and its filth seemed a glorious paradise to me."

The Boers set up camp that night in the shadow of a looming mountain and surrounded by low, ragged hills. They arranged their wagons in a square, much as the American pioneers had circled their own wagons to protect themselves from attack. Inside the square, they set up a hodgepodge of tents, all shapes and sizes and strikingly different from the uniformly white and sturdy tents of the British army. Then they gathered the prisoners before them.

They had decided that, because they were drawing closer to Pretoria, it was time to separate the prisoners into two groups. Addressing the ragged group of men, they demanded to know who among them were officers, and who enlisted men. Churchill once again had a decision to make. As a civilian, he could have chosen either group. As a former military man, however, he naturally gravitated toward the officers, a group that would include Haldane. He chose to be housed with the officers, a decision that, by nightfall, he would regret.

Once inside his tent, peering through the triangular flap at the flickering fires and the Boers who sat just outside, their guns in their laps, Churchill realized that he had made a mistake. Ladysmith was only five miles away. If he could slip past the wagons without being seen, he could make it there before morning. Because he was in the officers' tent, however, it would be impossible to move an inch without being noticed. Four guards were stationed outside, two at the back of the tent and two in front. He could hear them clicking the breech bolts on their Mausers, and he watched, dismayed, as they relieved one another at regular intervals throughout the night. Also, unlike the night before, when Haldane had considered escaping, the moon was now full and bright, illuminating every shrub and hollow where he might hide. "One could not help regretting," Haldane wrote, "the chance that had been lost twenty-four hours earlier."

→→

Early the next morning, they started out for Elandslaagte, a railway station midway between Ladysmith and Dundee where Haldane had been wounded in battle not even a month before and which would soon be the final stop in their long march. They spent one more night on the veld, and then, on the morning of November 18, three days after their capture, they walked into Elandslaagte, and saw a train already waiting for them in the station.

While arrangements for the final leg of the journey were being made, the Boers herded their uniformed prisoners into the baggage room, and, not sure what else to do with him, locked Churchill in the ticket office. "As I observed the ticket office with its copper bars under which the tickets were sold," a burgher named Keuzenkamp would later write, "I felt it answered to the appearance of a jail." Seeing where Churchill had been placed, Louis Botha ordered Keuzenkamp to stand guard at the door. From outside, he could hear Churchill in the small room, restlessly pacing the floors.

When it was finally time to leave, the enlisted men, who had been separated from their officers the night before, were directed toward six or seven closed cars, while the officers were given a first-class carriage. Soon after Churchill, Haldane and Frankland climbed in and sat down, the door opened and a man carried in what seemed to them, after their long, hungry march, to be extraordinary quantities of food—four tin cans, two of mutton and two of fish, several loaves of bread, six jars of jam and a big can of tea. "The reader will believe that we did not stand on ceremony," Churchill wrote, "but fell to at once and made the first satisfying meal for three days."

As the men ate, a crowd quickly gathered outside their windows. Churchill, desperately hungry, ignored them until one man identified himself as a doctor and asked about his hand, which had been grazed by a bullet just before his capture. It wasn't a large wound, but because it had not been cleaned or cared for in any way during their three-day march, it had begun to fester. After Churchill raised his hand to be examined through the window, the man hurried off, soon returning with bandages and hot water. "Amid the approving grins of the rough fellows who thronged the platform," Churchill wrote, "he soon bound me up very correctly."

Inside the train car, the prisoners had been joined by a rather tough and scrappy young man named Adam Brockie. Brockie was an Irish sergeant major, not an officer, and so belonged in one of the other cars. Churchill and Haldane knew his secret, but both for his safety and their own benefit they had decided to keep it. Brockie was smart and resourceful, and he would, they felt, prove useful.

Brockie was an unusual young man. His mother had died when he was very young, and he had enlisted in the British army in Dublin at just fourteen years of age. He had lived in South Africa for much of his adult life and, four years earlier, had taken part in the Jameson Raid, which had humiliated Joseph Chamberlain and nearly led to the imprisonment of Cecil Rhodes. He was now a prisoner of war like the rest of them, but he had been captured only after a stunningly long and effective streak of testing the Boers and, time and again, evading them.

In fact, Brockie had managed to do something that Churchill had only dreamed of attempting. Also stationed in Estcourt, Brockie had requested to be attached to General James Wolfe-Murray's staff as a scout. On November 4, eleven days before the train derailment, three Zulu whom Wolfe-Murray had sent to Ladysmith with messages for White had been captured by the Boers. Upon hearing this, Brockie had asked the general if he could give it a try. "He told me I would never get through," Brockie later wrote. "I said, Sir never try, never win. . . . He gave me the despatches." Brockie had to crawl on his hands and knees for at least a mile of the forty-some miles separating Estcourt and Ladysmith, but he made it through without being caught. White, astonished, asked him if he thought he could return to Estcourt. Not only did Brockie make it back, but he was so good at slipping past the Boers that Wolfe-Murray sent him four more times. Not until the sixth attempt was he finally caught.

When he was captured and asked his rank, Brockie, who had earlier removed the corps insignia from his hat and coat, had claimed to be a lieutenant of the Natal Carbineers. He was certain that if his captors had known who he was, and that he had taken part in the Jameson Raid, they would have shot him without hesitation. Inside the officers' first-class train car, Brockie's fellow prisoners agreed to "maintain the fiction." Not only was this new addition to their small group clever and brave, but he knew the land well and was fluent in both Dutch and Zulu. "We thought," Churchill would later write, "he was the very man for us."

As the train sped north toward Pretoria, passing Talana Hill, where Penn Symons had been killed, and then Majuba, where the British army had fallen in humiliating defeat to the Boers in the First Boer War, twenty years earlier, the four British prisoners thought of little else but escape. Speaking in undertones when they thought the two guards were not listening, they tried to make plans. It was impossible, though, to know what awaited them in Pretoria.

Churchill, who had quickly regained his old lust for life, found it impossible to simply bide his time. Continuously looking about the train car, he searched for an escape route even there. At one point, he considered climbing out a window while the train hurtled through a long tunnel. One of the guards, however, perhaps guessing his thoughts, stood, balancing on the swaying car floor, and reached up to close both windows. Looking pointedly at Churchill, he then opened the breech of his Mauser to show him that it was fully loaded, and to make it clear that he would not hesitate to use it if necessary. Although the Boers took pride in treating their prisoners well, they were not about to lose a single man, especially this one.

CHAPTER 14

"I REGRET TO INFORM YOU"

On November 18, the day that her son would reach Pretoria as a prisoner of war, Lady Randolph Churchill threw one of the most celebrated social events of the year in London. As the chairman of a fund-raiser to refurbish the *Maine,* a hospital ship that was scheduled to sail to South Africa the following month, she had designed a party so lavish it stunned even this jaded, society-weary city. The venue was Claridge's, but the everyday splendor of that legendary hotel was not sufficient for Lady Churchill. As a reporter covering the party for the *Daily Mail* would write, although Claridge's had "always been noted as the resort of kings and princes, [it] was really Royal in its preparations for this great occasion."

As Jennie's guests stepped into the hotel that afternoon, the vast entry hall was filled with the bright, lilting music of pipes, played by a contingent of Scots Guards, who, in their vibrant red dress jackets, lined the hotel's sweeping central staircase, tucked in among a lush array of potted palms and enormous flowers. As they were ushered inside, they found that the dining room, with its soaring ceilings and paneled walls, had been transformed for the afternoon into a magnificent concert hall. A large stage had been erected at one end of the room, over which two flags had been draped—not just the

Union Jack but, to the surprise of some guests and the indignation of others, the Stars and Stripes of Lady Churchill's own country as well. The rest of the room was filled with an elegant arrangement of tables, each topped with a vase of yellow and pink chrysanthemums, perfectly matching the shades on the lamps, which cast a soft, golden glow over the dazzled guests.

Although Jennie had billed the event as a "Thé-concert," this was still her party, which meant that there was quite a bit more than tea for sale. "Pretty women wearing the prettiest frocks moved deftly about to wait upon every newcomer," the reporter for the *Daily Mail* wrote, "and in the Royal room especially very high prices were paid." Guests could buy everything from alcohol, including a particularly strong drink that had been named for the *Maine,* at the "American bar" in the adjoining room, to cigarettes, five hundred boxes of which had been donated by the Virginia-based Pasquali Cigarette Syndicate, to souvenir programs bound in white vellum. On the program's cover was a striking portrait of a woman whom everyone in the city, let alone the room, would have known at a glance. Sketched in chalk by the most famous portrait painter of the Victorian era, John Singer Sargent, were the dark curls, heavily lidded eyes and famously full, sensuous lips of the hostess herself.

As beguiling as it was, however, Sargent's sketch was the only glimpse Jennie's guests would have of her that day. Nearly everyone she knew, or deemed worth knowing, was there, a glittering crowd that included the most prominent and powerful members of British society. Everyone from the Prince of Wales, who had arrived with the Duchess of Marlborough, dressed in ruby red and wearing a chic, narrow-brimmed black hat, to Sir Arthur Sullivan, who had written the music for two of the biggest theatrical hits of the century—*H.M.S. Pinafore* and *The Pirates of Penzance*—filled the concert hall. Only Lady Churchill herself was nowhere to be seen.

Two days earlier, a telegram had arrived at Jennie's home in London. It began with the five words that every mother fears most when her son is at war. "I regret to inform you," it read, "that Mr. Winston Churchill has been captured by the Boers." Although the author of the telegram, Oliver Borthwick, Churchill's editor at the *Morning Post,* had been able to assure Jennie that Winston had "fought gallantly," he could tell her nothing more. Nor could anyone else. Her younger son, Jack, who had been the first to see the telegram, had quickly written to her, hoping to stem her fears. "He is not wounded," he told her. "Don't be frightened. I will be here when you come home."

By the day of the benefit at Claridge's, news of the attack on the armored train was in every newspaper in London. From South Africa, Buller had referred to the decision to send out the train that morning as an example of "inconceivable stupidity." In London, however, there was far less interest in the attack itself than in Churchill's actions during it. He had become not only the talk of the city but the subject of widespread praise and admiration, something he had long felt deserving of, but had certainly never before been.

The wounded men who had been able to cling to the engine as it lurched back to Estcourt had told everyone who would listen of the heroism of Winston Churchill. In fact, on the same day as the attack, the platelayers had asked the railway inspector to write a special letter of tribute to the newspaper correspondent who had led the effort to free the engine, thus enabling them to escape, and quite possibly saving their lives. "The railway men who accompanied the armoured train this morning ask me to convey to you their admiration of the coolness and pluck displayed by Mr. Winston Churchill," the letter, which was reprinted in newspapers across England, read. "The whole of our men are loud in their praises of Mr. Churchill who, I regret to say, has been taken prisoner. I respectfully ask you to convey their admiration to a brave man."

Churchill's bravery was not just mentioned in every article about the attack on the train, it was the heart of the story and, usually, the headline as well. Instead of commenting on the fact that five men had been killed and nearly sixty taken prisoner, the headline in the *Yorkshire Evening Post* had shouted, "MR. CHURCHILL'S HERO-ISM." The *Standard* had reported that "Mr. Winston Churchill is said to have behaved during the skirmish with the greatest coolness and courage." He had "rallied the party frequently, and fearlessly exposed himself," the *Daily News* wrote, and the *Daily Telegraph* informed its readers that this "young man of brilliant promise" had not just helped to free the train but "manfully help[ed] to carry the wounded."

Churchill's own paper, the *Morning Post,* had not let the opportunity go to waste, boldly broadcasting the heroism of its man in the field. Its headline on the day of Jennie's benefit, "OUR CAPTURED CORRESPONDENT," was followed by a subtitle, in only slightly smaller type, that touted, "Mr. Winston Churchill's Gallantry." It also quoted from other newspapers' accounts of the attack, including the *Daily Mail,* the paper that had attempted to hire Churchill first. "The dangers of the modern war correspondent's work," the *Daily Mail* had argued, "are strikingly exemplified by the capture of the *Morning Post*'s brilliant young special, Mr. Winston Churchill."

Talk of Churchill's political career was also revived, with predictions for his soaring success, should he make it out of South Africa alive. "We wish him a safe return to England to contest Oldham in the Conservative interest," the *Nottingham Evening Post* wrote, "successfully we trust." Not surprisingly, Atkins had also chimed in, predicting in the *Manchester Guardian* that his friend and fellow correspondent would make a triumphant return to politics. "This is the way to Parliament," he wrote, "whither [Churchill] will carry, if he survive these perilous days."

So loud and universal was the praise for Churchill, in fact, that one newspaper felt it necessary to point out what the others in their excitement seemed to have forgotten: He wasn't even a member of the military. "We are very sorry that Mr. Winston Churchill should have been taken prisoner, and we have no doubt that he behaved with hereditary gallantry," an editorial in the *Globe* began sulkily, before launching into a bitter complaint. "But we protest against despatches which represent him, a correspondent, and therefore properly a mere spectator, as 'rallying' the troops and calling upon them to 'be men,' while no mention is made of the officers actually on duty. One might suppose, from such a message, that Mr. Churchill undertook the conduct of the fight, and that the real commanders were doing nothing while it was in progress."

Even at Jennie's sumptuous fund-raiser, the conversation revolved not around the *Maine,* or even the war, but young Churchill. "Everyone naturally discussed the achievement of Mr. Winston Churchill," the *York Herald* reported. There too, however, controversy was already brewing. Would Lady Churchill use her connections to try to free her son, as she had so often used them to send him to war? "The talk about the highest social influence being exerted in order to secure [Churchill's] release in preference to that of prisoners unconnected with noble families," one reporter wrote, "is most strongly deprecated."

→→

At home, for once in the spotlight not because of her own exploits but those of her son, Jennie suddenly found herself the object not of admiration, disapproval or jealousy, but pity. She was inundated with letters and telegrams, filled with a strange mixture of condolences for her son's capture and congratulations on his bravery. Among the letters was one from Thomas Walden, once her husband's valet and now her son's, who had joined the Imperial Light Horse after Winston's capture so that he could remain in South Africa to await, he hoped, his employer's release. "I came down in the armoured train with the driver, who is wounded in the head with a shell," he wrote to Jennie. "He told me all about Mr. Winston. He says there is not a braver gentleman in the Army." The editor of the *Daily News Weekly* apparently agreed, writing to Lady Churchill to ask if she would be willing to write a caption for a sketch he wanted to publish depicting "the gallantry of WSC."

The only letter Jennie took much notice of, however, was from her young lover, George Cornwallis-West. An officer in the Scots Guards, George was by then also in South Africa and had written to Jennie as soon as he heard the news of Winston's capture. "I am so grieved to see by today's paper that Winston has been taken prisoner," he wrote to her from the Orange River Camp. "I do hope he will be released soon as a non combatant and that nothing will happen to him—how anxious you will be, my poor darling. How I wish I could help you."

Had Churchill had his way, George would remain as far away from his mother as it was possible to be. He had known before leaving England that the dashing young officer wanted to marry Jennie, and that, despite some reservations, she was seriously considering the idea. "Of course, the glamour won't last forever," she had written breezily to a friend, "but why not take what you can?" The thought of his mother marrying a man who was not only his age but, as one of Jennie's later biographers would write, "a bit short on brain," made Churchill miserable, and he had not hidden his feelings on the subject. "I hate the idea of your marrying," he had told her.

George had not endeared himself to Churchill in recent months, as he had already begun to adopt the manner of a disapproving stepfather. After running into Winston a few days before he boarded the *Dunottar Castle,* George had reported the encounter to Jennie, clicking his tongue in avuncular dismay. "Don't tell him I said so, but he looked just a young dissenting parson, hat brushed the wrong way, and at the back of his head, awful old black coat and tie," George had written. "He is a good fellow but—very untidy."

Churchill's only hope lay in the fact that he was not alone in trying to prevent his mother from marrying George. George's family had done all they could to discourage the relationship. After trying and failing to keep George from seeing Jennie, and then to interest him in other, more suitable women, out of desperation George's father had turned for help to the only person he thought might be able to talk some sense into Lady Churchill: her older son. Knowing that he had no hope of changing his mother's mind, Winston had instead written to George. "I cannot tell you what he said as he refused me the right to disclose a word," George later told Jennie, but "his arguments were very strong."

Churchill had one other ally: the Prince of Wales, who had not only chided Jennie but warned George that he was making a terrible mistake. That summer, the prince had pulled George aside on his yacht, the HMY *Britannia,* and urged him to reconsider marrying a woman who was so much older than he was. He had also written to Jennie, sternly telling her that he hoped she would not continue her "flirtation" with George. In response, Jennie, bristling with indignation, had reminded the prince that it was her life they were discussing, not his own. "It has been my privilege to enjoy your friendship for upwards of quarter of a century," he wrote to her in reply, "therefore why do you think it necessary to write me a rude letter simply because I have expressed strongly my regret at the marriage you are about to make?"

The more their friends and family pushed, the more angry and obstinate Jennie grew, and the more lovesick George became. He referred to Jennie as "my darling little missie," swore that he could not live without her and loved her "more & more if possible." Churchill, however, still held out hope that the wedding would not happen. "After all I don't believe you will marry," he had written to his mother not long before setting sail for South Africa. "My idea is that the family pressure will crush George."

➤➤

The resistance to her relationship with George had, of course, only made Jennie more determined than ever to marry him. In fact, she hoped to be reunited with him soon. Although Jennie had not planned to accompany the *Maine* to South Africa, she was beginning to change her mind. While throwing herself into the fund-raising (the benefit at Claridge's alone had raised £1,500, around $200,000 in today's money), she had been able to forget for a time her worries about Winston. "Had it not been for the absorbing occupation of the *Maine,*" she would later write, "I cannot think how I could have got through that time." She also realized, however, that the ship could be useful to her in another way. Should she make the journey, she might be able to see George while she was there.

With the money Jennie and her committee had raised, the trip to South Africa need not be as onerous as it might otherwise have been. The ship, which had been donated by the American business-man Bernard Baker, had in its previous life been used to transport everything from cattle to baby elephants for the Barnum & Bailey Circus, and was therefore in desperate need not just of scrubbing but of an almost complete overhaul. With the help of the Royal Navy, the committee planned to add two decks, electric lighting and India-rubber flooring throughout the ship. There would be five wards, with more than two hundred beds, electric fans and refrigerators, and an operating theater with modern X-ray equipment.

Jennie, however, had some further renovations in mind that were perhaps not strictly medical in nature. Used to living in splendor her entire life, from her father's Brooklyn four-story to Blenheim Palace, she was not about to bunk down in a tiny, sparsely furnished cabin on the *Maine*. In the end, her room would look more like a small Fifth Avenue apartment than quarters on a hospital ship. Crowded in among the enormous silk pillows, heavy, cinched curtains and pot-ted plants was a surprising amount of furniture, from a tall, ornately carved cabinet that had a narrow, fold-out desk on hinges, to a richly upholstered sofa and even a large wooden pedestal table, crowded with clocks, framed photographs, tea trays and a cut-glass decanter. The room was, one nurse complained, "decorated in a manner sug-gestive of a lady's boudoir, rich in . . . luxuries."

What would create even more controversy than her lavish quar-ters was Jennie's open resistance to accommodating any religious sen-timent on board. Like her son, Lady Churchill had little interest in organized religion, and even less patience for its trappings. While she was happy to help the soldiers and officers of the queen's army, she certainly wasn't going to subject herself to the dour world of religious zealotry while she was at it. Before setting sail, Jennie, one outraged South African reporter would write, "had every scrap of religious literature—tracts, bibles, periodicals, leaflets etc—brought up on deck and the whole pitched overboard for the moral instruc-tion of the fishes."

Lady Churchill would soon be on her way to South Africa, wear-

ing an unusually fashionable nurse's uniform that she had designed
herself, with a lace blouse and a wide belt that accentuated her slim
waist. When she arrived, however, she would see neither her lover—
who would fall victim not to Boer bullets but to sunstroke and would
be invalided home before she had even set sail—nor her son. As Jennie began to oversee the packing of her bags and the decorating of
her cabin, Churchill was about to begin his life as a prisoner of war.
It would prove to be a strange and uncertain time, one that he would
hate, he later wrote, "more than I have ever hated any other period
in my whole life."

CHAPTER 15

A CITY OF THE DEAD

When his train pulled into Pretoria, Churchill listened as the door of his car was finally unlocked. Climbing out onto a dirt platform, blinking in the sunlight, he looked at the large crowd that had gathered around the station, and, for the first time since the war began, felt hatred for the enemy. "The simple, valiant burghers at the front, fighting bravely . . . claimed respect, if not sympathy," he wrote. "But here in Pretoria all was petty and contemptible." As he stood in a small space that had been carved out of the throng, his hands clasped behind his back and a look of contempt on his face, Churchill took in the people of Pretoria with a furious, raking glance. "Ugly women with bright parasols, loafers and ragamuffins, fat burghers too heavy to ride at the front," he would later write, remembering with scorn the Boers who had elbowed and squirmed their way through the crowd to get a better look at the prisoners. "Slimy, sleek officials of all nationalities—the red-faced, snub-nosed Hollander, the oily Portuguese half-caste." Glaring into their eager, curious faces, he bristled at the idea of being their captive.

As the men shuffled their feet uncomfortably, kicking up loose pebbles on the flat, open stretch of dirt where they had been ordered to wait, the heat from a midday summer sun bore down on them.

Haldane, trying with little luck to find some shade, pulled his hat low over his eyes. Peeking out from under the brim at the other prisoners, still divided into two groups, officers and soldiers, he suddenly spotted a man whom he knew to be an officer in the Natal Carbineers, the same regiment in which Brockie had claimed to be a lieutenant. Worried that the man would accidentally give their secret away, Haldane called him over and quickly muttered an explanation of the situation. Despite his efforts to protect the young sergeant major, however, Haldane watched in dismay as Brockie was pulled away and ordered to join the enlisted men. Minutes later, a large Boer policeman, one of the white-helmeted Zuid-Afrikaansche Republiek Politie, or ZARPs, singled out another man—Winston Churchill.

Startled from his angry reverie, Churchill looked up when the ZARP, who looked to him like a "broken-down constabulary," clapped a hand on his shoulder. Growling that Churchill was not an officer, the man demanded that he "go this way with the common soldiers." Churchill, who had been annoyed with the lower-ranking men since hearing them talking and laughing as they emerged from the train cars, took the opportunity of being thrust into their midst to correct their behavior. As if he were their commanding officer, he sternly urged them to be "serious men who cared for the cause they fought for" and was gratified by their immediate response. As he studied the men, now standing in quiet, sober rows, a thought occurred to Churchill, whose mind was never far from escape. "When I saw . . . what influence I possessed with them," he would later write, "it seemed to me that perhaps with two thousand prisoners something some day might be done."

While Churchill congratulated himself on his influence over the soldiers, Haldane, at the risk of his own safety, argued with the "burly, evil-looking police official" who had led him away. "I remonstrated with this Jack-in-office," Haldane wrote, "and pointed out to him that a war correspondent ranked as an officer." He made the mistake, however, of also telling the man exactly who Churchill was, forgetting for a moment how different the Boer attitude toward aristocracy was from the British. "We know and care nothing for your

lords and ladies here," the man barked at Haldane before walking
away.

After about twenty minutes, during which the "crowd had thoroughly satisfied their patriotic curiosity," the prisoners were ordered
to march. When the first British POWs had been brought to Pretoria
weeks earlier, they had been forced to take a long, meandering route
from the station to the prison, "a trophy," as Haldane would later
learn, "for the inhabitants to see." The Boers had been disappointed
in their captives, bitterly complaining that they were not wearing
the famous red coats. Since that time, the prisoners had been taken
directly to the prison.

The journey, which took them along two sandy, bisecting streets,
was nonetheless long enough for the men to see some of the town.
Angry and defiant as they were, they could not help but admit that
the Boer capital, while small, backward and astonishingly dusty, had
its charms. Even Churchill's father, who had had few good things to
say about anything he had seen in southern Africa, had been favor-
ably impressed with Pretoria, writing that it was "a pretty place,
much more attractive than any other Transvaal town." As it nestled
in its fertile green valley, sheltered by low hills dotted with mimosa
shrubs, the capital was, as Leo Amery would later write, "an attractive, if baking hot, townlet."

Nearly a thousand miles north of Cape Town, and four hundred
miles inland from the British-held eastern coast, Pretoria had as yet
been relatively untouched by the war. After the deadline for the ultimatum had passed, and thousands of burghers had thundered out
of the town in fierce, determined waves, it had been left "deserted,"
Amery wrote, "a city of the dead." Apart from the ZARPs, it was
also largely a city of women and children. The Boer women gathered,
their long skirts trailing in the red dust, at the bulletin boards that
had been erected to post updates on the war, searching for news of
their husbands, fathers and brothers. They drove the ox wagons that
rumbled down the dirt roads, the crack of their rawhide whips shat-
tering the town's unnatural quiet. The only exceptions were Pretoria's
two largest hotels—the Grand and the Transvaal—which were filled

with men, although there was rarely a Boer among them. "Soldiers of
fortune, Red Cross delegations, visitors, correspondents, and contrac-
tors," the American journalist Howard Hillegas wrote of the hotels'
patrons, "and almost every language except that of the Boers could
be heard in the corridors."

In the town itself, the public squares, the shops, the modest
houses that lined the streets, the fighting seemed to be so distant
it was at times difficult to believe it was happening. "When cannon
were roaring on the frontier," Hillegas wrote, "Pretoria itself seemed
to escape even the echoes." For the town's citizens, left behind to keep
life going as best they could, the only daily evidence that a war was
raging in their country was the almost palpable absence of Boer men,
and the very real presence of British prisoners.

➤➤

For Haldane, the march to the prison was, if humiliating, at least
useful. As he made his way along the dirt streets, he sized up the
town, gathering information he hoped might come in handy one day.
"The town is regularly laid out in parallelograms, the sides which
form them running nearly due north and south, and east and west,"
he noted, "a not inconsiderable advantage to those who may desire to
find their way out of the city in some particular direction." Haldane
also noticed that the town was "brilliantly lighted by electricity," a
modern convenience that had been introduced to Pretoria only seven
years earlier.

While they walked, Haldane took advantage of the opportunity
not only to study the city but to try again to retrieve Churchill.
Although the officer he approached, a man named Hans Malan,
seemed to Haldane to be a "still more ill-favoured-looking person"
than the ZARP who had seized Churchill, he was obviously a more
senior member of the force. Perhaps because he agreed with Haldane,
or more likely because Churchill's name and family status interested
him, Malan strode over to Churchill moments later and ordered him
to return to the officers.

Although happy to be reunited with Haldane, Churchill was as unimpressed with Malan as his friend had been. To Churchill, the ZARP "looked a miserable creature," a first impression that would only darken with time. In fact, it would not take long for Malan to become known to him as the "odious Malan," a crude, cruel and jeering guard who was also uniquely dangerous, because he was the grandson of Kruger, the president of the Transvaal.

Soon after Churchill rejoined the officers, the two groups were, for the first time since their capture, led in different directions. For the soldiers, the final destination would be a racetrack about a mile and a half away that had been enclosed in barbed wire and converted into an outdoor prison camp. Although, as an editor for the Johannesburg-based newspaper the *Standard and Diggers' News* wrote, "life on the racecourse was not an altogether miserable experience," the camp, which would hold some two thousand British prisoners, offered its captives far less in the way of shelter, food, sanitary conditions and medical care than the officers' prison. The conditions would leave the men angry and determined to escape by almost any means, a situation that Churchill would soon hope to turn to his advantage.

After watching their men disappear into the distance, the officers turned a corner and suddenly found themselves facing a large redbrick-and-sandstone building: their prison. Standing on about an acre of land at the corner of Skinner and Van der Walt Streets, the building, known as the Staats Model School, was more elaborate than most in the modest town. Built just three years earlier to be used as a teachers training college, it had been designed by the Dutch architect Sytze Wierda in the style of the Neo-Dutch Renaissance. It had a peaked roof with a collection of cupolas along the center, long windows on each side and, in the front of the building, a tall, narrow archway flanked by a recessed veranda.

In jarring contrast to the beauty of the building were the newly added fixtures of war. Ten feet in front of the veranda stood a breast-high iron fence that enclosed the entire west side, wrapping around it to the south. The north and east sides were surrounded by a roughly six-and-a-half-foot-tall corrugated-iron paling. Nine stony-faced

ZARPs patrolled the building, pacing in the dust and clutching their whistles and Lee-Metford rifles.

As the men took in the Staats Model School, what they noticed first, after the railings and the rifles, was the veranda, which was already crowded with prisoners. Bearded men, many still in their khaki uniforms, were leaning on their elbows over a long railing, watching as they approached. As Churchill would soon learn, the prison was already home to some fifty British officers, most of whom had been captured at the Battle of Nicholson's Nek two weeks earlier, the day the *Dunottar Castle* had entered Table Bay. In fact, Haldane recognized a few of them as men with whom he had fought before being injured at Elandslaagte. Others had been taken prisoner at Dundee, on the very first day of the war.

As soon as they stepped through the gate, Churchill and the officers in his group were immediately swarmed by the other prisoners. "Hullo!" they shouted. "How are you? Where did they catch you? What's the latest news of Buller's advance?" This welcoming party, a rite of passage for new prisoners, would be repeated many times over the coming months as the prison quickly filled to twice its original number and the men inside grew more and more desperate for news of the war. "All are mobbed, as they enter our prison gates," Charles Burnett, a captured officer from the Eighteenth Hussars, wrote in his diary. "This excess is perhaps excusable, as we bitterly feel our present situation. Could we but have one short period of our lives to act again . . . we would allow no such combination of circumstances to again take place, as those which landed us, in some cases so easily, in the Staats Model School."

Still tired from his long journey and sickened by the sight of the prison, Churchill wanted nothing more than to get away from the other prisoners. Their intensely curious, almost frantic greeting reminded him of "the sort of reception accorded to a new boy at a private school, or as it seemed to me, to a new arrival in hell." As soon as he could, he extricated himself and made his way inside the building, his new home.

As he walked past the front door, Churchill found himself in

a long, cool corridor that ran nearly the length of the building. On
each side of the corridor were six dormitories and at each end two
larger rooms, one of which was used as a dining hall and the other
as a gymnasium. All of the new prisoners were assigned to the same
dormitory—the second room on the west side. It was a group that
included Churchill, Haldane, Frankland and, to everyone's relief,
Brockie, who had also been returned to the officers, likely because of
Haldane's efforts on his behalf.

Although the four men were grateful that they were still together,
they were far from resigned to their fate. As soon as they entered
their room, they began a meticulous search, looking for anything—a
hole in the wall, a forgotten tool, a loose window frame—that might
help them. "We thought of nothing else but freedom," Churchill
wrote, "and from morn till night we racked our brains to discover a
way of escape."

→»

As determined as Churchill and his roommates were to flee the
Staats Model School, they quickly learned that life there was nothing
like the rumors of horrors and atrocities they had heard from fellow
soldiers. So eager were the Boers to prove that they were not the
savages the British had made them out to be, they went to extreme
lengths both on the battlefield and in their prison camps to dispel
the myth. Although during battle they did not always abide by the
newly signed Geneva Convention, sending their shells sailing into
field hospitals over which soared twelve-foot-high Red Cross flags,
when the damage had been done, they were surprisingly compassionate toward the dead and the dying.

After the death of Penn Symons, Joubert had sent his widow a
letter of sympathy. During the siege of Ladysmith, which was then
still ongoing, he allowed a train full of sick and injured to leave the
town every day, and he demanded that the Boers treat wounded British as they would their own men. To an astonishing degree, however,
the burghers were even more compassionate than their softhearted

commandant general. After the Battle of Nicholson's Nek, the *Daily Mail* correspondent George Warrington Steevens had marveled at the Boers' kindness toward their prisoners. They gave them "the water out of their own bottles," he wrote. "They gave the wounded the blankets off their own saddles and slept themselves on the naked veldt."

Despite their compassion, the depiction of them as unwashed and uneducated bumpkins, long encouraged by men like Randolph Churchill, persisted. The Boers bristled with wounded pride, deeply resenting even the slightest suggestion of condescension. There was one man among them, however, with whom even the most over-bred, meticulously educated Briton could not hope to compete. He was, in the words of Leo Amery, a "lean, fair-haired young man with angry blue eyes," and his name was Jan Smuts, the Transvaal state attorney. Smuts had been raised to be a cattle herd on his father's farm in Cape Colony, but his life had taken a dramatic turn when he was twelve years old and his older brother died. Because it was the Boer custom to educate only the oldest son, the death of Smuts's brother meant that he could go to school, a sudden turn of the hand of fate that eventually led him to Victoria College, just east of Cape Town, and then, after winning a scholarship, to Christ's College, Cambridge. Years later, the master of Christ's College, the Nobel Prize–winning chemist Alexander Todd, would say that in the college's five-hundred-year history only three of its students had been truly outstanding, a rarefied group that included John Milton, Charles Darwin and Jan Smuts. Even Albert Einstein had been impressed, insisting that only a few men in the world understood the theory of relativity, and Smuts was one of them.

Determined to prove to the British that, like Smuts, they were men of learning, the Boers allowed their prisoners almost unheard-of latitude. The men were permitted to receive visitors, to buy newspapers and to be waited on by their soldier-servants if those men had been captured with them. In fact, ten batmen were then living in tents in the yard behind the Staats Model School, where Thomas Walden would likely have set up camp had he joined Churchill on the armored train three days earlier.

The officers were even allowed to chart the progress of the war on a large and astonishingly detailed map of Natal and the Transvaal. The men, who had been carefully trained in cartography at military academies, sketched the map themselves, giving it a scale of five miles to one inch and taking up the better part of a wall in a room across the hall from Churchill's. A resident artist, likely the talented Tom Frankland, also drew a roughly six-foot-tall skeleton, one arm outstretched, the bony fingers pointing toward the map, above which had been written the hopeful words "The War in South Africa 1899–1900."

Although the food at the Staats Model School was adequate, and often far better than what the Boers were eating in the field, the prisoners were allowed to supplement it with purchases from a storekeeper in Pretoria named Mr. Boshof. They could buy almost anything they could afford, from cigarettes to bottled beer to even clothing. Although, upon entering the prison, every officer was handed bedding, towels and a new suit of clothes, Churchill immediately put in an order for a tweed suit in a "dark neutral colour, and as unlike the suits of clothes issued by the Government as possible." He had hoped to buy a hat as well, but here his captors finally drew the line. "What use could I find for a hat," he would recall them asking him, "when there were plenty of helmets to spare if I wanted to walk in the courtyard?"

Although Churchill acknowledged that he was the "least unfortunate kind of prisoner to be," from the moment he had raised his hands in surrender he had hated his captivity with an intensity that surprised even him. Not only was he eager to return to the war, but he couldn't bear the thought of being in another man's control. It had been hard enough to take orders from his superiors while he was in the army. To yield to the demands and whims of a Boer guard, in his eyes a mere troglodyte, was intolerable. "You are in the power of your enemy. You owe your life to his humanity, and your daily bread to his compassion," he later wrote, in an attempt to describe his sense of desperation. "You must obey his orders, go where he tells you, stay

where you are bid, await his pleasure, possess your soul in patience."
The prison was warm, dry, safe and clean, with plenty of food and
even little luxuries, but Churchill would have traded it in a heartbeat
for the heat, rain, filth and death of the battlefield. "The war is going
on," he wrote angrily, restlessly, "great events are in progress, fine
opportunities for action and adventure are slipping away."

Time was passing, and, even as a young man, Churchill could
feel his life slipping away. "I am 25 today," he wrote to Bourke Cockran, an American politician who was an old friend of Churchill's
mother, on November 30. "It is terrible to think how little time
remains."

So much did Churchill loathe his imprisonment that the experience would stay with him for the rest of his life. "Looking back on
those days I have always felt the keenest pity for prisoners and captives," he would write years later. "What it must mean for any man,
especially an educated man, to be confined for years in a modern
convict prison strains my imagination. Each day exactly like the one
before, with the barren ashes of wasted life behind, and all the long
years of bondage stretching out ahead." When, just ten years after his
own imprisonment, he was made home secretary and put in charge
of the British prison system, Churchill would be exceptionally compassionate to prisoners, especially those with life sentences, which he
believed to be a far worse fate than a sentence of death. He made sure
they had access to books, exercise and even occasional entertainment,
"to mitigate as far as is reasonable," he wrote, "the hard lot which, if
they have deserved, they must none the less endure."

His own imprisonment, Churchill passionately believed, was not
only unendurable but unjust. Although only a few days earlier he
had feared summary execution for taking part in a battle as a civilian, by the time he reached Pretoria, Churchill had already shrugged
off that very real, and still present, threat. As soon as he entered the
Staats Model School, he began again to demand his release, constantly reminding anyone who would listen that he was not a combatant but a correspondent.

In fact, on the very day Churchill arrived at the POW camp, he found pencil and paper and wrote a series of letters, all with the objective not just of explaining his situation but of making a case for his immediate release. To the *Morning Post,* he simply sent a telegram. "Captured unarmed 15th Frere detained Pretoria," it read. "Urge release." To his mother, who had always been the most constant and effective ally in his ambitions, he sent a longer letter. "Dearest Mama, a line to explain that I was captured in the armoured train at Frere," he began matter-of-factly, and then quickly took up his argument. "As I was quite unarmed and in possession of my full credentials as a Press correspondent, I do not imagine they will keep me." Well aware that the Boers would read his letters before sending them on, he was careful to praise his captors. "They have always treated press correspondents well and after Majuba Hill the *Morning Post* correspondent was released after a few days detention," he wrote. "You need not be anxious in any way but I trust you will do all in your power to procure my release."

Even when writing to Pamela Plowden, the beautiful young woman with whom he had fallen in love in India, Churchill could not resist using the letter as an opportunity to state his case. "Not a vy satisfactory address to write from," he began, "although it begins with a P." He assured Pamela, thousands of miles away and surrounded by rival suitors, that "among new and vivid scenes I think often of you," but not before slipping in information that was certainly more for the edification of a Boer reader than a London socialite. "I expect to be released as I was taken quite unarmed," he reminded his readers, "and with my full credentials as a correspondent."

The most important letter Churchill wrote that day, however, was to a man named Louis de Souza, the Transvaal secretary of state for war. De Souza, a quiet, thoughtful man who had been named head of the Prisoners Commission at the outset of war, had not only known of the attack on the armored train the day that it happened, but had known that Winston Churchill had been taken prisoner during it. "The burghers took an armoured train near Estcourt," his wife, Marie, had written in her diary on November 15. "56 prisoners, among them Winston Churchill, a son of the late Randolph Churchill." De Souza was well aware of Churchill's position and lineage, and understood what his capture might mean to the Transvaal.

Churchill, believing that de Souza might have the power to free him, or at least be willing to make an argument on his behalf, laid out his case in careful and, he hoped, persuasive detail.

18 November 1899
Pretoria

Sir

1. I was acting as a special correspondent of the *Morning Post* newspaper with the detachment of British troops captured by the forces of the South African Republic on the 15th instant at Frere, Natal, and conveyed here with the other prisoners.

2. I have the honour to request that I may be set at liberty and permitted to return to the British lines by such *route* as may be considered expedient, and in support of this request I would respectfully draw the attention of the Secretary of State to the following facts:

    a. I presented my credentials as special correspondent immediately after the British force surrendered and desired that they might be forwarded to the proper authority. This was promised accordingly.

    b. I was unarmed.

    c. My identity has been clearly established.

3. I desire to state that on my journey from the scene of the action to this town I have been treated with much consideration and kindness by the various officers and other burghers of the Republic with whom I have been brought into contact.

I am Sir, Your obedient servant

WINSTON SPENCER CHURCHILL
Special correspondent, *The Morning Post,* London

Churchill was not about to let a few inconsequential facts stand in the way of his freedom. No one need know that the only reason he had been unarmed at the time of his capture was because he had forgotten his pistol on the train when he jumped off to help the wounded men. In a later letter to de Souza, he would go even further, denying that he had played any role at all in the freeing of the engine. "I have consistently adhered to my character as a press correspondent, taking no part in the defence of the armoured train and being quite unarmed," he assured the secretary of state for war. "I have learned that it is alleged that I took an active part in the said defence. This I deny, although being for an hour and a half exposed in the open to the artillery of the Transvaal force, I naturally did all I could to escape from so perilous a situation and to save my life."

Searching for any weapon and willing to take any tactic, Churchill even set his sights on what he knew to be the Boers' Achilles' heel: their wounded pride. They wanted respect not only from the British Empire but from the powerful countries of Europe and North America, many of which they hoped would support them in the war. "My case while under detention as a prisoner of war has doubtless attracted a great deal of attention abroad and my release would be welcomed as a graceful act of correct international behaviour by the world's press," Churchill wrote to de Souza. "My further detention as a prisoner will most certainly be attributed in Europe and America to the fact that being well known I am regarded as a kind of hostage; and this will excite criticism and even ridicule."

The Boers were not buying it. In a telegram sent the day after Churchill's arrival in Pretoria, the commandant general himself warned the Transvaal secretary of state, Francis Reitz, that their aristocratic prisoner was not, as he claimed to be, merely an innocent correspondent. "I understand that the son of Lord Churchill maintains that he is only a newspaper reporter and therefore wants the privilege of being released," Joubert wrote. He had, however, received a full account of the attack from Louis Botha, the man who had led it, and had read the glowing newspaper accounts of Churchill's bravery and critical role in the defense of the armored train. Churchill "must be guarded and watched as dangerous for our war; otherwise he can still do us a lot of harm," Joubert urged Reitz. "In one word, he must not be released during the war."

The telegram took three days to find Reitz. By November 21, however, the secretary of state had not only received it but attached a note of his own. "The Government," he wrote, "will act accordingly."

CHAPTER 16

BLACK WEEK

From her house on Skinner Street, Marie de Souza, the wife of the Transvaal secretary of state for war, could almost see the prison. It was just four blocks away, and she knew the walk well. Her husband made it nearly every day.

A lifelong diarist, Marie had begun a new diary just thirteen days before the declaration of war. Instinctively, she knew there were horrors to come, and dangers that were particular to her own family. "War! What a terrible thing it is," she had written on October 30, the day the British had let the ultimatum pass. "And for what?"

The day after the new prisoners arrived in Pretoria, Louis de Souza visited them at the Staats Model School. Concerned about the treatment of the POWs, he considered the prison an important part of his responsibilities. On November 19, however, he stayed so long his wife remarked on his late return in her diary that night.

As soon as he met de Souza, Churchill knew that he had found his man. Not only was the secretary of state for war willing to listen to his story, but he sympathized with the young correspondent and did what he could to help him. As Churchill's time in captivity stretched from days to weeks, de Souza became increasingly indispensable to him. He gave Churchill news of the war, arranged for him to meet with high-ranking officials so that he could petition for his release in person, and even brought him baskets of fruit, many of which had a bottle of whiskey hidden in their depths, a forbidden gift that de Souza was also known to conceal in a pocket of his tailcoat.

In stark contrast to de Souza, the men directly responsible for running the prison had little interest in Churchill, or any of the men in their custody. The warden—the *commandant van de wacht,* or commandant of the guard—was a man named R. W. L. Opperman, who, Churchill wrote with disgust, was "too fat to go and fight." He was still a fierce proponent of the Boer cause, though, and, in the words of one of his prisoners, "a terrible hater of the English." Opperman's assistant, Dr. Jan Gunning, was more courteous to the British officers and well liked by many of them, but he had little say in how the prison was run, so had less potential value to Churchill. He also had problems of his own. In times of peace, Gunning was the director of the State Museum, a role that he relished but that had gotten him into trouble. Before the war, Cecil Rhodes, arguably the most hated man in the Transvaal, had offered him a lion for his pet project, a zoological garden that was to be built in Pretoria, and, unable to resist, he had accepted. When Kruger found out, Gunning nervously confided to Churchill, the president had been furious and had spoken "most harshly" to him.

Churchill's only hope for a sympathetic hearing was de Souza. The secretary of state for war was not only concerned about the prisoners, he seemed to have a broader perspective than most Boers. He was, Churchill wrote, "a far-seeing little man who had travelled to Europe, and had a very clear conception of the relative strengths of Britain and the Transvaal." Although de Souza had gone to Europe on an arms-buying mission three years earlier, when he was the first secretary in the Office of the Commandant General, like Joubert, he had continued to believe that war might be averted. When the end came, he had been devastated. "Louis is worried to death!" his wife had written in late September, just weeks before the Boers issued their ultimatum. "The General [Joubert] told him that he had given up all hope of peace tonight."

As interested as de Souza was, however, his ability to help Churchill was severely limited. Although he held a powerful position in the Transvaal government, he himself had long been on shifting ground. Since the war had begun, his status in Pretoria had only become more tenuous.

As a member of the Volksraad, de Souza was an anomaly. His family had come to the Transvaal by way of not the Netherlands or France but Portugal. In the early nineteenth century, his grandparents had moved from Lisbon to the small Indian state of Goa, where his father, Mariano Luis, was born and where, according to family history, the rest of the family had been killed in an epidemic. In the mid-nineteenth century, Mariano Luis traveled as an orphan to Portuguese East Africa, modern-day Mozambique, on the Indian Ocean coast. After making his way to the Transvaal, he had met and married Trui Joubert, the young daughter of a *Voortrekker* and the distant cousin of Piet Joubert, now the commandant general.

Although Louis de Souza, the first child of Mariano Luis and Trui, had coursing through him the blood of one of the Transvaal's oldest *Voortrekker* families, he still looked Portuguese. Small, thin, dark-haired and with a deep olive complexion, he instantly stood out among the pale, pink-cheeked Dutchmen who filled the streets of Pretoria. He was also, like his Portuguese grandfather, Catholic, a religious affiliation that the strongly Calvinistic Boers considered almost blasphemous. In fact, until 1858 no one outside the Dutch Reformed Church had even been allowed citizenship in the Transvaal, much less a place in its government.

Among his fellow Boers, de Souza also had one more strike against him: He was married to the daughter of an Englishman. Although Marie de Souza had been born in Durban, not far from where Louis Botha had grown up, in the minds of many of her neighbors she was as British as the queen of England. Now that they were at war with the British Empire, the de Souzas were looked at with even greater suspicion. Even Kruger did not fully trust them, asking Louis during an executive meeting of the Volksraad if his wife was English.

De Souza's situation was not improved by the fact that he felt compassion not just for the prisoners but for the British citizens who had long been living in the Transvaal. Life for so-called Uitlanders, Afrikaans for "outlanders," or "foreigners," had never been easy, but as the Boers and the British inched toward war, it had become increasingly difficult. Finally, on September 27, the Volksraad had passed a proclamation that ordered all British subjects to leave the country in the event of war. Although she had expected it, Marie had been horrified when, soon after the war began, she had watched as English citizens were crowded into cattle trucks and forcibly removed from the city.

Many Englishmen had come to de Souza, asking his advice and help. "He has been so dreadfully worried over the uitlanders," Marie confided to her diary. There was little de Souza could do, however, either for them or for himself. Even Churchill understood that his new friend had to be "very careful."

➤➤

Despite his precarious position, de Souza continued to visit the men at the Staats Model School, and to spend much of his time while there with the prison's most troublesome inmate. About a week and a half after Churchill had arrived in Pretoria, de Souza stopped by his dormitory, where he found his young friend standing before the map that had been drawn on the wall. Churchill had attached red and green paper squares to the map, indicating the various columns as he attempted to chart the war's course. On this day, he had new information to add to his collage.

The day before, Churchill had received an unexpected windfall. While standing on the veranda, leaning on the railings, he had noticed a man with a red mustache walking quickly down the street, two collies trotting after him. Since coming to Pretoria, Churchill had learned to pay careful attention to the townspeople. Although some, as Haldane wrote, looked "as if they would be glad to have a shot at us through the railings," a few showed the men not just sympathy but a willingness to help, even at great risk to themselves. As time went on, in fact, the sympathizers' efforts to communicate with the prisoners would become increasingly elaborate, from a man who used his walking stick to tap out messages by Morse code to two young women who lived across the street from the Staats Model School and signaled news with a white flag from their veranda.

As the man with the mustache approached Churchill, he did not alter his pace. Just before he passed by, however, he said something that made Churchill's heart soar. "Methuen beat the Boers to hell at Belmont," he muttered. Paul Methuen was the general officer commanding the First Division of the British army, and his victory was all Churchill needed to lift his spirits and convince him that the war was finally turning his way. "That night the air seemed cooler," he wrote, "and the courtyard larger."

When de Souza walked into his room the next day, Churchill was eager to discuss this new development in the war. "What about Methuen?" he asked de Souza. "He has beaten you at Belmont. Now he should be across the Modder. In a few days he will relieve Kimberley." De Souza, however, was unconcerned. Shrugging his shoulders, and without asking Churchill where he had gotten this information, he replied simply, "Who can tell?" Then, pressing his finger on the map, he said, "There stands old Piet Cronje in a position called Scholz Nek, and we don't think Methuen will ever get past him."

As it turned out, de Souza was right. The reason, however, was less Methuen and Cronjé than Joubert and Botha. Just a few days before de Souza and Churchill stood over the hand-drawn map in the Staats Model School, Piet Joubert's horse had stumbled and thrown him. The result of the Boers' humiliating defeat at Belmont and Joubert's injuries, which were so severe he had to return to Pretoria riding in a closed carriage, was that Botha was put in command. Botha's promotion would be made permanent a few months later, when Joubert succumbed to peritonitis.

Joubert's death devastated de Souza, who would be with him three months later when he died and would be a pallbearer at his funeral, but it freed Botha. The sudden turn of events meant that for the first time since the war began, Botha's hands were finally untied. Just days before his fall, the commandant general had ordered his intense young general to pull back from Estcourt, where Botha had been relentlessly and successfully attacking the British forces in the wake of the armored train derailment. At first, Botha had refused the order, but when Joubert threatened to relieve him of his command, he had given in. With Joubert gone, there was finally no one to tell him no, no one to hold him back. Botha knew that left to his own devices, he could advance the war, and teach the arrogant British what the Boers were capable of.

Little more than a week after Botha was put in command, the British, to their horror, found themselves lurching from one defeat to another, a staggering series of losses that would come to be known as Black Week. The first blow came on December 10, in the Battle of Stormberg, which, although the British had roughly three thousand men to the Boers' fewer than two thousand, ended with nearly seven hundred British killed or captured. The very next day, Methuen fell to Cronjé and the legendary Boer general Koos de la Rey in the Battle of Magersfontein, known to the Boers as Scholz Nek, where the British lost almost a thousand men.

It did not take long for news of Black Week to reach London, where the reaction was not only shock but utter bewilderment. This was, after all, the "British century," and no Briton then alive could remember a time when their empire had not dominated the world stage. As December 1899 brought with it news of devastating defeats at the hands of the Boers, an opponent they had dismissed as insignificant and unsophisticated, a chilling thought crept in: Would this, the last month of the century, mark the beginning of the end of the British Empire? To Queen Victoria, who had been on the throne for sixty-three of the past one hundred years, the question was one that must not even be asked. "Please understand that there is no one depressed in this house," she told Arthur Balfour, then leader of the

House of Commons. "We are not interested in the possibilities of defeat; they do not exist."

→►

For the men of the Staats Model School, the news of Black Week came as a particularly painful blow. They had learned to be wary of what they were told by the gloating guards or read for themselves in the shamelessly slanted Boer newspapers, but they could no longer deceive themselves that the war was going well. "All the news we heard in Pretoria was derived from Boer sources, and was hideously exaggerated and distorted," Churchill would later write. "However much one might doubt and discount these tales, they made a deep impression. A month's feeding on such literary garbage weakens the constitution of the mind. We wretched prisoners lost heart."

The guards, naturally, took great satisfaction in the course of the war, and rarely missed an opportunity to taunt their prisoners about the "huge slaughters and shameful flights of the British." Even in the best of times, the men now guarding the prison were not, for the most part, gentle men. Now, far from the war and surrounded by men who, although they were prisoners now, were at least fresh from the battlefield, they choked on their humiliation and barely contained their rage. Adrian Hofmeyr, a clergyman from Cape Colony who had been taken prisoner because of his British sympathies, so detested the guards at the Staats Model School that he would later devote an entire chapter in his book *The Story of My Captivity* to detailing their offenses. The ZARPs, he wrote, were "as brutal a lot of men, with very few exceptions, as one could find in a day's march."

The prisoners were not the guards' only targets. Knowing that they were carefully watched by de Souza, the ZARPs rarely indulged in physical violence, although they incessantly goaded and mocked the men under their control. Their rage, however, was in full, unthrottled display when it came to Pretoria's black and mixed-race inhabitants, especially those who made the mistake of passing by the Staats Model School. "How our blood boiled when we were forced to be passive spectators of this Zarpian ruffianism!" Hofmeyr wrote. "Poor fellow! He does not know that the street is not wide enough for his Majesty the Zarp and himself, and thus walks on with that apologetic air which every [black man] in the Transvaal wears, till he has passed the Rubicon—that rope which excludes him and forces him to walk a block round."

None of the guards, however, was as intolerable as Hans Malan. It did not take Churchill and Haldane long to be confirmed in their initial assessment of Kruger's grandson. "A foul and objectionable brute," Churchill wrote of Malan. "His personal courage was better suited to insulting the prisoners in Pretoria than to fighting the enemy at the front." Churchill was not alone in his contempt. Word had filtered down to the prisoners that, despite his close ties to Kruger, Malan had been openly scorned within the Volksraad for his cowardice. Even Marie de Souza, who had heard of his cruel treatment of native Africans, loathed him. "He is no man but a brute!!" she wrote in her diary. "Oh, if I could only speak or had power."

Although he did not want to place himself in danger, or fight anyone who could defend himself, Malan had been a vociferous proponent of the war. As the chief inspector of the roads, he had, in the words of John Buttery, an editor for the *Standard and Diggers' News,* "brought a great deal of influence to bear during the secret Raad [Volksraad] sittings on those members known to be wavering in the direction of peace, and whom it was necessary to intimidate and coerce into joining the war-gang." Malan, Buttery wrote, had made a practice of "button-holing the members as they went in and out, and there was no mistaking his truculent bearing."

While many of the officers found Malan intimidating and did their best to avoid him, Churchill found it difficult to swallow his incessant jeering without striking back. One day, when Malan had been particularly insufferable, Churchill rounded on him. Reminding the guard that in war either side might emerge victorious, he then asked him if it was wise to "place himself in a separate category as regards behavior to the prisoners." Should they win the war, Churchill said, looking pointedly at Malan, the British government might wish to make examples of a few Boers. The implication had clearly made Malan, a "great gross man [whose] colour came and went on a large over-fed face," nervous, and, Churchill later wrote, "he never came near me again."

As the war continued, however, Malan was the least of the men's worries. To their great dismay, they quickly learned that Commandant Opperman, who ran the prison, had little control over his wildly swaying emotions. If the Boers were winning, he was elated. If not, he looked, Churchill wrote, "a picture of misery." So tightly tied were Opperman's emotions to the outcome of the war that he had often told the prisoners that should the Boers lose, he would "perish in the defence of the capital." Although the officers had little concern for Opperman's fate, they were sickened when he told them that before dying in a blaze of glory, he would first shoot his own wife and children.

While Opperman threatened to kill his own family, his superiors, the men who were actually running the war, suddenly began to reconsider the lives of their prisoners. The day before Churchill had arrived in Pretoria, the British had captured a man named Nathan Marks, whom they accused of being a Boer spy. Disguised as an ambulance driver, Marks had infiltrated British lines, carrying with him a wounded man. When discovered, he had admitted that he had been sent there to find out if the Boer shells were as devastating as those of the British. When told of Marks's capture, the Boers not only vehemently denied that he was a spy but threatened to retaliate if anything happened to him.

Reitz, the Transvaal secretary of state, made clear his intentions to the governor of Cape Colony, Alfred Milner. If Marks were executed, Reitz assured Milner, the Boers would "put to death six British officers now held as prisoners of war at Pretoria." Although the men at the Staats Model School would continue to be fed, clothed and protected from the wrath of their guards, they understood that, from one day to the next, their lives could not be guaranteed.

➤➤

Not long after Reitz delivered his threat to Milner, he traveled to Pretoria, stopping in at the Staats Model School to see the men whose lives hung in the balance. Since Churchill had been demanding a meeting with Reitz since the day he was captured, the secretary of state decided to oblige him. Reitz's son Deneys, who had ridden out of Pretoria with Botha the day the war began, happened to be in the capital as well and accompanied his father as he walked from his office to the prison. The two men entered the building, walked past the guards and stepped into a large room, where they found Churchill "playing games," most likely chess, with the other prisoners.

Deneys already knew exactly who Churchill was, as did his father. Not only had Reitz read Joubert's telegram urging him to deny the correspondent his freedom, but he had since received several other angry complaints about Churchill. "I see a rumour in the papers that Lord Churchill's son . . . will soon be released by the government," a Boer general who had been with Botha at the attack on the armored train had written to Reitz on November 28. "If this person is released so can any other P.O.W. be released. He was most active in directing the soldiers in stultifying our operations. . . . He must therefore be treated as any other P.O.W. and if needs be guarded with even greater vigilance." Reitz even received a letter from a man named Danie Theron, who had witnessed Churchill's capture and now implored the secretary of state to ensure his continued captivity. "According to the *Volkstem* and *Standard and Diggers News* he [Churchill] now declares he took no part in the fight," Theron wrote. "This is a pack of lies; nor would he stand still when warned by Field-Cornet Ooosthuizen to surrender or do so till covered by the latter's rifle. In my opinion he is one of the most dangerous prisoners in our hands."

When Churchill looked up and saw Reitz, he quickly launched into what was by then a well-rehearsed argument for his release. Unlike de Souza, however, Reitz was not easily persuaded. After Churchill argued that he was a war correspondent, not a combatant, Reitz reminded him that he had been carrying a Mauser. Churchill replied that in the Sudan all correspondents had carried weapons for self-protection. This comparison had the opposite effect Churchill had hoped it would. Rather than changing Reitz's mind, it irritated him. Boers, he stiffly informed Churchill, were "not in the habit of killing non-combatants." In the end, Churchill succeeded only in persuading Reitz to take with him some articles he had written and that he hoped the secretary of state would send on to the *Morning Post*.

Churchill's last hope was a prisoner exchange then being discussed between the Boers and the British. "Unless I am regarded for the purpose of exchange as a military officer," he wrote to Colonel Frederick Stopford, Buller's military secretary, on November 30, "I am likely to fall between two stools. Pray do your best for me." Joubert, however, then still clinging to life, adamantly refused to let him go. "I agree to the exchange proposed," he wrote on December 10, the same day as the Battle of Stormberg, "but am resolved against the exchange of Churchill."

Churchill finally gave up. The Boers, he realized, would never willingly let him go. "As soon as I learned of [Joubert's] decision in the first week of December," he wrote, "I resolved to escape."

CHAPTER 17

A SCHEME OF DESPERATE
AND MAGNIFICENT AUDACITY

hurchill began pacing the courtyard after sundown. Every night, he would watch as the sun sank behind a fort that sat on a hill overlooking the prison, thus marking the end of "another wretched day." Then he would begin circling the building, following a path so well known to the prisoners that they had long ago estimated that nine times around equaled a mile. He slunk past the guards, carefully appraising them, disdainful of their "dirty, unkempt" uniforms, and he bitterly eyed the fences. "You feel a sense of constant humiliation in being confined to a narrow space," he would later write, "fenced in by railings and wire, watched by armed men." As his mind, like his feet, traced the same paths, over and over again, he thought that there must be some way, "by force or fraud, by steel or gold, of regaining my freedom."

In his fevered desire for escape, Churchill was far from alone. Ever since there have been prisoners and guards, men have tried everything, from climbing to digging, from bribery to brute force, to make their escape. In the end, if there is no hope that a prisoner will lose his shackles, he may lose his mind. Twenty years after Churchill traced his restless path around the Staats Model School, a Swiss surgeon named Adolf Vischer would write a small book titled

Barbed Wire Disease: A Psychological Study of the Prisoner of War. In it, Vischer, who had visited POW camps during World War I to study the psychological impact of captivity, would make the argument that almost without exception men exposed to long-term incarceration develop what he termed "barbed wire disease."

"They find intense difficulty in concentrating on one particular object; their mode of life becomes unstable, and there is restlessness in all their actions," Vischer wrote. "All in common have a dismal outlook and a pessimistic view of events. . . . Many are inordinately suspicious." Although the men affected most severely were those who had been imprisoned for months or years, to some degree all POWs were prey to the disease. Unlike "the criminal who knows to the day and hour the length of his imprisonment and can tick off each day," Vischer wrote, "the prisoner of war remains in complete uncertainty."

In the Boer War, there were, of course, Boer POWs as well as British, and they too thought obsessively about escape—although for them it was all but impossible. After first keeping their prisoners on barges anchored in Simon's Bay, just around the corner from Cape Town, the British soon moved them to a volcanic island twelve hundred miles off the coast of Africa: St. Helena. Despite the fact that St. Helena was, in many ways, a perfect prison—surrounded by thousands of square miles of ocean, ringed by cliffs and with very few places to land a boat—there were several escape attempts, one of which involved another of Kruger's grandsons, Commandant P. Eloff. None of them worked.

St. Helena, in fact, had a history of failed escape attempts, many of which revolved around its most famous prisoner, the French emperor Napoleon Bonaparte, who was imprisoned on the island in 1815 following the Napoleonic Wars. During his six miserable years on St. Helena, there were dozens of plots to free Napoleon, but he died, allegedly of poisoning but more likely from stomach cancer, before any of them could succeed.

After he walked through the doors of the Staats Model School, Churchill had quickly begun to exhibit the same characteristics described by Vischer. He was restless and irritable. Even the activities that came most naturally to him were suddenly a chore. "I could not write, for the ink seemed to dry upon the pen," he would later recall. "I could not read with any perseverance." Usually able to devour entire books in a single sitting, Churchill now struggled to read even two over the span of a month, "neither of which," he wrote, "satisfied my peevish expectations." He also took no interest in the other prisoners and had very little patience with them, especially when they whistled, which he particularly loathed. "He no doubt felt that such a display of lightheartedness did not sit well on those in the clutches of the enemy," Haldane wrote.

Churchill would allow nothing to distract him from his one overriding, all-consuming goal—escape. As he circled the grounds at night and studied the building by day, his plan began to emerge. It was, of course, no ordinary plan. An elaborate, multistep strategy, it was as bold as it was complicated. It was, in Churchill's own words, "a scheme of desperate and magnificent audacity."

->-

Every day, from the moment he woke up in his metal-frame bed, pushed into the wide hallway because it was cooler than his room, to the moment he climbed back into it at night, Churchill brooded over his plan. Whenever he could, he picked up more bits of information, slips of intelligence that gave him ideas or helped him refine his strategy. Although he made a careful study of the prison, no aspect of it interested him more than the ZARPs.

As little respect as Churchill had for the men who guarded him, he knew that they were dangerous. He also knew that they, and not the fences that encircled the prison, were his only real barrier to freedom. "No walls," he wrote, "are so hard to pierce as living walls." About forty ZARPs had been assigned to the Staats Model School, but only ten of them were on permanent sentry duty at any one time. The other thirty could be found wandering aimlessly around Pretoria or hanging listlessly about the prison, bored, irritable, angry and, Churchill hoped, easily distracted.

The ZARPs, Churchill knew, were at their most vulnerable at night. The thirty men not on duty slept in a tent that had been pitched in a corner of the rectangular prison yard. Before wrapping themselves in blankets, most of them took off their boots, their belts and even their clothes, and they stacked their rifles and bandoliers in piles around the tent poles. One of their number usually stood guard over them, but Churchill had noticed that there were times, often in the midst of a guard change, when they had no protection at all. "There were therefore periods in the night," he wrote, "when these thirty men, sleeping . . . within fifty yards of sixty determined and athletic officers, were by no means so safe as they supposed."

Even Churchill admitted that overwhelming the ten men who were awake and armed would be more difficult, but he had plans for them as well. The Staats Model School had a gymnasium with a "good supply" of dumbbells. These could be used, Churchill thought, in a surprise attack. "Who shall say that three men in the dark, armed with dumbbells, desperate and knowing what they meant to do," he wrote, "are not a match for one man who, even though he is armed, is unsuspecting and ignorant of what is taking place?"

Churchill's plan did not end at the Staats Model School. He had not forgotten the men languishing at the racecourse. Occasionally, soldier-servants who had run afoul of either the Boer guards or their own officers would be replaced by men from the racecourse, who brought with them news of the other POW camp in Pretoria. From these reports, the officers knew that these men were miserable, and prime for a rebellion. "Their life was monotonous, their rations short, their accommodations poor," Churchill wrote. "They were hungry and resentful." So bad, in fact, were the conditions at the racecourse that a small group of English sympathizers had secretly put together a fund to raise money for food and medical supplies for the men. There were also only about 120 ZARPs, with two machine guns between them, to guard about two thousand British soldiers. It would require "nothing but leading," Churchill thought, "to make them rise against their guards."

Churchill shared his plan with a few of the officers, and had little difficulty persuading them to join him. Although he was one of the youngest men in the prison, and the only civilian, he was an extraordinarily persuasive speaker. "He talks brilliantly," a journalist would write of Churchill just a few months later, "in a full clear voice, and with great assurance." Even to the point of stirring rebellion at the racecourse, the men were willing to follow his lead. Beyond that point, however, Churchill's plan took a sudden, staggering turn, taking on an almost fantastical sheen. It had become, in his mind, not just an escape but a "great and romantic enterprise."

Even years later, Churchill would write of the plan in a near frenzy of excitement, punctuating his descriptions of each stage with a feverish "What next?" or "What then?" The final phase, as he saw it, was not merely freedom but a full-scale takeover of the Transvaal capital, which included, of course, the kidnapping of its president. Were it realized to its fullest extent, his plan would, he believed, so stagger the Boers that it would bring the war to a sudden and decisive end. "What a feat of arms! President Kruger and his Government would be prisoners in our hands," he wrote. "Perhaps with these cards in our hands we could negotiate an honourable peace, and end the struggle by a friendly and fair arrangement which would save the armies marching and fighting. It was a great dream."

It was, in fact, too great, too dazzling, too theatrical—altogether too much. When some of the senior officers in the prison found out about the young correspondent's wildly ambitious plan, and the men he had already recruited for it, they quickly put an end to it all. Churchill was disappointed but, as ever, unrepentant. "Who shall say what is possible or impossible?" he wrote defiantly. "In these spheres of action one cannot tell without a trial."

→→

Although they had dismissed Churchill's dream of taking over Pretoria and defeating the Boers in one brilliant stroke, even the most levelheaded among them knew that escape from the Staats Model School was possible. In fact, it had been done. On December 7, three days before the start of Black Week, two soldier-servants had climbed over the back fence while the rest of the prisoners were eating dinner, a time when, Haldane had noticed, "the vigilance of the sentries was somewhat relaxed." The guards, perhaps embarrassed or worried that they would be punished, had said nothing about the escape to their superiors. The men were not well known and would not be quickly missed. They were, however, quickly caught. They hadn't made it far from Pretoria when they were picked up and, rather than being returned to the POW camp, were put in a Boer prison.

"The escape of these men," Haldane wrote, "made one feel that no time was to be lost." While Churchill had been indoctrinating the other officers, making his plan ever bigger, more ambitious and more wide reaching, Haldane had been working quietly with Brockie. It had not taken them long to come up with a plan that they were confident would work. With his natural resourcefulness and his command of both Dutch and Zulu, Brockie was exactly the man Haldane needed. Like Haldane, Brockie had no patience for theatrics. He was not interested in impressing anyone. He simply wanted to get out, quickly and quietly, and he certainly didn't want to do it with fanfare.

Haldane and Brockie's plan was as simple as Churchill's was elaborate. Like the soldier-servants who had escaped early in December, they planned to climb over the iron paling that formed the enclosure along the back of the prison yard. The problem was the sentries who, since the humiliation of the earlier escape, were more vigilant, and more than willing to shoot if given any excuse. Haldane had attempted to bribe one of the friendlier guards, offering him £100 to "look the other way," but while the man was sympathetic, he was, Haldane wrote with disappointment, "not to be tampered with." The ZARP also pointed out to Haldane the futility of his ambition. "He said that if I got out of the building I could never get out of the country, there were so many patrols and other precautions to prevent the escape of prisoners," Haldane wrote. "In any case the sentries on his right hand and left would see, and not be silent."

It was also true that even at night the prison yard was drenched in light. "The whole enclosure," Churchill wrote, "was brightly and even brilliantly lighted by electric lights on tall standards." When the prisoners discovered that the electrical wires for the lights had been threaded through the dormitories where they slept, one of the men who had been trained as an electrician insisted that he could "disconnect them at any moment and plunge the whole place in pitch darkness." They even went so far as to test the theory, causing the lights to go out one night in a sudden blackout, and then just as quickly blaze back on.

Haldane and Brockie, however, wanted no part of any plan that would attract attention or require complicated maneuverings and additional people. Nor, for their purposes, did they need the entire enclosure to be dark, just a corner of it. Although the security lights stood in the middle of the quadrangle, bathing nearly all of the enclosure in bright light, Haldane had noticed that they left a small slice of the eastern wall in shadow. "Only one sentry could possibly see any one climbing over," he observed, "and if his back were turned, provided he heard nothing, his eyes would certainly be of no avail."

Getting over the wall, the men knew, would require both skill and luck. But it would also be only the beginning of their journey. Even if they succeeded in eluding the ZARPs, they would still be far from their final destination—Portuguese East Africa, now known as Mozambique, situated almost due east on Africa's Indian Ocean coast. A territory of the Portuguese Empire, which had been the world's first global empire, it was Transvaal's closest neighbor, less than three hundred miles from Pretoria, and neutral territory in the Boer War. To get there, however, Haldane and Brockie would have to make their way out of Pretoria, navigate the countless guards and checkpoints that dotted hundreds of miles of Transvaal landscape, find the railroad that led to Delagoa Bay, on the coast of Portuguese East Africa, jump a train and hide on board during the long overland journey, hoping no one would search it.

To further complicate matters, the two men soon had another problem: Winston Churchill. After his own escape plan had been shut down, Churchill had immediately begun trawling for another.

Keeping his eyes and ears open for opportunities, he quickly figured out that two of his roommates had banded together and were planning an escape. Brockie, Churchill knew, would be resistant to his joining their plan. Haldane, on the other hand, would have a difficult time refusing him.

➤➤

Churchill knew things about Aylmer Haldane that nearly no one else knew. For whatever reason, soon after they had begun their friendship, Haldane had decided to confide in Churchill. In fact, he had told him the greatest secret, and burden, of his life: He was married.

More than a decade earlier, when Haldane was a twenty-six-year-old lieutenant stationed in Belfast, Ireland, he had met a young barmaid named Kate Stuart. The two had married on July 13, 1888, but apparently knowing even at the time that he had made a mistake, Haldane had insisted that they keep their marriage a secret. Soon after, he had returned to England, leaving behind not just his life in Ireland, but his new wife as well.

Kate, however, had refused to simply fade into the past. In 1893, after years of impatient waiting and unanswered letters, she had traveled to England and tracked her husband down at the Staff College, a military academy at Camberley, Surrey, where he was briefly in charge of the officers' mess. She wanted more money, she told him, but more than that, she wanted a home. Terrified that the other officers would find out about his wife, Haldane had told her that he would try to send more money, but he refused to make a life with her. The following year, he left for India, where he met Churchill and, feeling desperate and trapped, unburdened himself to his new friend.

Churchill was nothing if not sympathetic. "She tricked him on the same line as in Jude the Obscure," he had written to his mother after hearing Haldane's story. "Being conscientious he behaved 'honourably' and has been miserable ever since. He has never lived with her—hates the sight of her. Offers her half of all he has in the world to divorce him. Futile." Kate, who, Churchill delicately confided to his mother, was "not originally *virgo intacta,*" wanted more than money. She wanted to be a lady. As long as he was married to her, however, Haldane could never rise within the hierarchy of the British military, a situation that, to Churchill, was not only appalling but quite possibly worthy of drastic actions. "I questioned him about her health," he wrote with the pity of a pragmatist. "Excellent. I am afraid I could suggest nothing better than Murder—and there are objections to that of course."

After he and Haldane had left India and parted ways, Churchill had tried to express his concern in letters, but had ended up making his friend feel even worse. "It is all very sad. Nor do I see any light," Churchill had written to Haldane in 1898. "Who knows that if luck & fortune are on your side the stimulus may not be removed. . . . But this is trying to see a silver lining to a very black cloud." It was unfortunate, he wrote a few months later, that the problem could not forcibly be removed. "I hope the millstone is weighting lightly," he wrote. "You must not despair of its fretting through the cord that binds it to your neck—of its own weight. It is a pity you cannot cut it—one stroke. But people put cords to so many uses."

→→

Now Haldane was not the only man with a millstone around his neck. For all of the men, but especially for Churchill, prison was not only dangerous in the constantly shifting tide of war but an unbearable burden, denying him the glory of battle and the opportunity for recognition and advancement. This time, he was not about to let Haldane cut the cord around his own neck without also severing his.

Haldane knew that Churchill would insist that he take him along when he made his escape, but he did not know what to do about it. "I was loath to seem ungenerous," he wrote, "as would be the case if I went without him." He was grateful for Churchill's sympathy and friendship, and he admired his bravery during the attack on the armored train. He had tried to do all he could to help him secure his release, even writing an open letter vouching for Churchill's unblemished status as a noncombatant. "I certify on my honour," he had written the day after arriving at the Staats Model School, "that Mr. Winston Churchill, Correspondent of the Morning Post accompanied the armoured train on the 15 November as a non-combatant, unarmed and took no part in the defence of the train."

Despite his attachment to Churchill, however, Haldane had strong reservations about attempting to escape with him. If they were able to make it out of the prison without being shot, they would have an arduous journey ahead of them, and just getting Churchill over the fence would be difficult. Years earlier in India, Churchill had dislocated his shoulder while trying to jump onto land from a rocking boat, snatching at an iron ring nailed into a stone wall just as the boat had jerked out from beneath him. It was an injury that, Churchill later wrote, "was to last me my life . . . and to be a grave embarrassment in moments of peril, violence and effort."

Aside from his injured shoulder, Churchill was out of shape. Since their imprisonment, Haldane had noticed, Churchill had been utterly uninterested in exercise. While the other men in the prison played vigorous games—from fives, which is similar to racquetball without the racket, to the bat-and-ball sport rounders—to keep themselves fit, Churchill sat before a chessboard or stared moodily at an unread book. "This led me to conclude," Haldane wrote, "that his agility might be at fault."

Of even greater concern to Haldane than Churchill's fitness was his lack of discretion. Haldane worried that his "talkative friend" would be unable to keep their plans to himself. Even Churchill had to admit that he loved to talk. In fact, he had told a tent mate in Malakand that his only fear was "getting wounded in the mouth so he couldn't talk."

For Churchill, few topics of conversation would be more irresistible than a prison break, especially if it worked. When trying to persuade Haldane to take him along, he promised his friend that if they made it out alive, he would share the spotlight. Haldane would

Winston Churchill was born at Blenheim, the great palace in Oxfordshire built in the early eighteenth century for John Churchill, the 1st Duke of Marlborough (pictured above). More than just the source of his family status, Marlborough was Churchill's inspiration for success on a grand scale. "He never rode off any field except as a victor," Churchill wrote of his famous forebear.

Born into the highest ranks of British aristocracy, Churchill had an air of haughty self-confidence even at the tender age of seven. What he longed for most, however, was the love and attention of his father, Lord Randolph Churchill (pictured below), who was Chancellor of the Exchequer and had little time for his oldest son. One of the great regrets of Churchill's life was that Randolph died an early and tragic death, depriving Winston of the chance to know him.

Churchill's American mother, born Jennie Jerome, was a famous beauty, said to have "more of the panther than of the woman in her look." Although his mother used her influence with high-ranking men to help him secure military appointments, Churchill, like most of the men in her life, had to adore her "at a distance."

To Churchill's dismay, his widowed mother, still beautiful and restless at forty-five, became romantically involved with a young aristocrat named George Cornwallis-West, who was only two weeks older than Churchill. Despite ardent opposition from her sons and his parents, Jennie and George married before the Boer War was over.

As he set sail for South Africa, Churchill carried in his wallet this pencil sketch of the young socialite Pamela Plowden, the first great love of his life. "I must say," he had written to his mother after meeting Pamela in India, "that she is the most beautiful girl I have ever seen."

(Below, left) On October 9, 1899, Paul Kruger, president of the Transvaal, sent an ultimatum demanding that the British Empire withdraw its troops and cease interference in the affairs of the Boer republic, or prepare for war. When the British contemptuously allowed the deadline to pass, Kruger knew that war was inevitable. Bowing his head, he said, "So must it be."

(Right) Soon after war was declared, Sir Redvers Buller was named commander in chief of Her Majesty's army in South Africa. Buller, who had won the Victoria Cross in South Africa twenty years earlier, during the Anglo-Zulu War, was nicknamed the Steamroller, in the expectation that he would quickly flatten the Boers.

Anticipating an easy victory, the British did not consider the extraordinary fighting skills of the Boers, strikingly personified in Louis Botha, the youngest commander in their ranks. Nearly six feet tall with violet-blue eyes, Botha's quiet confidence quickly earned him the respect and trust of his men, and his relentless attacks on the enemy forces would leave the vaunted British army reeling.

The Boers were well known not only for their fierce independence but for their harsh treatment of native Africans and Indians. Among the most effective advocates for these groups in southern Africa were Solomon Plaatje *(right)*, a brilliant young journalist and linguist who would become the first secretary of the African National Congress (ANC), and Mohandas Gandhi, seated exact center *(below)*, who led a team of stretcher-bearers on some of the most blood-soaked battlefields of the war.

Churchill set sail for South Africa just two days after war was declared. Hired as a correspondent by the *Morning Post,* he quickly made his way to the heart of the war, settling into a bell tent with two other journalists. "I had not before encountered this sort of ambition," one of his tent mates would later write of Churchill, "unabashed, frankly egotistical, communicating its excitement, and extorting sympathy."

Soon after arriving in South Africa, Churchill was reunited with an old friend, Aylmer Haldane *(left)*, who had already been injured in one of the first battles of the war. Assigned to take command of an armored train on a reconnaissance mission, Haldane invited Churchill to come along. Churchill immediately agreed, notwithstanding the grave danger involved.

(Below) "Nothing looks more formidable and impressive than an armoured train," Churchill wrote, "but nothing is in fact more vulnerable and helpless." Crowded into open cars with little more than their peaked helmets to protect them, the men were sitting targets for the Boers, who needed only wait for them to come rattling along the tracks into their sights.

(Facing page) On November 15, 1899, just a month after Churchill arrived in South Africa, Louis Botha led a devastating attack on the armored train that carried Churchill, Haldane and his men. In the midst of a hailstorm of bullets and shells, the train was thrown from the tracks, leaving several men dead and dozens more seriously wounded. Rushing down from the surrounding hills, the Boers captured some sixty men, among them Winston Churchill.

(Below) Three days after the attack on the armored train, Churchill arrived in Pretoria, the Boer capital, with the other British prisoners of war. Surrounded by curious Boers eager to see the new prisoners, he glared back at them with unconcealed hatred and resentment. Although he respected the enemy on the battlefield, the idea that ordinary Boers would have any control over his fate enraged him.

Churchill was imprisoned with about a hundred British officers in the Staats Model School. Used as a teachers college before the war, the building was now surrounded by a corrugated-iron paling and heavily armed Boers. Churchill hated his imprisonment, he later wrote, "more than I have ever hated any other period in my whole life."

Furious and frustrated at finding himself captive while the war raged on without him, Churchill turned for help to Louis de Souza, the Transvaal secretary of state for war. Although he befriended Churchill, even bringing him a bottle of whiskey hidden in a basket of fruit, de Souza could not give the young reporter the only thing he wanted—his freedom.

(Facing page) Finally realizing that the Boers would never let him go as long as they were at war, Churchill decided to escape. To the Boers' fury, he not only slipped through their fingers but left behind an insouciantly arrogant note, addressed directly to de Souza. "Regretting that circumstances have not permitted me to bid you a personal farewell," he wrote before scaling the prison fence, "Believe me Yours vy sincerely, Winston S. Churchill."

State Schools Prison
Pretoria.

Dear Mr. de Souza,

I do not consider that your Government was justified in holding me, a press correspondent and a non combatant as a prisoner, and I have consequently resolved to escape. The arrangements I have succeeded in making in conjunction with my friends outside are such as give me every confidence. But I wish in leaving you thus hastily & unceremoniously to once more place on record my appreciation of the kindness which has been shown me and the other prisoners by you, by the commandant and by Dr. Gunning and my admiration of the chivalrous and humane character of the Republican forces. My views on the general question of the war remain unchanged, but I shall always retain a feeling of high respect for the several classes of the burghers I have met and, on reaching the British lines I will set forth a truthful & impartial account of my experiences in Pretoria. In conclusion I desire to express my obligations to you, and to hope that when this most grievous and unhappy war shall have come to an end, a state of affairs may be created which shall preserve at once the national pride of the Boers and the security of the British and put an final stop to the rivalry & enmity of both races. Regretting that circumstances have not permitted me to bid you a personal farewell, Believe me

Yours very sincerely

Winston S. Churchill.

Dec. 11th 1899

After striking out on his own and attempting to cross hundreds of miles of enemy territory without a map, compass, weapon or food, Churchill stumbled upon the Transvaal and Delagoa Bay Colliery. Taking a wild chance that he might find help there, he forced himself to come out of hiding, stepping out of "the shimmering gloom of the veldt into the light of the furnace fires."

(Above, left) By an incredible stroke of luck, Churchill knocked on the door of John Howard, the mine's manager and one of the few Englishmen who had been allowed to remain in the Transvaal during the war. When Howard agreed to help him, Churchill would later write, "I felt like a drowning man pulled out of the water."

(Above, right) After hiding Churchill in a rat-infested coal mine shaft, Howard finally found a way to secret him out of the country—burrowed deep inside the wool trucks of the mine's storekeeper, Charles Burnham. Burnham not only agreed to let Churchill hide in his trucks, but rode with him all the way to Portuguese East Africa, bribing guards and inspectors at every stop.

When Churchill finally arrived in Lourenço Marques, the capital of Portuguese East Africa, he quickly made his way to the British consulate. Although Britons and Boers alike were desperately trying to find him, when Churchill arrived at the consulate, covered in coal dust, the secretary did not recognize the filthy young man standing before him. "Be off," he sneered. "The Consul cannot see you to-day."

As soon as the success of his escape was known, Churchill became a national hero. He was greeted in Durban, the largest city in British-held Natal, by cheering throngs. "I was nearly torn to pieces by enthusiastic kindness," he later recalled. "Whirled along on the shoulders of the crowd, I was carried to the steps of the town hall, where nothing would content them but a speech."

After delivering his speech in Durban, Churchill returned to the scene of his capture, inspecting the wreckage of the armored train he had fought to save and spending Christmas Eve in a tent erected on the same railway cutting where he had been forced to surrender.

This wanted poster, distributed in the wake of Churchill's escape, offered a reward for his capture, "dead or alive." When he saw the poster, Churchill's only complaint was that the reward was so small. "I think you might have gone as high as £50," he wrote to the poster's author, "without an overestimate of the prize."

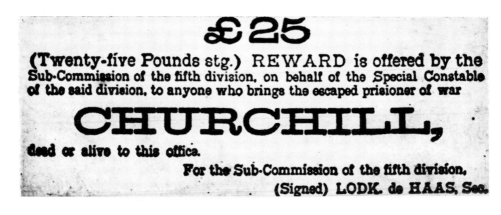

As soon as he was free, Churchill wanted to fight. After convincing Buller to give him a commission in the South African Light Horse, he took part in several battles before returning to Pretoria, where he and his cousin, the 9th Duke of Marlborough, freed the jubilant men who had so recently been Churchill's fellow prisoners.

Just six months after his escape, Churchill ran for Parliament for the second time. This time, to no one's surprise, least of all his own, he won. "It is clear to me from the figures," he wrote to the prime minister, "that nothing but personal popularity arising out of the late South African War, carried me in."

later recall Churchill assuring him that his "name would not be hidden under a bushel—in other words, I would share 'in a blaze of triumph.'"

Haldane also knew that Churchill would be missed far sooner than either he or Brockie, or any other man in the prison. Not only was he the son of Lord Randolph, but he had made himself known, incessantly and doggedly, to every high-ranking official in the Transvaal. "I do not exaggerate when I say that the major part of the anxiety which I felt at this time about the success of our escape was due to his accession to the party," Haldane wrote. "With Brockie only as my associate there was nothing to fear, but with a third accomplice and that accomplice the talkative Churchill, the situation was a very different one."

Finally, with Churchill relentlessly pressing him, Haldane told him that because he had come up with the plan with Brockie, he would have to consult him before making a decision. Knowing before he even asked what Brockie's reaction would be, Haldane approached him when they were alone one day. Brockie had the same objections Haldane did—Churchill was unfit, too famous, and he couldn't keep a secret—but, if anything, he felt them even more strongly. He wanted nothing to do with Churchill.

Haldane's conscience, however, was weighing heavily on him. He told Brockie that Churchill had been on the armored train because of him, and he could not "repay him by leaving him in the lurch." He would make it clear to Churchill that neither he nor Brockie wanted him to come with them, but he would leave the final decision up to him.

When Haldane pulled Churchill aside, he was blunt. "I did not hide from him," he later wrote, "how greatly, in my opinion, his presence would add to the risk of capture." Neither Haldane and Brockie's reluctance, however, nor the additional danger he posed gave Churchill a moment's hesitation. He would join the escape. Haldane knew that this sudden change in their plans could prove disastrous, but he could see no way out of it. "The wine was drawn," he wrote, "and it had to be drunk."

CHAPTER 18

"I SHALL GO ON ALONE"

Although Haldane and Brockie had slowly and carefully planned their escape, they chose the date spontaneously. When they woke on the morning of December 11, they decided, this was the day. "These things," Churchill understood, "are best done on the spur of the moment."

As eager as Churchill was to rejoin the war, and as confidently as he had spoken not just of escape but of wholesale revolt, now that the time had finally come, he was sick with anxiety. He hated the idea of "stealing secretly off in the night like a guilty thief," and he could not help but think of the ZARPs' highly accurate Lee-Metford rifles, which, at a range of just fifteen yards, would certainly not miss their target. Churchill had also begun to think about what life would be like on the run. If they made it over the fence alive, he knew that he could look forward to nothing better than "severe hardship and suffering." Worse, he was now willing to admit, there was little hope of success. "I passed the afternoon," he wrote, "in positive terror."

Churchill also had a lingering suspicion that Haldane and Brockie were not telling him everything. Although paranoia was one of the most common symptoms of barbed-wire disease, in this case at least, Churchill was right. His partners in escape were very consciously keeping the full details of their plan from their "talkative friend." After making it very clear to Churchill that he expected him to follow orders, Haldane had told him "in general terms what the plan was, but not in detail, as he would be in my company." As far as Churchill knew, the plan covered only the escape and nothing else. "Everything after this," he wrote, "was vague and uncertain."

Even with limited information, Churchill, as Haldane and Brockie had feared, was constitutionally incapable of keeping their plans secret. He immediately began telling the other prisoners that he was about to make his escape. "Churchill is in a great state of excitement," Haldane wrote in frustration in his diary, "and letting everyone know that he means going to-night." Haldane had hoped to keep their plans quiet not only to lessen the risk of the guards finding out but also because he knew that there were officers who would be jealous and would worry that if they succeeded in escaping, those left behind would suffer.

Haldane and Brockie were also worried that Churchill, especially in his current nervous state, would make a sudden, potentially dangerous move that would jeopardize the entire plan. While he had never questioned Churchill's bravery, Haldane knew that his friend was not as judicious as he could have hoped, or as their escape attempt would demand. "I perhaps have seen Churchill in a situation of greater danger than have others, and can affirm with confidence that he possesses one at least of the attributes of his great ancestor," Haldane wrote, referring to Churchill's famously courageous forebear, the 1st Duke of Marlborough. "He can be splendidly audacious at times and, sometimes, at the wrong time."

�»

Churchill tried with little luck to while away the hours until dinner, when they planned to make their escape. He played chess and was "hopelessly beaten." He attempted to read one of his favorite authors, W. E. H. Lecky, an Irish historian who had written about everything from Jonathan Swift to the moral history of

Europe. Churchill had somehow obtained a volume of Lecky's *History of England in the Eighteenth Century,* but even it couldn't claim his attention. "For the first time in my life," he wrote, "that wise writer wearied me."

Finally, the time came. The sky grew dark, the dinner bell clanged, and the men began to file listlessly into the large, open room at the end of the wide hallway. It was the time of day that Churchill hated most at the Staats Model School. Each night, they "crowded again into the stifling dining hall for the last tasteless meal of the barren day," he wrote. "The same miserable stories were told again and again . . . until I knew how the others came to Pretoria as well as I knew my own story."

On this night, for the first time, a current of excitement coursed through Churchill when the sun began to set. At ten minutes to 7:00, he and Haldane slipped away. They were accompanied by a few of the other officers, who knew what they intended to do and were willing to help them. Brockie would follow when he had received word from these men that his cohorts had made it over the fence.

Once in the yard, the men headed straight for the lavatory. A small, circular building, it was next to the iron paling and in that crucial sliver of darkness that Haldane and Brockie were counting on to conceal them. Although night had fallen, the electric lamps were on, flooding the enclosure with a blue-white light that left only a few, velvety black shadows. As the men strode across the grass, passing the tents of the soldier-servants and then those of the ZARPs, no one stopped them.

Nonchalantly entering the lavatory, they quickly closed the door and peered through a small gap in the metal casing. From their hiding place, they could see one of the ZARPs standing directly across from the section of fence they hoped to climb. Most nights, the guard would eventually leave, moving toward the double row of trees that lined the fence just north of the lavatory. On this night, however, he seemed maddeningly content to stay in his corner.

One by one, the other officers left the lavatory, hoping that the guard would believe that it was now empty and would himself move on to another part of the enclosure. Breath held, hearts racing, Haldane and Churchill waited in silence for what seemed to Haldane to be a quarter of an hour and to Churchill two hours, but the sentry never moved. Finally, the two men put their heads together for a whispered conference. It was no use, they decided. They would have to try another night.

As Churchill climbed back into bed that night, still in his dormitory in the Staats Model School, he was overwhelmed not with anger or frustration but with "a most unsatisfactory feeling of relief." He could not help but be grateful that the tension and uncertainty of the day had at last slipped off his shoulders. At the same time, he steeled himself to take up the yoke once again as soon as the sun rose. "I was determined," he wrote, "that nothing should stop my taking the plunge the next day."

➤➤

When he woke on the morning of December 12, Churchill was even more tightly wound than he had been the day before. "Another day of fear," he wrote, "but fear crystallizing more and more into desperation. Anything was better than further suspense." That evening, instead of listlessly circling the building, Churchill strode agitatedly up and down the yard in a straight line in front of the fence. Haldane watched him nervously, all too aware that his excitement was fully apparent to everyone in the enclosure. "We *must* go to-night," Churchill snapped under his breath. "There are three of us to go," Haldane calmly replied, "and we will certainly do so if the chance is favourable."

As soon as the sun set, Churchill's anxiety only heightened. He haunted Haldane and Brockie's every step, determined to be ready at any moment to escape. "W.C. never lost sight of self or Brockie," Haldane wrote in his diary, "as if he feared we might go without him!"

At 7:00 that night, the men gathered on the back veranda, staring out at the fence and the guards. Churchill and Haldane, again accompanied by a few officers who would serve as lookouts, started out for the lavatory, leaving Brockie behind to wait for his signal. As had happened the night before, however, the sentry posted across from the lavatory did not stir. After waiting as long as they safely could, they once again agreed to postpone the escape and crossed the yard to rejoin Brockie on the veranda.

When Haldane began to explain their decision to Brockie, his reaction was swift and withering. "You're afraid," he sneered. "I could get away any night." Haldane, by this time irritated with both of his partners, replied, "Very well; go and see for yourself." Brockie immediately stalked off, headed in the direction of the lavatory. Haldane stood quietly watching him, but Churchill could not stand to be left behind. Turning suddenly to Haldane, he said, "I am going over again," then added, "Don't follow immediately."

When he had first agreed to bring Churchill with them, Haldane had made at least one aspect of their plan perfectly clear. Although they could not all three climb over at the same time, he and Churchill were to go together, with Brockie following. There was no question, at least in Haldane's mind, that whatever happened, Churchill would not go alone. Churchill, he believed, understood this as well as he did. Now, as he watched his young friend walk away, Haldane simply stared after him, nonplussed.

Churchill had not gotten very far when Brockie suddenly emerged from the lavatory. As Haldane watched, the two men walked up to each other, stopped for a moment, apparently in tense conversation, and then continued in opposite directions. When Brockie rejoined Haldane on the veranda, he was furious. "That damned fool Churchill wanted to stop and talk within earshot of the sentry," he spat. "I told him that it was useless to try to escape then."

By that time, Churchill had already disappeared into the lavatory. Confident that he understood the plan and would not attempt anything while he was alone, Haldane turned away, deciding to take the opportunity to have a quick meal before trying again. As he and Brockie stepped inside the building and made their way toward the dining hall, they assumed that Churchill would be right behind them.

→→

Some twenty years later, a prolific British author known only as Mrs. Stuart Menzies would write a book titled *As Others See Us* in which she would compare Churchill to the famous king of Scotland Robert the Bruce. According to legend, Bruce, who had ruled from 1306 to 1329, defeated the English in the Battle of Bannockburn only after hiding in a cave and watching a spider repeatedly try and fail to spin a web. In Sir Walter Scott's version of the story, *Tales of a Grandfather*, Bruce decides that if the spider tries a seventh time and succeeds, he will "venture a seventh time to try my fortune in Scotland." If the spider fails, he will "never return to my native country again."

Churchill, Menzies believed, was even more determined than either the king or the spider. There was no limit to how many times he would try. He would never give up. "Unlike Robert the Bruce, Winston has nothing to learn from spiders in the way of perseverance," she wrote. "The spider in that case tried seven times, but I say unto you that Churchill will try seventy times seven, so it saves trouble to give into him at once."

As he stood alone in the prison lavatory, Churchill found himself again nervously watching the guards through a chink in the metal frame. It looked as if they would never move. Half an hour passed, and still they remained "stolid and obstructive." Then, suddenly, one of the men turned, walked over to the other guard and began talking to him. For the moment at least, both of the men had their backs to Churchill.

In an instant, Haldane and Brockie's plan and Churchill's promise to his friend were completely forgotten. The only thought that rushed through Churchill's head was "Now or never." Bolting out of the lavatory, he rushed to the fence, the sentries standing just fifteen yards away. As their voices drifted on the warm night air right behind him, Churchill, using every bit of strength he had, pulled himself to the top of the paling. "Twice I let myself down again in sickly hesitation," he later wrote, "and then with a third resolve scrambled up."

When he finally got to the top, Churchill glanced down at the guards one last time. Then, as quietly as he could, he lowered himself over the side. Behind the Staats Model School was a private house, which the men believed to be unoccupied, and Churchill now found himself in its garden, crouching in a low shrub that stretched along the fence. It was far from the perfect hiding place, but it would have to do until Haldane and Brockie got word that he had made it over and were able to join him.

As he hid among the short, sharp branches, the voices of the ZARPs still floating over the prison wall, Churchill had a startling thought. Although this sudden turn of events was thrilling, it was also irrevocable. As difficult as it had been to climb out of the prison without being seen, it would be all but impossible to climb back in.

→→

Sitting in the dining hall with Brockie, Haldane began to wonder where Churchill was. After about ten minutes, he finally went to their room to see if he had gone there instead of following them into dinner. Not only did he not find Churchill in the dormitory, but, even more disturbing, he did not find Churchill's hat.

To the prisoners of the Staats Model School, a hat was an object of immeasurable value—uniquely useful and almost impossible to acquire. If a man was fortunate enough to have one, Haldane wrote, he kept it "carefully preserved." After trying unsuccessfully to convince the Boers to let him order a hat with his suit of clothes, Churchill had persuaded Adrian Hofmeyr, the clergyman who had been imprisoned for his English sympathies, to let him borrow his. It was exactly what he had hoped for—soft, drooping felt that covered his face and would make him indistinguishable from any Boer on the streets of Pretoria. It could also be easily hidden.

Haldane knew that as soon as he had acquired a hat, Churchill had begun keeping it under his pillow. Looking at the bed, Haldane first saw something on top of the pillow—a letter. Unable to leave without having the last word regarding his imprisonment, Churchill had written a letter to Louis de Souza, the secretary of state for war, and left it where it would not be missed. It was an impudent, not to mention dangerous, thing to do, but Haldane ignored it for the time being. Quickly slipping his hand under the pillow, he searched for Hofmeyr's hat. All he felt was the rough, cool sheet underneath.

As he stood next to Churchill's bed, wondering where he could be and why he still had his hat with him, one of the other prisoners stepped inside the room. Churchill had escaped, he told Haldane. Then another man appeared, claiming to have spoken to Churchill through the fence. Before Haldane could absorb either of these reports, he got another one: The guard had moved from his place next to the lavatory. "If Brockie and I were to escape," he wrote, "we must at all costs do so without losing a moment."

Haldane quickly slipped out the back door with three other officers and walked as fast as he could to the lavatory. Believing that the sentry was still gone, he reached up and began to pull himself to the top of the fence. At that moment, the rising moon shone fully on his face. A guard who had been hidden in shadow stepped forward and, raising his rifle to his shoulder, pointed it at Haldane's head. "Go back you . . . fool," he barked.

→→

Kneeling in the shrubs on the other side of the fence, Churchill waited impatiently for Haldane and Brockie. "Where were the others?" he wondered. "Why did they not make the attempt?" The moonlight, which had revealed Haldane to the sentry on the other side, was a friend to Churchill, throwing his hiding place into deep shadow. Still, he was terrified that he would be found. The house was only twenty yards away and, he realized with a sickening jolt, it was occupied. More than that, it was filled with people.

Peering through the leaves, Churchill could see light pouring through the windows of the house, and against that bright background he saw dark figures moving around inside. Then, to his horror, a man opened the door, light spilling out of the house and into the garden. Stepping into the moonlit night, he walked across the grass and stopped directly in front of Churchill. He was just ten yards away and, Churchill was certain, looking directly at him. "I cannot describe the surge of panic which nearly overwhelmed me," he wrote. "I must be discovered. I dared not stir an inch. My heart beat so violently that I felt sick."

Terrified, Churchill realized that the only chance he had of remaining undiscovered was the invisibility that, he fervently hoped, the darkened shrubs provided. "Amid a tumult of emotion," he later wrote, "reason, seated firmly on her throne, whispered, 'Trust to the dark background.'" He briefly considered speaking to the man, whispering to him that he was a detective and that he was waiting to catch a prisoner whom he believed would attempt to escape that night. Catching himself just in time, however, he realized that a Boer detective would certainly speak Dutch, a language he did not know.

Trying to remain as motionless as he possibly could, Churchill suddenly saw yet another man leave the house, and walk directly toward him. Lighting a cigar, he joined the man standing in front of Churchill and then, to Churchill's immense relief, they both began to walk away. Just at that moment, a dog chased a cat into the bushes, and the cat, tearing blindly through the underbrush, crashed into Churchill's silent, crouching figure. Shocked, the cat "uttered a 'miaul' of alarm" and tore back out of the shrub, rattling the branches and making a tremendous racket as he went. The two men who had been walking away stopped short when they heard the commotion, but when the cat dashed past them, they continued on their way. As they stepped through the garden gate and into the town, Churchill watched them go, hoping that he would soon follow in their footsteps.

Now that disaster had, at least for the moment, been averted, Churchill glanced down at his watch and realized that an hour had passed since he had climbed over the fence. Where were Haldane and Brockie? Just then, he heard a voice, a British voice, on the other side. "All up," it said tersely. Scrambling closer, Churchill could hear two men talking in a strange mixture of English, Latin and nonsense, laughing as they paced back and forth just in front of him. Then he distinctly heard them say his name. Coughing to let them know he was there, Churchill listened intently as one man continued to jabber while the other spoke in a slow, clear voice. It was Haldane.

"Cannot get out," Haldane said. "The sentry suspects. It's all up. Can you get back in?" On the opposite side of the fence, alone and terrified of being found, Churchill knew that he had no one and nothing to help him, and was truly on his own. Instead of panicking, however, he suddenly felt freed. "All my fears fell from me at once," he wrote. "To go back was impossible. . . . Fate pointed me onward." There was nothing to do now but test his luck. Whispering through the iron paling for the last time, he told Haldane, "I shall go on alone."

PART FIVE

In the Heart
of the Enemy's Country

CHAPTER 19

TOUJOURS DE L'AUDACE

As he climbed out of his tangled hiding place, straightening his back and turning toward the garden gate, Churchill knew only one thing with any certainty: He would be caught. "Of course, I shall be recaptured, but I will at least have a run for my money," he said to himself. "Failure being almost certain, no odds against success affected me. All risks were less than the certainty."

Taking Hofmeyr's hat out of his pocket, Churchill put it on and strode into the garden as if he were as free as any man in Pretoria. As he passed the house, its lights glowing, voices drifting through the windows, he made no attempt to hide or even keep to the shadows. "I said to myself, *'Toujours de l'audace,'*" he wrote, quoting the famous words of Georges Danton, a leader of the French Revolution who was eventually guillotined. "Always more audacity."

Churchill passed through the same gate he had watched the two men walk through just minutes earlier, and then turned left into the street. He was, he thought with exultation, "at large in Pretoria." There was a sentry only five yards away, but Churchill did not give him a second look. Although he was known to most of the ZARPs by sight, he walked with such confidence that if the sentry did see him, his suspicions were not aroused. Outwardly, Churchill continued on his way, utterly unruffled. Inwardly, he resisted "with the utmost difficulty an impulse to run."

As Churchill made his way through the town, wearing the brown flannel suit he had ordered from the prison, his hat slouching low over his eyes, no one paid any attention to him. He sauntered down the middle of the road and, because he hated whistling, hummed a carefree tune. Looking the picture of comfort and ease, he kept walking east on Skinner Street until everything in Pretoria that he most feared and hated, and that represented his loathed imprisonment, slowly disappeared behind him—President Kruger's house, the train station where he had first arrived nearly a month earlier and, above all, the Staats Model School.

Even walking at a leisurely pace, Churchill soon reached the outskirts of Pretoria. There were fewer stone buildings here, more shanties and modest cottages, and, in the distance, the steep banks of a low, muddy river—the Apies. The river, whose name means "little ape" in Afrikaans, flows north into the Pienaars, a tributary of the thousand-mile-long Limpopo. Narrow and shallow, the Apies could easily be forded, but as Churchill approached the river, he noticed that a small bridge had been built over it. Stepping onto the bridge, he sat down and tried to figure out what to do next.

Although in many ways he was an optimist, even a dreamer, Churchill was also a realist. He had no illusions about how difficult it would be simply to get out of Pretoria, let alone cross hundreds of miles of enemy territory. "I was in the heart of the enemy's country," he wrote. "All exits were barred. The town was picketed, the country was patrolled, the trains were searched, the line was guarded."

He was also painfully aware that he was completely unprepared. Escaping with Haldane and Brockie had been one thing. Escaping alone was something else altogether. His friends not only had the compass and the map, they had opium tablets and even meat lozenges. Tinned disks of dried meat that one British company advertised as "a meal in the vest pocket . . . for tourists, athletes, invalids," the lozenges could sustain a hungry man on the veld for days. Taking an inventory of his own pockets, Churchill found that beyond £75, four slabs of melting chocolate and a crumbling biscuit they were empty. Even if he wasn't quickly recaptured, he wondered, how could he find his way to freedom, or survive the journey?

Only one direction offered any prospect of success. The closest city of the British-held Cape Colony, where he had landed with Buller, lay almost five hundred miles to the south. Rhodesia, now known as Zimbabwe, was closer, about three hundred miles northeast of Pretoria, but the Boers fiercely patrolled its border. In fact, the city of Mafeking, which sat on its border, was, like Ladysmith, under siege. To the west, below the Kalahari Desert, the British protectorate of Bechuanaland was teeming with Boers. Churchill knew that he had to go east, to Portuguese East Africa. What he did not know was how he could possibly get there.

As he contemplated the hopelessness of his situation, his feet dangling over the Apies, Churchill looked up and caught sight of an old friend in the night sky: Orion. A year earlier in Egypt, he had become separated from his unit and lost his way in the desert. Growing more and more desperate for water, he had found Orion, one of the brightest constellations in the northern sky, and followed it to the Nile. Now, in southern Africa rather than northern, he again looked to Orion for help. "He had given me water," he wrote. "Now he should lead me to freedom. I could not endure the want of either."

Strengthened by the help of this welcome celestial guidepost, Churchill summoned the courage he needed to keep going. Leaving the bridge behind, he began walking again, still east but also south this time, moving steadily farther from the center of town. The land surrounding Pretoria was very different from the view he had had from Estcourt. Instead of mile after mile of flat veld, the landscape here was broken by hills, dells and valleys, even trees and shrubs. The climate was much milder, but the nights, he knew, would be colder.

After walking for half an hour, Churchill suddenly came upon a set of train tracks. It was an opportunity, but also a danger. He could follow the tracks, but it was impossible to know with any certainty where they would lead him. Three railway lines ran through Pretoria. Only one carried trains in the direction Churchill needed to go—east, to the Indian Ocean coast and the neutral Portuguese colony. The other, however, ran north, toward a town called Pietersburg, which was just south of Rhodesia and the assiduously patrolled border.

Churchill stood for a while, peering into the distance, trying to determine in what direction the tracks beside him were headed. Unlike railways in the relatively featureless Natal, where he was captured, trains in the Transvaal were forced to climb low mountains and skirt deep valleys, and rarely went in one direction for long. A man without a compass could very easily follow a railway line for miles in the wrong direction without knowing it. As far as Churchill could tell, and farther than he could see, the set of tracks at his feet traveled north. "Still," he thought, ever the optimist, "it might be only winding its way out among the hills."

Either way, Churchill had little choice in the matter. This was the only railway line he had seen since his escape, and he had no idea where, or if, he would find another. The only thing he could do as he set off along the tracks was hope against hope that they would, eventually, lead him in the right direction.

→→

Although he could not have been more vulnerable or in greater danger, Churchill clung to the theory that had brought him over the wall, out of the garden and through Pretoria. *Toujours de l'audace.* "When hope had departed," he wrote, "fear had gone as well." As he followed the tracks, he ignored the picket fires, bright and flickering against the night sky, and he walked without flinching past the "watchers," the men who were posted at every bridge.

Reveling in the cool night air as it swept against his face and listening to the red dirt crunch beneath his boots, Churchill gloried in his release from captivity. He knew that he could be caught at any moment, but for now he was free. Even if he had only a single hour alone, outside the walls that had so recently penned him in, it seemed to him well worth the risk.

More even than his freedom, Churchill delighted in the thrill of adventure, which he had longed for since the war began. "A wild feeling of exhilaration took hold of me," he wrote. Flush with the success of the first phase of his escape, he boldly began to plan the next. He knew that if he was ever going to make it to Portuguese East Africa, he could not do so by walking. It was too far. The obvious, and only, answer was a train. "I would board a train in motion," he thought, "and hide under the seats, on the roof, on the couplings—anywhere."

It would be a grand adventure, an exploit of the most romantic kind. He at once imagined himself as one of the principal characters in the 1882 novel *Vice Versa*. In the book, a father and son switch bodies after coming in contact with a magical stone from India. While his son runs his company, the father, Paul Bultitude, is forced to go to the boy's boarding school, and run away by hiding on a train. "I thought of Paul Bultitude's escape from school," Churchill wrote. "I saw myself emerging from under the seat, and bribing or persuading some fat first-class passenger to help me."

Although he could not jump on a train that was moving at full speed, Churchill thought that if it slowed down long enough, he might make it. Haldane and Brockie had worried about his fitness and his injured shoulder, but he had climbed over the fence of the Staats Model School without their help. He was young and thin and, most important of all, determined.

For the next two hours, Churchill followed the tracks with no sign of a train. Finally, in the distance, he saw something that instantly stood out among the natural surroundings of rocks, dirt and trees—the unmistakable bright red and green flashing of signal lights. He had found a station.

For the first time since his escape, Churchill decided that the best strategy would be to hide. Quickly making his way around the back of the station, he found a ditch about two hundred yards from the tracks and, sliding down its crumbling sides, settled in to wait for a train. "What train should I take?" he asked himself, and instantly answered, "The first, of course."

→►

At the outset of war, southern Africa had about forty-six hundred miles of railway lines, about thirteen hundred miles of which were in the Boer republics of the Transvaal and the Orange Free State. In times of peace, the railway system was carefully maintained and run with the same precision and consistency with which it would have been managed in Europe. Now that there was war, however, everything was, in the words of Sir Édouard Girouard, a railway builder and chronicler of the war, "suddenly and entirely altered."

From one day to the next, there could be profound and completely unpredictable changes to the lines, changes that had a devastating effect on the trains' ability to run on time, or at all. It was impossible to know, for instance, if a watering station, as essential as coal in keeping the steam engines running, still existed, had accidentally been destroyed during the fighting or was intentionally sabotaged. Instead of carrying a small number of passengers, the trains now shuttled tens of thousands of men across the republics, often making unscheduled stops during which they unloaded enormous quantities of supplies. The trains themselves had also become dangerous to ride. The drivers were overworked and exhausted, and even the most unreliable engines could not be spared and so were rarely pulled off the line for repairs.

As he crouched in the ditch near the station, Churchill did not know any of this. He knew only that an hour had passed and still there was no train in sight. With each passing minute, his impatience grew. Not only was he eager to try his luck, but he was running out of time. Even if no one at the Staats Model School had yet noticed his absence, as soon as the sun rose, they would know that he was gone. "My escape must be known at dawn," he wrote. "Pursuit would be immediate."

Straining his ears for the sound of an approaching train, Churchill suddenly heard something: the deep-throated, wet whistle of a steam engine, and the heavy, rhythmic rattle of wheels on tracks. Looking up from his ditch, he saw two large yellow headlights swing into view. After waiting for an hour, he would now have only minutes, perhaps seconds, to make his move.

As the train came closer, Churchill climbed out of his ditch and scrambled over to the tracks. "I argued that the train would stop at the station," he wrote, "and that it would not have got up too much speed by the time it reached me." Counseling himself to be patient, to wait until the train had passed by him before jumping so that he would not be seen, he mentally rehearsed what he was about to do. The train would pass, he thought, and then he would "make a dash for the carriages."

As had so often happened in Churchill's young life, however, nothing turned out quite as he had planned. When the engine pulled away from the station, "with much noise and steaming," it picked up speed quickly, much more quickly than Churchill had anticipated. In what seemed like a mere heartbeat, the blinding lights were upon him, the pleasant rattle had grown into a thunderous roar, and he was staring up at the "dark mass" of the engine. Everything came in a massive, churning, irresistible rush—"the engine-driver silhouetted against his furnace glow, the black profile of the engine, the clouds of steam."

Crouching next to the tracks, Churchill knew that it was, once again, now or never. Before he could hesitate or even think, he leaped. What happened next was a blur of wheels, smoke and terror. "I hurled myself on the trucks," he wrote, "clutched at something, missed, clutched again, missed again, grasped some sort of hand-hold, was swung off my feet—my toes bumping on the line." Finally, with a surge of effort, he pulled himself off the tracks and onto the couplings of the fifth car.

His body surging with fear and adrenaline, Churchill crawled as quickly as he could into the interior of the boxcar. It was a goods train, and the car was filled with sacks, all of which were coated in coal dust. They were filthy, but Churchill did not care as he tunneled his way into their depths. In just a few minutes, he was all but invisible, tucked deep within the mass of warm, soft bags, comfortable and, for the moment, safe.

As he lay in his cocoon, breathing in coal dust and sweat and feeling the bulky bags heavy on his legs and uneven beneath his back, Churchill's mind churned with questions. Had the engine driver seen him as he jumped onto the train and struggled to pull himself onto the couplings? Would they unload the car at the next station? Would they search it? Where was the train taking him? To Delagoa Bay or Pietersburg?

"Ah, never mind that," he finally told himself. "Sufficient for the day was the luck thereof." Lying in his dusty nest, Churchill listened to the soothing sound of the train clattering along the tracks, carrying him away from Pretoria at twenty miles an hour. Exhausted, triumphant and content, he quickly fell asleep.

When Churchill awoke with a start several hours later, he was a different man from the one who had drifted off to sleep among the coal bags. The rush of excitement, the thrill of his newly won freedom, the feelings of triumph and invincibility, had all gone. All that was left, he wrote, was "the consciousness of oppressive difficulties heavy on me."

Disoriented and frightened, Churchill had no idea how long he had been sleeping, or where the train had taken him. Peering out from the boxcar, he was relieved to see that it was at least still dark. No longer full of swagger, he took comfort in the night, relying on it to hide him while he did what he knew he had to do—jump from the train.

Unwilling to risk being found at the next station and desperate for water, Churchill reluctantly crawled from his "cosy hiding place" and climbed back onto the same couplings that had been his savior a few hours earlier. The train was still moving fast, but he knew that he did not have the luxury of waiting for it to slow down. Grasping an iron handle at the back of the boxcar with his left hand, he pulled it as hard as he could and jumped. He struck the ground hard, took two "gigantic strides" and found himself sprawled in a ditch next to the tracks. Looking up, he watched as the train, "my faithful ally of the night," hurtled on without him, quickly disappearing in the dark.

As he stood, his legs shaky beneath him, Churchill tried to take stock of his surroundings. He was standing in a broad valley, encircled by low hills and filled with tall, dew-covered grass. He had no idea where he was, but, he thought with a small twinge of consolation, neither did anyone else. He also noticed with even greater relief that the tracks he had been traveling on ran toward the rising sun. At some point as he had slept, the train had turned from north to east, carrying him in the direction of Portuguese East Africa and freedom.

Savagely thirsty, Churchill's first thoughts were of water. Finding a clear pool in a nearby gully, he drank more than he wanted, and then he drank some more. He knew that after the sun had risen, he would have to spend the entire day in hiding. Walking toward the surrounding hills, the grass drenching his pant legs, he came upon a small grove of trees that bordered a deep ravine. It would have to do as a hiding place until the sun set once again.

It was now 4:00 in the morning. Roughly nine hours had passed since his escape, but he would have to wait at least fourteen more before he could continue his journey. When he had first jumped from the train, he had felt the cold night air sharp on his hands and face and stealing through his thin flannel suit. With little humidity in the air, there was nothing to hold the heat after the sun went down. As it came up, however, Churchill knew that he would soon long for the chill of night.

He had experienced extreme heat before. In India, he had described it in tactile, almost anthropomorphic terms. "You could lift the heat with your hands," he had written, "it sat on your shoulders like a knapsack, it rested on your head like a nightmare." Now it was not only oppressive, it was a threat. The pool from which he had drunk before the sun rose was only about half a mile away, beckoning him, but it was too dangerous to walk even that short distance in the daylight. By 10:00, even in the shade of his grove, Churchill was boiling, and his thirst had returned with a vengeance. Because he had had nothing to eat since before dinner the previous day, he ate one of his four precious bars of chocolate, but it did little to satisfy his hunger and only heightened his thirst.

Exhausted from his ordeal, Churchill lay down among the trees and tried to sleep, but it was too hot, and he was too anxious. "I had scarcely slept, but yet my heart beat so fiercely and I was so nervous and perplexed about the future that I could not rest," he wrote. "I thought of all the chances that lay against me; I dreaded and detested more than words can express the prospect of being caught and dragged back to Pretoria."

Even here, in the middle of nowhere, the likelihood of Churchill being captured, or even shot, was high. Although he was many miles from Pretoria and far from the fighting, he was not alone. From his hiding place, he could see the silhouettes of men, some walking, others on horseback, crossing the valley. One man, hunting birds, came right up to the grove of trees in which he was hidden. He fired twice, but left without seeing the British escapee who was silently watching him between the branches.

At the moment, the only creature paying careful attention to Churchill was a large, ferocious-looking bird of prey, which, he wrote, "manifested an extravagant interest in my condition." Churchill believed it was a vulture, but whatever it was, it "made hideous and ominous gurgling" sounds at it stared intensely at the frightened young man standing before it.

As Churchill hid among the trees, a hunted man, the hopelessness and peril of his situation became almost too much to bear. His famously strident confidence had left him, leaving behind only the impossibility of finding his way to freedom, or even surviving the attempt. "I found no comfort in any of the philosophical ideas which some men parade in their hours of ease and strength and safety," he wrote. "I realized with awful force that no exercise of my own feeble wit and strength could save me from my enemies." Finally, desperate and nearly defeated, Churchill turned for hope and help to the only source he had left: his God.

Churchill was not a religious man. "If the human race ever reaches a stage of development—when religion will cease to assist and comfort mankind," he had written to his mother two years earlier, "Christianity will be put aside as a crutch which is no longer needed, and man will stand erect on the firm legs of reason." As a child, he had been forced to spend many hours in church, and would later say that he was grateful for them only because, aside from weddings and funerals, he had felt little need to return. "I accumulated in those years so fine a surplus in the Bank of Observance," he wrote, "that I have been drawing confidently upon it ever since."

Churchill had, however, room not only in his heart but in his mind for a God. He had never been able to understand why his intellect and his soul must be in conflict. "It seemed good to let the mind explore so far as it could the paths of thought and logic, and also good to pray for help and succor, and be thankful when they came," he wrote. "I could not feel that the Supreme Creator who gave us our minds as well as our souls would be offended if they did not always run smoothly together in double harness. After all He must have foreseen this from the beginning and of course He would understand it all."

Now, with no new ideas, no clever plans, no strutting confidence in the strength of his mind and the agility of his young body, Churchill was forced to admit to himself that he needed help. "Without the assistance of that High Power which interferes in the eternal sequence of causes and effects more often than we are always prone to admit," he wrote, "I could never succeed." He was, by all measures but one, alone, and so he did the only thing he could think to do. He prayed, "long and earnestly."

CHAPTER 20

"TO TAKE MY LEAVE"

When the sun rose over the Staats Model School, the alarm did not sound as Churchill had thought it would. In fact, only a handful of men knew that anything was amiss, and they were not talking. While Churchill had been strolling through Pretoria, doing his best imitation of a man enjoying a summer evening, Haldane and Brockie had been scrambling to buy him time. They did this even though the mere mention of Winston Churchill's name filled them with fury.

Since Churchill's escape the night before, the two men had been stunned to find themselves shut out of their own plan. Brockie, who had been adamantly against even including Churchill, was unable to choke back his rage. He let loose "a full dose of opprobrious epithets of which [he] had a liberal command," Haldane wrote. There was, in fact, "a chorus of vituperation" against Churchill, because the officers who had wanted to join the plan themselves felt certain that it would be far harder for any of them to escape now. Haldane, while enduring Brockie's "sneering allusions to 'Your trusted friend—a nice kind of gentleman!'" struggled to tamp down his own anger. "I said little," he wrote, "swallowing my chagrin as best I could."

What was done was done. They could not get Churchill back,

and they could no longer use the same plan. There was nothing to do but find another way out and, in the meantime, try to help Churchill succeed. Working as fast as they could, Haldane and Brockie fashioned a "dummy figure" and tucked it into Churchill's bed, its head on the same pillow that had once hidden Hofmeyr's hat.

It was apparently an effective disguise. When a soldier-servant stepped into their room that morning, carrying a cup of coffee, he spoke to what he believed was Churchill, still wrapped, motionless, in blankets on his bed. When there was no answer, he simply set the coffee on a chair and walked away.

Churchill's next visitor, however, was not so easily discouraged. While at the Staats Model School, Churchill had not only made purchases, from clothing to alcohol, he had arranged for services from local vendors. For the past month, he had been receiving regular haircuts and shaves from a Boer barber. In the excitement of his escape, he had forgotten that he had an appointment for the morning of December 13.

One of the many reasons Haldane and Brockie had not wanted to take Churchill with them was that he was well known within the prison not just for his aristocratic background but for his aristocratic tastes. Whether he was in Blenheim Palace or on a battlefield, Churchill expected certain amenities, and he saw no reason why he should not have them simply because he was in prison. The day he arrived in Pretoria, he had written to his mother asking her to ensure that his credit would be good in the Transvaal capital. "Cox's should be instructed to cash any cheques I may draw," he had explained to her. "Their cheques are the ones cashed here easiest."

Churchill had developed a taste for fine things seemingly from birth, with little concern for how much they cost. When he was just fifteen years old, he had written to his mother complaining bitterly because he had been forced to travel in the second-class compartment of a train. "I won't travel 2d again by Jove," he had railed. By the following year, his spending had become so extreme that his father had sternly reprimanded him for his lavishness. "You are really too extravagant," Randolph had written to his son. "If you were a millionaire you could not be more extravagant."

Even after joining the army, Churchill had not outgrown his profligate ways. In India, like many young officers, he had turned to the services of moneylenders, even though they had all been warned against it. Any money they needed "had to be borrowed at usurious rates of interest from the all-too-accommodating native bankers," Churchill would remember years later. "All you had to do was sign little bits of paper, and produce a polo pony as if by magic. The smiling financier rose to his feet, covered his face with his hands, replaced his slippers, and trotted off contentedly till that day three months [later]."

When the barber arrived at the Staats Model School at 8:00 a.m. on December 13, he went straight to Churchill's room, accompanied as always by a guard. Haldane tried to turn him away, telling him that Churchill would not need his services that day, but the barber was insistent. "Unfortunately, he was an inquisitive, persistent fellow," Haldane wrote, "who was unwilling to depart before earning his expected fee."

After not finding Churchill in his room, the barber went up and down the hallways, the ZARP trailing behind him as he asked everyone he met if he had seen Churchill. "Some gave him no answer, just looked him up and down," Hofmeyr would later recall. "Others referred him to the most unlikely corners." Finally, Tom Frankland, who had been captured with Churchill and was his roommate at the Staats Model School, stepped in, hoping to put the barber off by telling him that Churchill was bathing. The barber, however, was not about to give up so easily. Hurrying to the bathroom, he and the now mildly interested guard stood outside the door, patiently waiting for Churchill to emerge. After half an hour, the barber knocked, "gently and apologetically" at first, and then louder. When there was no answer, he and the sentry began pounding on the door. Finally, they decided to go in. The guard turned the handle and slowly, nervously pushed the door open, "inch by inch, peeping in gingerly," Hofmeyr wrote. "Is the man perhaps dead? Has he cut his throat? What ghastly sight am I doomed to see? He opens the door a little more. There is no one."

After frantically searching every inch of the tiny, eight-by-three-foot room, peering under a chair and behind the door, carefully examining bath towels and slivers of soap, the ZARP was forced to admit that Churchill was not there. What had at first seemed a minor mystery suddenly turned darker. "Consternation is now changed into panic," Hofmeyr wrote. "The gaoler is called; the guard is alarmed; there is bustle and confusion." One by one, the prisoners were questioned. When did they last see Winston Churchill? Again and again, they gave the same answer: last night.

The widespread alarm that Churchill had expected now spread quickly, not just through the prison, but throughout Pretoria. The Staats Model School was soon swarming with government officials and police inspectors. One man, a field cornet who had raced to the prison when he heard that Churchill was missing, was, in Hofmeyr's words, "in a great rage." Storming into Hofmeyr's room with the jailers Opperman and Gunning in tow, he demanded to know when the clergyman had last seen Churchill. When Hofmeyr gave him the same answer as every other prisoner—"last night"—the man turned with a vengeance on Opperman and Gunning. "You must produce Churchill," he hissed, glaring at them until they trembled with fear. "If not General Joubert will hang you!"

For Opperman and Gunning, as for any guard who had shown the prisoners a moment's leniency or kindness, it seemed as though the situation could not get any worse. Churchill was missing, but he would be found. Surely he could not have gone far. Then they found the letter.

Handwritten in Churchill's small, distinctive script, it was addressed directly to the Transvaal secretary of state for war.

State Schools Prison
Pretoria

Dear Mr. de Souza,

I do not consider that your Government was justified in holding me, a press correspondent and a non combatant a prisoner,
and I have consequently resolved to escape. The arrangements
I have succeeded in making in conjunction with my friends
outside are such as give me every confidence. But I wish in leaving you thus hastily & unceremoniously to once more place on
record my appreciation of the kindness which has been shown
me and the other prisoners by you, by the Commandant and by
Dr. Gunning and my admiration of the chivalrous and humane
character of the Republican forces. My views on the general
question of the war remain unchanged, but I shall always retain
a feeling of high respect for the several classes of the burghers
I have met and, on reaching the British lines I will set forth
a truthful & impartial account of my experiences in Pretoria.
In conclusion I desire to express my obligations to you, and to
hope that when this most grievous and unhappy war shall have
come to an end, a state of affairs may be created which shall
preserve at once the national pride of the Boers and the security
of the British and put a final stop to the rivalry & enmity of
both races. Regretting that circumstances have not permitted
me to bid you a personal farewell, Believe me

Yours vy sincerely

WINSTON CHURCHILL,
Dec. 11th 1899

On the envelope, Churchill could not resist adding a small, smug
postscript: p.p.c., or *pour prendre congé*. French for "to take my leave," it
was often used by members of the British aristocracy, who scribbled
it on their calling cards, dropping them on a table or in the white-
gloved hand of a butler as they walked out the door. The postscript,

as Churchill well knew, was exactly the kind of over-bred, aristo-cratic gesture that the Boers despised.

Although Churchill would later admit that he had taken "great pleasure" in writing the letter, it did not have the effect he had imag-ined it would. Far from being charmed by his cleverness or mollified by his compliments and wishes for a speedy end to this "grievous and unhappy war," the Boers were outraged. The idea of being humili-ated by the son of Lord Randolph Churchill was simply too much to bear. They were determined that nothing, not even the war, would prevent them from finding Winston Churchill.

In fact, the Transvaal government was so shocked and infuriated by Churchill's escape that tracking him down suddenly became the first order of business. "So great was the Government's . . . desire to capture [Churchill]," Haldane wrote, that "the whole State machin-ery came to a standstill." To Hofmeyr, the Boer officials appeared to be almost paralyzed with rage. "It seemed to me," he wrote, "that even the war was forgotten."

Despite Churchill's attempts to protect his friends, the Boers' fury fell first on those closest to him. He had hoped that by referring to his "friends on the outside," he would make it seem as though he had had no help from inside the prison, either from his fellow inmates or from the guards. The letter, however, had done more harm than good. It was immediately apparent to the men Churchill had left behind that life for them would change dramatically. "Vengeance was now to be taken on us," Hofmeyr wrote. "Everybody and every-thing was suspected." They could no longer have visitors or walk out-side after 8:30 p.m., buy newspapers or sleep on the veranda on the hottest nights. Nearly all of the privileges they had come to expect from the Boers were now stripped from them. "We were subjected to many petty annoyances," Haldane wrote, "which displayed to fine advantage the narrow-minded and malicious nature which actuated our warders."

What worried Haldane and Brockie, however, was that it would now be a thousand times harder to escape. Additional sentries were added not just to the enclosure but to the neighboring yards. Several guards were accused of taking bribes and removed from the prison altogether. Even de Souza's wife, Marie, believed that they were guilty, writing in her diary that Churchill "must have bribed the guards, who are policemen!" The new ZARPs were angrier, more vigilant and less easily distracted than their predecessors. They were not about to be humiliated again.

The prisoners could also no longer count on any help or news from their small group of friends within Pretoria. The Boers launched a massive search of homes, especially those with any English connections. Even Dr. Gunning, the assistant jailer of the Staats Model School, endured the humiliation of having his house ransacked by ZARPs because his wife was English. In a warrant, P. Maritz Botha, the first criminal *landdrost,* or magistrate, wrote that "there is reason to believe that W. Churchill . . . is hidden in a certain house in this town inhabited by certain parties. You are hereby authorized in the name of the Government of the South African Republic to enter the said house during the day, and there thoroughly to search the house [for articles] of the said W. Churchill and in case of the said articles being found there to bring the same together with the party in whose possession they are found, before the Landdrost to be dealt with according to law."

Moving quickly through the town, ZARPs knocked on one door after another, looking for Churchill or any sign of him. For the rest of her life, Catherine Holmes, who was six years old at the time, would remember waking in the middle of the night and listening to the tense voices of her parents as they discussed the escape. "As there was a 7 o'clock curfew nobody could be out late," she wrote years later. "My cousin had crept through the windows of the houses to warn us all that the Boer soldiers were coming to search the houses for Sir Winston."

When the Boers reached the home of one English family, the family's daughter, who spoke Dutch, whispered to her father to stay silent and still. Opening the door, she calmly addressed the men before her in High Dutch. "Well gentlemen," she said, "what can I do for you?" One of the ZARPs told her that an English prisoner had escaped, and they had reason to believe that he was hiding in her house. "So in the name of the State," he barked, "we demand an entrance." After turning to her father to explain to him in English what was about to happen, she opened the door wider and said, "Follow me gentlemen." The ZARPs searched every inch of the house, thrusting their swords through nightgowns, stripping beds, emptying drawers, pushing aside bookcases to peer into their shadows and climbing into the attic, from which they emerged, to the girl's delight, covered in dust. There was no indication that Churchill was or had ever been in the house, or in any of the houses in Pretoria, but still the search continued.

Although many Pretorians suffered in the wake of Churchill's escape, some even forced out of the Transvaal, no one endured more suspicion and hostility than the man to whom Churchill's letter had been addressed: Louis de Souza. Already considered highly suspect as a Catholic and the husband of a woman with English parents, de Souza was an easy and immediate target for the Boers' fury. As soon as Hans Malan, the loathed ZARP who was President Kruger's grandson, read Churchill's letter, he flew into a rage, accusing de Souza of aiding Churchill in his escape. Although de Souza angrily denied the accusations and did all he could to help in the investigation, the rumor, prompted by Malan, quickly spread. Finally, de Souza was forced to defend his honor before the president himself. "Louis had an awful row with Monsieur le P[resident]," Marie wrote in her diary that night. "Louis made up his mind to send in his resignation but he thought they might perhaps say he was a coward."

It was Churchill, however, that the Boers wanted to demean. It would not be enough to recapture him. They were intent on humiliating him in the process. Rumors quickly spread that he had escaped by dressing as a woman. A wanted poster was printed that not only offered a reward for his capture, "dead or alive," but described him in the most unflattering terms the Boers could think up. Beyond just giving a basic description of Churchill, his height, complexion, hair color, the poster included details that were clearly calculated to humiliate the arrogant young Briton. Churchill had a "stooping gait," the poster read, "almost invisible moustache, speaks through his nose, cannot give full expression to the letter 's,' and does not know a word of Dutch." An earlier description, in a telegram sent by the commandant general's department the day after the escape, had also mentioned that Churchill "occasionally makes a rattling noise in his throat."

Finally, in a desperate attempt to protect its fiercely guarded reputation and stem the potential damage, the Transvaal government claimed that, before Churchill's escape, it had planned to let him go. Although for weeks everyone from Reitz to Joubert had adamantly denied Churchill's constant requests for release, ordering instead that he be closely guarded until the end of the war, after his escape Joubert suddenly produced a letter that gave Churchill his freedom. Claiming that he had known nothing of the correspondent before seeing the glowing accounts of his defense of the armored train in the newspapers, Joubert shrugged and said that if Churchill denied these accounts, he would have to take his word for it. "If I accept his word, then my objections to his release cease," he wrote. "I have no further objections to his being set free." The letter was carefully dated December 12, the very day Churchill had climbed over the fence of the Staats Model School, and released the following day. "It is certainly an odd coincidence," Churchill would later write, "that this order should only have been given publicity *after* I had escaped."

--➤--

While Pretoria seethed with fury and frustration and launched a sprawling manhunt for Winston Churchill, hundreds of miles to the south, in the thick of the war, Louis Botha was doing what the British Empire had thought impossible: winning. Standing on Hlangwane Hill, a five-hundred-foot-high, scrub-covered kopje on the outskirts of Colenso, halfway between Estcourt and Ladysmith, Botha was planning a new battle. For the British, it would be the most devastating yet.

Even John Atkins, Churchill's friend and fellow journalist,

could feel the battle coming. He was in Frere, the little town where Churchill had been captured and where the British army had moved after Buller finally arrived at the front. They had twenty thousand men now, enough, Buller hoped, to finally free Ladysmith. Botha, however, had nearly as many, an arsenal that was the envy of Europe, and a string of victories behind him. Even Buller, who had as much experience fighting in South Africa as any man in the British army, did not know what to expect. "At Frere we are now spending a period of deep and peculiar calm, a calm significant because it is itself a symptom of the storm," Atkins had written just a week before Churchill's escape. "It is a period of preparation—the machine is being perfected—and it will end, if the Boers stay in their present position near Colenso, in one of the great battles, perhaps the greatest battle of the campaign."

As the British army, with Atkins in tow, had shifted its camp from Estcourt to Frere, warily moving north, they had passed the destruction that the Boers had left in their wake. Their enemy had used explosives to blow up the little iron railway bridge at Frere. "It is a beautiful job," Atkins had to admit. "The bridge has been lifted bodily from its masonry piers and lies in the river bed, the iron framework and girders contorted like a tangle of forest creepers." They had also destroyed the six-hundred-foot-long bridge that spanned the Tugela and led to Colenso, and that had cost £80,000 to build.

Colenso itself was a disaster scene, with every house looted and vandalized, not, it seemed, to prevent those who lived in the largely English town from helping the enemy, but simply to punish them. "They pulled drawers out of chests and broke them; they ripped open mattresses and distributed the flock with amazing industry equally over the floors and stairs," Atkins wrote. "They burned photographs; they broke the glass of pictures and windows; they stuffed clocks upside down into flower-pots; and they pulled up flowers in the garden and threw them in at the windows."

No scenes of destruction, however, affected Atkins like the sight of the wreckage of the armored train. It lay just a mile north of the

Frere station, "a melancholy heap." Little had changed since the day
he and Amery had watched, shocked and sickened, as the engine
limped back to Estcourt alone, its broken cars and broken men left
in smoking, bloody heaps behind it. The car that had been knocked
over on its side, wedging the third car between it and the tender, was
now home to a military cobbler who had set up a small shop within
its shattered interior. The first car that had been knocked off the
rails when it plowed into the boulders still lay on its back, its wheels
in the air like the stiff legs of a dead animal. All the cars, whether
on the tracks or off, were riddled with huge holes from the Boer
shells that had ripped through them—"clean as a whistle where the
shells came in," Atkins wrote, "and jagged and gaping where they
passed out." Next to the wreckage lay a small mound, the grave that
had been dug by the Boers for the British soldiers who had died in
the attack. Men from Buller's Border Regiment had since added a
stone border and a tombstone upon which they had carved the words
"Here lieth the remains of those who were killed in the armoured
train on Nov. 15th, 1899."

In the month that had passed since the Boers had buried those
men and imprisoned Churchill, Botha had never stopped fighting.
In that time, he had won not just battles but the respect and loyalty
of his men. For most Boer generals, it was a daily struggle to persuade the fiercely independent burghers to follow orders, or even to
stay with their regiment rather than simply riding off on their own
horses, returning by the hundreds to their families and farms. For
Botha, they stayed. Although, at thirty-seven years of age, he seemed
to most Boers to be extraordinarily, even ridiculously, young to be
leading a regiment, let alone the entire southern force, it was apparent to all who met him that he was a natural leader. His men, both
those he led and those he was supposed to follow, loved him. Jan
Smuts, the brilliant young Transvaal state attorney, wrote of Botha
that he had a natural sympathy that made it possible for him to "get
extremely close to others and to read their minds and divine their
characters with marvellous accuracy. It gave him an intuitive power
of understanding and appreciating men which was very rare."

Botha also had a quality that would have been extremely rare if not unheard of in a British general: genuine modesty. Everyone, regardless of rank, achievement or, certainly, social standing, was welcome in his tent. It was the simplest sort of tent. He had found it at Penn Symons's camp at Dundee, and it held little more than a packing case and a single chair. Botha himself rarely sat in the chair, insisting on giving it to any elderly burgher who visited him and quietly taking a seat for himself on the ground.

Botha knew that in the coming months he would need all the goodwill his strength and humility had engendered. In fact, even he was struggling to hold his men at the Tugela River as Buller marched toward them with sixteen battalions of infantry, the largest force the British army had sent into battle in fifty years. On December 13, the day after Churchill's escape, they had retreated from Hlangwane Hill, which was central to their defense. Telegraphing Pretoria for advice, Botha had received in reply only religious fervor and dire warnings from Kruger. "God will fight for you," the president promised his young general. "So give up position under no circumstances . . . dead or alive." The next morning, Kruger sent a second telegram, again urging Botha and his men to hold fast. "Understand please, if you give up position there, you give up the whole land to the enemy," he wrote. "Fight in the name of the Lord. . . . Fear not the enemy but fear God."

That night, with just eight hundred men, Botha reoccupied Hlangwane Hill. His force was waiting there now, watching in tense silence for Buller's khaki army to appear below them. Buller knew they were there, the only real obstacle in his path. "Only this we know, that at the end of this calm we advance to relieve Ladysmith," Atkins wrote. "The Boers wait for us on the hills."

CHAPTER 21

ALONE

As Botha looked to God for help in the coming clash of thousands of men at Colenso, Churchill was on his knees alone on the northern veld, praying that he would survive his solitary trial. When he looked up, the sun had begun to set. "The western clouds flushed into fire," he wrote. "The shadows of the hills stretched out across the valley."

Even for the Boers, whose idea of a good neighbor was one who lived at least a day's wagon ride away, Churchill was in the middle of nowhere. Since escaping from the Staats Model School, he had been following the Delagoa Bay Railway, the line that connected Pretoria with the Portuguese port of Delagoa Bay on the Indian Ocean and that had opened only four years earlier. If he had been able to sit down with a map, a pencil and a ruler, he could have drawn nearly a straight line, roughly following the 25° latitude, between Pretoria and Lourenço Marques, the capital of Portuguese East Africa. Even after riding for hours on a train, however, Churchill was less than a third of the way there. He had jumped off in an area called Witbank, a small farming and mining community that was about seventy miles east of Pretoria, but still more than two hundred miles west of Lourenço Marques.

As Churchill cautiously stepped out of the grove in which he had been hiding, he could see for some distance in every direction. Not that there was much to see. A small town lay perhaps three miles to the west, its tin roofs catching the last of the fading light. A rough Boer wagon trundled heavily across the landscape in the direction of the town. In between were a few farms, scattered here and there and marked by their own groupings of trees, which, Churchill wrote, helped to "relieve the monotony of the undulating ground."

At the bottom of the hill, apart from the town, lay a kraal. Adopted by the Boers from the Portuguese word *curral,* a cognate of the Spanish, and later English, word "corral," the African kraal was a circular livestock enclosure or rural village surrounded by a mud wall or a fence, often made of thornbush branches. Churchill could see the people of the village, tiny figures in the distance, rounding up their cows and goats as they headed home for the night. Occasionally, the wind would catch part of a word or a cry and carry it up to him, but it quickly faded, leaving him as isolated and alone as before.

Churchill carefully watched the people in the kraal, regarding anyone, Boer or African, as a potential danger. Most of his attention, however, was consumed by the railway track that cut through the little tableau stretched out below him. Throughout the day, he had eagerly counted the trains as they passed, four heading east and four west. If that many trains ran during the day, he told himself, the same number would likely operate at night. He planned to be on one of them before sunrise.

Having waited to leave his hiding place until the sun had fully set and it was "quite dark," Churchill finally began to make his way down the hill and toward the tracks. Nightfall had itself been a mercy because it meant he could finally venture out to find water. Ravaged by thirst after the long, hot day, he found a stream that, even years later, he would remember as running with "cold, sweet water" and stopped to drink deeply before continuing on.

Churchill was headed not for the valley, where the trains ran straight and swift, but for the summit of a nearby hill. The night before, he had noticed that not far from his promontory the tracks ran up this steep gradient. Here, the trains, especially the long, heavy freight trains such as the one he had hidden on the night before, inched up the hill like oxen straining against a heavy yoke. "Sometimes," he noted with satisfaction, "they were hardly going at a foot's pace." It would certainly be far easier to hop on a train car as it struggled up a hill than it had been to lunge at one while the engine rushed straight at him with mounting speed.

The plan came together quickly in Churchill's mind. "I saw myself leaving the train again before dawn, having been carried forward another sixty or seventy miles during the night," he wrote. "That would be scarcely one hundred and fifty miles from the frontier." After that, he'd catch another train, and another, as many as it took to deliver himself safely and triumphantly into Portuguese territory. "Where was the flaw?" he thought. "I could not see it."

Reaching the top of the hill, Churchill found a small bush near a curve in the track and sat down behind it. The bush would have to do as a hiding place while he waited, and the curve, he hoped, would shield him from the eyes of the engine driver when he leaped. "I could board some truck on the convex side of the train," he wrote, "when both the engine and the guard's van were bent away." For the first time since he had awoken, afraid and depressed, on the speeding train, Churchill felt relatively optimistic. He even had a little food to carry him through, not much, but enough "to keep body and soul together at a pinch." There were several pieces of chocolate left, and one of his pockets was still bulging with the crumbling biscuit. It would not sustain him nearly as well as Haldane's meat lozenges, but at least he would not be forced to steal food and risk being captured in the process.

It seemed to be a perfect plan, and it was, but for one problem: No trains came. Churchill waited for an hour, his spirits and hope strong. Then a second hour passed with no vibrating tracks, no telltale steam whistle, no train. He could not understand it. Throughout the day, he had watched the trains steaming along this very line, and he had carefully kept track of their times. The last one had passed by six hours earlier. Something was wrong. Another two hours passed without a single train in sight. As the minutes ticked by, Churchill slowly turned from puzzled to desperate. "My plan began to crumble," he wrote, "and my hopes to ooze out of me."

➤➤

Finally, after sitting at the side of the railway tracks for four hours without a single train in sight, Churchill decided that he had no other choice. He would have to abandon his plan and walk. To remain on top of the hill, with nothing more than a bush to hide him when the sun rose, would be tantamount to surrender. His visions of traveling swiftly and securely, burrowed deep inside the snug car of a freight train, vanished.

As soon as he began his journey, Churchill realized that it was going to take even longer than he had imagined. Although the area was sparsely populated, there were occasional huts, kraals and even small towns, all of which he had to trace wide circles around. So brightly did a full moon illuminate the veld that it seemed as though it were the middle of the day, making it far too dangerous for him to follow the train tracks, or even to cross bridges, all of which were guarded by armed Boers, almost certainly sent there for no other reason than to search for Churchill. He crawled through high, wet grass, waded across rivers and splashed through bogs and swamps. Before long, he was soaking wet from the waist down and, as Haldane and Brockie had predicted, completely exhausted after spending the past month doing nothing more physically taxing than slouching in slow circles around the perimeter of the Staats Model School. He still had two hundred miles of enemy territory to cross, and he had no idea how he was going to do it on foot, alone and with nothing to eat.

Forcing himself to keep trudging forward, dodging huts and bridges, crossing rivers, Churchill finally saw a train station up ahead. It was as simple as the towns he had seen, nothing more than a platform surrounded by a handful of buildings and huts. On the sidings, however, were three trains, sitting perfectly still, clearly silenced for the night. As he stared at the trains, Churchill suddenly understood why he had waited for hours on top of the hill without seeing a single engine. After his escape had become known, the Boers had shut down rail service after sundown.

As the war intensified, even British trains would be forbidden to operate at night. A manual distributed by the Royal Engineers Institute declared that, with very few exceptions, "no trains are to run after 7 p.m. until daylight and until permission has been given . . . that traffic may be resumed." The hope was that the trains would be safer during the day than at night, even though the derailment of Churchill's armored train had been just one of dozens of attacks that had been carried out by the Boers in the full light of day.

As he stood looking at the trains, remembering the plan that earlier in the night had seemed to be so perfect, so infallible, Churchill was struck by the thought that although he was free, he was still far from master of his own fate. No matter how clever his plans, how "fine and sure," there was no guarantee that they would work. On the contrary, they were far more likely to fail. Too much was out of his hands. There were too many factors that he could not control, or even anticipate.

Even the trains before him, "motionless in the moonlight," held a legion of unanswerable questions. He had no idea where they were going, at what stations they would stop, or when they would be unloaded. He could choose one at random, climb into it and hide, waiting for it to carry him away, but he knew that if he did, he would be taking a tremendous risk. "Once I entered a wagon," he wrote, "my lot would be cast." He would have to gather as much information about the trains as he could before boarding one. Even this seemingly simple venture, however, held inestimable risks.

Crouching low, Churchill slipped into the station and wound his way between the trains. He was looking for labels, either on the freight cars themselves or on the goods they held, anything that would tell him where they were headed. As he was studying the markings on one of the trains, he suddenly heard voices, perilously near. He wasn't sure, but it sounded as if there were two African men, laughing, and a Boer arguing with someone, or perhaps giving orders. Whoever they were and whatever they were doing there, Churchill had heard enough. As quickly and quietly as he could, he left the station and slid back between the tall stalks of grass, no better off than he had been but at least still unseen.

"There was nothing for it but to plod on," he thought, "in an increasingly purposeless and hopeless manner." Not just the desperateness of his situation but the loneliness of it had begun to bear down on him. As he passed the small houses scattered across the veld, he looked longingly at their windows, glowing with warm, welcoming light. As much as he wished for help, comfort or even simple companionship, he knew that every sign of human habitation or industry he came across "meant only danger to me."

Even in this remote corner of the Transvaal, Churchill saw signs of human life all around him. In the distance shone the lights of what he guessed must be another train station, either Witbank or Middelburg. Some eight lights, lined up in a row on the wavering horizon, shone like bright, alien eyes. Then he saw something nearer, the softer light of fire. He could see two or three, glowing in the night. He could not tell how far away they were, but he was certain they were not coming from houses. Perhaps, he thought with a rush of hope, they might be the fires of another kraal.

Churchill knew that he would be taking a risk making any human contact, and he had gone to great lengths since his escape to avoid it. But if there was any safe place for him in the hundreds of miles that stretched between Pretoria and Portuguese East Africa, it was an African kraal. "I had heard," he recalled, that native Africans "hated the Boers and were friendly to the British." Although what Churchill had heard was true, it was not because the British had become Africans' champions or even their protectors. They were simply the lesser of two evils.

➻

More than half a century earlier, the British Empire had done one thing that had redeemed it in the eyes of the Africans, and vilified it in the eyes of the Boers: It had abolished slavery. This decision had ignited fury among the Boers and, just a year after the law was enacted in South Africa, prompted the Great Trek. The famous Scottish missionary and explorer David Livingstone had continually clashed with the Boers over slavery, spending much of his time in Africa fighting what he called the "open sore of the world." Randolph Churchill had openly criticized Boer treatment of native Africans, writing in his dispatches from the Transvaal that "the Boer does not recognize that the native is in any degree raised above the level of the lower animals. His undying hatred for the English arises mainly from the fact that the English persist in according at least in theory equal rights to the coloured population as are enjoyed by whites."

Nearly twenty years later, Lord Randolph's son had come to the same conclusion. Before reaching the Staats Model School, Churchill had had a long, spirited conversation with a Boer guard that had quickly turned into a debate about equal rights. The guard was openly disgusted by the rights Britain's law afforded its black citizens, and astonished that the British expected the Boers to do the same. "Brother! Equal! Ugh!" he had spat. "Free! Not a bit." Churchill believed he had finally gotten to the heart of what seemed to him to be the Boers' bewilderingly vehement opposition to British rule. "It is the abiding fear and hatred of the movement that seeks to place the native on a level with the white man," he wrote. "British government is associated in the Boer farmer's mind with violent social revolution. Black is to be proclaimed the same as white. The servant is to be raised against the master. . . . The dominant race is to be deprived of their superiority; nor is a tigress robbed of her cubs more furious than is the Boer at this prospect."

Despite the Boers' fierce determination to deny native Africans their freedom or, certainly, any rights under their laws, change had already begun to take place within the African community itself. Throughout the Transvaal, Africans, unwilling to wait to be freed by an Anglo-Saxon empire, which had motives of its own, or for the Boers to finally find their way to enlightenment and reason, had taken matters into their own hands. Among them, no man was more effective, or more striking for his shining intelligence, quiet courage and innate, unassailable dignity, than Solomon Tshekisho Plaatje.

Although he was only twenty-three years old at the outset of the Boer War, Plaatje was already as well known among Boers as he was among Africans. Raised in a Lutheran mission, he had received only three years of formal education but had somehow managed to teach himself not just all of the major African vernaculars but also eight European languages, including Dutch, English and German. In fact, in any examination he took—from typing to a civil service test— Plaatje unfailingly received the top score, even though the other candidates were European and the tests given in their native languages.

When the Boer War began, Plaatje was sent to Mafeking to serve as a court interpreter. In this position, he interpreted the proceedings not just between Boers and Britons but for native defendants as well, who, for the first time, could actually understand the charges being leveled against them. During this time, Plaatje, whose childhood in a mission and his own striking achievement had shielded him from the harshest realities of native life, saw firsthand the brutal injustices native people endured under Boer rule. Having earned extra money by working as a typist and assistant for foreign correspondents, Plaatje began writing his own articles on native issues and, soon after, started his own newspaper, *Koranta ea Becoana,* the first paper written in both English and Setswana, the language of Plaatje's own tribe, the Barolong.

During the war, Plaatje believed that if he and his fellow Africans were to have any ally, it would have to be the British Empire, but he was under no illusions that even the British could be trusted. Although the Boers continued to think of native people as slaves or, at best, a pestilence on the land that God had given to them, the British were rarely much better. During the siege of Mafeking, two hundred miles north of Pretoria, Plaatje watched as the British army made sure that when the suffering began, the Africans were first in line. General Robert Baden-Powell, later founder of the Boy Scouts, drastically cut African rations in an attempt to spare not just his own men but any white civilians trapped in the town with them. His plan was to starve the native population until they were forced to break out of the besieged city in search of food, thus reducing the number of mouths to feed.

Plaatje witnessed Baden-Powell's cruelty to the town's black inhabitants firsthand. At one point, he watched as a gaunt group of nearly a thousand people, who had been living for weeks on little more than porridge made from oat husks, hungrily devoured a slaughtered horse. "It looked like meat with nothing unusual about it," Plaatje wrote, "but when they went to the slaughter-pole for the third time and found that there was no more meat left and brought the heads and feet, I was moved to see their long ears and bold heads, and those were the things the people are to feed on. The recipients, however, were all very pleased to get these heads and ate them nearly raw."

Despite the fact that the British were losing the war and treated Africans only marginally better than did the Boers, from tribe to tribe, native Africans had made it clear that should they be forced to choose a side, it would be England. It was a situation that made the Boers, who knew that they were not only greatly outnumbered but deeply hated by the Africans, increasingly nervous. "The attitude of the natives causes some uneasiness [among the Boers]," the journalist George Warrington Steevens had written before the war even began. "Every Basuto . . . has returned to his tribe, one saying, 'Be sure we shall not harm our mother the Queen.'"

→→

As Churchill stood alone on the veld, the fires seemingly within easy reach, he wondered if he might find help in an African kraal, if nowhere else. Knowing the native Africans' hatred of the Boers, he thought it was at least unlikely that they would arrest him and turn him over to their common enemy. He wouldn't ask for much. In fact, without Brockie there to translate, he wouldn't be able to. Thinking

question, or any other. When he had been sitting on the veld, agonizing over whether he should reveal himself or remain hidden, he had never really considered what he would say if he were to find himself in exactly this situation. To his own astonishment, however, a fully formed story slid easily off his tongue.

"I am a burgher," Churchill told the man. "I have had an accident." From there, the tale seemed to take on a life of its own, expanding and becoming more detailed, and no doubt less believable, as he spoke. "I was going to join my commando at Komati Poort [the last train station in the Transvaal]," he continued. "I have fallen off the train. We were skylarking. I have been unconscious for hours. I think I have dislocated my shoulder."

Churchill could not help but marvel at his own ability to spin a story out of whole cloth. "It is astonishing how one thinks of these things," he later wrote. "This story leapt out as if I had learnt it by heart. Yet I had not the slightest idea what I was going to say or what the next sentence would be." He had even managed to weave into the story a reference to the injured shoulder that he really did have, although he had dislocated it years earlier, on a different continent.

What Churchill most wanted was simply an opportunity to talk to this man quietly, in the privacy of his home. If he could only persuade him to invite him inside, he thought, he might have a chance to win him over. Out here, in the night, within hearing distance of curious neighbors, the man was more likely to turn him away, or perhaps even sound the alarm.

After a moment's pause while he carefully scrutinized Churchill, the man finally said, "Well, come in." Moving deeper into shadow as he walked back along the hallway, he came to a door on one side and opened it, silently motioning with his hand for Churchill to enter. As Churchill stepped into the room, he wondered what would happen to him. Would this place be his salvation, or his prison?

The first thing Churchill saw when he walked through the door was a large table standing in the middle of the room. He walked to the far side of it and watched as the man struck a match and lit a lamp, producing a dim, wavering light that revealed more of the small room. It seemed to Churchill that it must serve as both an office and a dining room. Besides the table, there was a rolltop desk, a few chairs and an oddly shaped device—a vertical stack of two glass globes covered with wire netting—which he guessed must be used for making soda water. There was one object in the room, however, that consumed his attention. When he had stepped in behind Churchill, the man had set a revolver on top of the table. Churchill now realized that he must have been carrying it all along.

With the gun lying on the table in front of him, the man sat down and, finally breaking the silence, said, "I think I'd like to know a little more about this railway accident of yours." Churchill immediately understood that he had no hope of fooling this man, whoever he was. He had not given his story a moment's thought before blurting it out, and he knew that if he tried to spin it any further, it would quickly come unraveled. It would also be impossible to hide the fact that although he had said he was a burgher, he could not speak a word of either Afrikaans or Dutch.

There was nowhere left to turn. "I think," Churchill finally said, "I had better tell you the truth." "I think you had," the man replied.

As soon as he made the decision to confide in this perfect stranger, Churchill held nothing back. "I am Winston Churchill, War Correspondent of the *Morning Post,*" he said, in a rush of confession. "I escaped last night from Pretoria. I am making my way to the frontier. I have plenty of money. Will you help me?" Another long, tension-filled moment passed while the man stared at Churchill, saying nothing. Finally, he pushed out his chair, stood up slowly, turned and locked the door. It was an act, Churchill wrote, that "struck me as unpromising."

Turning back around to face Churchill, the man took a few steps toward him. To Churchill's surprise, however, instead of reaching for the gun that still lay on the table, he abruptly thrust out his empty hand. "Thank God you have come here!" he said as he clasped Churchill's hand in his. "It is the only house for twenty miles where you would not have been handed over. But we are all British here, and we will see you through."

→→

By an incredible stroke of luck, Churchill had stumbled upon one of the few places in the 110,000 square miles of the Transvaal where it was still possible to find an Englishman. Since the proclamation ordering British subjects to leave the country had been passed nearly two months earlier, thousands of men, most of whom worked in mines, had been forced to leave their homes and lives in South Africa. Bracing themselves for the long journey, they had made their way in droves to Cape Colony, from where they had set sail for England. "They had been turned out of work, packed in cattle-trucks, and had come down in sun by day and icy wind by night, empty-bellied, to pack off home again," George Warrington Steevens had written. "Faster than the ship-loads could steam out the train-loads steamed in."

It was not just the men working in the mines who had been forced to leave but those who owned the mines as well. They too had wandered, shocked and angry, through the streets of Cape Town, loudly, bitterly, and usually drunkenly, complaining to anyone who would listen. "They spoke now of intolerable grievance and hoarded revenge," Steevens wrote, "now of silent mines, rusting machinery, stolen gold."

As eager as the Boers were to rid themselves of the British, they knew that there was a price to pay for this forced mass exodus. They would not have a hope of winning the war if the largely British-run mines ground to a halt. Their concern, moreover, was less for the glittering gold and diamonds that had brought wave after wave of Englishmen to South Africa than for the black prehistoric remains of swamp and bog vegetation that lay hundreds of feet below the earth's surface.

Because most of the war was being played out in Natal—from Dundee to Ladysmith—the Boers were now forced to rely heavily on the collieries of the Transvaal. Witbank, the part of the Transvaal where Churchill had found himself after jumping from the train, had one of the richest coal deposits in South Africa, with seams that ran both thick and shallow, at a depth of just three hundred feet or less. In fact, so well known would the region become for its coal that more than a century later it would be renamed eMalahleni, Zulu for "place of coal."

The furnaces whose bright light Churchill had followed for miles across the veld belonged to the Transvaal and Delagoa Bay Colliery. Although it had only been operating for four years, having opened in anticipation of the completion of the railway that ran between Pretoria and Portuguese East Africa, it was already one of the most productive collieries in Witbank. Its owner, Julius Burlein, was German, but he had hired a British man to run the place. That man, John Howard, was now shaking hands with Winston Churchill.

→►→

So shocked was Churchill by Howard's warm offer of refuge that he felt a "spasm of relief" sweep over him. Not only was this man not going to shoot, or even arrest, him, he was going to help him. He was no longer alone. "I felt," Churchill would later write, "like a drowning man pulled out of the water."

After introducing himself to Churchill, Howard explained to him how he had managed to remain in the Transvaal when most Britons had been forced out. Not only was he uniquely skilled, capable of keeping the mine in perfect condition until the war had ended and it could again run at full capacity, but the Boers trusted him. Howard had lived in the Transvaal for many years. He spoke the language and had even become a naturalized citizen.

Howard's decision to become a burgher, however, could now have consequences that he had never anticipated. Because he had been born British, the Boers had excused him from fighting in the war, but if he were caught harboring a fugitive, he could not hope to be shown any leniency. He would be tried for treason, and, very likely, shot. By helping Churchill, Howard was not only risking his freedom, he was risking his life.

The threat to both their lives, moreover, was even closer than Churchill knew. The weary fugitive was not the first visitor Howard had had that day. Just hours before Churchill had knocked on the mine manager's door, a Boer field cornet had come looking for him. The Boers were scouring the veld, searching for an escaped prisoner, the man had said, and if Howard saw any sign of him, he was to report it immediately. "They have got the hue and cry out," Howard now told Churchill, "all along the line and all over the district."

Realizing the danger he was placing Howard in simply by being there, Churchill said that he would leave that night. If he could have "food, a pistol, a guide, and if possible a pony," he said, "I would make my own way to the sea." Howard would not hear of it. With the help of four other British citizens who had also been allowed to stay and work at the colliery—a secretary and an engineer as well as two Scottish miners—he would find a way to get Churchill out. "Never mind," he assured the exhausted young man before him. "We will fix it up somehow."

As determined as Howard was to help Churchill, he was not reckless. They would have to be extraordinarily careful, he warned. "Spies were everywhere." Even in this very house, two Dutch maids were sleeping. It had been a miracle that Churchill had not awakened them with his knock.

Having fallen into a reverie about the dangers they faced, Howard suddenly remembered that his guest had been on the run for two days. "But you are famishing," he said. Disappearing from the room as he called back to Churchill to use the whiskey bottle and soda water machine to make himself a drink, he soon reappeared with enough food to feed several men. As Churchill fell gratefully upon a cold leg of mutton, Howard left again, this time slipping out the back door.

Nearly an hour later, he returned with good news. "It's all right," he told Churchill. "I have seen the men, and they are all for it." The other Englishmen who worked at the colliery had also taken an oath to "observe strict neutrality" during the war, but they were not about to let that stop them from helping Winston Churchill. The most immediate problem was how to keep him hidden until they could come up with a plan. "We must put you down the pit tonight," Howard said, "and there you will have to stay till we can see how to get you out of the country."

→>

As soon as he finished his meal, Churchill found himself following Howard out of the house and across a small yard. The sun was just beginning to rise, and the world could not have looked more different to him than it had just a few hours earlier. "The message of the sunset is sadness," he would write years later. "The message of the dawn is hope."

For Churchill, hope now came in the form of a Transvaal colliery that lay deep in the heart of his enemy's land. As soon as he opened the door, he could see, looming above him in the pale pink light, the mine's processing plant, a roughly fifty-foot-tall, heavily weathered building with long, vertical windows. Rising over the roof was the large winding wheel that had been his first glimpse of the colliery when he had stepped out of the veld.

As he and Howard neared the mine, Churchill could see a rather round, short man waiting for them. Howard introduced him as Mr. Dewsnap, the mine engineer. To Churchill's astonishment, it turned out that Dan Dewsnap was not only British but from Oldham, the constituency that Churchill had lost in the parliamentary election. Although it seemed a lifetime ago, the election had taken place less than six months earlier, and even in South Africa Dewsnap had heard about it. Now, grasping Churchill's hand "in a grip of crushing vigour," he leaned in and whispered, "They'll all vote for you next time."

Together, the three men walked into the building and made their way toward a large, metal cage that would carry them down into the mine shaft. Stepping into the cage, which was wide enough to hold fifteen men, they could feel it sway slightly beneath them as their boots hit the barred floor. The door clanged shut, and "down we shot," Churchill wrote, "into the bowels of the earth."

The seam was only about ninety feet deep, but as the men descended the shaft, it looked as if they were entering not just a mine but the underworld. With each foot they dropped down, it became progressively darker, as if a cloak were being wound ever more tightly around the cage. By the time they reached the bottom, it was as black as night, but with no South African stars to guide them.

Although there were no stars in the shaft, there were lanterns. Churchill could see them now, swinging in the hands of two men, the Scottish miners—Joe McKenna and Joe McHenry—whom Howard had told him about. When the cage clattered to a halt, the two Scotsmen, each carrying a bulky bundle as well as a lantern, led the small party into the tunnel.

For his four guides, this dark, eerie world was as familiar as life aboveground. For Churchill, everything he saw or couldn't see, heard or couldn't hear, was strange and new. As he walked deeper into the mine, he found himself in a "pitchy labyrinth," he wrote, "with frequent turns, twists, and alterations of level." It was, however, surprisingly spacious. There was no need for the men to stoop as they walked through the tunnel because it was between eight and ten feet high. It was also wide enough to allow them to easily proceed two by two rather than being strung out single file.

Despite the roominess, it would have been extremely easy for Churchill to become lost. Not only was it pitch-black, but there was no way to distinguish between the narrow timber pillars that lined the tunnels and held up the roof, each one looking very much like the last. It was also almost completely silent. But for the sound of their footfalls, which echoed through the tunnels, Churchill could hear nothing but the faint drip of water and the rare, startling crash as a flake of shale fell and smashed to bits on the tunnel floor.

The floor itself was smooth and hard-packed under Churchill's feet, its natural bumps and divots beaten flat not by boots but by hooves. As the Boers found more coal and the tunnels had become longer, they had begun breeding ponies to haul their carts under-

ground. So essential had the ponies become that stables with feeding
and watering troughs had been built for them near the ventilation
shafts. The ponies, which were brought down by the same cage that
had just carried Churchill, lived in the tunnels for five and a half
days at a time, with just a day and a half aboveground.

With so many ponies, teams of men were needed to clean up
their droppings, and the men who worked in the mines had long
since ceased to notice the smell. To someone like Churchill, however,
who had never been in a coal mine, the stench would have been overwhelming, easily overpowering the mine's naturally damp, musty
scent.

By the time Churchill's guides finally stopped, he had no idea
where he was, and would not have been able to find his way back out
if his life depended on it, which they all hoped it would not. They
had come to a sort of chamber where the air was surprisingly fresh,
and it was noticeably cooler than it had been in the tunnel. The miners had decided he would be most comfortable in one of the pony
stables. Fortunately for Churchill, this one was newly built and as
yet unused. It would be his home until they could figure out what
to do next.

In the meantime, the men promised to keep him supplied with
everything he would need. The large bundles that McKenna and
McHenry had been carrying turned out to be a mattress and blankets. Howard had brought from the house a few candles, a bottle of
whiskey and a box of cigars, all of which he now handed to Churchill.
"There's no difficulty about these," he said. "I keep them under lock
and key." The problem would be the food, or, as Howard referred
to it, the *skoff*. There was plenty of it to go around, but its absence
would not go unnoticed. "The Dutch girl sees every mouthful I eat,"
Howard had told Churchill. "The cook will want to know what has
happened to her leg of mutton. I shall have to think it all out during
the night."

With that, and a warning to stay put, "whatever happens," the
men took their leave. Standing in the stable with his small pile of
supplies, Churchill watched as they walked away, his life having

taken another sudden and completely unexpected turn, his fate now resting in the hands of men he did not know but would have to trust. He could see their lanterns bobbing as they disappeared into the mazelike tunnel, leaving him alone in the "velvety darkness of the pit."

CHAPTER 23

AN INVISIBLE ENEMY

On December 15, scarcely twenty-four hours after Churchill had knocked on John Howard's door, John Black Atkins awoke before dawn in Colenso to the sound of men preparing for war. From his thin-walled tent, Atkins, the correspondent for the *Manchester Guardian*, could hear the coughing and tramping of horses, native drivers calling to their mules, and men quietly rallying each other for the day that lay ahead. "The camp was filled with a steady, continuous, sweeping noise, which resembled silence," Atkins wrote. "This was the morning of a battle."

As the men moved across the plain, adjusting their helmets and swinging their rifles over their shoulders, a pall of dust rose up around them. "The column at my tent door passed through [the dust] like men wading through a white level tide which reached the middle of men and the bellies of horses," Atkins wrote. Before them, the veld sloped gently toward the winding Tugela River. Although it was neither deep nor wide near Colenso, the river was more than three hundred miles long, running west to east before emptying into the Indian Ocean. It was the only thing separating Buller from the Boers and, beyond them, Ladysmith.

Rushing to catch up, Atkins found the infantry sitting on the plain, arranged in neat rows in the order of advance. In many ways, the young men before him were indistinguishable from his friend Winston Churchill—shining with youth, excitement, confidence and, in their own minds, immortality. "Chaffing and smoking," Atkins wrote, they propped "themselves up on their elbows to inquire when the 'fun' was going to begin."

→>

Across the river, a few hours earlier, a messenger had stepped into Louis Botha's small tent with news that the enemy was stirring. Within minutes, having given orders to put the laager on alert, the young Boer commander was standing on a ridge, field glass to his eye, scanning the opposite bank of the Tugela.

What Botha saw as the sun began to rise was a vast enemy army, some sixteen thousand men, laid out before him like a military pageant from a picture book. The northern side of the river, where the Boers were encamped, was broken and bulging with ravines, hills and, in the distance, the dark, looming Drakensberg Mountains. The southern side, however, was flat, open veld interrupted by only a few low, solitary hills. Stretched out over this plain, impossible to miss despite their khaki uniforms, was line after line of British soldiers and officers, forming a front that was two miles wide and a mile deep.

Although in the past week alone they had already lost two battles to an invisible and devastatingly effective enemy, the British army had continued to fight in line formation. Even Atkins marveled at the lines' uncompromising precision. "Each man [was] the appointed distance from his neighbour," he wrote, "and each row the appointed distance from the next." For the Boers, the sight was utterly bewildering, bearing no resemblance to their battles with the Zulu, from whom they had learned how to hide.

Mesmerized by the scene unfolding before them, the Boers watched as the most revered and reviled army in the world slowly advanced across the veld. Now more than three times larger than Botha's force, Buller's army seemed to be "sweeping on in majestic motion, like a resistless flood, over the resounding veldt," the Irish journalist Michael Davitt, who was traveling with the Boers, wrote. "It was war in all its spectacular glory, as seen from where the little force of warrior farmers and beardless boys behind the Tugela gazed with fascinated but fearless eyes."

Despite the impressive show of force, the Boers made no move to respond in kind, or even reveal themselves. Botha had made it clear that not a shot would be fired until he had given the signal—a single, reverberating blast from the howitzer that stood, sandbagged and ready, beside him. Until then, they would have to wait for the enemy to come to them.

Suddenly a low, rumbling sound rolled across the hills. It was coming not from the British field guns, which they could clearly see behind the lines of soldiers, but from within the Boers' own camp. A group of burghers, who had spent most of their lives fighting a formidable enemy, had begun to sing their morning hymn, an "invocation of Divine help" for the battle before them. Deep and stirring, it stole across the river and over the plains below like a heavy mist. It seemed to be an "echoing response to some chant of giants from mountain tops behind," Davitt wrote, "and then [it] died away, leaving a more deathlike stillness in the morning air."

→–

To gain a sweeping view of the coming battle, Buller had climbed to the top of Naval Gun Hill, a low, sloping promontory that was one of the few elevated spots on his side of the river, and was peering back at the Boers. As carefully as he scanned the northern stretches, however, he could see nothing. There was no sign of life, not a helmet, not a horse. "What a conspiracy of invisibility!" Atkins wrote.

As they had been throughout the war, the Boers now surrounding Colenso were as invisible as their enemy was conspicuous. Not only did they have the topographical advantage, but they knew instinctively how to fade away into the dusty landscape. Everything was camouflaged. They had dug their trenches in the long grass near the river, carefully scattering the excavated soil so that there were no obvious mounds. Unlike the British, whose twinkling lights had telegraphed their intentions across the Tugela well before the sun rose, the Boers had been strictly forbidden to make fires, or even smoke a cigarette, after the sun went down. They even used dummy gun barrels that were made of corrugated iron or tree trunks, propped on hilltops and pointed south so that the British would have no way of knowing where the gunfire was really coming from when the fighting began.

Not only did Buller not know where Botha and his men were, but he had done very little to find out. While Botha had scouts scattered across the veld, on both sides of the Tugela, reporting to him day and night on the enemy's movements, Buller, who did not even have a reliable map of the area, had shown little interest in reconnaissance. "Practically no attempt was made to find out anything about the river itself or what lay behind," Leo Amery, Churchill's old schoolmate from Harrow and the correspondent for the London *Times,* wrote, "though there were dozens of young officers who would have given a quarter's pay to be allowed to swim the Tugela at night and crawl over the Boer positions."

Buller did have a plan, but it was based on centuries-old military strategy rather than any understanding of the land, the river or the enemy. As Botha had expected, the British commander in chief had decided on a frontal attack. Led by General Henry Hildyard, it was to be supported by several flanking brigades, to the left and the right, overhead and behind. Although any British general would have thoroughly approved of the strategy, it had one devastating stumbling block: The highly decorated officers Buller was sending into battle had no idea where the enemy was. "Buller's plan of attack resembled the wild swings of a blindfolded pugilist in the general direction of his opponent," a later historian of the war would write. "Of the river in front of him and the burghers who guarded it, he had only the vaguest notion."

As the sun revealed the plains below, Buller could see that it was going to be an achingly beautiful day. There was not a cloud in the sky or a breath of wind sweeping across the veld. His men seemed to be moving not through an actual scene but through a painting of a perfect day. Most of them had left their greatcoats in the wagons that trundled slowly behind them, and, with their bandoliers slung over their shoulders and their ammunition pouches bouncing from their belt hooks, they marched at an easy pace, as though they had no cares in the world.

➤➤

While Buller's men were at ease, confident in their innate superiority and their commander's wisdom, Buller himself was tense as he watched them make their way toward the seemingly empty hills. After a week of devastating losses, he was still no closer to Ladysmith, and he knew that every move he made, every miscalculation, every slip of the tongue or sword, was being watched not only by the Boers and the British but by most of the Western world.

It was no secret to the British that few European countries were rooting for them to win the war. Although the governments of most of the great colonial powers were outwardly civil to England, hatred and resentment seethed just below the surface. The British Empire was the largest and most powerful in the world, and everyone was waiting for the Boers to expose even the slightest sign of vulnerability. With Black Week, they had gotten far more than they had hoped for. "The tidings of British reverses were received everywhere with a fierce clamour of exultation," Amery wrote. "The imminent dissolution of the British Empire, the pricking of the great bubble which had so long imposed upon the world by its appearance of solidity and strength, was everywhere proclaimed."

Other countries were motivated less by hatred for the British than by sympathy for the Boers. Although the president of the United States, William McKinley, had vowed to stay out of the war, many Americans saw in it glimpses of the American Revolution and their own struggle for freedom from British rule little more than a hundred years earlier. Even Theodore Roosevelt, then governor of New

York, could not take his eyes off South Africa. Writing to his friend Cecil Spring Rice, later British ambassador to the United States, he admitted that he had been "absorbed in interest in the Boer War."

Although both the British and the Boers would have liked to have American help, the national opinion that mattered to them most was Germany's. The Boers had not only acquired many of their weapons from Germany but openly and actively sought out the Germans' help just days before the first battle had begun. Dr. Willem Johannes Leyds, then state secretary of the Transvaal, had traveled to Berlin in mid-October to ask the German government to intervene in the war on the Boers' behalf. Although Kaiser Wilhelm II, son of Queen Victoria's oldest daughter, had refused the Boers' request, after watching the British lose battle after battle, he had sent his grandmother a personal message. "I cannot sit on the safety valve for ever," he warned her. "My people demand intervention. You must get a victory."

The nearer the British came to the Tugela, however, the further out of reach victory seemed to be. Standing near Buller on Naval Gun Hill, Atkins looked out over the battlefield, beyond the plain, and was stunned by what he saw on the other side. "Ridge upon ridge, top upon top, each one looking over the head of the one in front of it," he wrote. "Simply desperate!" He knew that the Boers were somewhere in there, thousands of them hidden in trenches and behind hills. The fact that he could not see them made them all the more terrifying.

->->-

With his columns mobilized and his plan in place, there was little for Buller to do but begin the battle, with or without a visible enemy. At 5:30 a.m., when they had come within three miles of the river, his men abruptly stopped. The field guns pulled up behind them and, with little fanfare, opened fire. Instantly, the hills across the Tugela erupted like a roaring volcano, alive with sprays of red dust, a column of gray smoke rising hundreds of feet into the air, and a greenish plume of lyddite, the explosive used in British shells. "The cry of the shell through the air; the upheaval of smoke and earth and dust," Atkins wrote. "These are the things that clamp your soul and will be the visions afterwards of wakeful nights."

If the British had believed that the fury and grandeur of their opening bombardment would bring out the Boers at last, they were mistaken. "No guns opened in reply," Amery wrote. "Not a sign showed whether the pall of smoke covered torn and mangled bodies or a bare, untenanted hump of earth and rocks." To Buller, the silence was inexplicable. He had used even more explosives than had been employed at Magersfontein, a battle that the Boers had won just four days earlier, but at the cost of hundreds of lives. How could Botha's men fail to respond? Perhaps, he thought, they had already fled.

On the plain below him, Buller's plan continued to unfold. Although he had several brigades in action, like long, splayed fingers reaching for the river, he quickly found himself training his field glasses, in horror, on just two. The first was led by Major General Arthur Fitzroy Hart, who had been ordered to force his way across a broad ford and move down the river's left bank. The second was led by none other than Colonel Charles Long, the man who, just a month earlier, had been censured for sending his armored train from Estcourt into the arms of the Boers.

Buller, who would later say in a court of inquiry that blame for the armored train disaster lay "entirely on Colonel Long," had given Long very clear orders in Colenso. Placed in charge of the artillery, he was to take five hundred men and eighteen guns and follow to the right of the frontal attack, keeping well away from the river. Anticipating very little action on the part of Long and his men, Buller assumed there would be even less risk.

Unfortunately, Long had a theory. He believed that the closer he could get to the enemy, the better. Atkins, who, along with Churchill, had sailed to South Africa with Long on the *Dunottar Castle,* had heard Long's theory firsthand, as had many others. "The only way to smash those beggars," the colonel had often been heard to say, "is to rush in at 'em."

Secure in his theory, and ignoring repeated requests from his infantry escort to wait for them to catch up, Long ordered his men to advance quickly across the plain, well beyond where Buller had told him to wait. When he was within seven hundred yards of the river, he called to his men to stop. Then, eager to put his theory to the test, he gave the order for attack.

As soon as Long issued his order, a single shot rang out from across the river. It was Botha's signal. Seconds later, although the British could still see no sign of the enemy, they no longer wondered whether they were there. So sudden and devastating was the firestorm of shells and bullets that descended on Long's brigade that it tore his men to pieces before they even understood what was happening. "Men and officers . . . seemed to melt down into the ground under some deadly sirocco," Atkins wrote, referring to the hurricane-force wind that blasts out of the Sahara. "They were bullets at close quarters, in the full strength of life, bullets that splashed and drummed and spattered."

Among the first wave of fallen was Long himself. Shot through the liver, he lay shouting orders and encouragement to his men over the roar of the fusillade. "Abandon be damned!" he cried when implored to fall back and leave the field guns behind. "We never abandon guns!" Even when he was being dragged to a ditch, already brimming with the wounded and dead, Long continued to cry out, as if in a delirium. "Ah my gunners!" he called. "My gunners are splendid! Look at them!"

→→

As soon as the attack began, an unusual collection of daring men without rifles or rank began to dart across the plain, dodging bullets as best they could. These men, dressed in wide-brimmed hats and simple, loose-fitting khaki uniforms, a white band with a red cross on it wrapped around their left arms, were known to Buller's troops as "body-snatchers," retrieving not just bodies from the battlefield but, they hoped, young men from the jaws of death. In all, there were about eight hundred of them in Colenso that day, and they were led by one man: a thirty-year-old Indian lawyer and civil rights activist by the name of Mohandas Karamchand Gandhi.

Gandhi had been living in South Africa for six years when the Boer War began, and had already begun to develop his ideas of non-violent resistance. He had come to Africa in a desperate attempt to save his floundering law career but had been stunned by the injustices and cruelties to which the Boers subjected Indians as well as native Africans. In fact, just two years earlier he had nearly been lynched by a mob of angry Boers for his efforts to actively recruit, organize and lead the Indian community.

When the war broke out, Gandhi felt strongly that, because he was demanding rights as a British citizen, it was his duty to defend the British Empire. Although his convictions would not allow him to fight, he had gathered together more than a thousand men to form a corps of stretcher bearers. When he had learned of Gandhi's efforts, Buller had not only approved, he had asked Gandhi's men to serve within the firing line. "General Buller sent the message that though we were not bound to take the risk," Gandhi later wrote in his autobiography, "Government would be thankful if we would do so and fetch the wounded from the field. We had no hesitation."

Now, rushing across the veld in the midst of Botha's devastating attack, Gandhi and his team of stretcher bearers had more wounded than they could carry. As Atkins watched them, along with the nurses and doctors who worked at their side, risking their own lives again and again, he marveled at their bravery. "Anywhere among the shell fire," he wrote, "you could see them kneeling and performing little quick operations that required deftness and steadiness of hand."

Those British soldiers who survived the Boer guns, at least long enough to be carried out of range, found as much horror in the hospital tent as they had on the battlefield. Atkins watched as they were rushed in by the hundreds, carried, pulled and dragged from every direction. "Men with waxen grey faces and clotted bandages swathed about them," he wrote, "men who smiled at their friends and instantly

changed the smile for a gripping spasm; men who were clinched
between life and death; men who had died on the way and were
now carried hurriedly and jerkily, since it no longer mattered; . . .
men who were mere limp, covered-up bundles, carried on stretchers
through which something dark oozed and dropped."

↠

As crushing and instantaneous as Long's defeat proved to be, it
was not the only disaster that day. At the same time that his brigade was being bombarded on the right, General Hart's was being
slaughtered on the left. Ordered to cross the Tugela, Hart made the
disastrous decision to march his men into a loop in the river. It was
a baffling mistake for Hart, who had been in the army for thirty-five
years and who certainly knew as well as any man that a salient, or
open end of a loop, was one of the most dangerous places to be on a
battlefield. "To march into a well-defended salient," a historian of the
war would later write, "is like putting your head into a noose."

The repercussions were as immediate as they were catastrophic.
It did not take long for Botha's men to realize that Hart's brigade
was trapped. The loop was only a thousand yards wide, and Hart
had four thousand men. There was no way out when the bullets and
shells came raining down on them. "Nothing could have saved them
from the flanking fires and the guns in front," Atkins wrote. "At last
the river bank was reached—reached by those who were left."

Even those who were able to stagger out of the loop alive found
that death was waiting for them at the river's edge. The ford that
they had expected to find was not there, having been flooded, as the
British would later learn, by the Boers, who had dammed the river.
The fleeing men's only hope was to try to swim across, but they were
weighed down by their heavy ammunition and weapons. Instead of
fighting to the death in a heroic battle, most of them, Atkins wrote,
"drowned like dogs."

↠

Watching this second, almost simultaneous tragedy unfold from Naval Gun Hill, Buller prepared to order a wholesale retreat. Little more than two hours had passed since he had sent his opening salvo across the river, and the battle was already lost.

If he was forced to admit defeat once again at the hands of the Boers, however, Buller was not willing to leave twelve field guns for the enemy on his way out. Despite Long's fevered cries that he would never abandon his guns, Buller could see them now, alone on the plain, surrounded only by items that had been dropped by the men as they ran or fell, and a group of terrified and apparently abandoned horses. As Atkins looked more closely at the horses, he realized that their riders had not left them behind but had dropped, dead, from their saddles and were now being dragged, still harnessed to their horses as they galloped in frenzied circles around the guns.

Climbing on his own horse, which he had brought from England on the *Dunottar Castle,* Buller left Naval Gun Hill and rode in the direction of the abandoned guns. As soon as he arrived, Botha's men, clearly recognizing the British commander in chief's entourage, redoubled their attack. "You oughtn't be here," Lieutenant David Ogilvy, who was in charge of the naval guns, gasped when he saw Buller. "I'm all right, my boy," Buller replied.

Shouting to his men, the shells and bullets pounding the ground so loudly that he could barely be heard above the din, Buller said, "Now, my lads, this is your last chance to save the guns; will any of you volunteer to fetch them?" A tense moment passed, and then one man stood up, a corporal, and with him six more. It was an incredible display of bravery, but it was not enough. There were twelve guns out there, and Buller needed more men if he was to have any hope of retrieving them.

Turning to his own staff, which had followed him from Naval Gun Hill, Buller now said, "Some of you go and help." Three men volunteered for the extraordinarily dangerous mission, among them Lieutenant Freddy Roberts, the only son of Lord Frederick Sleigh Roberts, a renowned combat leader and one of the most respected and admired men in the British army. Just twenty-seven years old,

Freddy Roberts was not known for the kind of military precision and sobersided devotion to his job that had made his father famous. He was handsome, lighthearted and charming, qualities that might not have impressed his commanders but that endeared him to his fellow officers and his men. As he set out on his horse toward the guns, Roberts looked back at the British lines, laughing as he swung his riding stick in circles, trying to persuade his horse to plunge into the barrage of bullets. "He was in the full exhilaration," Atkins wrote, "that is to say, of a man riding to hounds."

As they approached the guns, the men were quickly separated in the onslaught, which intensified as soon as the Boers realized what they were attempting to do. The devastation was immediate, leaving one man and twelve horses dead, with five men wounded. Freddy Roberts seemed to vanish in the tumult of beating hooves and drumming bullets, a broad smile on his face. By 3:00, the last of the men had retreated, and the sounds of war had been silenced. The men could hear the river again, rushing between the crumbling red banks that still separated the two armies. Even the birds were back, but while some brought relief from the horrors of battle, others only heightened it. "The aasvogels gathered in numbers," Atkins wrote, referring to the hook-beaked vultures, "wheeling overhead with an eye on the horrid banquet."

In the silence, with the full brunt of the South African sun now bearing down on the wounded and the dead, the men finally found Freddy Roberts. He was unconscious, but still alive. He had been shot three times, once in the stomach, and he was lying alone on the veld. His friends rushed out to him, dragged him to shelter, and used his coat to shade his head from the merciless sun. He would die two days later.

Even Buller himself had not been spared the Boers' bullets. While he had been standing with his men, watching the artillery fire, a bullet had grazed his side, severely bruising his ribs. When his staff doctor, a man whom Buller loved and would watch die just minutes later, asked if there was anything he could do for him, Buller had assured him that he was fine and that the bullet had "only just taken his wind a bit." When Atkins saw Buller return to camp, he did not know that he had been injured, because Buller had refused to tell anyone, but he was struck by the sight of him, climbing "limply and wearily from his horse like an old, old man."

Across the river, Louis Botha quietly made his way out of the hills toward the town of Colenso. Here, he sent President Kruger a wire with news of his triumph. "The God of our fathers has to-day granted us a brilliant victory," he wrote. "We repulsed the enemy on every side, and from three different points. . . . The enemy's loss must have been terrible. Their dead are lying upon each other." Before signing off, Botha asked that a national day of prayer be proclaimed, as a sign of gratitude to "Him who gave us this victory." Two days later, a Sunday, the day Freddy Roberts would die, a day of prayer was observed throughout the Transvaal.

CHAPTER 24

THE LIGHT OF HOPE

When news of the Battle of Colenso reached Cape Town, its governor, Sir Alfred Milner, was in the middle of hosting a luncheon party at Government House. He was "in tremendous form," Leo Amery, who attended the luncheon, later wrote, "making light of our reverses and keeping up every body's spirits." In private, however, Milner, who had pushed hard for war with the Boers and had scoffed at the idea that there was any danger of defeat, was distraught. Pulling Amery aside at the first opportunity, he led him into the library and told him what had happened at Colenso. "The gay mask dropped from his face as he told me that Buller had just blundered into a trap," Amery wrote, "and had not only lost heavily in men, but had abandoned his guns in the open and fallen back."

What neither Amery nor even Milner knew, however, was that Buller had not only lost the battle, he had, it seemed, lost hope. His cable to London in the aftermath of the fighting was as somber as Botha's had been triumphant. "I regret to report serious reverse," he wrote. Although the War Office was concerned by news of yet another loss, far more troubling than Buller's defeat was his obvious dejection. Not only had he given up just a few hours into the battle, but he had then urged General White, who was still trapped in Ladysmith with thirteen thousand men, to do the same.

"I tried Colenso yesterday but failed. The enemy is too strong for my force," Buller had cabled to White. "I suggest your firing away as much ammunition as you can, and making the best terms you can." Although White was outraged by Buller's suggestion that he surrender to the Boers and made it clear that he had no intention of doing so, Buller's seemingly complete collapse sent waves of panic through the War Office.

Buller's hopelessness was dangerously contagious. "Overwhelmed by the successive tidings of disaster," Amery wrote, "the War Office seemed almost inclined to acquiesce in Buller's despair." Instead, it decided to relieve him of his duties. A few days after the battle, Buller received a cipher telegram from London. He had been relegated to the British force in Natal and was being dismissed as commander in chief. The War Office had already selected his replacement: Lord Frederick Roberts.

Roberts could not have been more different from Buller. At sixty-seven years of age, he was still as fit as he had been more than thirty years earlier, when he won his Victoria Cross during the Indian Mutiny. While Buller gave the impression of a favorite uncle, Roberts had the steely manner that most Britons expected to see in their commander in chief. "I have never seen a man before with such extraordinary eyes," Ian Hamilton, acting adjutant general of the Natal Field Force, wrote of Roberts. "The face remains perfectly motionless, but the eyes convey the strongest emotions. Sometimes they blaze with anger, and you see hot yellow fire behind them. Then it is best to speak up straight and clear and make an end quickly."

Even Roberts, however, was powerless to undo the damage that had already been done or to save the lives that had already been lost, including that of his own son. When Buller received the cable from London informing him of his dismissal, he had already sent his own telegram to Roberts, bearing the devastating news of Freddy's death. "Your gallant son died today," it read simply. "Condolences, Buller." The secretary of state for war, Henry Lansdowne, was with Roberts when he was handed the telegram. "The blow was almost more than he could bear," Lansdowne later wrote, "and for a moment I thought he would break down, but he pulled himself together. I shall never forget the courage which he showed."

→→

If there was anything Britons knew how to do, it was to show courage in the face of tragedy. Black Week required a particularly stiff upper lip. Not only were they stunned by the number of young men already killed in the war, but they could not believe that it was possible for the British Empire to lose to anyone, let alone a small, isolated republic on a faraway continent. "It is impossible to describe the feeling of dismay with which the news of Sir Redvers Buller's defeat was received," one London correspondent wrote. "So much had been expected of him, and so much depended on his success, that it could scarcely be credited that he had failed disastrously."

In a desperate attempt to rebound from the shock of Black Week and to reassure themselves that theirs was still the greatest empire in the world, Britons put on a feverish display of patriotic pride. "Deep as was the gloom of that 'Black Week,' humiliating as was the sense of defeat and failure," Amery wrote, "one may wonder whether the thrill of a common sympathy and a common purpose throughout the whole length and breadth of the Empire may not have been worth more than many easily won victories." Shopwindows were plastered with posters depicting square-jawed generals and handsome young officers. Men and boys who were too old or too young to fight wore badges on their lapels with rallying cries of "Only one order, forward!" and "England expects every man to do his duty," or bracing assurances that "we hold a vaster Empire than has been." Parents bought their children books, comics, toy soldiers and even board games to teach them about the war. One game of skill, billed as "a new South African War game," came in a red box with drawings of a burgher and a soldier on the front and was named Boer or Briton— the question that was on everyone's mind.

Even Queen Victoria did her part. She not only knit eight khaki-wool scarves for "the best all-round men taking part in the South African campaign" but sent all her men in the field a gift for the New Year, and the new century. It was a small, rectangular gold-and-red-painted tin with a portrait of the queen stamped on the front, "South Africa 1900" printed in large letters to one side and a message from the queen herself—"I wish you a happy new year"—in her royal script below. Inside the tin, beneath two layers of stiff paper and bright foil, were six bars of chocolate, most of which had already melted by the time they reached her subjects on the blazingly hot veld, a world away from wintry England.

There would be more mouths for the queen to feed in South Africa in 1900 than there had been in 1899. As soon as news of the Battle of Colenso reached England, the British army was overwhelmed with men wanting to sign up to fight the Boers. "For this far-distant war, a war of the unseen foe and of the murderous ambuscade, there were so many volunteers that the authorities were embarrassed by their numbers and their pertinacity," Sir Arthur Conan Doyle wrote. "It was a stimulating sight to see those long queues of top-hatted, frock-coated young men who waited their turn for the orderly room with as much desperate anxiety as if hard fare, a veld bed, and Boer bullets were all that life had that was worth the holding."

As 1899 came to a dismal close, however, what England needed most was not patriotic posters, chocolate from the queen or even thousands of additional soldiers. What it needed was a hero. The Boers had theirs. After the Battle of Colenso, Botha had risen to fame seemingly overnight. Throughout the Transvaal, he had become a figure of national pride, the face of the war that the Boers wanted to present to the world. He was young, smart, handsome and brave, and he had done something dramatic, something that had galvanized his people and strengthened their will to keep fighting.

The British now realized to their dismay that they had no Botha. Buller, the great "steamroller" who was supposed to have effortlessly ended the war before Christmas, had been humiliated and dismissed from his duties after less than three months in South Africa. There had been more than enough heroic and heartrending deaths, dashing young men sacrificing their lives for their empire as they had been taught to do since childhood. But there were no thrilling success stories, no stunning feats of heroism, of jaw-dropping risk, that, instead of ending in tragedy or defeat, had actually worked.

→→

The only exception to the seemingly endless series of disasters that had befallen the British Empire since the beginning of the war was the escape of Winston Churchill. The story of his audacious flight from the Staats Model School had riveted both nations. He had reminded the world what it meant to be a Briton—resilient, resourceful and, even in the face of extreme danger, utterly unruffled. "I have no doubt that he knows what he is about and will turn up with an extra chapter of his book finished in a few days time," his editor, Oliver Borthwick, had assured Churchill's mother after his escape.

As confident as Borthwick had tried to sound when writing to Jennie, few people, whether in London or Pretoria, actually believed that Churchill would make it to safety. "Although Mr. Winston Churchill's escape was cleverly executed," a reporter for the *Manchester Courier* wrote, "there is but little chance of his being able to cross the border." More than that, they feared that when Churchill was caught, he would pay for his audacity and the humiliation he had caused the Boers not just with his freedom but with his life. "With reference to the escape from Pretoria of Mr. Winston Churchill," a London newspaper reported, "fears are expressed that he may be captured again before long and if so may probably be shot."

It was less than a week before Christmas, and it was difficult to imagine how the war could be going any worse. England had already suffered a series of defeats, a staggeringly long list of casualties, a disgraced and dispirited commander in chief and a hero who had disappeared into the veld. "We are on the eve of the saddest Christmas within the memory of man," one correspondent wrote. "The

Star of Bethlehem is the star of hope, the sign of redemption, and never more was the light of hope needed than in this dark day of our history."

→→

Thousands of miles away, ninety feet belowground in the mine shaft of the Transvaal and Delagoa Bay Colliery, Winston Churchill awoke in absolute darkness, darker than any night he had ever known. When he reached out a hand to search blindly for the candle that Howard had given him, he found that it was gone. He had no idea how long he had been sleeping or what time it was, and he could not find out because it was too dangerous to venture into the maze-like tunnels alone and without light of any kind.

When Churchill had fallen asleep the night before, settling onto the mattress that McKenna and McHenry, the two Scottish miners, had left with him, he had felt not just relieved but triumphant. "Life seemed bathed in rosy light," he wrote. "I saw myself once more rejoining the Army with a real exploit to my credit, and in that full enjoyment of freedom and keen pursuit of adventure dear to the heart of youth." Now, in the deep gloom of the mine, he realized that he was so dependent on the strangers he had met the night before that he could not even leave his bed. "I did not know what pitfalls these mining-galleries might contain," he wrote, "so I thought it better to lie quiet on my mattress and await developments."

Churchill lay there for hours, listening to the heavy silence of the mine and staring into its impenetrable blackness. Finally, he saw a faint glimmer of light, traveling toward him in the dark like an errant star. When it came close enough, he could see that it illuminated the friendly face of John Howard, holding a lantern and asking him why he had not lit his candle. When Churchill told him he could not find it, Howard asked, "Didn't you put it under the mattress?" "No," Churchill replied. "Then"—Howard shrugged—"the rats must have got it."

Churchill had not spent the night alone after all. Several years earlier, Howard had introduced into the mine a species of white rat that was, in Churchill's words, "an excellent scavenger." The rats had thrived in the dark recesses of the mine and had quickly added to their numbers until there were now swarms of them, clever, quick and able to make a living off anything they could find, including Churchill's candle.

Fortunately, Howard had brought with him half a dozen more candles along with a cooked chicken. The chicken, Howard told Churchill, sitting down to keep him company as he ate, had not been easy to get. The largely eaten leg of mutton had, as Howard had feared it would, aroused suspicion in his Dutch servant girls. To avoid further questioning, he had gone all the way to the house of an English doctor, twenty miles away, to get the chicken Churchill was now eating. If he had difficulty getting another chicken the next day, he would have to resort to taking double helpings, and stuffing them into a bag when the servants were out of eyesight.

Howard was not being overly cautious. Not only had the Boers not given up their search for Churchill, but knowing that Middelburg and Witbank were among the few places in the country where Britons were still living, they had narrowed in on the very region where Churchill was hiding. As in Pretoria, everyone of English origin was under suspicion. "He said inquiries were being made for me all over the district by the Boers," Churchill wrote. "The Pretoria Government was making a tremendous fuss about my escape." In fact, three thousand copies of Churchill's picture had been printed for distribution so that any Boer could recognize the fugitive instantly.

Although Howard assured Churchill that as long as he was in the mine, he was "absolutely safe," even this was not completely true. Howard knew that it was quite possible, even likely, that the Boers would search the mine, although if that happened, he had a plan. "Mac," he told Churchill, referring to one of the Scottish miners, Churchill did not know which one, "knows all the disused workings and places that no one else would dream of. There is one place here where the water actually touches the roof for a foot or two. If they searched the mine, Mac would dive under that with you into the workings cut off beyond the water. No one would ever think of looking there."

Even if the Boers didn't come rattling down the mine elevator, workers would be in and out all the time, their movements very difficult to anticipate or control. For this problem, Howard planned to rely less on the mine's hidden corners than his workers' own fears. He would tell them that the mine was haunted, perhaps even inhabited by a *Tokoloshe*. One of the most feared creatures in Zulu mythology, a *Tokoloshe* is a small, malevolent spirit believed to cause not only mischief wherever it goes but also physical harm, perhaps even death. A *Tokoloshe,* Howard hoped, would discourage his workers from wandering too deep into the mine, and keep their curiosity in check.

→-

The next morning, after a restless night spent fending off the rats as they tried to snatch his candles from beneath his pillow, Churchill was glad to see another lantern approaching, this time accompanied by the two Scottish miners, McKenna and McHenry. Would he "like to take a turn around the old workings and have a glimmer?" they asked Churchill. Eager to tour the mine, or do anything that would allow him to leave his, by now, filthy mattress for a few hours, Churchill quickly agreed, and they set off down the tunnel.

Mostly what they saw were rats. Fortunately, Churchill had "no horror of rats" and thought that the ones scurrying around the mine were "rather nice little beasts." He admired their sleek white fur and their dark eyes. His guides, however, assured him that if he could see the rats in natural light, he would find that their eyes were in fact bright pink. They were albinos, and so had even worse eyesight than most rats as well as a unique sensitivity to light, all of which made them, unlike Churchill, perfectly suited to life in the mine.

After more than an hour of touring what Churchill referred to as the "subterranean galleries," the three men ended up at the bottom of the shaft, two hundred feet below the surface. One of the Macs had told Churchill that, in some parts of the mine, there were disused shafts through which daylight was visible. As promised, when they reached the bottom, Churchill was able to stand beneath a shaft and peer up at the outside world. He stayed there for a quarter of an hour, surrounded by darkness as he gazed longingly at the "grey and faint . . . light of the sun and of the upper world," the world he had been forced to leave behind and to which he was so desperate to return.

CHAPTER 25

THE PLAN

For the next two days, the rats were Churchill's constant companions. Although they neither frightened nor disgusted him, he quickly tired of fending them off. "The patter of little feet and a perceptible sense of stir and scurry were continuous," he wrote. As long as he had a lit candle, they kept to the shadows, but as soon as he extinguished the flame and lay down to sleep, they rushed at him, trying to take anything he had. At one point, Churchill wrote, he was wrenched from his sleep when he felt a rat "actually galloping across me."

One of the few pleasures Churchill would allow himself were the cigars Howard had brought him. Even these proved to be potentially dangerous. This particular type of cigar was extremely fragrant, and one day a young mine worker smelled the smoke and followed it to where Churchill was hidden. It did not take him long to find the fugitive, the glowing end of his cigar lighting his pale face. The stories that Howard and the Scottish miners had planted among their crew, however, must have made an impression because as soon as he saw Churchill, the worker fled in terror. Word of the ghost in the mine quickly spread, and Churchill was left to himself. In fact, Howard later wrote, "for a long time afterwards we could not get any of the boys to move in that vicinity at all."

Although he did not yet know how he was going to smuggle Churchill out of the country, Howard had begun to worry about the young man's mental health. "I noticed that he was becoming nervy," Howard would later write, "this being probably due to his solitary confinement." As lonely as the days were, the nights were far worse. Churchill could hardly sleep because of the rats, which surrounded him, he told one of Howard's friends, playing "leap-frog [and] hide-and-seek," leaping and pouncing. They had to get him out of the mine, Howard finally decided, even if it was just for a few hours.

That night, Churchill was allowed to come to the surface for the first time since he had gone underground. Walking next to Howard along the veld, he had a full, unimpeded view of the stars, their light supernaturally bright in comparison to the pale, filtered sunlight he had seen from the bottom of the mine shaft. Churchill had "a fine stroll in the glorious fresh air and moonlight," but it was not enough. He couldn't bear the thought of going back down into the dark.

Taking pity on his young friend, Howard told Churchill that, although he would still need to remain carefully hidden, they would move him to a secure location aboveground. The Boers were still spread out across the region, searching for Churchill, but most of them believed that he had never left Pretoria. He was still hiding in the capital, they thought, doubtless in the house of an Englishman or, an object of even greater loathing, a British sympathizer.

Soon after, Howard made a small hideout for Churchill in a spare room at the back of his office, behind a barrier of packing cases. He gave him a key, and they agreed upon a secret knock. Unless he heard that knock, Churchill was to remain hidden, with the door always locked.

→»

Even though he was now out of the mine, the days passed slowly for Churchill, filled with fear that he would be found and frustration that he had so little control over his own fate. Although he had repeatedly tried to persuade Howard to give him a pony and a guide and let him set off on his own, Howard refused to listen, determined to help Churchill no matter what the risk. While Howard and his friends discarded plan after plan as too difficult or too dangerous, Churchill tried to tamp down his growing restlessness. Every night, he slipped outside to walk on the veld with Howard or one of his friends. Every day, he waited behind the packing cases, trying to forget even for a moment the desperation of his situation by losing himself in the pages of a book—a borrowed copy of Robert Louis Stevenson's *Kidnapped*.

For most of his life, Churchill had taken refuge in books. He had never liked school, finding it a grim, joyless struggle, and himself more often than not at the bottom of his class. He wasn't well liked by the other boys, and his parents had all but abandoned him, so he was left with few places to turn for solace and friendship. "The greatest pleasure I had in those days was reading," he later wrote. In particular, he loved poring over the pages of *Treasure Island*, which had been a rare gift from his father when he was only nine years old. "My teachers saw me at once backward and precocious," he wrote, "reading books beyond my years and yet at the bottom of the Form."

Churchill had again turned to books when he was a young officer in India, hoping that they might fill in what he perceived to be the gaps in his education. Every month, he asked his mother to send him more books, books on history, philosophy, economics and evolution. He read for four or five hours every day, everything from Plato's *Republic* to Aristotle's *Politics* to Schopenhauer, Malthus and Darwin. In history, he began with Edward Gibbon. "Someone had told me that my father had read Gibbon with delight; that he knew whole pages of it by heart, and that it had greatly affected his style of speech and writing," Churchill later recalled. "So without much more ado I set out upon the eight volumes of Dean Milman's edition of Gibbon's *Decline and Fall of the Roman Empire*."

Now, in Stevenson's *Kidnapped*, Churchill found something more than refuge or even knowledge. He found shared understanding. Although David Balfour, the hero of *Kidnapped*, was a fictional character, through him Stevenson expressed the same feelings of foreboding, powerlessness, even shame, with which Churchill was struggling as he sat alone in Howard's office. "Those thrilling pages . . . awakened sensations with which I was only too familiar," he wrote. "To be a fugitive, to be a hunted man, to be 'wanted,' is a mental experience by itself. The risks of the battlefield, the hazards of the bullet or the shell are one thing. Having the police after you is another. The need for concealment and deception breeds an actual sense of guilt very undermining to morale. . . . Feeling that at any moment the officers of the law may present themselves . . . gnawed the structure of self-confidence."

There were enough moments in his new hiding place alone to keep Churchill's nerves constantly on edge. One day, he heard what he thought was the secret knock that he and Howard had agreed upon. Slipping out from behind the packing cases, he put the key in the lock and opened the door. Instead of Howard standing before him, however, Churchill found the young man Howard had hired to do odd jobs. As he had stood outside the office, sweeping the floors, the man had either placed his broom against the door or let it fall, making a noise that, to Churchill's ears, had sounded like Howard's signal. When he saw Churchill standing at the open door, the man, as shocked as the mine worker had been, immediately fled, rushing to tell his bosses that a stranger was hiding in the office. As soon as Howard learned what had happened, he pulled the young man aside, promising him a new set of clothes if he would keep their secret. He agreed and, Howard later said, received his clothes in due course.

-+-

One morning while talking with Churchill, Howard suddenly had an idea. Although he, Dan Dewsnap and John Adams, the colliery's secretary, had spent the past few days discussing little else than how they were going to get Churchill out of the Transvaal, nothing they had suggested seemed plausible. Now, however, as he sat alone with Churchill, Howard remembered something: The man who ran the store at the mine, Charles Burnham, had a small busi-

ness on the side—buying wool for a German firm and shipping it to
the coast. At that moment, Burnham had several bales waiting to be
sent to Delagoa Bay, on the coast of Portuguese East Africa. There
was enough wool to fill seven large boxcars, and it seemed to Howard
that they should be able to hide Churchill inside one of them.

The more Howard thought about the idea, the more he liked
it. They could load the cars at the mine's railroad siding, packing
the bales so that a hole was left in the center of one of them, big
enough for Churchill to crawl inside and survive for the roughly sixteen hours it would take him to reach the border. They could tie a
tarpaulin over the top of each car after it had been loaded, so if the
train was stopped for inspection, it would be obvious that the fasten-
ings had not been tampered with since they were first secured.

The only thing left to do was talk to Burnham. Although the
shopkeeper had no idea that Winston Churchill was even hiding
at the colliery, Howard was confident that they could rely on him.
Burnham too was of English origin, although his family had been in
South Africa for several generations. In fact, his grandfather Jeremiah
Cullingworth had brought the first printing press to Durban, using
it to print the *Natal Mercury*, which he had helped to found in 1852.
Burnham was smart and resourceful, and he had never been one to
shy away from a little adventure.

As soon as he learned of the situation, Burnham immediately
agreed to help. After four tense days, constantly worrying about
keeping their secret guest hidden and fed, dodging questions from
curious employees, hoping against hope that the Boers would not
search the mine, the men finally had a plan. The only person who was
not thoroughly relieved by the sudden turn of events was Churchill
himself.

Although Churchill agreed that this was the best hope they had,
rather than alleviating his anxiety, Howard's plan had only heightened it. Since climbing over the fence of the Staats Model School,
Churchill had lived in constant fear of being recaptured. He had
been wet, cold and hungry. He had lain alone for hours in complete
darkness, fighting off swarms of rats. As miserable as he had been,

however, he had at least been free. Howard's plan placed that freedom in imminent peril. "I was more worried about this than almost
anything that had happened to me so far," Churchill would later
write. "When by extraordinary chance one has gained some great
advantage or prize and actually had it in one's possession . . . the idea
of losing it becomes almost insupportable."

Had the plan given Churchill some measure of control, he could
have borne the risk with far less fear. When he had been on his own
on the veld, hiding in copses and perching on train couplings, ready
to jump at the first sign of trouble, he had at least been master of
his own fate, if only to some small degree. As soon as he burrowed
into the wool bags like a frightened rabbit, he would be obliged to
rely on chance, or, worse, someone else's intelligence and cunning.
This state of affairs was far less appealing to him than the dangers
he would face if he were once again on his own. "The idea of having
to put myself in a position in which I should be perfectly helpless,"
he wrote, "without a move of any kind, absolutely at the caprice of a
searching party at the frontier, was profoundly harassing."

Churchill understood that his new friends had gone to great
trouble and risk on his behalf, and he could not repay their generosity by sneaking off as soon as the sun went down as he had in Pretoria. Knowing that he had no other options, however, did not make
his situation any easier. "I dreaded in every fibre the ordeal which
awaited me," he wrote, "and which I must impotently and passively
endure if I was to make good my escape from the enemy."

➤➤

A few days after Howard had explained his plan, Churchill was
sitting alone in the back office, struggling to read *Kidnapped* while
he agonized over the powerlessness of his situation, when he heard
the sound of gunshots. They were nearby, and they came one after
another, in a halting series of jarring blasts. The first thought that
raced through Churchill's mind was that the Boers had discovered
that he was hiding at the colliery, and Howard and his friends had

refused to give him up, engaging "in open rebellion in the heart of the enemy's country."

Having been repeatedly warned to stay in his hiding place no matter what happened outside his door, Churchill remained crouched behind the packing cases, listening desperately for another sound that would tell him his fate—more gunfire, a shout, the violent rattling of his doorknob. Instead, he heard voices, calm and measured, and then laughter. A few minutes later, there was again silence outside, and Churchill heard a key turn in the lock and his door slide open. Peering around the packing cases, he saw the pale face of John Howard.

Locking the door behind him, Howard walked quietly toward Churchill, a broad smile lighting up his face. "The Field Cornet has been here," he said. "No, he was not looking for you. He says they caught you at Waterval Boven yesterday." Despite the apparent innocence of the Boer's visit and his insistence that Churchill had already been captured, Howard had wanted him off the property as quickly as possible. The best way to do this, he had decided, was to challenge him to a rifle match, shooting at glass bottles, and let him win. "He won two pounds off me," Howard told Churchill with obvious pleasure, "and has gone away delighted."

Before leaving, Howard turned once more to Churchill and, as if it were little more than an afterthought, told him, "It's all fixed up for to-night." "What do I do?" Churchill asked, realizing that the moment he had been dreading had finally come. "Nothing," Howard replied. "You simply follow me when I come for you."

CHAPTER 26

THE RED AND THE BLUE

At 2:00 on the morning of December 19, the door to Churchill's hidden room opened once again. Churchill, already fully dressed and waiting, looked up to find Howard standing in the doorway. Without speaking, Howard motioned for him to follow, and the two men walked silently into the outer office that lay just beyond Churchill's hiding place and then out the door.

Stepping outside beneath a bright moon, Churchill could see the railroad siding in the distance, the cars already waiting on the tracks. Nearby, three men were walking in different directions across the veld. Although Churchill could not tell with any certainty from that distance, he believed that it was Dewsnap, McKenna and McHenry, the men who had shown him such kindness while he was hiding in the mine shaft. Along with them was a group of native workers, busy loading a gigantic bale of wool onto the last car.

Crossing the veld, which stretched low and green between the mine office and the siding, Churchill and Howard quickly reached the train. As he walked in front of Churchill along the tracks, Howard passed the first boxcar and crossed behind it, nonchalantly pointing to it with his left hand as he did. Understanding that this was his cue, Churchill scrambled onto the couplings. As soon as he had pulled himself up, he could see, between bulging bales of wool and the side of the car, a hole just big enough for him to crawl into. Beyond the opening was a tight tunnel running between bales and ending in the middle of the car. Slithering through the narrow space, Churchill came to a small hollow that his friends had made for him, just tall enough to sit up in and long enough to lie down. "In this," he wrote, "I took up my abode."

Outside, Charles Burnham, the shopkeeper in whose wool Churchill was now hiding, climbed into the guard's van, a small carriage attached to the back of the train. After agreeing to help Howard, Burnham had decided that not only would he turn a blind eye as Churchill crawled into one of his boxcars before it headed to Delagoa Bay, but he would ride with him to make sure that he actually made it there. The train would have to stop at several stations along the way, and Burnham knew that it would be inspected by armed guards. Someone would have to intervene.

As well as being prepared to help Churchill along the route, Burnham had tried to pave the way for him ahead of time. The best way to protect his stowaway, he had decided, was to ensure his swift journey. Toward that end, after applying for his travel permit, Burnham sat down with the local railway officials, making the case to them that this particular delivery was urgent. "I made representation to the railway people that it was essential to have it delivered at once," he would later explain, "as there was a likelihood of a fall in the market." The cost to him could be substantial, he said, urging them to help him avoid any unnecessary delays and, wherever possible, inspections.

Hours passed before Churchill even left the colliery. Crouching in his tight burrow, unable to see much of anything beyond the walls of his boxcar, he waited in silence for something to happen. Finally, thin rays of sunlight began to seep through the chinks in the walls and the cracks in the floorboards. Daylight had come, and with it the sound of an engine rumbling down the tracks. Soon after, Churchill could feel his car being bumped about as it was coupled to the colliery's engine.

There was another pause and then the distinctive, stomach-clenching sensation of movement as the train began to roll forward. Track by track, it slowly left the colliery behind. The mine began to recede in the distance, its winding wheel looming over the coal-blackened processing plant; Howard's office with its hidden back room, dark and empty now; and, standing in silence as they watched the train disappear, the men who had risked their lives to help Winston Churchill, a man they barely knew and would never see again.

→→

As he settled into his hiding place, Churchill looked around and began to examine the provisions his friends had smuggled into the boxcar. The first item he noticed was from Dan Dewsnap, the engineer from Oldham who had predicted his victory in the next election. Dewsnap had given Churchill the one thing he feared he might need on the final leg of his escape: a revolver. Although he was grateful for the gift, Churchill could not imagine that he would actually use it. "This was a moral support," he wrote, "though it was not easy to see in what way it could helpfully be applied to any problem I was likely to have to solve."

Along with the revolver, Churchill found enough food to sustain him for a journey that was twice as long. As well as two roast chickens, cooked by Burnham's mother, a loaf of bread and a melon, his friends had tucked into the car sliced meat, three bottles of tea and, from Howard, a bottle of whiskey. "Smokes were taboo," Howard later explained, worried that cigar smoke might give Churchill away on the train as it had in the mine shaft. Whiskey, however, could do little harm and might bolster his courage.

Howard had also given Churchill a compass. Although he was not going to be able to see where he was going, Churchill could at least keep track of the train's direction. He also happened to know every stop it would make on its way to the coast.

While at the Staats Model School, Churchill and Haldane had memorized every station along the Delagoa Bay Railway line. It had been an easy task for Churchill, who had always had a remark-able memory. When he was at Harrow, he had learned by heart twelve hundred lines of Macaulay's *Lays of Ancient Rome.* He could remember entire lectures if they interested him, and, decades after the Boer War, he would still be able to reel off the names of the Transvaal stations in order of appearance, beginning with Wit-bank and running west to east, from Middelburg to Bergendal, Belfast, Dalmanutha, Machadodorp, Waterval Boven, Waterval Onder, and on and on, all the way to the border town of Komati-poort.

When the train made its first stop at Witbank, the branch line Churchill had been riding on joined the main railway line. While he waited for his freight cars to be coupled to another train, Burnham saw one of the railway men approaching him. He knew it wasn't likely to be good news, and he was right. It would be impossible, the man told Burnham, to continue his journey that day. His trucks would have to wait by the siding until the following morning.

Burnham had expected to bribe a few men before he and Churchill reached their final destination, but he now realized that he would have to open his wallet before they had even left Wit-bank. Turning to the man, Burnham used "a little gentle persuasion" and then slipped him some cash—"a Christmas box," he would later say, "as it was near Christmastide." It worked. Soon after, the man returned, this time with much better news. "Look here, Burnham," he said, "I'll put your wool on the next train that passes through."

Burnham had no way of communicating with his stowaway with-out risking his discovery, so Churchill had to simply wait in silence, hoping that nothing had gone wrong as the boxcars sat idly in the Witbank station. Finally, after about an hour had passed, he felt his car being hooked to a train. Then, to his relief, he could tell that they were not only moving again but chugging along at what seemed to him to be a "superior and very satisfactory pace."

After a short delay at the next station, Middelburg, where Burn-ham was forced to bribe yet another railway man to keep his cars moving, they finally began to roll quickly through the countryside.

In his wool cocoon, Churchill was not missing anything he had not already seen countless times over the past three months. Mile after mile of flat veld, bordered by distant, jagged mountains, spooled out behind them.

As he was jostled around on the floor of the car, growing progressively more soot stained from the coal dust that coated everything, Churchill tried to distract himself from his fears by imagining his triumphant return to the larger world. In his mind, he painted "bright pictures of the pleasures of freedom, of the excitement of rejoining the army, of the triumph of a successful escape." Despite the satisfaction of imagining himself the hero of every scene, he could not forget the fact that his trial was far from over. No matter what he did, he could not rid himself of his "anxieties about the search at the frontier, an ordeal inevitable and constantly approaching."

Sometime between 6:00 and 7:00 that night, the train pulled into Waterval Onder. Stepping out of the guard's van, Burnham, who, like Churchill, had with him a bottle of whiskey, offered a drink to a Boer guard standing nearby. The man gratefully accepted, and Burnham, who had already been told once again that his boxcars would be detained, took the opportunity to ask his help. Could the guard hook his cars onto the next train that came into the station? Unfortunately, he couldn't, the man told Burnham, because he would not be traveling any farther that night. He would, however, introduce him to the man who was to relieve him. If Burnham happened to have another bottle of whiskey on hand, they should be able to sort things out to everyone's satisfaction.

Told that he had enough time to have dinner in a nearby hotel, Burnham took advantage of the chance to buy more whiskey for the new guard. To his amazement, as he sat down to his dinner, he overheard the hotel's proprietor talking about Winston Churchill. As Burnham listened, the man informed his astonished guests that not only was Churchill still on the run, but he had passed through their little town of Waterval Onder just two days earlier, disguised as a Catholic priest. Finishing his meal, Burnham happily watched as the hotelier's story was accepted and thus passed into the general circulation of the Boer rumor mill. "So long as it was believed," he wrote, "I had little fear of my charge being discovered or disturbed in his truck."

→→

It would have surprised both Burnham and the proprietor of the Waterval Onder hotel to know that, at that moment, Boer officials not only believed that Winston Churchill was no longer on the run, they thought he was in their possession, on his way back to Pretoria. Soon after Churchill had left the colliery that morning, Howard had boarded a train traveling in the opposite direction, getting on at Brugspruit, less than ten miles west of Witbank, with the intention of taking it all the way to Pretoria. When he had stepped into his train car, he had found to his surprise that among the other passengers was a British prisoner. Perhaps knowing that Howard was English, one of the men had excitedly explained to him that this was no ordinary prisoner of war. This man, he told Howard, was none other than Winston Churchill.

Saying nothing to clear up the mistake, Howard kept his thoughts to himself as the train rumbled on toward Pretoria. When they finally reached the Transvaal capital, he watched as a Boer official approached the train to take custody of the famous escapee. The Boers might have been humiliated by the escape of this insufferable young British aristocrat, but, they believed, his recapture would right that wrong, and restore their dignity in the eyes of the world.

Howard would never forget the look on the official's face when he "met the train at Pretoria Station expecting to receive his illustrious prisoner." For Howard, who had done little else but feed, protect and hide Churchill for the past five days, the coincidence of his being there to witness the moment when the Boers realized they had the wrong man could not have been more delicious. Although he knew that he would immediately be arrested if they had any idea that he had helped Churchill escape, it was all Howard could do to keep a straight face as he watched the farce play out. "I would have given much," he later wrote, "to have had a hearty laugh."

→→

As much as Churchill had already overcome, both Howard and Burnham knew that he was still far from free. Although Burnham had managed to befriend the new guard at Waterval Onder with his new bottle of whiskey, when the train pulled in to Kaapmuiden the next morning, less than fifty miles from the border, he was met with a sickening sight. As soon as he climbed out of the guard's van and began walking toward Churchill's boxcar, he saw to his horror that someone had already beaten him to it. Leaning against the side of the car, holding a rifle with a bandolier strapped across his chest, was a leathery old burgher.

Seized by fear that Churchill had already been discovered, Burnham tried his best to mask his apprehension as he approached the guard. Forcing himself to speak calmly and casually, he asked the man if he knew where he could get a cup of coffee. Staring at Burnham as if he had lost his mind, the guard said, "Why there it is," glancing at the coffee stall that was directly in front of them. "All right, Oom," Burnham replied, using the Afrikaans word for "uncle," a sign of respect among the Boers. Then, in the hope that he might lure him away from the boxcar, he asked the guard if he'd like to join him. To Burnham's relief, he accepted, and the two men walked together to the coffee shop, apparently in easy camaraderie. When the train was ready to depart, Burnham offered a quick apology and slipped away.

It was late in the afternoon by the time they reached Komatipoort, the station Churchill had been dreading more than any other. It was the last stop before Portuguese East Africa, and he knew that if the Boers were going to catch him anywhere, it would be here. Peering through a chink in the wall of his car, he surveyed the station. It was much larger than the others, and everywhere he looked, he could see people, trains, tracks and a bustle of activity. It was also much louder, the sounds of shouting voices and the bright, piercing whistle of steam engines filling the station. There was little Churchill could do but trust in Burnham and hide himself as best as he could. Moving to the center of the boxcar, he pulled a piece of sacking over the length of his body and lay perfectly still.

Quickly alighting from the train, Burnham immediately sought out the chief customs officer, a man named Morris. Unlike the other station officials along the route, Morris was not a stranger to Burnham. In fact, he had already discussed with him his concerns about getting his wool to the capital as quickly as possible. After Burnham reminded Morris of their conversation, the customs officer ordered his men not to search the shopkeepers' personal property. Burnham, however, was far from satisfied. It was not his own suitcase but his boxcars that he wanted the burghers to stay as far away from as possible. "I gave a very plausible excuse for that being kept intact," he wrote, "especially as I wanted to have it delivered at its destination with the minimum of delay." Finally, he asked Morris if he could talk to the stationmaster, perhaps use his influence to ensure that his wool would go through. Morris agreed, and although the rest of the train was carefully searched, Burnham's cars were left untouched.

While Burnham used every means at his disposal to avoid an inspection, Churchill lay alone under his sacking, as vulnerable and impotent as he had feared he would be. Time passed, the sun set, and still he waited in agonizing suspense. "It was tantalizing to be held so long in jeopardy after all these hundreds of miles had been accomplished," he wrote, "and I was now within a few hundred yards of the frontier."

As he waited for hours with no news, Churchill's fears only intensified. "Perhaps they were searching the train so thoroughly that there was consequently a great delay," he thought. "Alternatively, perhaps we were forgotten on the siding and would be left there for days or weeks." Desperate to peer out of his hiding place and have his fears dispelled or even confirmed—anything was better than not knowing—Churchill resisted the temptation with great effort and remained tucked away until he finally felt his car being coupled up and, at long last, resume its journey.

Although, relying on his knowledge of the railway line, the stations that he and Haldane had memorized, Churchill thought that he had finally crossed the border and was in Portuguese territory, he had no way of knowing for sure. After being on the run for days, constantly hiding and living in fear, he was filled with self-doubt. He worried that he had made a mistake, that he had somehow miscounted the stations and that the train had not yet left the Transvaal. "Perhaps there was still another station before the frontier," he thought. "Perhaps the search still impended."

It was not until the train reached the next station that Churchill's fears fell away. Putting his eye to a crack in the wall of his boxcar, he saw two things that made his heart leap: the distinctive uniform caps of the Portuguese officials, bobbing through the crowded station, and, written in large letters upon a wall, the words "Ressano Garcia," the first train station in Portuguese East Africa.

Churchill continued to crouch silently in his hiding place until the train had pulled out of the station. As soon as he was certain that no one could see or hear him, however, he forced his head out of the tarpaulin and felt the wind rushing through his hair as they rattled toward Lourenço Marques. Lifting Dewsnap's revolver into his hands, he suddenly realized that he did, after all, have a use for it. Pointing it into the air, he shot it again and again and again, literally screaming for joy. "I . . . sang and shouted and crowed at the top of my voice," he later wrote, "carried away by thankfulness and delight."

--->--

Even as he celebrated his escape from the Transvaal, Churchill knew that he was not yet out of his enemy's grasp. Until he stepped inside the doors of the British consulate in Lourenço Marques, he could still be recaptured. Boers flooded the streets of the Portuguese capital, and they would like nothing more than to haul the young fugitive all the way back to Pretoria on the next train out. What

Churchill did not know was that his situation was even more perilous now than it had been when he climbed into his wool-filled boxcar at the colliery. The man who had watched over him for two days
and had made it possible for him to make it this far without being
discovered was no longer aboard his train.

With a little help from his bribes and his whiskey, Burnham's
luck had held until they crossed the border, but it had run out in
Ressano Garcia. "The station master there," he would explain years
later to Churchill, "was the only one on the whole journey who was
proof against a bribe." When the man told Burnham that passengers
were not allowed to travel through Portuguese East Africa on freight
trains, and passenger trains could not carry goods, Burnham had
asked him to make an exception. "If I allowed you to do that," the
man replied, "I would be fined." Even after Burnham offered him
£20, more than any fine he might receive, he had remained stead-
fast. "All my pleadings and inducements were of no avail," Burnham wrote, "but he promised me faithfully that he would send the
trucks on by the next goods train, which was due to reach Lourenco
Marques at 4 p.m." Deeply worried about Churchill but unable to do
anything about it without exposing them both, Burnham was forced
to continue on to the capital alone.

When Burnham's train pulled into Lourenço Marques, he
quickly made his way to the section of the station where the goods
trains came in. Knowing that he risked arrest if he was found to be
loitering in this area, which was for staff only, he looked for someone who could be his eyes and ears. Inside the station, he found a
native worker and enlisted his help. Handing the man a half crown,
Burnham explained that a freight train would soon be arriving with
wool. If he saw a man emerge from one of the boxcars, he was to say
nothing to anyone, but quickly bring him to Burnham at the goods
gate. Promising the man another half crown if he did as he asked,
Burnham slipped back out into the yard and sat down among some
goods that had been heaped into teetering piles.

Soon after Burnham settled in, he saw a Portuguese soldier
approaching him. As he had feared, the man ordered Burnham to

follow him, intending to arrest him for loitering. Just as he was about
to be led out of the station, the native worker who was keeping an
eye out for Churchill saw what was happening and hurried over. A
heated argument in Portuguese, which Burnham could not understand, ensued. By the end of it, Burnham was released, but ordered
to leave the station immediately and not return.

Relieved that he had not been arrested, Burnham left, but he did
not go far. Standing just outside the goods gate, he kept a careful
watch until, at 4:00 p.m., as promised, he saw his own seven trucks
being shunted into the station yard. Knowing that if the soldier saw
him return, he would not have a hope of avoiding arrest, Burnham
quietly slipped back through the gate and quickly walked toward
the freight cars, weaving his way between them until he came to the
one that he knew was Churchill's.

The boxcar had barely stopped moving when Churchill leaped
from it, covered in coal dust and looking, Burnham thought, as
"black as a sweep." As he emerged from his "place of refuge and
of punishment," Churchill would later write, he felt "weary, dirty,
hungry, but free once more." He had somehow already managed to
discard his leftover food, and other waste, and had done his best to
rearrange the truck so that it wouldn't be obvious that someone had
been living in it for nearly three days. Walking up to Churchill,
Burnham muttered that he should follow him, and the two men
quickly left the train station, going out the same way Burnham had
just come in.

➤➤

As an Englishman living in the Transvaal, not far from Portuguese East Africa, Burnham understood the importance of Lourenço
Marques. A three-hundred-year-old seaside town, it had been named
for the Portuguese navigator who explored the region in the sixteenth
century. For much of its existence, the town had been poor and largely
forgotten, its narrow streets and grass huts little populated.

With the completion of the rail line to Pretoria, however, Lourenço Marques had transformed into a thriving metropolis, uniquely important not just to the Portuguese but, even more so, to the land-locked Boers. "As an outlet to the sea and as a haven for foreign ships bearing men, arms, and encouragement it was invaluable," the journalist Howard Hillegas had written at the beginning of the war. "Without it, the Boers would have been unable to hold any inter-course with foreign countries, no envoys could have been despatched, no volunteers could have entered the country, and they would have been ignorant of the opinion of the world."

As Churchill followed Burnham through the streets of Lou-renço Marques, he passed sign after sign of modern development and progress. The piers were crowded with tall, arching cranes and large landing sheds. There were hotels and warehouses, broad, tree-lined streets, electric streetlamps and thin, metal trolley tracks.

Since the beginning of the war, however, the city had been over-whelmed by refugees, coming in ever-growing waves of increasingly desperate British subjects. In his offices at the British consulate, in the heart of the city, the consul general, Alexander Carnegie Ross, was harried and exhausted, with no idea what to do with them all. "Without shelter, badly fed, crowded together," he had wired to the governor of Natal in mid-October. "Local Authorities impatient. Military called out to maintain order. Several collisions last night. Populace and police both injured."

As the war had progressed, the situation had only become worse. Now, instead of receiving help or even a sympathetic hearing from Natal, Cape Colony or the War Office in London, Ross had only been getting bad news. Another loss, another reverse, thousands dead, millions spent. Buller had been humiliated. Roberts had not yet even reached South African soil. No one seemed to know what to do, or how to stem the tide of disaster flowing out of the Transvaal.

The streets that Burnham and Churchill now navigated were crowded with Portuguese, Britons, Boers and Africans, a potent cock-tail of races, languages, prejudices and ambitions. As Churchill fol-lowed Burnham through this churning chaos, the two men did not exchange a single word or even acknowledge each other's existence.

With no idea where he was, Churchill turned tight corners, passed small houses, crossed street after street until, suddenly, Burnham stopped. Standing in silence, the older man gazed across the street, his eyes on the roof of a large building. It was white and two stories tall, with wide verandas on both the bottom and the top floors and an expansive lawn in front. It sat well away from the street, behind a metal fence, and, Churchill suddenly realized with a catch in his throat, flying from its roof were the bright red and blue colors of the Union Jack.

Crossing the street, Churchill passed through the gates, across the garden and up to the front door. Thin, exhausted, covered in soot from head to toe and with a crazed gleam of triumph in his eyes, he demanded to see the consul general. Ross's secretary, who had no idea who this filthy madman was, attempted to turn him away. "Be off," he said contemptuously to Churchill. "The Consul cannot see you to-day. Come to his office at nine to-morrow, if you want anything."

Instantly filled with outrage and fury, Churchill did not even acknowledge the fact that the secretary had spoken. Shouting at the top of his lungs, he simply repeated his demand, insisting that he see "the Consul personally at once." So great was his indignation and so loud his voice that it carried up to an open window on the second floor of the consulate. Wondering who could possibly be making such a racket, the consul general himself, his nerves already frayed, put his head out the window.

A moment later, the consul had descended the stairs, walked past his secretary, stepped up to the young man standing at his door and asked his name. It was one of the last times in a long life that anyone would ever again need to ask Winston Churchill that question.

EPILOGUE

As soon as Churchill was free, he wanted to fight. It wasn't enough
to have escaped from the Boers, he wanted to help win the war for
his country, and, if possible, a medal or two for himself. First, however, he had to get out of Lourenço Marques.

News of his arrival at the British consulate spread quickly, and
the consul general was rattled when, just hours after Churchill had
first appeared at his door, he looked outside during dinner to see
armed men gathering on his lawn. They were not, as Ross had feared,
Boers who had come to recapture Churchill. On the contrary, they
were Englishmen, there to make sure their new hero made it safely
into British territory. After Churchill had finished his dinner, the
men escorted him to the quay, marching along some of the same
streets through which he had followed Burnham, and watched pro-
tectively as he boarded a steamship for the British colony of Natal.

To Churchill's great surprise, an enormous, raucous welcoming
party awaited him in Durban, Natal's largest city, when he arrived
on Saturday, December 23. At first, he couldn't understand why the
harbor was so choked with boats, some anchored, others restlessly
circling while they waited to be pulled in, and the dock filled with
crowds of people. Everywhere he looked, there were cheering throngs

and waving flags, even a band was playing. "It was not until I stepped on shore," he wrote, "that I realised that I was myself the object of this honourable welcome." An admiral, a general and the mayor were all there to congratulate Churchill on his escape, but they were not allowed to keep him long. "I was nearly torn to pieces by enthusiastic kindness," Churchill wrote. "Whirled along on the shoulders of the crowd, I was carried to the steps of the town hall, where nothing would content them but a speech."

After "a becoming reluctance," Churchill agreed to address the crowd. Wearing a clean new suit, his hat doffed and his hands on his hips, he regarded the men and women before him. "I need not say how deeply grateful I am for the great kindness you have shown in your welcome to me," he said. "When I see this great demonstration, I regard it not only as a personal kindness to me, and as a demonstration of hospitality to a stranger [at which point he was interrupted by a shout of "You're not a stranger!"] but as a token of the unflinching and unswerving determination of this Colony to throw itself into the prosecution of the war." He spoke for only a few minutes, proclaiming that they were now "outside the region of words," and then he wound his way through the cheering crowd and set off, he later wrote, "in a blaze of triumph" for the front.

Before the sun had risen the next morning, Churchill had passed through Estcourt and, as daylight broke, stopped in Frere, the small town where he had been captured a month earlier. Stepping off the train, he made his way down the tracks and after some inquiries found that the tent that had been pitched for him sat on the exact same cutting where he had been forced to raise his hands in surrender. That night was Christmas Eve, and Churchill spent it celebrating "with many friends my good fortune."

Churchill had returned to the scene of his capture not to revel in his personal triumph but to meet with Sir Redvers Buller, who, after the disaster at Colenso, was trying once again to free Ladysmith. Since their journey to Cape Town together on the *Dunottar Castle,* Churchill had lost some of his early admiration for Buller. "I am doubtful," he wrote, "whether the fact that a man has gained the

Victoria Cross for bravery as a young officer fits him to command an army twenty or thirty years later." Buller, on the other hand, had been impressed by Churchill's act of daring, which had given his men a much-needed boost, and was more than willing to meet with him. "Winston Churchill turned up here yesterday escaped from Pretoria," he wrote to a friend. "He really is a fine fellow and I must say I admire him greatly. I wish he was leading regular troops instead of writing for a rotten paper."

Buller would quickly learn that Churchill actually wanted to do both—write for his paper and fight for his country. After asking the young correspondent to tell him everything he had witnessed in enemy territory during his escape, Buller finally asked the question Churchill had been waiting to hear. "You have done very well," he said. "Is there anything we can do for you?" Churchill was ready with his reply. He wanted a commission. The Boers had nearly killed him, imprisoned him and hunted him down. Now he wanted to fight back.

Clearly surprised by Churchill's request, Buller paused for a moment before asking, "What about poor old Borthwick?" Churchill knew that the general was referring to his editor at the *Morning Post*. He also knew that the War Office had a rule barring correspondents from being soldiers and soldiers from being correspondents. Churchill was particularly aware of this rule because it had been established primarily because of him. He had never shied away from openly criticizing military leaders, but he had been especially harsh in his assessment of Herbert Kitchener's conduct during the Sudan campaign a year earlier. "The victory at Omdurman was disgraced by the inhuman slaughter of the wounded," he had written to his mother at the time, "and Kitchener is responsible for this." It was after the release of Churchill's book *The River War* that the War Office finally put its foot down. No more soldier correspondents.

Churchill knew that by asking Buller to give him a commission, he was putting the general in an "awkward" position. "Here then was the new rule in all its inviolate sanctity," Churchill would later write, "and to make an exception to it on my account above all others—I who had been the chief cause of it—was a very hard proposition." Still, in very Churchillian fashion, he wanted both jobs, and he wasn't about to withdraw his request simply to spare Buller discomfort. Buller paced the room, circling it several times while he studied the impertinent young man before him. Finally, he made up his mind. "All right," he said. "You can have a commission. . . . You will have to do as much as you can for both jobs. But you will get no pay for ours." It was a deal.

->>-

As soon as Churchill had his commission, having been made a lieutenant in the South African Light Horse, he wasted no time in going straight to the heart of the conflict. A month later, he was fighting in, and writing about, one of the most infamous battles of the war: Spion Kop. Played out on a fourteen-hundred-foot rocky hilltop overlooking Ladysmith, the Battle of Spion Kop left nearly six hundred men dead and some fifteen hundred wounded. So great was the carnage that both sides were stunned as they called a temporary truce so that they could collect their dead. "The scenes on Spion Kop," Churchill admitted in a letter to Pamela Plowden, "were among the strangest and most terrible I have ever witnessed."

In fact, so horrific were the stories coming out of southern Africa that Pamela begged Churchill to come home. After news of his safe arrival in Lourenço Marques had reached her, she had telegraphed just three words to Churchill's mother: "Thank God—Pamela." Now, having endured his capture, his escape and his participation in one of the bloodiest battles of the war, in which a bullet had come so close to his head it severed the jaunty feather on his hat, she had had enough.

As much as he loved Pamela, Churchill was shocked that she would think for a moment that he would abandon the war. "I read with particular attention your letter advising and urging me to come home," he wrote to her. "But surely you would not imagine that it

would be possible for me to leave the scene of war. . . . I should for-
feit my self respect forever if I tried to shield myself like that behind
an easily obtained reputation for courage. . . . I am really enjoying
myself immensely and if I live I shall look back with much pleasure
upon all this."

It was certainly no accident that, for the remainder of his time in
South Africa, wherever there was an opportunity for an epic battle,
a heroic triumph or a great story, there was Churchill. Just a month
after the Battle of Spion Kop, he rode triumphantly into Ladysmith
at the head of the relief column. He would never forget watching
with a mixture of pity and exaltation as heartbreakingly thin, weak
men in tattered clothing raced through the streets, some laughing,
some crying, all cheering the relieving troops and the end of the devastating four-month siege. It was, Churchill would later write, "one
of the most happy memories of my life."

Not even being present at the relief of Ladysmith, however, could
compare with the day, three months later, when Pretoria fell to the
British. Early that morning, Churchill and his cousin Sunny, the 9th
Duke of Marlborough, rode as victors into the Transvaal capital. It
was the first time Churchill had been there since his escape from the
Staats Model School, and his first thoughts were for the men he had
left behind.

Churchill knew that not long after he had climbed the prison
fence, the Boers had moved their British captives to a new location.
After asking for directions, he and Sunny rode through the largely
abandoned streets, looking for the POW camp. Finally, they found
it: a long, low tin building encircled with a heavy wire fence.

Inside the prison, Charles Burnett, an officer in the Eighteenth
Hussars, was watching from a window. He and the other prisoners
had been in a frenzy of excitement for days, ever since they had first
heard guns booming just outside the Transvaal capital and witnessed
the panic that had gripped Pretoria, with stores looted and entire
families frantically fleeing the city. The guards, as furious as they
were frightened, had threatened to move the prisoners to yet another

location, but nothing had happened. Now, from his window, Burnett thought that he could see troops in the distance. Through a heavy morning mist, he could not be sure.

Suddenly out of the fog appeared not an army or even a regiment but just two men on horseback. "Then, and then only," Burnett wrote, "we knew that our deliverance was at hand." As soon as he saw the prison, Churchill raised his hat into the air and let out a loud cheer. Instantly, he heard it echoed within the prison walls. "Hats were flying in the air," Burnett wrote, "and we were all shouting and cheering like madmen." Moments later, although they were surrounded by fifty-two armed Boer guards and only two men had come to set them free, the prison gates sprang open, and 180 prisoners swept out the doors and into the yard, surrounding Churchill and Sunny in a cheering, shouting, crazed throng. "Some in flannels, hatless or coatless," Churchill wrote, "but all violently excited."

Surrendering to their inevitable fate, the Boer guards were quickly disarmed and forced inside the prison. The men they had once held hostage now carried the guards' rifles and wore their bandoliers, joyfully assuming the role of jailers to their former captors. Churchill's great pleasure at watching this transformation take place was marred only by the fact that Opperman, the warden who had been "too fat to go and fight" and had taken pleasure in making known his hatred of Englishmen, and Hans Malan, Kruger's malicious grandson, were already gone, having fled the city in terror of the advancing troops.

While the chaotic celebration unfolded, one of the POWs tore down the prison flag and hoisted in its place the Union Jack. It was a handmade version, secretly stitched together from a Transvaal flag found in a prison cupboard and kept carefully hidden. As he watched his own flag now waving over the Boer prison, Churchill carefully marked the moment. "Time: 8:47, June 5," he would remember many years later with perfect clarity. "Tableau!"

➼

Among the jubilant prisoners flocking around Churchill and Sunny in the prison yard, two were strikingly absent—Adam Brockie and Aylmer Haldane. Both men, along with one other prisoner, Lieutenant Frederick Le Mesurier of the Dublin Fusiliers, had escaped from the Staats Model School more than three months earlier. When they had been forced to come up with another plan after Churchill's escape, their thoughts had turned from the prison fence to the floor beneath their feet.

After learning that the Boers were going to move the POW camp, Haldane suggested that they make use of a trapdoor they had found under one of the beds. They could hide in the shallow space beneath the floorboards in the hope that the guards would think they had already escaped. When the camp left without them, they would emerge from their hiding place and make their way to freedom. In late February, believing that the prison would be moved in a matter of days, they had opened the trapdoor and slipped into the dark, damp world beneath the Staats Model School.

As soon as they climbed in, the three men realized that they had not been prepared for what awaited them. Their roommates had agreed to help them, providing food and information, but that did little to change the fact that their new home was little better than a torture chamber. Just two and a half feet high, it was divided into five narrow, eighteen-foot-long compartments. They could not sit up, talk above a whisper or wash themselves. There was no light or fresh air, and it was so damp that their leather boots soon turned green. The only way they could stand it was by constantly reminding themselves that it wouldn't last long.

Their absence was discovered the next morning. As the three men listened intently to the sounds above them, a fruitless search ensued. They were never found, but, to their despair, the Boers' plan to move the prisoners was delayed. Then it was delayed again, and again, until, in Haldane's words, they were "doomed to occupy this earthly chamber for nearly three weeks."

When the prisoners were finally moved and the three men were able to emerge, filthy and weak, from the trapdoor, it took them less time to make their way to Portuguese East Africa than it had to hide beneath the prison floor. Just two weeks later, two of the men, Haldane and Le Mesurier, climbed out of a train in Lourenço Marques. Following essentially the same path that Churchill had taken three months earlier, the men had received assistance from native Africans, and ultimately made contact with the same underground network of Englishmen that John Howard had organized to help their former prison mate. Emboldened by the success of their first, improvised scheme, Howard and his trusted neighbors simply repeated their dangerous adventure, hiding the fugitives in their colliery and spiriting them across the border as stowaways in Charles Burnham's wool trucks.

Not long after leaving the empty prison, Haldane and Le Mesurier had become separated from Brockie. Although he would later say that he searched for the two English officers for four days, the scrappy Irish enlisted man might have concluded he was better off without them. Able to speak Dutch and Zulu and with a good grasp of the terrain, he had found his own way to Kaapmuiden, one of the last stops on the railway line to Portuguese East Africa, and even worked briefly in the train station bar. By the time Haldane and Le Mesurier boarded the steamship to Durban, Brockie was already on it.

When the three men reached the Natal port, no welcoming party with bands and cheering crowds was waiting to celebrate their escape. Haldane did, however, find a letter from Winston Churchill. "My heartiest congratulations on your wonderful exploit which will mark you as a man of daring, endurance and resource among all soldiers," Churchill had written. "I am delighted to think you are safe. I feared they had murdered you in the veldt."

They had survived the veld, but soon after reaching Durban, both Haldane and Le Mesurier nearly lost their lives to illness. Le Mesurier was immediately invalided home with enteric fever, and a few days later Haldane was hospitalized in Pietermaritzburg with malaria. Only Brockie appeared to be wholly unaffected, Haldane wrote in astonishment, "having suffered not at all during our adventures."

✈

Little more than a week after the fall of Pretoria in June 1900, having taken part in one last battle, Churchill decided it was time to go home. "Our operations were at an end," he wrote. "The war had become a guerrilla and promised to be shapeless and indefinite." By now, even the most stalwart Britons were forced to admit that the war was far from over. Worse, it was quickly becoming clear that it would finally end not with pageantry, precision or gallantry but with cruelty of the most brutal and modern kind.

Six months after Churchill left, Lord Roberts himself, the commander in chief, sailed back to England, declaring the war over, or near enough. In his place, he left in command Lord Kitchener, the man Churchill had attacked for his brutality in the Sudan campaign. In command of overwhelmingly superior firepower, but frustrated by the Boers' unrelenting guerrilla tactics, Kitchener took a route that would hasten the end of the war, at a staggering cost.

To prevent Boer civilians throughout the veld from providing shelter and provisions to the elusive burghers who harassed his forces, Kitchener expanded with a vengeance a policy of farm burning that Roberts had begun. So extreme was Kitchener's version that by the end of the war some thirty thousand Boer farms would be left in black smoldering ruins. The problem then was what to do with the homeless families, mostly women and children, who were left behind. To the horror of the Boers and, soon after, the rest of the world, the British came up with a stunning solution: concentration camps.

The idea behind concentration camps was not new, but this was the first time the term had been used. More than that, it was the first time the camps had targeted a whole country and depopulated entire regions. Although the British did not intentionally kill their captives, they committed what Louis Botha called "slow murder." The camps quickly multiplied until there were some forty-five of them scattered across southern Africa. They did not have nearly enough food for their thousands of inmates. There was little to no medical care, and the sanitary conditions were not only appalling but deadly.

By the end of the war, more than twenty-six thousand Boer civilians would die in British concentration camps, some twenty-two thousand of whom were children. Those statistics, however, do not even take into account the roughly twenty thousand Africans who, having been forced to fight in a war that was not their own, subsequently died in separate black concentration camps.

Outraged, Botha repeatedly wrote to his British counterparts protesting the concentration camps, but to no avail. "At our meeting at Middleburg I verbally protested against forcible removal of our families, and against the cruel manner in which it was done," Botha wrote to Kitchener. "These families were given no opportunity of providing themselves, from their homes and goods, with sufficient necessaries for a long journey and complete change of dwelling; but on the contrary they were, notwithstanding the prevailing inclement weather, removed mostly on open trollies, by which they were exposed to every discomfort and misery, while their houses were also looted by the British soldiers. . . . This convinces me that the British troops under Your Excellency's Chief Command wish to do all in their power to make our helpless women and children suffer as much as possible." In response, Kitchener just shrugged. "As I informed Your Honour at Middleburg," he replied to Botha five days later, "owing to the irregular manner in which you have conducted and continue to conduct hostilities . . . I have no other course open to me and am forced to take the very unpleasant and repugnant steps of bringing in the women and children."

It was not until a British social worker named Emily Hobhouse visited the camps and publicized their inhumanity that the conditions slowly began to improve. Horrified by the thin tents, open sewage and starving children, Hobhouse returned to England to tell both the British people and their representatives in Parliament exactly what was happening in southern Africa. Later that year, Henry Campbell-Bannerman, who would become prime minister in 1905, excoriated the leaders of the British army for their use of concentration camps. "When is a war not a war?" he asked. "When it is waged in South Africa by methods of barbarism."

➤➤

As reprehensible as Kitchener's methods were, they took a heavy toll on the fiercely defiant Boers. Even Botha had to admit that the scorched-earth strategy was working. As fast, invisible and skilled as they were at fighting in the open veld, even the self-reliant burghers could not survive without the farms that had fed and sheltered them. Their inability to protect their wives and children from such tactics led even the toughest Boer fighters to despair. "Fight to the bitter end?" one Boer general asked. "But has the bitter end not come?"

Finally, in the fall of 1902, two and a half years after the war had begun, a delegation of ten men, including Louis Botha, met Kitchener in Pretoria to sign the Treaty of Vereeniging. Among the concessions the Boers were forced to make was that both the Transvaal and the Orange Free State would be annexed by the British. In return, the British pledged to give the Boers £3 million to compensate for the thousands of farms lost during Kitchener's raids. They also promised that eventually the Boers would be allowed to once again govern their own people.

Noticeably missing from the signatures on the Treaty of Vereeniging was that of Paul Kruger, the president of the Transvaal. Fearing capture, he had fled to Europe on September 11, 1900, little more than three months after the fall of Pretoria. Although he was greeted as a hero in France, the German kaiser had refused even to see him. The kaiser's grandmother, England's revered Queen Victoria, had died more than a year before the Treaty of Vereeniging at the age of eighty-one, thus ending what was at the time the longest reign of any British monarch. Kaiser Wilhelm now had to forge a working relationship with his cousin the playboy prince, who had finally been crowned King Edward VII at the age of fifty-nine.

After being rebuffed by the kaiser, Kruger found sanctuary in the Netherlands with his wife and eight of his grandchildren. The children had been living with their mother, one of Kruger's sixteen children, in a concentration camp. Their mother had not survived the camp's brutal conditions, and her children were so sick that five of them died soon after joining their grandparents in Europe. Not long after, Kruger's wife also died, leaving him, nearly deaf and partially blind, to face the end of the war alone. He lived for two and a half more years, never again setting foot on African soil.

➤➤

The country that Kruger had once led would eventually free itself from Britain's grip, but it would happen so slowly that many of the men who had fought for independence would not live to see South Africa become a sovereign state. After the war had ended, eight years would pass before the Boer republics Kruger had left behind— the Transvaal and the Orange Free State—were finally reunited with Natal and Cape Colony to form the Union of South Africa. The union was better than being a colony, but it was still a dominion of the British Empire. It wasn't until 1931, when the empire reluctantly became a commonwealth, that South Africa could shake off the last vestiges of British control. Even then, Queen Victoria's silk-gloved hand still rested on the dusty backs of the Boers for another thirty years. Her great-great-granddaughter Queen Elizabeth II would continue to hold the title of queen of South Africa until 1961, when the Union of South Africa officially became the Republic of South Africa.

For the great majority of the inhabitants of southern Africa—the Zulu and Xhosa peoples, the mixed-race "coloreds," and the other nonwhite populations that included even the large Indian community of which Gandhi was a part—it would take still longer to win the most basic rights of freedom and equality within their own country. During the war, the British had promised that as soon as the Boers were defeated, life for nonwhites would change dramatically. They would, at long last, be treated as citizens, with respect, rights and, most important, suffrage. Instead, the situation grew steadily worse.

With the same insular, defiant worldview that had marked their fight against the British, the Boers did not relinquish their harsh, race-based social views, but instead worked to expand and codify them. Just a few years after the Treaty of Vereeniging, the Boers began a concerted push toward segregation, forming the South African Native Affairs Commission, which proposed dividing the republic, its rural land as well as its cities, into black and white sections. By 1913, the infamous Natives Land Act was passed, forcing nonwhite Africans, who made up 67 percent of the population, to live on just 7 percent of its arable land.

Emboldened in part by the new international attention that the war had focused on South Africa, the communities that were the target of such policies began to build their own strength. But they faced a long, uphill struggle against the well-organized regime, which began to trade the now-pejorative Boer identity for an updated image as "Afrikaners." In 1912, the year before the act passed, leaders within the black community had gathered in Bloemfontein, less than three hundred miles south of Pretoria, to form the South African Native National Congress, which would later become the African National Congress, or ANC. Among the founding members of the ANC, and its first secretary-general, was Solomon Plaatje, the brilliant young linguist and journalist who had chronicled the Boer War from the African point of view. Taking advantage of his prodigious language skills, Plaatje traveled widely to help native Africans make their case abroad. After touring England, however, and, later, the United States, Plaatje returned to a South Africa run by and for the Afrikaners.

Resistance to the government's hardening racial policies was initially spontaneous and largely peaceful, particularly in the Indian community, where Mohandas Gandhi used the combination of humanitarianism and courage that he had learned on the Boer War battlefield to define an entire new movement based on nonviolent protest. After a new law was passed in 1906 forcing Indians to register with the government, Gandhi, who had founded the Natal Indian Congress twelve years earlier, organized a mass meeting of

his own to protest the law. For the next seven years, Indians in South
Africa, following Gandhi's methods of nonviolent resistance, defied
prejudicial laws and suffered the consequences. Thousands were
imprisoned, beaten and even killed for their defiance, but nothing
changed. Finally, in the summer of 1914, after more than twenty
years in South Africa, Gandhi returned to India, where his peaceful
protests would, in the end, find more success. When he heard that
Gandhi had left, Jan Smuts felt nothing but relief. "The saint has left
our shores," he wrote. "I sincerely hope forever."

Among South African whites, wide-scale prejudice became
increasingly rationalized and institutionalized, first with Smuts's
United Party, which ruled from 1934 until 1948, and then with the
National Party. Dominated by Afrikaners, the National Party imple-
mented an official, state-run program of racial segregation that it
called apartheid, Afrikaans for "apartness." The blatant discrimina-
tion and dangerous inequalities inherent in apartheid, however, only
fueled support for the ANC, which swelled with popular support
despite ever-harsher government measures to suppress it.

Finally, in the 1960s, under the leadership of a charismatic
young lawyer named Nelson Mandela, a faction of the ANC abandoned peaceful methods and declared that it would take up armed
struggle as the only realistic means of winning change. In response,
the National Party banned the ANC from South Africa and imprisoned Mandela for twenty-seven years, embarking on a bitter and
escalating conflict against the majority of its country's own citizens
and transforming itself into an international pariah. It was not until
1990, nearly a hundred years after the Boer War and just ten years
before the beginning of another new century, that a new president,
F. W. de Klerk, would lift the ban and free Mandela. Four years
later, South Africans would finally win universal suffrage, and, in a
moment that would stir the hearts and hopes of people of all races
across the world, Nelson Mandela would become the first black president of South Africa.

→→

In the summer of 1900, another man who would leave his mark on world history left Africa to return home to England, where he was given a hero's welcome. Among Churchill's first stops was Oldham, where, just a year earlier, he had lost his first election. Now he was carried through the streets in a procession of ten carriages. "10,000 people turned out . . . with flags and drums beating," he wrote to his brother, Jack, "and shouted themselves hoarse for two hours." The procession ended at the Theatre Royal, the same theater where he had spoken during the last campaign, and where he was now expected to tell the people of Oldham the story of his escape.

Churchill had told the story many times before, but this was the first time he was able to use the names of the men who had helped him. By that time, the British had occupied Witbank, and he need no longer fear reprisals. As he described the colliery and the mine shaft in which he had hidden, Churchill mentioned that Dan Dewsnap, an Oldham native, had been among the men who had risked their own lives to protect him. As soon as he said the name, the audience erupted. "His wife's in the gallery," they cried. "There was," Churchill later wrote, "general jubilation."

Dan Dewsnap had been right. They did all vote for Churchill the next time, or at least enough of them did to win the election. Two months after his second speech at the Theatre Royal, Churchill won his first seat in Parliament, coming in second by just sixteen votes to one of the Liberal candidates, Alfred Emmott. "It is clear to me from the figures," Churchill wrote to Prime Minister Salisbury the day after the election, "that nothing but personal popularity arising out of the late South African War, carried me in."

Churchill had also won the election without the help of his mother. Although he no longer needed her celebrity because he now had his own, he had nonetheless begged her to come to Oldham. "I write again to impress upon you how very useful your presence will be down here," he had written to her just before the election. Jennie, however, would not be swayed. She was, after all, on her honeymoon.

Despite the adamant objections of her family and his, or perhaps in part because of them, Jennie had married George Cornwallis-

West in July, soon after Winston returned from southern Africa. Some three thousand people had swarmed the London church just to get a look at the bride. "The wedding was very pretty and George looked supremely happy in having at length obtained his heart's desire," Churchill wrote to his brother, who was still fighting in Africa. "As we already know each other's views on the subject, I need not pursue it."

Churchill's own romantic hopes did not turn out as well, at least in the short term. Although he told his mother that Pamela Plowden was "the only woman I could ever live happily with," it seemed that he was not the kind of man the sparkling young socialite was destined to marry. "She ought to be a rich man's wife," one of Churchill's friends wrote of Pamela soon after the election, and within the year she was. In the spring of 1902, Pamela married Victor Bulwer-Lytton, 2nd Earl of Lytton and the godson of Queen Victoria. "Miss Plowden frequently has been said to have been engaged," a reporter for the *Daily Chronicle* wrote, "but she now makes an alliance that was well worth waiting for."

Like Churchill, who would marry Clementine Hozier six years later, Pamela had a long and apparently happy marriage, but her friendship with Churchill would continue for the rest of their lives. In fact, she was among the first people to whom he wrote after proposing to Clementine. "Secret till Sat[urday]," he told her. "I am going to marry Clementine. . . . You must always be our best friend." In the end, the correspondence between Pamela and Churchill would span sixty-three years, ranging from his first lovesick missives to her congratulations on his election as prime minister—"All my life I have known you would become PM, ever since the days of Hansom cabs"—to his condolences after the death of one of her sons during World War II.

"The first time you meet Winston you see all his faults," Pamela would explain years later to Edward Marsh, Churchill's private secretary, "and the rest of your life you spend in discovering his virtues."

Churchill was not one to forget old friends. Even in the heady days following his escape, he never forgot the men who had made it possible. Soon after returning to England, Churchill wrote to Howard, telling him that he was sending him a package that contained eight gold watches, presents for those who had risked their lives to help him. "I hope you will all do me the honour to accept these small keepsakes of our remarkable adventure," he wrote, "and believe that they also represent my sincere gratitude for the help and assistance you all afforded me." On the back of the watches, Churchill had inscribed each name followed by "from Winston S. Churchill in recognition of timely help afforded him in his escape from Pretoria during the South African War, Dec. 13, 1899."

Churchill's friends in Witbank had certainly earned his gratitude. After the young aristocrat had been swept up into the grand celebration at Durban, Charles Burnham and his English neighbors had remained unprotected in the Boers' heartland, concealing Churchill's secret and even taking new risks to help Haldane and Le Mesurier follow the path he had blazed. As a result, Burnham and John Howard had barely escaped prison, and possibly execution, at the hands of the increasingly suspicious Boer authorities.

After the train car in which Churchill had been hiding continued on to the firm that was buying Burnham's wool, someone found what appeared to be greasy finger marks on the bales, indicating that the car had been carrying more than just wool. When Churchill's escape became known, it was also remembered that Burnham had been spotted walking with a stranger through the streets of Lourenço Marques. Burnham was questioned, but he insisted that if someone had slipped into one of his trucks, he certainly knew nothing about it. Although the Boers were deeply suspicious, they had no proof and so were forced to let him go.

For Howard, it had been an even closer call. Not long after he had helped Haldane and Le Mesurier on their way to Lourenço Marques, he heard a knock on the door of his office and opened it to find a Boer commandant and five burghers. They had come to arrest him and take him to Pretoria for interrogation. Realizing that if he went to Pretoria he might never come back, Howard decided that his best chance was to try to bribe the men. If that didn't work, he was not going to go without a fight. "Should they not fall in line with his suggestions, then it was a matter of his life for theirs," Howard's son would explain years later. "He would shoot it out with them."

Inviting the men into the dining room, the same room where he had brought Churchill on the night he arrived at the colliery, Howard gave them food and whiskey and then told them he was going to pack a bag. He returned a few minutes later with two revolvers in his pockets. Standing at the room's only door, next to where he had stacked the men's rifles, he made his proposition: If they would let him go, he would give them £50 now and another £200 after the war. The men agreed, not knowing that Howard was prepared to shoot them if they had turned him down. Soon after, they returned to Pretoria to explain to their superiors that John Howard had somehow slipped through their grasp.

->>

As grateful as Churchill was to his old friends, he was equally respectful and generous to his old enemies. Although during the war he had defended Kitchener's scorched-earth policies, writing to his brother that by burning a few farms, they might persuade more burghers to stay home rather than go out and fight, he also argued strongly that as soon as the war was won, they should be as compassionate in victory as they had been unflinching in battle. "We embarked on the stormy ocean of war to find true peace," he reminded his readers in an article at the end of 1900. "Beware of driving men to desperation. . . . Those who demand 'an eye for an eye, and a tooth for a tooth' should ask themselves whether such barren spoils are worth five years of bloody partisan warfare and the consequent impoverishment of S. Africa." Churchill's advice was not well received by his fellow Englishmen, but he did not care, nor ever would.

For the rest of his life, after every war in which England fought,

Churchill would exhort his country to offer "the hand of friendship to the vanquished." For the Boers, he argued, "the wise and right course is to beat down all who resist, even to the last man, but not to withhold forgiveness and even friendship from any who wish to surrender. . . . Therein lies the shortest road to 'peace with honour.'"

Churchill himself extended the hand of friendship not just to the Boers as a people but directly to the man who had personally been responsible for many of the battlefield defeats that had kept the war going for so long—Louis Botha.

The two men met for the first time in 1903, not long after the end of the Boer War, when Botha visited England to ask his former enemies for help in rebuilding his country. Although Botha had been responsible for the attack on the armored train that had led to Churchill's capture and imprisonment, the two men quickly became friends.

"Few men that I have known have interested me more than Louis Botha," Churchill would write many years later. "An acquaintance formed in strange circumstances and upon an almost unbelievable introduction ripened into a friendship which I greatly valued." Churchill and Botha understood each other, perhaps better than anyone else they knew. Although they had had strikingly different childhoods, their young adult lives had been defined by war, and they both seemed destined to lead their nations in the new century.

In 1907, just over seven years after he had sat astride his horse on that rain-swept hillside in Frere, watching Churchill's train steam toward the trap he had laid, Botha was elected prime minister of the Transvaal. Now a high official of the same British Empire he had sought to defy, Botha traveled to England to take part in the Imperial Conference, a meeting of the leaders of the self-governing colonies. Churchill, then undersecretary of state for the colonies, also attended the banquet, which was held in Westminster Hall, the oldest building in the Palace of Westminster, whose six-foot-thick stone walls, vast spaces and delicate statuary were designed to overawe visitors with tangible proof of British power.

Striding through the great hall to the place that had been

reserved for him, the former Boer commander paused when he saw Lady Randolph Churchill, standing next to the man who was once his battlefield prisoner. With the simplicity of a burgher, and the courtesy of the international statesmen he and Churchill had both become, Botha acknowledged to Jennie the strange, intertwined history he shared with her son. "He and I," Botha said, "have been out in all weathers."

ACKNOWLEDGMENTS

The prospect of writing about Winston Churchill, even a small part of his life, is as daunting as it is thrilling. I took courage from the fact that, throughout the process, I was never alone. Some of the greatest minds not just in Churchill studies but in the field of history have gone before me, revealing Churchill in all his brilliance, boldness, originality and lust for life. After spending years reading an ever-expanding library of books about Churchill, I owe a tremendous debt of gratitude to a great number of historians and writers. Although it would be impossible to list them all here, I would be remiss if I did not mention at least those who had the most profound impact on this book.

My first and greatest debt is to Sir Martin Gilbert, whose death just last year was a great loss to his many friends and admirers. Gilbert was not only the most trusted and respected Churchill biographer, he was an incredibly skilled and prolific historian, and what I learned from him went far beyond the events of Churchill's life. Gilbert was first brought to the subject, as a young Oxford graduate student, by Churchill's son, Randolph, who hired him as a research assistant. Before he died at the age of fifty-seven, just five years after his father's death, Randolph had completed the first two volumes of the definitive Churchill biography that Gilbert continued. These two volumes, as well as the related

Documents, cover Churchill's early life and, as such, were an invaluable resource, guide and friend to me as I conducted my own research.

As indebted as I am to Martin Gilbert and Randolph Churchill, my first introduction to Winston Churchill, decades ago, was through the work of William Manchester. I have rarely encountered a writer with the ability to describe a scene with as much dazzling detail or conjure a moment from the murky depths of history as confidently and magisterially as Manchester. His writing is absolutely irresistible, and, even more than a decade after his death, his unforgettable three-volume series, *The Last Lion,* which was finished with impressive skill and devotion by Paul Reid, continues to thrill loyal readers and attract new ones.

To understanding the intricacies and endless complications of the Boer War, I could not have hoped for a more assured, trustworthy or fascinating guide than Thomas Pakenham. Pakenham is perhaps best known for *The Scramble for Africa,* but of equal power and reach is his book *The Boer War,* which is, in my opinion, the definitive modern history of the war. This book is not only thoroughly researched, it is incredibly engrossing reading, brilliant, rich and utterly compelling. I read it as much for pleasure as for work.

For a uniquely intimate and knowing perspective on Winston Churchill, it would be impossible to do better than the works of his granddaughter, Celia Sandys. Through her books—most notably *Churchill: Wanted Dead or Alive*—lectures and television appearances, Sandys has told Churchill's story in a way that no one else could. Sandys not only knew her grandfather well, she has traveled in his footsteps, a personal mission that has taken her around the world, greatly enriching both her work and our understanding of Churchill. I am grateful to Sandys not only for her contribution to Churchill studies but for her kindness and generosity to me as I began my research.

I was very fortunate to be able to speak with family members of several of the central characters in this book. I would like to thank Keith Burgess, the great-grandson of Joe McKenna, one of the two Scottish miners who helped hide Churchill at the Transvaal and Delagoa Bay Colliery; Nicholas Woodhouse, the grandson of Pamela Plowden, later

Lady Lytton, the first love of Churchill's life; and Judith Crosbie, the great niece of Adam Brockie, who, along with Aylmer Haldane, laid the plan that led to Winston Churchill's escape from the Staats Model School. Crosbie wrote an insightful article for *The Irish Times* about her great uncle and was kind enough to share additional information with me.

I would also like to say a special word of thanks to Jonathan and Beth de Souza. Jonathan is the grandson of Louis de Souza, the Transvaal secretary of state for war who showed Churchill such kindness while he was imprisoned by the Boers. Jonathan and his wife not only invited me to their beautiful home in Johannesburg, they allowed me to copy in full the diary of Marie de Souza, Louis's wife and Jonathan's grandmother. This diary was extremely important to my understanding not only of Churchill's life at the Staats Model School and his relationship with de Souza but the atmosphere in Pretoria before and during the war. The de Souzas also introduced me to the work of Jonathan's cousin, Francis Hugh de Souza, who researched their grandfather's life during the Boer War and wrote a very thought-provoking book about it titled *A Question of Treason*. Hugh also generously shared with me photographs of his grandparents as well as a copy of the letter Churchill left for Louis de Souza upon his escape.

While conducting my research, I had the great fortune to work with some of the most distinguished experts and archivists in the fields of Churchill and military studies, in England, South Africa and the United States. First and foremost in this category is the Churchill Archives Centre in Cambridge, to which any book on Churchill owes a tremendous debt of gratitude, and without which I would have been utterly lost. The extraordinarily complete and meticulously organized collection is overseen by its director, Allen Packwood, who is widely respected among Churchill scholars and students. I would also like to thank Ceci Humphries, Sarah Lewery and Sophie Bridges, archivists at the center who were exceptionally helpful to me both at the archives and, later, long distance, as I repeatedly called and e-mailed them with questions and requests for materials. I am also grateful to the archivists who guided my research at the National Army Museum; the National Archives at Kew; Clare Fleck at the Knebworth House; and John Hoy, the chief executive at Churchill's ancestral home, Blenheim Palace. At Blenheim, I am particularly grateful to John Forster, who, as well as personally giving me a tour of the house and its archives and taking me to see Churchill's grave, generously agreed to read sections of my manuscript. Finally, I would like to offer a special note of thanks to Phil Reed, director of the extraordinary Churchill War Rooms. Phil gave me excellent advice, suggested several archives and experts, and even treated me to a delicious and absolutely enormous English breakfast.

In South Africa, I have a long list of highly skilled and knowledgeable archivists to thank, from Jennifer Kimble at the Brenthurst Library to Isle Cloete at the War Museum in Johannesburg, Johan Cronje and Elsje van der Merwe at Kimberley's Sol Plaatje Museum, Gabriele Mohale in the historical papers at the University of Witwatersrand, Bernice Nagel at the Africana Research Library and the archivists at the Killie Campbell Museum in Durban.

I learned just as much outside of South Africa's museums and archives, however, as I did within them. In Ken Gillings, I had an extremely knowledgeable, absolutely fascinating and very fun guide to the Boer War battlefields of South Africa. Through Ken, I also had the great good fortune to meet Sandy Buchanan, who is uniquely knowledgeable about the South African railway system, and John Bird, who not only has a deep understanding of the history of South African coal mining but has studied Churchill's escape and his days as a wanted man in Witbank more closely, I believe, than anyone else in the world. Ken, Sandy and John answered countless questions for me over many years and were three of my most essential readers for this manuscript.

John Bird also introduced me to two South African mining consultants, John Wallington and John Sparrow, who provided critical details about what Churchill would have seen, smelled and heard as he hid in the coal mine shaft. I would also like to thank the mining historian Jade Davenport, who helped guide my research into South African mines and whose carefully researched and fascinating book, *Digging Deep*, was an excellent resource for me. I am also grateful to João das

Neves, the head of the history archives in Maputo, Mozambique, who was my guide to the seaside town that was once Lourenço Marques and the two-story white building that is still today the home of the British consulate. My thanks as well to the consulate staff who allowed me to walk the grounds, which has a wonderful plaque commemorating Churchill's escape, and even tour sections of the building.

In the United States, I would like to express my gratitude to the National Churchill Museum in Fulton, Missouri, where Churchill gave his famous Iron Curtain speech in 1946 and where there is now a world-class museum that has been host to many of the most respected Churchill scholars in the world. In particular, I would like to thank two of the museum's former directors, James Williams and Rob Havers. I am also grateful to Karen Font, who did a brilliant job fact-checking this book.

I would like to say a special word of thanks to the Churchill Centre in Chicago, which has been extremely supportive and encouraging to me since I first began work on this book five years ago. In particular, I would like to thank Laurence Geller, the center's chairman, and Lee Pollock, its executive director. Lee introduced me to a wide range of scholars and archivists as well as Churchill family members. He opened countless doors for me, making the early days of my research infinitely easier. I am also grateful to Lee for introducing me to James Muller, a professor of political science at the University of Alaska, Anchorage, and a preeminent Churchill scholar. James gave me the great benefit of his tremendous knowledge while reading the manuscript for this book.

I am very grateful for the extraordinarily talented publishing team with which I have the honor and great pleasure to work: my editor, Bill Thomas; my agents, Suzanne Gluck and Alicia Gordon; and my publicist, Todd Doughty. This is our third book together over fifteen years, and during that time they have become not only my advisers and allies but my friends.

I would also like to thank my niece and nephew, Tori and Aaron Shaffer; my dear friends Stacy Benson and Jodi Lewis; the extremely talented and creative artist Brett McGuire; and two of the smartest, coolest people I know, Susie and Denis Tinsley, who invited me to stay in their incredibly beautiful home while I was doing research in London. Finally, I am forever grateful to my loving parents, Larry and Connie Millard, and mother-in-law, Doris Uhlig; my three amazing sisters, Kelly Sandvig, Anna Shaffer and Nichole Millard; and my precious children, Emery, Petra and Conrad, whom I love with all my heart. My deepest, most heartfelt thanks go to my husband, Mark Uhlig, the most extraordinary person I will ever know.

NOTES

MANUSCRIPT SOURCES

AHD, Aylmer Haldane Papers, National Library of Scotland
BHL, Brenthurst Library, Johannesburg
CAC, Churchill Archives Centre, Cambridge
KCM, Killie Campbell Museum, Durban
LOC, Library of Congress, Manucript Division, Marlborough Papers
NAM, National Army Museum, London
NAR, National Archives Repository, Pretoria
NAS, National Archives, Surrey
SPM, Sol Plaatje Museum, Kimberley
WIT, Louis de Souza Papers, University of Witwatersrand, Johannesburg

CHAPTER 1: DEATH BY INCHES

7   "There is no ambition": WSC to Jack, Dec. 2, 1897, CAC.
7   "From very early youth": Winston Churchill, *My Early Life,* 76.
7   "that it all had to be make-believe": Ibid., 44.
8   "not so much *in spite* of": WSC to Lady Randolph Churchill, Aug. 29, 1897, CAC.
8   "The immortal Barnum himself": Scott, *Winston Spencer Churchill,* 11.
9   He was called a "self-advertiser": Cowles, *Winston Churchill,* 55; Scott, *Winston Spencer Churchill,* 15; Winston Churchill, *My Early Life,* 162.
9   "melancholy to be forced to record": Winston Churchill, *My Early Life,* 162.
9   "the swift road to promotion": Ibid., 74.

9   "bullets strike flesh": Ibid., 83.

10   "3rd rate watering place": WSC to Lady Randolph Churchill, April 14, 1897,
        CAC.

10   "a magnificent pink and white": WSC to Lady Randolph Churchill, Oct. 14,
        1896, in Churchill and Gilbert, *Churchill Documents,* 2:688.

10   "as big as a prize turnip": Winston Churchill, *My Early Life,* 105.

10   The 5th and 6th Dukes of Marlborough: Randolph S. Churchill, *Youth,*
        14, 96.

11   "We each have a 'Butler' ": WSC to Jennie, Oct. 14, 1896, in Churchill and
        Gilbert, *Churchill Documents,* 2:688.

11   It was a perfect day: Winston Churchill, *My Early Life,* 122.

12   "I am certainly not": WSC speech in the House, Nov. 11, 1942, quoted in
        Coote and Batchelor, *Maxims and Reflections of Winston Churchill,* 34.

12   "In my interest": Winston Churchill, *My Early Life,* 151–52.

12   "Having realized, that if": Winston Churchill, *Story of the Malakand Field
        Force,* 73.

12   "Very difficult; no vacancies": Winston Churchill, *My Early Life,* 123.

13   "hell fiends": Winston Churchill, *Story of the Malakand Field Force,* 18, 99.

13   The night before, the Pashtun: Ibid., 97.

14   "Death by inches": "Pathan" is the English term for "Pashtun."

14   "literally cut to pieces": Coughlin, *Churchill's First War,* 210–11.

14   "those impartial stars": Winston Churchill, *Story of the Malakand Field Force,*
        100.

15   As Blood divided his thousand men: Ibid., 101.

15   "about trying to attract attention": WSC to Jack, Dec. 2, 1897, CAC.

15   "The boy seemed to look": *Harper's,* July 1900.

16   "I have faith in my star": WSC to Lady Randolph Churchill, Sept. 5, 1897, in
        Churchill and Gilbert, *Churchill Documents,* 2:784.

16   In fact, soon after arriving: Coughlin, *Churchill's First War,* 150.

16   "I rode on my grey pony": WSC to Lady Randolph Churchill, Sept. 19, 1897,
        in Churchill and Gilbert, *Churchill Documents,* 2:792.

17   "Mud villages and castles": Winston Churchill, *My Early Life,* 138.

17   "This kind of war": Ibid., 180.

17   As Churchill stared intently: Ibid., 139.

18   "Now suddenly": Winston Churchill, *Story of the Malakand Field Force,* 103.

18   "From high up on the crag": Winston Churchill, *My Early Life,* 140.

18   Turning, Churchill watched in outrage: Winston Churchill, *Story of the Mal-
        akand Field Force,* 103.

18   "I forgot everything else": Winston Churchill, *My Early Life,* 141.

18   "It was a horrible business": WSC to Lady Randolph Churchill, Sept. 19, 1897,
        in Churchill and Gilbert, *Churchill Documents,* 2:792.

19   "Bullets—to a philosopher": WSC to Lady Randolph Churchill, Dec. 22,
        1897, CAC.

CHAPTER 2: THE GRAVEN PALM

20   He published his first book: Newspaper clipping of review from "Our Library Table," Sir Winston Churchill Archive Trust, CHAR 28/24.

20   "I am somewhat impatient": WSC to Lady Randolph Churchill, Jan. 26, 1898, quoted in Randolph S. Churchill, *Youth,* 64.

21   "horses spouting blood": Winston Churchill, *My Early Life,* 193.

21   "You cannot gild it": WSC to Lady Randolph Churchill, Sept. 4, 1898, in Churchill and Gilbert, *Churchill Documents,* 2:973.

21   "Nothing touched me": Ibid., quoted in Randolph S. Churchill, *Youth,* 415.

21   "set fair" and "On what do these things depend": WSC to Charles Spencer-Churchill, Sept. 29, 1898, LOC.

21   "I have sent my papers": WSC to Charles Spencer-Churchill, Jan. 24, 1899, LOC.

22   the Clock Tower: Parliament's famous Clock Tower is now called Elizabeth Tower, in honor of Queen Elizabeth's Diamond Jubilee in 2012.

23   "To me": Winston Churchill, *My Early Life,* 46.

23   "Everything he said": Ibid., 32.

24   When at Harrow: WSC to Lady Randolph Churchill, June 24 and July 8 [?], 1887.

24   "The darling of democracy": Scott, *Winston Spencer Churchill,* 10.

24   "Mr. Moore, who was devoted": Quoted in Randolph S. Churchill, *Youth,* 86.

25   "write four plays": *Isle of Wight Observer,* March 5, 1898.

26   Wilde wrote: Wilde wrote a letter, *De Profundis,* from prison, and, after his release, a final poem, *The Ballad of Reading Gaol.*

26   "expecting four guineas": Ibid.

26   "strange skill in Palmistry": WSC to Mrs. Robinson, May 3, 1899, in Churchill and Gilbert, *Churchill Documents,* 2:1023.

26   "would rather not have": WSC to Mrs. Robinson, May 6, 1899, in Churchill and Gilbert, *Churchill Documents,* 2:1024.

27   "very little hope": "Court Circular," *Times,* June 15, 1899.

27   "There is no doubt": WSC to Lady Randolph Churchill, June 25, 1899, CAC.

CHAPTER 3: THE SCION

28   "If ever the Industrial Revolution": N. J. Frangopulo, *Tradition in Action: The Historical Evolution of the Greater Manchester County* (Wakefield: EP, 1977), 154.

29   Inside, three horseshoe-shaped galleries: *Morning Post,* June 28, 1899.

29   Churchill's life on the public stage: Winston Churchill, *My Early Life,* 206.

29   Unable to pronounce the letter *s:* Randolph S. Churchill, *Youth,* 293.

30   "Where is the London twain?": Winston Churchill, *My Early Life,* 69.

30   Although he would become famous: Just four years later, Churchill would have a disastrous experience while pretending to make an impromptu speech in the House of Commons. After just a few lines, he forgot what he had planned to say next and was forced to sit down without finishing the speech.

The situation had been shocking to the other members of the House, who already saw him as a great speaker, and devastating to Churchill. He never attempted to make another speech without his notes.

30   "Winston has spent the best years": Nicholas Soames, "Sweat and Tears Made Winston Churchill's Name," *Telegraph,* May 4, 2011.

30   "Personally I am very popular": WSC to Charles Spencer-Churchill, June 29, 1899, CAC.

30   "I improve every time": WSC to Pamela Plowden, July 2, 1899, CAC.

31   "was proud to stand": Winston Churchill, *My Early Life,* 223.

31   "We shall see": *Manchester Evening News,* June 26, 1899, quoted in Churchill and Gilbert, *Churchill Documents,* 2:1029.

31   his hands either placed confidently: John Hulme, "Mr. Churchill: A Portrait from 1901," *Finest Hour,* no. 49 (Autumn 1985).

31   "Throughout he was listened to": *Morning Post,* June 28, 1899.

32   "a touch of mysticism": *Harper's New Monthly Magazine,* 1900, clipping without further information, CAC.

32   "recognize in Mr. Winston Spencer Churchill": *Morning Post,* June 28, 1899.

32   "Mrs. Runciman goes everywhere": WSC to Lady Randolph Churchill, July 2, 1899, in Churchill and Gilbert, *Churchill Documents,* 2:1035.

33   "more of the panther": Winston Churchill, *My Early Life,* 4–5.

34   Major Caryl Ramsden: Sebba, *American Jennie,* 223.

34   "You had better have stuck": Prince of Wales to Lady Randolph Churchill, Feb. 25, 1898, quoted in Ridley, *Bertie,* 315.

34   Patsy Cornwallis-West: Ibid.

34   "You are evidently up to your old game": Prince of Wales to Lady Randolph Churchill, March 30, 1898, quoted in Sebba, *American Jennie,* 814.

34   "I suppose you think": Quoted in Manchester, *Visions of Glory,* 320.

35   "She shone for me": Winston Churchill, *My Early Life,* 5.

35   At his insistence, she had charmed: Randolph S. Churchill, *Youth,* 340.

35   "This is a pushing age": Ibid., 426.

35   Jennie arrived in Oldham: Sebba, *American Jennie,* 882.

35   "Lady Randolph Churchill was": *Sheffield Evening Telegraph,* July 7, 1899.

35   "as big as was known": Winston Churchill, *My Early Life,* 225.

36   "a bottle of champagne": Ibid., 226.

36   "I thought he was a young man": Ibid.

36   "What an awful thing": WSC to Lady Randolph Churchill, Jan. 11, 1899, CAC.

CHAPTER 4: BLOWING THE TRUMPET

37   "Looking at the lake": Mrs. George Cornwallis-West, *The Reminiscences of Lady Randolph Churchill,* 236–47.

38   "Winston is going back to school": Duchess of Marlborough to Lord Randolph, Jan. 23, 1888, in Randolph S. Churchill, *Youth,* 104.

38   "We shape our buildings": Forster and Bapasola, *Winston and Blenheim,* 2.

38   Now, however, as he wandered: WSC to Lady Randolph Churchill, Aug. 13, 1899, in Churchill and Gilbert, *Churchill Documents,* 2:1040.

38   "Amid all the chances": Winston Churchill, *Marlborough,* 15.

40   "You are young": WSC to Charles Spencer-Churchill, Jan. 24, 1899, LOC.

40   "It is a fine game to play": WSC to Lady Randolph Churchill, Aug. 16, 1895, CAC.

40   In late July, Churchill received: In 1908, while attending another of Lady Jeune's gatherings, Churchill would become reacquainted with the woman who would become his wife, Clementine Hozier.

41   "An introduction to her": www.kosmoid.net/lives/jeune.

41   "His conversation was a practical": Winston Churchill, *My Early Life,* 227.

41   When Lady Jeune pointed out: Ibid.

43   About two decades after the Eureka Diamond: The Witwatersrand is now known as the Rand, which is also the term for South Africa's currency.

43   "The discovery of an El Dorado": Winston Churchill, "Our Account with the Boers," 8, CAC.

44   "I longed for the day": Winston Churchill, *My Early Life,* 99.

44   "It is not yet too late": Winston Churchill, "Our Account with the Boers," CAC.

45   "A war in South Africa would be": Chamberlain to the House of Commons, May 1896, quoted in Pakenham, *Boer War,* 27.

45   "It is no use blowing the trumpet": Winston Churchill, *My Early Life,* 227.

45   "Sooner or later": Winston Churchill, "Our Account with the Boers," CAC.

46   His opportunity had come: "Conservative Fete at Woodstock," *Oxford Journal,* Aug. 19, 1899.

46   "Inspired possibly by memories": *Manchester Evening News,* Aug. 18, 1899.

47   "very great power": "Conservative Fete at Woodstock."

47   "If he would encourage": *Manchester Evening News,* Aug. 18, 1899.

47   "The atmosphere": Winston Churchill, *My Early Life,* 229.

48   "The Government must press": "The Ultimatum: Full Official Text," *Diamond Fields Advertiser,* Oct. 12, 1899.

48   After reading the telegram: Marie de Souza, diary, Oct. 11, 1899, courtesy of Jonathan de Souza.

49   "The age of Peace": Winston Churchill, *My Early Life,* 75.

CHAPTER 5: "SEND HER VICTORIOUS"

53   Since early that morning: *London Daily News,* Oct. 16, 1899.

53   Waterloo Station, where he had been given a grand send-off: Ibid.

54   When Buller's special five-car train: Ibid.

54   Those who had resorted to sitting: *Lancashire Evening Post,* Oct. 16, 1899.

54   A rope that had been strung: *London Daily News,* Oct. 16, 1899.

54   Although dressed for the chill, early autumn air: *Yorkshire Evening Post,* Oct. 16, 1899; *London Daily News,* Oct. 16, 1899.

54   The ship itself had arrived: *Dundee Courier,* Oct. 16, 1899.

54   The *Dunottar Castle* could sail: *London Daily News,* Oct. 16, 1899.

55   "worse than a flogging": Gilbert, *Churchill: A Life,* 101.

55   "with the chance of being drowned": Randolph S. Churchill, *Youth,* 454.

55   At 6:00 p.m., with the final cry: Winston Churchill, *London to Ladysmith,* 7.

55   As Buller stood on the captain's deck: *Yorkshire Evening Post,* Oct. 16, 1899.

55   "back towards the shores": Winston Churchill, *London to Ladysmith,* 7.

56   Inside his stitched brown leather wallet: Photographs and information about them and the wallet from the Churchill Archives Centre.

56   "I was introduced yesterday": WSC to Lady Randolph Churchill, Nov. 4, 1896, CAC.

56   "the brightest star": "Society News and Gossip," *New York Times,* Feb. 26, 1905.

56   "You dare not walk": WSC to Lady Randolph Churchill, Nov. 4, 1896, CAC.

57   "very much impressed": WSC to Lady Randolph Churchill, May 3, 1899, CAC.

57   "I quite understand": WSC to Plowden, June 28, 1899, CAC.

57   In an attempt to make up: WSC to Plowden, Nov. 28, 1898, CAC.

57   "Why do you say I am incapable": Ibid.

57   "I am lonely without her": WSC to Lady Randolph Churchill, Sept. 3, 1899, CAC.

57   "while not madly in love": WSC to Lady Randolph Churchill, Aug. 22, 1899, in Churchill and Gilbert, *Churchill Documents,* 2:1043.

57   "Jack dined with me last night": George to Lady Randolph Churchill, Aug. 24, 1899, CAC.

58   On September 18, nearly a month: WSC to Lady Randolph Churchill, Sept. 18, 1899, in Churchill and Gilbert, *Churchill Documents,* 2:1049.

58   As soon as he received Harmsworth's telegram: Ibid.

59   Responding immediately: Winston Churchill, *My Early Life,* 230.

59   Not only would more journalists: National Army Museum, London.

59   Edgar Wallace: National Army Museum, London.

59   Kipling would also raise £250,000: National Army Museum, London.

60   "exceedingly brilliant": *Evening News Post,* Dec. 6, 1899.

60   "the greatest living master": *Times,* Feb. 15, 1927, quoted in "Finest of the Empire," *Finest Hour* (Summer 2012): 25.

60   "faith in my pen": WSC to Lady Randolph Churchill, April 25, 1898.

60   "an astonishing triumph": *Daily Mail,* Nov. 7, 1899, quoted in Randolph S. Churchill, *Youth,* 457.

60   "My literary talents": WSC to Lady Randolph Churchill, April 25, 1898, CAC.

60   He had gone shopping: WSC to Lady Randolph Churchill, Sept. 18, 1899, in Churchill and Gilbert, *Churchill Documents,* 2:1049.

61   At the famous optical shop: Randolph S. Churchill, *Youth,* 453.

61   "grievously sick": WSC to Lady Randolph Churchill, Oct. 17, 1899, in Churchill and Gilbert, *Churchill Documents,* 2:1055.

61   Buller could usually be found: Details taken from a sketch that appeared in
       the *Illustrated London News,* Oct. 1899.
62   "v[er]y amiable": WSC to Lady Randolph Churchill, Oct. 17, 1899, in
       Churchill and Gilbert, *Churchill Documents,* 2:1055.
62   "a characteristic British personality": Winston Churchill, *My Early Life,* 234.
62   "The idea that time": Ibid., 235.
62   "may well be too late": Ibid., 231.
63   "infatuated step": Quoted in Pakenham, *Scramble for Africa,* 567.
63   "healthy and amusing": Winston Churchill, *London to Ladysmith,* 8–9.
63   "Some of our best officers": Winston Churchill, *My Early Life,* 235.
63   So certain were they: Amery, *My Political Life,* 119.
63   Even now, their enemy faced: Randolph S. Churchill, *Youth,* 456.
63   "Evidently the General expects": WSC to Lady Randolph Churchill, Oct. 17,
       1899, in Churchill and Gilbert, *Churchill Documents,* 2:1055.
63   "violently to and fro": Winston Churchill, *London to Ladysmith,* 9.
63   "plunging . . . 'with neck out-thrust'": Atkins, *Incidents and Reflections,* 122.
63   "knew everything about South Africa": Winston Churchill, *My Early Life,*
       231–32.
64   "talked Boer": Pakenham, *Boer War,* 117.
64   "The Army at large": *Daily Telegraph,* Oct. 9, 1899.
64   "Whatever the estimate": Amery, *Times History of the War in South Africa,* 2:42.
65   "Personally, I don't believe": Quoted in Pakenham, *Boer War,* 118.

CHAPTER 6: "WE HAVE NOW GONE FAR ENOUGH"

66   When he left for war, a Boer: Hillegas, *With the Boer Forces,* 37–38.
67   The home of the president: Pakenham, *Boer War,* 121.
68   "it was magnificent to see": Reitz, *Commando,* 23.
68   In particular, the Boers had been amassing: National Army Museum,
       London.
68   In 1895 alone, the Boers bought: Amery, *Times History of the War in South
       Africa,* 2:28.
68   The following year, the secretary: Francis de Souza, *A Question of Treason,* 40.
69   "the finest mass of rifle-armed horsemen": Winston Churchill, *My Early
       Life,* 96.
69   "stagger humanity": Quoted in Pakenham, *Scramble for Africa,* 569.
69   He could trace his family: There is some disagreement about Botha's ancestry,
       with some sources saying that he was German rather than Huguenot.
70   So infuriated were the Huguenots: Spender, *General Botha,* 14.
70   "In their manner of life": Amery, *Times History of the War in South Africa,*
       1:25.
71   Great Karoo: The word "karoo" probably comes from the San word *garo,*
       which also means "desert."
71   It was here, about halfway: Spender, *General Botha,* 16.

71   He grew up in a family: Trew, *Boer War Generals,* 137.

72   Louis himself had fought: Dinuzulu had promised Botha and his men land in return for their help, giving them more than four thousand square miles of Zulu land. More than twenty years later, in 1906, Dinuzulu would be imprisoned by the British for his involvement in a rebellion. As soon as Botha became prime minister in 1910, he released Dinuzulu and granted him a farm in the Transvaal.

72   In fact, Botha had nearly been killed: Meintjes, *General Louis Botha,* 14. Few men, in fact, would have been more affected had Botha been killed that night than Dinuzulu himself, who had formed so strong a friendship with Botha that it would last until Dinuzulu's death nearly thirty years later.

72   When tensions with the British: *Liverpool Mercury,* Oct. 11, 1899.

72   He had even been among: Spender, *General Botha,* 58.

72   "The Transvaal has done all it can": Meintjes, *General Louis Botha,* 27.

73   It was raining in heavy sheets: Rayne Kruger, *Goodbye Dolly Gray,* 74.

73   "As far as the eye could see": Reitz, *Commando,* 24.

73   By the time they merged: Amery, *Times History of the War in South Africa,* 2:58.

73   "Goodbye dear old lady": Quoted in Pakenham, *Boer War,* 120.

74   In Dundee, Penn Symons ran his brigade: Ibid., 132.

74   "I feel perfectly safe": Rayne Kruger, *Goodbye Dolly Gray,* 76.

74   At 5:00 on the morning of October 20: Meintjes, *General Louis Botha,* 33.

74   Penn Symons was just about to sit down: Rayne Kruger, *Goodbye Dolly Gray,* 77.

74   Outraged by the Boers' impudence: Pakenham, *Boer War,* 155–56.

74   No man among them: Ibid., 156.

74   "literally rising in dust": Ibid., 158.

75   "severely, mortally, wounded": Amery, *Times History of the War in South Africa,* 2:62–63.

75   Two days later, a Boer commander: Rayne Kruger, *Goodbye Dolly Gray,* 80.

75   "He had already won confidence": Davitt, *Boer Fight for Freedom,* 241.

CHAPTER 7: THE BLACKEST OF ALL DAYS

77   "who should say what tidings": Winston Churchill, *London to Ladysmith,* 10.

77   Desperate for news of the war: Pakenham, *Boer War,* 190.

77   When the two ships: Winston Churchill, *London to Ladysmith,* 10.

77   "It was the most dramatic encounter": Atkins, *Relief of Ladysmith,* 34.

78   "Under Heaven": Winston Churchill, *London to Ladysmith,* 10.

78   "it would only have taken ten minutes": Winston Churchill, *My Early Life,* 237–38.

78   "Man Who Knew": Winston Churchill, *London to Ladysmith,* 12.

78   While his audience stood transfixed: Ibid., 12; Atkins, *Relief of Ladysmith,* 37.

79   It was a stunningly long list: Winston Churchill, *London to Ladysmith,* 13.

79   Churchill had met Haldane: WSC to Lady Randolph Churchill, March 7, 1898, CAC.

79   After that first meeting: Ibid.

80   "I am entitled to a medal": WSC to Haldane, Aug. 11, 1898, CAC.

80   "We shall meet anon": WSC to Haldane, May 24, 1898, CAC.

80   "My idea is that my reputation": WSC to Lady Randolph Churchill, March 7, 1898, CAC.

81   "the picture of war": Winston Churchill, *London to Ladysmith,* 13.

81   In the midst of the pomp and circumstance: *Grantham Journal,* Nov. 4, 1899; *Sussex Agricultural Express,* Nov. 3, 1899.

81   In the month of October 1899 alone: Mahan, *Story of the War in South Africa,* 95.

81   As, one after another, ships left Southampton: Ibid.

83   "Knowing the meager way": Reitz, *Commando,* 32–33.

83   To carry all these supplies: Pakenham, *Boer War,* 196; Mahan, *Story of the War in South Africa.*

83   In an attempt to keep them calm: *Diamond Fields Advertiser,* Jan. 3, 1900; "Horses on Board Ship," *Baily's Magazine,* March 1903, 186.

83   Those that survived the journey: http://www.bwm.org.au/site/Horses.asp.

83   The crowd in Cape Town watched in excitement: WSC speech to Parliament, Jan. 1902; *Yorkshire Evening Post,* Oct. 16, 1899; *London Daily News,* Oct. 16, 1899.

84   he was surrounded by the hum of electric cars: The electric vehicle was built in the United States in 1899, and only in 1899. It had an electric cab, front-wheel drive, and rear-wheel steering.

84   "It seemed half Western American": Steevens, *From Capetown to Ladysmith,* 5.

84   "not to be a young ass": Griffith, *Thank God We Kept the Flag Flying,* 97.

84   "Sir Alfred Milner told me": Quoted in Pakenham, *Boer War,* 191.

85   Slipping into the city with Atkins: Atkins, *Incidents and Reflections,* 123; Winston Churchill, *London to Ladysmith,* 16.

85   When the other journalists learned: Winston Churchill, *My Early Life,* 241; Winston Churchill, *London to Ladysmith,* 16.

CHAPTER 8: LAND OF STONE AND SCRUB

87   When Churchill awoke: Winston Churchill, *London to Ladysmith,* 16.

87   "It is only to the eye": Steevens, *From Capetown to Ladysmith,* 8.

87   "The scenery would depress": Winston Churchill, *London to Ladysmith,* 16.

87   "horrible Antarctic gale": Winston Churchill, *My Early Life,* 241.

88   "most appalling paroxysms": Ibid.

88   "Here are wide tracts of fertile soil": Winston Churchill, *London to Ladysmith,* 19.

90   In many ways, Shaka both: Although he was the son of a Zulu chieftain, while he was still a child, he and his mother, an orphaned Langeni princess, were cast out of the tribe and forced to live with the Langeni, who did not want them and made their lives miserable. Shaka, who grew up to be a powerful and feared warrior, was filled with hatred and resentment and eager to exact

his revenge. His chance finally came in 1816, when his father died. After killing his half brother, who had been the only real threat to his ascension, Shaka seized control of the Zulu military and, soon after, the throne.

90   Shaka also redesigned the most essential: Morris, *Washing of the Spears,* 47.

91   "No fetters or cords": Quoted in Greaves and Mkhize, *Zulus at War,* 14–15. Shaka, moreover, had a long memory. As soon as he had risen to power, he had had everyone who had been abusive or cruel to his mother executed, impaling men on their own fences and burning down their villages. Several years later, when his mother died, the entire Zulu tribe, by then many thousands strong, were forced not just to mourn for weeks without relief, wailing and writhing, but to engage in wholesale massacre. At least seven thousand people were killed, for months filling the streams and kraals with rotting bodies. On the day of her burial, Shaka ordered twelve thousand men to guard his mother's grave, and ten young women were buried alive with her, their arms and legs broken so they could not claw their way out.

93   "I was too late": Winston Churchill, *My Early Life,* 242.

93   " 'As far as you can' ": Winston Churchill, *London to Ladysmith,* 20.

93   "As I approached": Reitz, *Commando,* 34.

94   Because Buller had yet to arrive: Winston Churchill, *London to Ladysmith,* 23.

94   Even with this welcome addition: Amery, *Times History of the War in South Africa,* 2:113.

94   "The enemy crouches": Atkins, *Relief of Ladysmith,* 60.

94   "It was a period of strained waiting": Romer and Mainwaring, *Second Battalion Royal Dublin Fusiliers in the South African War,* 15.

94   "We live in expectation of attack": Winston Churchill, *London to Ladysmith,* 22.

CHAPTER 9: THE DEATH TRAP

97   "Fancy how lucky I am": Winston Churchill, *My Early Life,* 168.

98   "tiny tin township": Ibid., 242.

98   "of mean and insignificant aspect": Winston Churchill, *London to Ladysmith,* 22.

98   "exceedingly clever": WSC to Lady Randolph Churchill, Nov. 3, 1899, CAC.

98   The young reporter had watched: Atkins, *Incidents and Reflections,* 112.

99   "most unusual young man": Ibid., 122.

99   "When the prospects of a career": Ibid.

99   "I don't like the fellow": Randolph S. Churchill, *Youth,* 354. It seemed that wherever he went, from Harrow to Bangalore, Churchill was judged a little too clever, and far too confident. Bishop Welldon, who had been the headmaster of Harrow when Churchill was a student there, once told a friend of Churchill's that he had been forced to whip him more often than any other boy and that "this obstreperous, irresponsible pupil had . . . even had the audacity to tell him how to perform his duties."

100   Churchill had only been at the school: Winston Churchill, *My Early Life*, 17–18; Amery, *My Political Life*, 39.

100   "outrage on my dignity": Amery, *My Political Life*, 39.

101   "for the first time meet": Winston Churchill, *My Early Life*, 243.

101   "I had an effective team": Amery, *My Political Life*, 115.

101   "could laugh at his dreams of glory": Atkins, *Incidents and Reflections*, 123.

101   It was difficult enough: Riall, *Boer War*, 23.

102   The camp had a bleak tin building: Ibid.

102   Occasionally, they were even forced to resort: http://17thdivision.tripod.com/rationsoftheageofempire/id5.html.

102   From the hills surrounding the town: Atkins, *Relief of Ladysmith*, 61.

102   From Estcourt, Churchill watched the flashes: The men in Estcourt also had a heliograph, which looked like a round, brass-framed vanity mirror on a tripod, with an arm on a swivel that held another, identical mirror. It was usually operated by a young officer named Malcolm Riall, who had undergone additional training in signaling while at Sandhurst and would calmly sit before his heliograph, smoking a pipe and wearing a flat-brimmed hat to shade his eyes as he attempted to communicate with White. It was not a perfect system. There were often cloudy or stormy days, and the high hills that lined the northern bank of the Tugela River, just south of Ladysmith, obstructed their view, but Riall was usually able to make it work. "Fortunately I am a fairly good signaler myself," he wrote to his mother, "and if there was any difficulty . . . I could generally rely on getting the message through." Riall, *Boer War*, 10.

102   "spent years in pigeon culture": "Carrier Pigeons in the British-Boer War," *Collier's Weekly*, Dec. 23, 1900, 15.

103   "brown speck floating": Winston Churchill, *London to Ladysmith*, 28.

103   "favourite diet": Steevens, *From Capetown to Ladysmith*, 34.

103   Bicycles, which had been used: Caidin and Barbree, *Bicycles in War*, 12.

104   "Nothing looks more formidable": Winston Churchill, *My Early Life*, 244.

104   "the advantage of drawing first blood": Winston Churchill, *London to Ladysmith*, 14.

104   "seriously underrated the nature": "Boers at Kraaipan," *Diamond Fields Advertiser*, Oct. 14, 1899.

104   "Wilson's death-trap": T. A. Heathcote, *British Admirals of the Fleet, 1734–1995: A Biographical Dictionary* (Barnsley, South Yorkshire: Leo Cooper, 2002), 80.

104   "It was not really an armored train": Atkins, *Relief of Ladysmith*, 65–66.

105   "Day after day": Haldane, *How We Escaped from Pretoria*, 6.

105   "chief diversion of our life": Atkins, *Relief of Ladysmith*, 65–66.

105   "How relieved the occupants": Haldane, *How We Escaped from Pretoria*, 6.

105   "should get to the front": Winston Churchill, *Ian Hamilton's March*, 123.

106   "An armoured train!": Winston Churchill, *London to Ladysmith*, 23. "Mr. Morley" refers to John Morley, 1st Viscount Morley of Blackburn, who had been

chief secretary for Ireland and would, in 1905, become secretary of state for
India. Morley was known for his opposition to imperialism in general and the
Boer War in particular and, as such, was an object of scorn and derision for
Churchill.

106 "Beyond Chieveley": Winston Churchill, *London to Ladysmith*, 24.
106 When they finally reached Colenso: Ibid.
107 When they pulled back in: Ibid., 25.
107 "could see nothing": Amery, *My Political Life*, 117.
107 As they climbed out of the car: Ibid.

CHAPTER 10: A PITY AND A BLUNDER

108 One night soon after arriving in Estcourt: Winston Churchill, *My Early Life*,
     243.
108 During the Battle of Elandslaagte: Haldane, *Soldier's Saga*, 137.
109 "I can never doubt": Winston Churchill, *Story of the Malakand Field Force*, 81.
109 "Instantly the camp sprang to life": Atkins, *Relief of Ladysmith*, 68.
110 The day before, a new battalion: Amery, *Times History of the War in South
     Africa*, 2:115.
110 "A dense, paralyzing mist of uncertainty": Ibid.
110 "A moment of confidence": Ibid.
111 All around them guy ropes: Atkins, *Relief of Ladysmith*, 67–69.
111 "Lord, O poor Tommy!": Steevens, *From Capetown to Ladysmith*, 39.
111 "I saw the flash of lightning": "Notes on Lightning-Strike in South Africa,"
     AngloBoerWar.com, Jan. 25, 1902, http://www.angloboerwar.com/forum/13
     -miscellany/4611-notes-on-lightning-stroke-in-south-africa.
111 In the end, eighty-six British servicemen: Stephen Adams, "Boer War Records
     Show 86 Were Struck by Lightning," *Telegraph*, June 24, 2010.
112 "As for their boots": Steevens, *From Capetown to Ladysmith*, 25.
112 "perhaps thirty harmless shots": Atkins, *Relief of Ladysmith*, 69.
112 "with an unblushing assurance": Atkins, *Incidents and Reflections*, 122.
113 "a pity and a blunder": Ibid., 127.
113 "There could be only one explanation": Ibid.
113 "There was to be no retreat": Atkins, *Relief of Ladysmith*, 71.
113 Later that night, not long before midnight: Haldane, *Soldier's Saga*, 138.
114 "with a heart full of misgivings": Ibid., 139.
114 "hanging about to pick up": Ibid., 140.
114 When he grimly told Churchill: Winston Churchill, *My Early Life*, 244.
114 "I need hardly point out": Haldane, *Soldier's Saga*, 139.
114 "When I approached him": H. W. Kinsey, "Churchill and Ladysmith," *Mili-
     tary History Journal* 7, no. 3 (June 1987).
115 "more disappointed than I": Ibid.
115 "eager for trouble": Winston Churchill, *My Early Life*, 244.
115 "I accepted the invitation": Ibid.
115 "It was no possible use": Amery, *My Political Life*, 117.

115   Churchill, already up and ready to go: Atkins, *Incidents and Reflections,* 128–29.

116   Quickly assessing the situation: Winston Churchill, *London to Ladysmith,* 31.

116   There was some confusion and difficulty: Haldane, *Soldier's Saga,* 141; Winston Churchill, *London to Ladysmith,* 31.

117   "In dispatching the train": Haldane, *Soldier's Saga,* 140.

CHAPTER 11: INTO THE LION'S JAWS

118   "a sign of opposition or indeed of life": Winston Churchill, *My Early Life,* 244.

118   "If the veld can only be compared": Maurice, *History of the War in South Africa,* 47.

119   "went out in a businesslike way": Amery, *Times History of the War in South Africa,* 2:24.

119   Where there was no natural feature in the landscape: Ibid., 2:38.

119   "a people whose only mode of warfare": Letter to the editor, *Diamond Field Advertiser,* clipping, no date given, Africana Library, Kimberley, South Africa.

120   "The actual conditions of warfare": Amery, *Times History of the War in South Africa,* 2:16–19.

120   "These experienced soldiers": Comaroff, *Boer War Diary of Sol T. Plaatje,* 38.

121   "When this siege is over": Steevens, *From Capetown to Ladysmith,* 39.

121   "long brown rattling serpent": Winston Churchill, *London to Ladysmith,* 32.

121   "It would be hard": Amery, *Times History of the War in South Africa,* 2:115.

122   "When God holds out a finger": Reitz, *Commando,* 43–44.

123   "Had I been alone": Haldane, *Soldier's Saga,* 142.

123   "A long hill was lined": Winston Churchill, *London to Ladysmith,* 32.

123   "Certainly they were Boers": Winston Churchill, *My Early Life,* 244.

123   Whenever they were forced to go on foot: Hillegas, *With the Boer Forces,* 82.

124   "There were men in the Boer forces": Ibid., 51.

124   Ordering his men to find as many stones: Amery, *Times History of the War in South Africa,* 2:116.

125   When their work was finished: Ibid.

CHAPTER 12: GRIM SULLEN DEATH

126   "Remain at Frere": Haldane, *Soldier's Saga,* 141–42.

126   "Everything about the station": Ibid., 142.

126   Ordering the telegraphist to report to Long: Ibid.

127   When the train reached the crest of a hill: Ibid.

127   "This noisome beast always lurks": Steevens, *From Capetown to Ladysmith,* 34.

127   Urgently pressing the button: Haldane, *Soldier's Saga,* 142.

127   "rather elated": Ibid., 143.

128   Churchill, standing on a box: Winston Churchill, *My Early Life,* 245; Winston Churchill, *London to Ladysmith,* 32.

128   "very nearly the last": Winston Churchill, *My Early Life,* 245.

128   "When all is said": Steevens, *From Capetown to Ladysmith,* 36.

128   "nice surprise": Winston Churchill, *London to Ladysmith,* 32.

128   As the train picked up speed: Winston Churchill, *My Early Life,* 245.

129   The first thing Churchill saw: Ibid., 246.

129   "He was a civilian": Winston Churchill, *London to Ladysmith,* 33.

129   Realizing that they were about to lose: Winston Churchill, *My Early Life,*
      246–47. Ten years later, when Churchill became home secretary, he remem-
      bered his promise to the train driver and suggested to the king that he be
      awarded the Albert Medal, the highest award for gallantry that a British citi-
      zen can receive.

130   "This arrangement gave us": Winston Churchill, *London to Ladysmith,* 34.

130   Turning on his heels: Winston Churchill, *My Early Life,* 247.

130   "I knew him well enough": *A Soldier's Saga,* 143–44.

130   "Any direct shell": Winston Churchill, *London to Ladysmith,* 33.

130   As if to prove that theory: Ibid., 34.

131   "It took more than verbal persuasion": Haldane, *Soldier's Saga,* 144.

131   The enemy quickly surrounded: Winston Churchill, *London to Ladysmith,*
      34–35.

131   "I know myself pretty well": WSC to Lady Randolph Churchill, Dec. 22,
      1897, CAC.

131   "Winston is like a strong wire": Atkins, *Incidents and Reflections,* 131.

132   "one of the bitterest disappointments": Winston Churchill, *My Early Life,*
      248.

132   "There was a grinding crash": Winston Churchill, *London to Ladysmith,* 35.

133   "the expectation of destruction": Ibid.

133   Climbing out of his battered truck: Haldane, *Soldier's Saga,* 145.

133   "standing in the cab": Winston Churchill, *London to Ladysmith,* 35–36.

134   "The whole arm was smashed": Ibid., 36.

134   "No shouting on my part": Haldane, *Soldier's Saga,* 145.

134   "Several screamed": Winston Churchill, *London to Ladysmith,* 36.

135   "What a shame!": Steevens, *From Capetown to Ladysmith,* 28.

135   "there has been a great deal": Winston Churchill, *London to Ladysmith,* 37.

135   "crying out about the number": Atkins, *Relief of Ladysmith,* 193.

135   As soon as they spotted the handkerchief: Winston Churchill, *London to Lady-
      smith,* 36.

136   "Full of animated movement": Ibid., 37.

136   "Death stood before me": Ibid.

136   "When one is alone and unarmed": Winston Churchill, *My Early Life,* 252.

136   Standing before the man: Winston Churchill, *London to Ladysmith,* 37.

CHAPTER 13: TO SUBMIT, TO OBEY, TO ENDURE

139   Just two miles outside Estcourt: Atkins, *Relief of Ladysmith,* 73.

139   When they were finally close enough: Amery, *My Political Life,* 117; Atkins,
      Incidents and Reflections, 129.

140   "shortly and stumblingly": Atkins, *Relief of Ladysmith,* 73–74.

140   "Well, I devoutly hope": Ibid., 75–76.

140   "All military pride": Winston Churchill, *London to Ladysmith,* 38.

140   Furious with himself: Winston Churchill, *My Early Life,* 253.

141   The two men had not gone far: Haldane, *Soldier's Saga,* 146.

141   "deep and dreary dungeon": Haldane, *How We Escaped from Pretoria.*

141   "I had not helped anybody": Winston Churchill, *My Early Life,* 257.

142   "Something at least was saved": Winston Churchill, *London to Ladysmith,* 38.

142   "meditated blankly upon the sour rewards": Winston Churchill, *My Early Life,* 257.

142   "like cattle!": Quoted in Randolph S. Churchill, *Youth,* 475.

142   "You need not walk fast": Winston Churchill, *London to Ladysmith,* 38.

142   "Behind every hill": Ibid., 39.

143   "I am a newspaper correspondent": Ibid., 40.

143   "A civilian in a half uniform": Winston Churchill, *My Early Life,* 258.

143   "a name better known": Winston Churchill, *London to Ladysmith,* 39.

144   "from the depths of the ground": "The African Diamond Mines," *Scientific American,* Aug. 22, 1891, 13042.

144   Although he was more than justified: Randolph Henry Spencer Churchill, *Men, Mines, and Animals in South Africa,* 92.

144   "The Boer farmer . . . is perfectly uneducated": Ibid., 94.

144   "Lord Randolph Churchill": Quoted in Manchester, *Visions of Glory,* 165–66.

145   "I have composed here": Randolph Churchill to Lady Randolph Churchill, July 2, 1891.

145   "You cannot imagine": WSC to Randolph Churchill, July [8?], 1891, CAC.

145   "I hear the horrid Boers": WSC to Randolph Churchill, Sept. 28, 1891, CAC.

145   "prey to gnawing anxiety": Winston Churchill, *My Early Life,* 258.

146   "Oh, we do not catch lords' sons": Winston Churchill, *London to Ladysmith,* 40.

147   "English by race": Ibid., 40–41.

147   "It seemed that love of life": Ibid., 40.

147   "if any officer": Haldane to Knutford, April 22, 1931.

148   "I think that it is a cardinal fact": Haldane, *Soldier's Saga,* 147–48.

148   "Why not lie buried": Winston Churchill, *London to Ladysmith,* 42.

148   Soon after a breakfast: Ibid.

149   Later in the day, as they drew nearer: Haldane, *Soldier's Saga,* 148.

149   "Beleaguered Ladysmith": Winston Churchill, *London to Ladysmith,* 44.

149   Once inside his tent: Ibid., 46.

150   "One could not help regretting": Haldane, *Soldier's Saga,* 148.

150   While arrangements for the final leg: Randolph S. Churchill, *Youth,* 475.

150   "The reader will believe": Winston Churchill, *London to Ladysmith,* 47.

151   "Amid the approving grins": Ibid.

151   Also stationed in Estcourt: Judith Crosbie, "The Great Escape: How My Family Gave Churchill a Leg Up," *Irish Times,* nd.

151   "He told me I would never": Brockie to his father, May 15, 1900, CAC.

152   Brockie had to crawl: Ibid.

152   When he was captured: Ibid.

152   "maintain the fiction": Haldane, *Soldier's Saga,* 148.

152   "We thought he was the very man": Winston Churchill, *My Early Life,* 261.

152   Speaking in undertones: Ibid.

152   Continuously looking about the train car: Winston Churchill, *London to Lady-smith,* 51.

CHAPTER 14: "I REGRET TO INFORM YOU"

153   "always been noted as the resort": "The 'Maine's' Concert," *Daily Mail,* Nov. 20, 1899.

153   As Jennie's guests stepped: "Mrs. Brown Potter's Concert," *Gloucestershire Echo,* Nov. 20, 1899; "'Maine's' Concert."

154   "Pretty women wearing the prettiest": "'Maine's' Concert."

154   Everyone from the Prince of Wales: Ibid.

154   "I regret to inform you": Randolph S. Churchill, *Youth,* 475–76.

155   "The railway men who accompanied": *Morning Post,* Nov. 18, 1899.

155   Instead of commenting on the fact: "Mr. Churchill's Heroism," *Yorkshire Evening News,* Nov. 17, 1899.

155   "Mr. Winston Churchill is said": Quoted in the *Morning Post,* Nov. 18, 1899.

155   "rallied the party frequently": Quoted in ibid.

156   "The dangers of the modern war correspondent's work": Ibid.

156   "We wish him a safe return": "Mr. Winston Churchill," *Nottingham Evening Post,* Nov. 17, 1899.

156   "This is the way to Parliament": Atkins, *Incidents and Reflections,* 130.

156   "We are very sorry": Quoted in the *Morning Post,* Nov. 18, 1899.

157   "Everyone naturally discussed": "The Capture of Mr. Winston Churchill," *York Herald,* Nov. 20, 1899.

157   "I came down in the armoured": Walden to Lady Randolph Churchill, Nov. 17, 1899, in Churchill and Gilbert, *Churchill Documents,* 1:466.

157   "the gallantry of WSC": *Daily News Weekly* editor to Lady Randolph Churchill, Nov. 21, 1899, CAC.

157   "I am so grieved": Quoted in Sebba, *American Jennie,* 241.

158   "Of course, the glamour": Quoted in ibid., 230.

158   "a bit short on brain": Ibid.

158   "I hate the idea": WSC to Lady Randolph Churchill, April 25, 1898, in Churchill and Gilbert, *Churchill Documents,* 2:923.

158   "Don't tell him I said so": George to Lady Randolph Churchill, Oct. 6, 1899, CAC.

158   "I cannot tell you what he said": George to Lady Randolph Churchill, Sept. 16, 1899, CAC.

159   That summer, the prince: Sebba, *American Jennie,* 237–38.

159   "It has been my privilege": Ridley, *Bertie,* 315.

159   "my darling little missie": George to Lady Randolph Churchill, Aug. 24, 1899, CAC.

159   "After all I don't believe": WSC to Lady Randolph Churchill, Sept. 3, 1899, CAC.

159   "Had it not been for the absorbing occupation": Mrs. George Cornwallis-West, *The Reminiscences of Lady Randolph Churchill,* 409.

159   She also realized, however: *Gloucestershire Echo,* Nov. 20, 1899.

160   The ship, which had been donated: Sebba, *American Jennie,* 241.

160   In the end, her room: Celia Lee, "90th Anniversary Talk on Jennie, Lady Randolph Churchill," June 29, 2011, http://www.winstonchurchill.org/support?catid=0&id=1205.

160   "decorated in a manner": Quoted in Sebba, *American Jennie,* 243.

160   "had every scrap of religious literature": Quoted in ibid.

160   Lady Churchill would soon be on her way: Lee, "90th Anniversary Talk on Jennie."

161   "more than I have ever hated": Winston Churchill, *My Early Life,* 259.

CHAPTER 15: A CITY OF THE DEAD

162   "The simple, valiant burghers": Winston Churchill, *London to Ladysmith,* 53.

162   "Ugly women with bright parasols": Ibid.

163   Worried that the man would accidentally: Haldane, *How We Escaped from Pretoria,* 22; Haldane, *Soldier's Saga,* 148–49.

163   "broken down constabulary": Winston Churchill, *London to Ladysmith,* 53.

163   "serious men who cared": Ibid.

163   "burly, evil-looking police official": Haldane, *How We Escaped from Pretoria,* 22.

164   "a trophy for the inhabitants": Ibid., 23.

164   "a pretty place": Randolph Churchill to Lady Randolph Churchill, July 2, 1891, CAC.

164   "an attractive, if baking hot, townlet": Amery, *My Political Life,* 105.

164   "deserted, a city of the dead": Ibid., 112.

165   "Soldiers of fortune": Hillegas, *With the Boer Forces,* 27.

165   "When cannon were roaring": Ibid., 26.

165   "The town is regularly laid out": Haldane, *How We Escaped from Pretoria,* 21.

165   While they walked: Winston Churchill, *London to Ladysmith,* 53.

165   "still more ill-favoured-looking person": Haldane, *How We Escaped from Pretoria,* 23.

166   "looked a miserable creature": Winston Churchill, *London to Ladysmith,* 53.

166   "odious Malan": Ibid., 56.

166   "life on the racecourse": Buttery, *Why Kruger Made War,* 30; Winston Churchill, *My Early Life,* 264.

166   In jarring contrast to the beauty: Haldane, *Soldier's Saga,* 150; Winston Churchill, *My Early Life,* 268. In *My Early Life,* Churchill writes that the fence was ten feet tall, but two other sources, including Haldane, say that it was six and a half.

166   Nine stony-faced ZARPs patrolled: Hofmyer, *Story of My Captivity,* 116; Haldane, *How We Escaped from Pretoria,* 26.

167   As the men took in the Staats Model School: Winston Churchill, *London to Ladysmith,* 54.

167   "All are mobbed": Burnett diary, http://www.angloboerwar.com/books/27 -burnett-18th-hussars-in-south-africa/696-burnett-appendix-1.

167   "the sort of reception": Winston Churchill, *London to Ladysmith,* 54.

168   On each side of the corridor: *Sir Winston Churchill and Pretoria: Sixty Years Ago.* http://repository.up.ac.za/bitstream/handle/2263/13262/007_p083-096 .pdf?sequence=4.

168   "We thought of nothing else but freedom": Winston Churchill, *My Early Life,* 261.

168   Although during battle they did not: Pakenham, *Boer War,* 172.

168   After the death of Penn Symons: Rayne Kruger, *Goodbye Dolly Gray,* 87–88; Griffith, *Thank God We Kept the Flag Flying,* 98.

169   "the water out of their own bottles": Steevens, *From Capetown to Ladysmith,* 27.

169   "lean, fair-haired young man": Amery, *My Political Life,* 106.

169   Even Albert Einstein had been impressed: Smuts, *Memoirs of the Boer War,* 19. By then, Smuts would have already been elected as prime minister of South Africa and served on the British War Cabinet during World War I, helping to form the Royal Air Force.

170   A resident artist: Frankland would also draw two smaller cartoons on the walls of the Staats Model School. These, because they depicted Kruger fleeing from a ZARP, whip in hand, were later destroyed, but pictures of them still exist.

170   "dark neutral colour": Winston Churchill, *London to Ladysmith,* 54–55.

170   "You are in the power of your enemy": Churchill, *My Early Life,* 259.

171   "I am 25 today": Cockran to WSC, Nov. 30, 1899, CAC.

171   "Looking back on those days": Churchill, *My Early Life,* 259.

172   "Captured unarmed": De Souza archive, Witwatersrand University.

172   "Dearest Mama": WSC to Lady Randolph Churchill, Nov. 18, 1899, CAC.

172   "Not a vy satisfactory address": WSC to Plowden, Nov. 18, 1899, CAC.

172   De Souza, a quiet, thoughtful man: Marie de Souza, diary, Jonathan de Souza notes, Oct. 23, 1899.

172   "The burghers took an armoured train": Marie de Souza, diary, Nov. 15, 1899.

174   "I have consistently adhered": Randolph S. Churchill, *Youth,* 480.

174   "My case while under detention": Ibid.

174   "I understand that the son": Ibid., 479.

175   "The Government will act accordingly": Ibid.

CHAPTER 16: BLACK WEEK

176   "War! What a terrible thing it is": Marie de Souza, diary, Oct. 30, 1899.

176   The day after the new prisoners arrived: Ibid., Nov. 19, 1899.

177   He gave Churchill news of the war: Winston Churchill, *London to Ladysmith,* 54.

177   R. W. L. Opperman: Hofmeyr, *The Story of My Captivity,* 117; Winston Churchill, *London to Ladysmith,* 55.

177   "a terrible hater of the English": Hofmeyr, *The Story of My Captivity,* 117.

177 Before the war, Cecil Rhodes: Winston Churchill, *London to Ladysmith,* 55; Hofmeyr, *Story of My Captivity,* 117.

177 "a far-seeing little man": Winston Churchill, *London to Ladysmith,* 55.

177 Although de Souza had gone to Europe: Francis de Souza, *A Question of Treason,* 49.

177 "Louis is worried to death!": Marie de Souza, diary, Sept. 27, 1899.

178 Although Marie de Souza had been born: Ibid., April 2, 1900.

179 Finally, on September 27: Ibid., Sept. 30, 1899.

179 "He has been so dreadfully worried": Ibid., Oct. 13, 1899.

179 "very careful": Winston Churchill, *London to Ladysmith,* 55.

179 Despite his precarious position: Ibid.

180 "as if they would be glad": Haldane, *How We Escaped from Pretoria,* 28.

180 "That night the air": Winston Churchill, *London to Ladysmith,* 56.

180 "What about Methuen?": Ibid.

180 Just a few days before de Souza: Amery, *Times History of the War in South Africa,* 2:119.

181 Joubert's death devastated de Souza: Meintjes, *General Louis Botha,* 41.

181 The first blow came: Pakenham, *Scramble for Africa,* 570–71.

181 "Please understand that there is no one": Ibid., 571; National Army Museum, London.

182 "All the news we heard": Winston Churchill, *London to Ladysmith,* 65.

182 "huge slaughters and shameful flights": Ibid.

182 "as brutal a lot of men": Hofmeyr, *Story of My Captivity,* 117.

182 "How our blood boiled": Ibid., 153.

183 "A foul and objectionable brute": Winston Churchill, *London to Ladysmith,* 56.

183 "He is no man but a brute!!": Marie de Souza, diary, Oct. 19, 1899.

183 "brought a great deal of influence": Buttery, *Why Kruger Made War,* 45.

183 "place himself in a separate category": Winston Churchill, *London to Ladysmith,* 56.

184 "a picture of misery": Ibid., 55.

184 The day before Churchill had arrived: "A Captured Boer Spy," *Age,* Nov. 18, 1899.

184 If Marks were executed: Ibid.; Marie de Souza, diary, Nov. 30, 1899.

185 "I see a rumour in the papers": Joubert to Reitz, Nov. 28, 1899, quoted in de Souza, *No Charge for Delivery,* 90.

185 "According to the *Volkstem*": Theron to Reitz, Nov. 28, 1899, quoted in ibid. Danie Theron was at this time a captain in the Transvaal Cyclist Corps. He later commanded a highly successful scouting unit known as Theron's Verkenningskorps (Theron's Scouting Corps). Information courtesy of Ken Gillings.

186 "not in the habit of killing": Reitz, *Commando,* 49. Later that night, after reading the articles, Reitz would tell his son that Churchill was a "clever young man, in which," Deneys wrote, "he was not far wrong, for soon after the prisoner climbed over a wall and escaped out of the Transvaal."

186 "Unless I am regarded": WSC to Stopford, Nov. 30, 1899, quoted in Randolph S. Churchill, *Youth,* 481.

186   "I agree to the exchange": Joubert to Acting Commandant General Pretoria, Haldane's journal, 14OE and 14OF, AHD.
186   "As soon as I learned": Winston Churchill, *My Early Life,* 268.

CHAPTER 17: A SCHEME OF DESPERATE
AND MAGNIFICENT AUDACITY

187   they had long ago estimated: Burnett, diary, 1, angloboerwar.com.
187   "You feel a sense of constant humiliation": Winston Churchill, *My Early Life,* 259.
187   "by force or fraud": Winston Churchill, *London to Ladysmith,* 57.
188   "They find intense difficulty": Vischer, *Barbed Wire Disease,* quoted in Walter Wood. *The Enemy in Our Midst* (London: 1906), 127.
188   "the criminal who knows": Ibid.
188   After first keeping their prisoners: A. J. Nathan, "Boer Prisoners of War on the Island of St. Helena," *Military History Journal* 11, no. 3/4 (Oct. 1999).
188   None of them worked: When the first contingent of Boer prisoners arrived there, a group that included General Cronjé, the British magazine *Punch* published a cartoon showing Cronjé saluting the ghost of Napoleon and saying, "Same enemy, Sire! Same result!" Ibid.
188   During his six miserable years: Mike Dash, "The Secret Plot to Rescue Napoleon by Submarine," *Smithsonian Magazine,* March 8, 2013.
189   "I could not write": Winston Churchill, *London to Ladysmith,* 57.
189   "He no doubt felt": Haldane, *Soldier's Saga,* 154.
189   "a scheme of desperate": Winston Churchill, *My Early Life,* 261.
189   "No walls are so hard to pierce": Ibid., 268.
190   "There were therefore periods": Ibid., 262.
190   "Who shall say that three men": Ibid., 264.
190   "Their life was monotonous": Ibid.
190   So bad, in fact, were the conditions: Burnett, diary, 6, angloboerwar.com.
190   "nothing but leading": Winston Churchill, *London to Ladysmith,* 55.
191   "He talks brilliantly": Mortimer Menpes, "Young Winston in South Africa, 1900," *Finest Hour,* no. 105 (Winter 1999–2000).
191   "What a feat of arms!": Winston Churchill, *My Early Life,* 266.
191   "Who shall say what is possible": Ibid., 262.
191   On December 7, three days before: Haldane, *How We Escaped from Pretoria,* 30.
192   "The escape of these men": Ibid., 31.
192   Like Haldane, Brockie had no patience: Crosbie, "Great Escape."
192   "look the other way": Haldane, *How We Escaped from Pretoria,* 30.
193   "The whole enclosure": Winston Churchill, *My Early Life,* 263.
193   "disconnect them at any moment": Ibid., 263–64.
193   "Only one sentry could possibly": Haldane, *How We Escaped from Pretoria,* 30.
193   To get there, however, Haldane and Brockie: Ibid., 30–31.
194   More than a decade earlier: "Capt. Aylmer Haldane Divorced," *Glasgow Herald,* Dec. 21, 1901.

194   In 1893, after years of impatient waiting: Haldane, *Soldier's Saga,* 59.

194   She wanted more money: "Capt. Aylmer Haldane Divorced."

194   "She tricked him": WSC to Lady Randolph Churchill, March 31, 1898, CAC.

195   "It is all very sad": WSC to Haldane, May 24, 1898, CAC.

195   "I hope the millstone": WSC to Haldane, Aug. 11, 1898. Kate Stuart would finally sue Haldane for divorce in December 1901, CAC.

195   "I was loath to seem ungenerous": Haldane, *Soldier's Saga,* 155.

196   "I certify on my honour": Quoted in Randolph S. Churchill, *Youth,* 481.

196   "was to last me my life": Winston Churchill, *My Early Life,* 102.

196   "This led me to conclude": Haldane, *Soldier's Saga,* 155.

196   "talkative friend": Ibid.

196   "getting wounded in the mouth": Douglas S. Russell, "Lt. Churchill: 4th Queen's Own Hussars," www.winstonchurchill.org.

197   "name would not be hidden": Haldane, *Soldier's Saga,* 154.

197   "I do not exaggerate": Ibid., 155–56.

197   Brockie had the same objections: Ibid., 155.

197   "repay him by leaving him": Ibid.

197   "I did not hide from him": Ibid., 155–56.

CHAPTER 18: "I SHALL GO ON ALONE"

198   "These things are best done": Winston Churchill, *London to Ladysmith,* 66.

198   "stealing secretly off": Ibid.

199   "in general terms what the plan": Haldane, *Soldier's Saga,* 155.

199   "Everything after this": Winston Churchill, *My Early Life,* 270.

199   "Churchill is in a great state of excitement": Haldane, diary, Dec. 11, 1899, AHD.

199   "I perhaps have seen Churchill": Ibid, 140U.

199   "hopelessly beaten": Winston Churchill, *London to Ladysmith,* 66.

200   "crowded again into the stifling": Winston Churchill, *My Early Life,* 57.

200   Once in the yard, the men headed: Ibid.

200   One by one, the other officers left: Haldane, *Soldier's Saga,* 150; Haldane, diary, 140H; Winston Churchill, *London to Ladysmith,* 66.

201   "a most unsatisfactory feeling": Winston Churchill, *London to Ladysmith,* 66.

201   "I was determined": Winston Churchill, *My Early Life,* 270.

201   "Another day of fear": Winston Churchill, *London to Ladysmith,* 66.

201   "We *must* go to-night": Haldane, diary, 140H.

201   "W.C. never lost sight": Ibid., 125.

202   "You're afraid": Ibid., 140H.

202   When he had first agreed: Haldane, diary, 140Q.

202   "That damned fool": Ibid.

203   "venture a seventh time": Walter Scott, *The Prose Works of Sir Walter Scott, Bart: Tales of a Grandfather,* 109.

203   "Unlike Robert the Bruce": Excerpt from Mrs. Stuart Menzies, *As Others See Us* (London: H. Jenkins, 1924).

203   "Now or never": Winston Churchill, *London to Ladysmith,* 66.

204   As he hid among the short, sharp branches: Ibid., 66–67.

204   Sitting in the dining hall with Brockie: Haldane, diary, 140H.

204   "carefully preserved": Ibid.

204   After trying unsuccessfully: Hofmeyr, *Story of My Captivity,* 133; Haldane, diary, 140H.

205   "If Brockie and I were to escape": Haldane, diary, 140I.

205   "Go back you . . . fool": Ibid.

205   "Where were the others?": Winston Churchill, *My Early Life,* 271.

206   "I cannot describe the surge": Winston Churchill, *London to Ladysmith,* 67.

206   "Amid a tumult of emotion": Ibid.

206   "uttered a 'miaul' of alarm": Ibid.

206   Now that disaster had: Ibid.; Haldane diary, 140I.

207   "Cannot get out": Winston Churchill, *London to Ladysmith,* 67.

CHAPTER 19: *TOUJOURS DE L'AUDACE*

211   "Of course, I shall be recaptured": Winston Churchill, *My Early Life,* 271.

211   "I said to myself, '*Toujours de l'audace*'": Ibid., 271–72.

211   "at large in Pretoria": Ibid., 272.

212   Even walking at a leisurely pace: Winston Churchill, *London to Ladysmith,* 68. There is an old story that claims that when describing his escape, Churchill said he swam the "mighty Apies." The story has become a source of hilarity and ridicule among South Africans, who know the thin, narrow river, but Churchill himself said that it was the product of a reporter's exaggeration, and he had never described the river in those terms.

212   "I was in the heart": Ibid.

212   He was also painfully aware: Ibid.

213   "He had given me water": Ibid.

214   "Still, it might be only winding": Ibid.

214   "When hope had departed": Ibid.

215   "A wild feeling of exhilaration": Ibid.

215   "I would board a train in motion": Ibid.

215   "I thought of Paul Bultitude's escape": Winston Churchill, *My Early Life,* 273.

216   "suddenly and entirely altered": Girouard, *History of the Railways During the War in South Africa,* 9–10.

216   From one day to the next: Ibid., 10–11.

216   "My escape must be known at dawn": Winston Churchill, *London to Ladysmith,* 68.

217   When the engine pulled away: Ibid.

218   "the consciousness of oppressive difficulties": Ibid., 69.

218   "cosy hiding place": Ibid.

219   "You could lift the heat": Winston Churchill, *My Early Life,* 132.

220   "manifested an extravagant interest": Winston Churchill, *London to Ladysmith,* 70.

221   "If the human race ever reaches": WSC to Lady Randolph Churchill, Jan. 14,
       1897, CAC.
221   "I accumulated in those years": Churchill, *My Early Life,* 113–14.
221   "It seemed good to let the mind": Ibid., 117.

CHAPTER 20: "TO TAKE MY LEAVE"

222   "a full dose of opprobrious epithets": Haldane, diary, 140I.
223   When a soldier-servant stepped: Haldane, *How We Escaped from Pretoria,* 33.
223   "Cox's should be instructed": WSC to Lady Randolph Churchill, Nov. 18,
       1899, CAC.
224   "I won't travel 2d again": WSC to Lady Randolph Churchill, Dec. 27, 1891,
       quoted in Randolph S. Churchill, *Youth,* 171.
224   "You are really too extravagant": Randolph to WSC, March 29, 1892, CAC.
224   Any money they needed: Churchill, *My Early Life,* 105.
224   "Unfortunately, he was an inquisitive": Haldane, *How We Escaped from Preto-
       ria,* 33.
224   "Some gave him no answer": Hofmeyr, *Story of My Captivity,* 134.
224   "gently and apologetically": Ibid., 134–35.
225   "Consternation is now changed into panic": Ibid., 135.
225   "in a great rage": Ibid., 135–36.
226   On the envelope, Churchill could not resist: Sandys, *Churchill,* 95.
227   "So great was the Government's": Haldane, *How We Escaped from Pretoria,* 34.
227   "It seemed to me": Hofmeyr, *Story of My Captivity,* 132.
227   "Vengeance was now": Ibid., 136–37.
227   "We were subjected": Haldane, *How We Escaped from Pretoria,* 35.
227   Additional sentries were added: Ibid., 34.
228   "must have bribed the guards": Marie de Souza, diary, Dec. 13, 1899.
228   The Boers launched a massive search: Marie de Souza, diary, Jonathan de
       Souza's notes, Dec. 15, 1899.
228   "there is reason to believe": Churchill and Gilbert, *Churchill Documents,* 2:1089.
228   "As there was a 7 o'clock": Ibid., 2:1089–90.
228   "Well gentlemen": Mrs. T. J. Rodda, "Memoires," *Pretoriana,* no. 20 (1956).
229   As soon as Hans Malan: Marie de Souza, diary, Jonathan de Souza's notes,
       Dec. 15, 1899.
229   "Louis had an awful row": Marie de Souza, diary, Dec. 13, 1899.
230   "If I accept his word": Churchill and Gilbert, *Churchill Documents,* 2:1086.
230   "It is certainly an odd coincidence": Winston Churchill, *My Early Life,* 300.
231   "At Frere we are now spending": Atkins, *Relief of Ladysmith,* 121–22.
231   "It is a beautiful job": Ibid., 122–23.
231   "They pulled drawers out of chests": Ibid., 124.
232   "a melancholy heap": Ibid., 125.
232   "get extremely close to others": Quoted in Meintjes, *General Louis Botha,*
       43–44.
233   It was the simplest sort of tent: Pakenham, *Boer War,* 268.

233   In fact, even he was struggling: Ibid., 267.

233   "God will fight for you": Ibid., 269–70.

233   That night, with just eight hundred men: Ibid., 270.

233   "Only this we know": Atkins, *Relief of Ladysmith,* 133.

CHAPTER 21: ALONE

234   "The western clouds flushed": Winston Churchill, *London to Ladysmith,* 70.

235   As Churchill cautiously stepped: Ibid.; Winston Churchill, *My Early Life,* 276.

236   "I saw myself leaving the train": Winston Churchill, *My Early Life,* 277.

236   "I could board some truck": Ibid.

236   "to keep body and soul together": Ibid.

237   "My plan began to crumble": Ibid.

237   As soon as he began his journey: Ibid., 278.

238   "no trains are to run after 7 p.m.": *Detailed History of the Railways in the South African War,* 104.

238   "fine and sure": Winston Churchill, *My Early Life,* 278.

239   "There was nothing for it but to plod on": Ibid., 279.

239   "I had heard": Ibid.

240   "the Boer does not recognize": Randolph Henry Spencer Churchill, *Men, Mines, and Animals in South Africa,* 92.

240   Churchill had had a long, spirited conversation: Winston Churchill, *London to Ladysmith,* 47–49.

241   Although he was only twenty-three: South African History Online, Solomon Tshekisho Plaatje; Comaroff, introduction to *Boer War Diary of Sol T. Plaatje.*

241   During the siege of Mafeking: Warwick, *Black People and the South African War,* 35.

242   "It looked like meat": Comaroff, *Boer War Diary of Sol T. Plaatje,* 124.

242   "The attitude of the natives": Steevens, *From Capetown to Ladysmith,* 14.

243   "They might give me food": Winston Churchill, *My Early Life,* 279.

243   "Suddenly without the slightest reason": Ibid., 280.

243   "It was certainly by no process of logic": Ibid.

245   "the shimmering gloom of the veldt": Ibid., 281.

CHAPTER 22: *"WIE IS DAAR?"*

246   Churchill stood in the moonlight: Winston Churchill, *My Early Life,* 282.

248   "I am Winston Churchill": Ibid.

249   "They had been turned out of work": Steevens, *From Capetown to Ladysmith,* 7.

249   "They spoke now of intolerable grievance": Ibid.

249   Witbank, the part of the Transvaal: Lang, *Power Base,* 41–43.

250   Its owner, Julius Burlein: Sandys, *Churchill,* 126.

250   "I felt like a drowning man": Winston Churchill, *My Early Life,* 283.

251   "They have got the hue and cry out": Ibid.

251   "food, a pistol, a guide": Ibid.

251   As determined as Howard was to help: Ibid., 284.

252   "The message of the sunset": Ibid., 81.

252   "in a grip of crushing vigour": Ibid., 284.

252   Stepping into the cage: Interview with John Bird.

253   "down we shot": Winston Churchill, *My Early Life*, 284.

253   The seam was only about: Interview with Bird.

253   "pitchy labyrinth": Winston Churchill, *My Early Life*, 284.

253   It was, however, surprisingly spacious: Interview with Bird.

253   Despite the roominess: Ibid.

254   With so many ponies, teams of men: Ibid.

254   They had come to a sort of chamber: Lang, *Power Base*, 46.

254   The large bundles that McKenna: Winston Churchill, *My Early Life*, 284–85.

254   "whatever happens": Ibid., 285.

CHAPTER 23: AN INVISIBLE ENEMY

256   "The camp was filled": Atkins, *Relief of Ladysmith*, 148–49.

256   "The column at my tent door": Ibid., 149.

257   "Chaffing and smoking": Ibid., 155.

257   Across the river, a few hours earlier: Davitt, *Boer Fight for Freedom*, 258.

257   What Botha saw as the sun: Barnard, *General Botha at the Battle of Colenso*, 6.

257   "Each man [was] the appointed distance": Atkins, *Relief of Ladysmith*, 155.

257   "sweeping on in majestic motion": Davitt, *Boer Fight for Freedom*, 260.

258   "invocation of Divine help": Ibid.

259   Unlike the British, whose twinkling lights: Barnard, *General Botha at the Battle of Colenso*, 3.

259   "Practically no attempt": Amery, *Times History of the War in South Africa*, 2:159.

259   "Buller's plan of attack": Barnard, *General Botha at the Battle of Colenso*, 5.

260   "The tidings of British reverses": Amery, *Times History of the War in South Africa*, 1:15.

261   "absorbed in interest": "Taking Sides in the Boer War," *American Heritage*, April 1976.

261   Willem Johannes Leyds: "Leyds's Last Card," *Diamond Field Advertiser*, Oct. 26, 1899.

261   "I cannot sit on the safety valve": Quoted in Winston Churchill, *My Early Life*, 303.

261   "Ridge upon ridge, top upon top": Atkins, *Relief of Ladysmith*, 150.

261   At 5:30 a.m.: Amery, *Times History of the War in South Africa*, 2:165.

262   "The cry of the shell": Atkins, *Relief of Ladysmith*, 155–56.

262   "No guns opened in reply": Amery, *Times History of the War in South Africa*, 2:165.

262   He had used even more explosives: Rayne Kruger, *Goodbye Dolly Gray*, 137.

262   "entirely on Colonel Long": *Reports from Commissioners, Inspectors, and Others,* 409.

262   "The only way to smash": Atkins, *Relief of Ladysmith,* 163.

263   "Men and officers": Ibid., 165.

263   "Abandon be damned!": Quoted in Rayne Kruger, *Goodbye Dolly Gray,* 139.

264   "General Buller sent the message": Gandhi, *Autobiography,* 215.

264   "Anywhere among the shell fire": Atkins, *Relief of Ladysmith,* 179.

265   "To march into a well-defended salient": Pakenham, *Boer War,* 276.

265   "Nothing could have saved them": Atkins, *Relief of Ladysmith,* 159.

265   "drowned like dogs": Ibid., 160.

266   As Atkins looked more closely: Ibid., 170.

266   "You oughtn't be here": Ibid., 171.

267   "He was in the full exhilaration": Ibid.

267   "The aasvogels gathered": Ibid., 176.

267   In the silence, with the full brunt: Pakenham, *Boer War,* 289.

267   "only just taken his wind": Barnard, *General Botha at the Battle of Colenso,* 9.

268   "limply and wearily from his horse": Atkins, *Relief of Ladysmith,* 169.

268   "The God of our fathers": Davitt, *Boer Fight for Freedom,* 271–72.

CHAPTER 24: THE LIGHT OF HOPE

269   "in tremendous form": Amery, *My Political Life,* 118.

269   "I regret to report": "British Disaster; Battle at Colenso," *Belfast News-Letter,* Dec. 16, 1899.

270   "I tried Colenso yesterday": Quoted in Pakenham, *Boer War,* 292.

270   "Overwhelmed by the successive tidings": Amery, *My Political Life,* 119.

270   "I have never seen a man": Winston Churchill, *Ian Hamilton's March,* 281.

270   "Your gallant son died today": National Army Museum, http://www.nam .ac.uk/exhibitions/online-exhibitions/dads-army/roberts-family/freddy-roberts.

271   "It is impossible to describe": *Sheffield Daily Telegraph,* Dec. 18, 1899.

271   "Deep as was the gloom": Amery, *Times History of the War in South Africa,* 2:174.

271   "Only one order, forward!": Boer War badges, British Museum.

271   Parents bought their children books: National Army Museum.

272   She not only knit: National Army Museum.

272   "For this far-distant war": Doyle, *Great Boer War,* 102–3.

273   "I have no doubt": Borthwick to Lady Randolph, Dec. 14, 1899, quoted in Randolph S. Churchill, *Youth,* 497.

273   "Although Mr. Winston Churchill's escape": *Manchester Courier,* Dec. 18, 1899.

273   "With reference to the escape": Winston Churchill, *My Early Life,* 290.

273   "We are on the eve": *Gloucester Journal,* Dec. 23, 1899.

274   When he reached out a hand: Winston Churchill, *My Early Life,* 286.

274   "Life seemed bathed in rosy light": Ibid., 285.

274   "I did not know what pitfalls": Ibid., 286.

274   "Didn't you put it": Ibid.
274   "He said inquiries": Ibid.
275   In fact, three thousand copies: Winston Churchill, *London to Ladysmith*, 71.
275   "absolutely safe": Winston Churchill, *My Early Life*, 287.
276   He would tell them that the mine was haunted: Ibid.
276   "like to take a turn": Ibid., 288.
276   "subterranean galleries": Ibid.

CHAPTER 25: THE PLAN

278   "The patter of little feet": Winston Churchill, *My Early Life*, 287.
278   "for a long time afterwards": "Man Who Befriended Churchill," *Johannesburg Star*, Dec. 11, 1923.
279   "I noticed that he was becoming nervy": Ibid.
279   "leap-frog [and] hide-and-seek": "Winston Churchill's Escape," *Johannesburg Star*, Dec. 22, 1923.
279   "a fine stroll": Winston Churchill, *My Early Life*, 288.
280   "The greatest pleasure I had": Ibid., 12–13.
280   "Someone had told me that my father": Ibid., 111.
281   "Those thrilling pages": Ibid., 290.
281   One day, he heard what he thought: "Man Who Befriended Churchill."
281   One morning while talking: "Winston Churchill's Escape."
282   The more Howard thought: Winston Churchill, *My Early Life*, 289.
282   The only thing left to do: In a 1921 interview for the *Johannesburg Star*, Burnham says that not only had he known about Churchill's presence at the mine for some time, but smuggling him in the wool cars had been his idea, not Howard's. I chose Howard's version of events because, in *My Early Life*, Churchill backs him up.
282   Burnham too was of English origin: "Churchill Rescuer Gives Watch to Museum," newspaper clipping in the archives of the Killie Campbell Africana Library, Durban; http://www.superbrands.com/za/pdfs/NATALMERCURY.pdf.
283   "I was more worried about this": Winston Churchill, *My Early Life*, 289.
283   "The idea of having to put myself": Ibid.
283   "I dreaded in every fibre": Ibid., 290.
284   "in open rebellion": Ibid., 292.
284   "The Field Cornet has been here": Ibid.
284   "It's all fixed up": Ibid.

CHAPTER 26: THE RED AND THE BLUE

285   At 2:00 on the morning of December 19: Winston Churchill, *My Early Life*, 292–93.
286   "I made representation": "Winston Churchill's Escape."
287   "This was a moral support": Winston Churchill, *My Early Life*, 293.

287 "Smokes were taboo": "Man Who Befriended Churchill."

287 While at the Staats Model School: Randolph S. Churchill, *Youth*, 112; Winston Churchill, *My Early Life*, 18.

288 He could remember entire lectures: Winston Churchill, *My Early Life*, 293.

288 "a Christmas box": "Winston Churchill's Escape."

288 "superior and very satisfactory": Winston Churchill, *My Early Life*, 293.

289 "bright pictures of the pleasures": Ibid., 294.

289 Sometime between 6:00 and 7:00: "Winston Churchill's Escape."

290 "So long as it was believed": Ibid.

290 "met the train at Pretoria Station": "Mr. Churchill's Escape," *Star*, March 9, 1907.

291 Although Burnham had managed: "Winston Churchill's Escape"; Burnham to WSC, March 8, 1908, quoted in Randolph S. Churchill, *Youth*, 503–4.

291 It was late in the afternoon: Winston Churchill, *My Early Life*, 294.

292 Quickly alighting from the train: Burnham to WSC, March 8, 1908, quoted in Randolph S. Churchill, *Youth*, 503–4.

292 Unlike the other station officials: "Winston Churchill's Escape."

292 "I gave a very plausible excuse": Burnham to WSC, March 8, 1908, quoted in Randolph S. Churchill, *Youth*, 503–4.

292 "It was tantalizing": Winston Churchill, *My Early Life*, 295.

292 "Perhaps they were searching": Ibid.

293 "Perhaps there was still another station": Ibid.

293 "I . . . sang and shouted": Ibid.

294 "The station master there": Burnham to WSC, March 8, 1908, quoted in Randolph S. Churchill, *Youth*, 503–4.

294 "If I allowed you": "Winston Churchill's Escape."

294 When Burnham's train pulled in: Ibid.

294 Soon after Burnham settled in: Burnham to WSC, March 8, 1908, quoted in Randolph S. Churchill, *Youth*, 503–4.; "Winston Churchill's Escape."

295 "place of refuge and of punishment": Winston Churchill, *London to Ladysmith*, 72.

295 He had somehow already managed: Winston Churchill, *My Early Life*, 296.

295 Walking up to Churchill: "Winston Churchill's Escape."

296 "As an outlet to the sea": Hillegas, *With the Boer Forces*, 20.

296 "Without shelter, badly fed": Quoted in Cammack, *Rand at War*, 119.

297 "Be off": Winston Churchill, *My Early Life*, 296.

297 "the Consul personally at once": Ibid.

EPILOGUE

299 News of his arrival: Winston Churchill, *My Early Life*, 297.

300 "It was not until I stepped": Winston Churchill, *London to Ladysmith*, 74.

300 "I was nearly torn to pieces": Winston Churchill, *My Early Life*, 297.

300 "a becoming reluctance": Ibid.

300 "in a blaze of triumph": Ibid.

300   "with many friends": Ibid.

300   "I am doubtful": Ibid., 303.

301   "Winston Churchill turned up here": Buller to Lady Londonderry, Dec. 26, 1899, in Churchill and Gilbert, *Churchill Documents,* 2:1093.

301   "The victory at Omdurman": WSC to Lady Randolph Churchill, Jan. 26, 1899, in Churchill and Gilbert, *Churchill Documents,* 2:1004.

301   "Here then was the new rule": Winston Churchill, *My Early Life,* 305.

302   "The scenes on Spion Kop": WSC to Plowden, Jan. 28, 1900, CAC.

302   "Thank God—Pamela": Churchill and Gilbert, *Churchill Documents,* 2:1093.

302   Now, having endured his capture: WSC to Plowden, Jan. 28, 1900, CAC.

302   "I read with particular attention": Ibid.

303   "one of the most happy memories": Winston Churchill, *My Early Life,* 318.

303   Inside the prison, Charles Burnett: Burnett, *18th Hussars in South Africa,* 263.

304   "Then, and then only": Ibid.

304   "Hats were flying in the air": Ibid.

304   "Some in flannels": Winston Churchill, *My Early Life,* 352.

304   While the chaotic celebration: Burnett, *18th Hussars in South Africa,* 263.

304   "Time: 8:47, June 5": Winston Churchill, *My Early Life,* 352.

305   After learning that the Boers: Haldane, *Soldier's Saga,* 168.

305   "doomed to occupy": Haldane, *How We Escaped from Pretoria,* 38.

306   Although he would later say: Brockie to his father, May 15, 1900, CAC.

306   By the time Haldane and Le Mesurier: Haldane, *How We Escaped from Pretoria,* 125.

306   "My heartiest congratulations": WSC to Haldane, April 9, 1900, CAC.

306   Le Mesurier was immediately invalided: Haldane, *Soldier's Saga,* 185.

307   "Our operations were at an end": Winston Churchill, *My Early Life,* 353.

307   The idea behind concentration camps: South African History Online, http://www.sahistory.org.za/dated-event/523-people-die-black-concentration-camps-second-anglo-boer-war.

307   The camps quickly multiplied: There were an additional sixty concentration camps for Africans.

308   "At our meeting at Middleburg": Botha to Kitchener, April 11, 1901, National Archives, Kew.

308   "As I informed Your Honour": Kitchener to Botha, April 16, 1901, National Archives, Kew.

308   "When is a war not a war?": "The Tempest in the Liberal Teacup," *Review of Reviews* 26 (July–Dec. 1901): 151.

309   "Fight to the bitter end?": Quoted in Pakenham, *Boer War,* 707.

312   "The saint has left our shores": Gandhi was someone else's problem now. In fact, he would one day be Churchill's. In 1942, when told that Gandhi, who was then imprisoned for protesting India's involvement in World War II, was on a hunger strike and might starve to death, Churchill would shrug and say that if it was up to him, he would "keep him there and let him do as he likes." England would finally grant India its independence five years later, the year before Gandhi was shot to death by a Hindu nationalist while walking to a prayer meeting.

313   "10,000 people turned out": WSC to Jack, July 31, 1900, *Churchill Documents,* 2:1188–89.

313   The procession ended: Winston Churchill, *My Early Life,* 356.

313   By that time, the British had occupied Witbank: Ibid., 356–57.

313   "It is clear to me from the figures": WSC to Salisbury, Oct. 2, 1900, *Churchill Documents,* 2:1204.

313   "I write again to impress upon you": WSC to Lady Randolph Churchill, Sept. 21, 1900, CAC.

314   Some three thousand people: "Lady Randolph Churchill's Marriage," *York Herald,* July 30, 1900.

314   "The wedding was very pretty": WSC to Jack, July 31, 1900, in Churchill and Gilbert, *Churchill Documents,* 2:1188.

314   "the only woman I could ever": WSC to Lady Randolph Churchill, Jan. 1, 1900, CAC.

314   "She ought to be a rich man's wife": Colonel J. P. Brabazon to Mrs. John Leslie, Oct. 1900, quoted in Churchill and Gilbert, *Churchill Documents,* 2:1209.

314   "Miss Plowden frequently": "Miss Plowden Engaged," *Daily Chronicle,* Feb. 2, 1902.

314   "The first time you meet Winston": Quoted in Gilbert, *Churchill,* 174.

315   "I hope you will all": WSC to Howard, Feb. 26, 1901, quoted in Sandys, *Churchill: Wanted Dead or Alive,* 140.

315   On the back of the watches: Many years later, Celia Sandys, Churchill's grand-daughter and the author of a number of illuminating books on him, would travel to South Africa and, while there, track down several of these gold watches. She tells the story in *Churchill: Wanted Dead or Alive.*

315   After the train car in which Churchill: Haldane, *How We Escaped from Pretoria,* 106; "Winston Churchill's Escape."

315   Not long after he had helped Haldane: "Man Who Befriended Churchill"; L. C. B. Howard to Randolph Churchill, May 31, 1963, quoted in Churchill and Gilbert, *Churchill Documents,* 2:1132.

316   Although during the war he had defended: WSC to Jack, June 28, 1900, CAC.

316   "We embarked on the stormy ocean": *Johannesburg Star,* Dec. 1900.

317   "the wise and right course": Winston Churchill, *My Early Life,* 329–30.

317   The two men met for the first time: Churchill would write in his memoir *My Early Life* that Botha insisted that not only had he led the attack on the armored train, but he had personally taken Churchill prisoner. Years later, while writing his biography of his father, Churchill's son, Randolph, would find that it would have been impossible for Botha to have captured Churchill. All evidence instead points to a field cornet by the name of Sarel Oosthuizen, who was killed later in the war.

317   In 1907, just over seven years: In 1910, Botha became the first prime minister of the newly formed Union of South Africa, the precursor to the Republic of South Africa.

318   "He and I have been out": Winston Churchill, *My Early Life,* 254.

SELECTED BIBLIOGRAPHY

Amery, L. S. *My Political Life*. Vol. 1. London: Hutchinson, 1953.

Amery, L. S., ed. *The Times History of the War in South Africa, 1899–1902*. Vols. 1–2. London: Sampson Low, Marston, 1900.

Atkins, J. B. *Incidents and Reflections*. London: Christophers, 1947.

———. *The Relief of Ladysmith*. London: Methuen, 1900.

Balsan, Consuelo Vanderbilt. *The Glitter and the Gold*. Kent: Gutenberg Press, 1973.

Barnard, C. J. "General Botha at the Battle of Colenso 15 December 1899." *Military History Journal* 1, no. 7 (Dec. 1970).

Beevor, Antony. *Inside the British Army*. London: Chatto & Windus, 1990.

Boyden, Peter B., Alan J. Guy, and Marion Harding. *Ashes and Blood: The British Army in South Africa, 1795–1914*. Coventry: Clifford Press, 1999.

Brendon, Piers. *The Decline and Fall of the British Empire*. New York: Alfred A. Knopf, 2008.

Brink, Elsabé. *1899, the Long March Home: A Little-Known Incident in the Anglo-Boer War*. Goodwood: National Book Printers, 1999.

Bryce, James, et al. *Briton and Boer: Both Sides of the South African Question*. New York: Harper & Brothers, 1900.

Buchan, John. *A Book of Escapes and Hurried Journeys*. London: Thomas Nelson & Sons, 1925.

Burnett, Charles. *The 18th Hussars in South Africa: The Records of a Cavalry Regiment During the Boer War, 1899–1902*. Winchester: Warren & Son, 1905.

Burnham, Frederick Russell, and Mary Nixon Everett. *Scouting on Two Continents*. New York: Garden City Publishing, 1926.

Buttery, John. *Why Kruger Made War; or, Behind the Boer Scenes*. London: William Heinemann, 1900.

Buxton, Earl. *General Botha*. London: John Murray, 1924.

Caidin, Martin, and Jay Barbree. *Bicycles in War*. New York: Hawthorn Books, 1974.

Cairnes, William Elliot. *Social Life in the British Army*. New York: Harper & Brothers, 1899.

Cammack, Diana Rose. *The Rand at War, 1899–1902: The Witwatersrand and the Anglo-Boer War*. London: James Currey, 1990.

Churchill, Peregrine, and Julian Mitchell. *Lady Randolph Churchill: A Portrait with Letters*. New York: Saint Martin's Press, 1974.

Churchill, Randolph Henry Spencer. *Men, Mines, and Animals in South Africa*. London: Sampson Low, Marston, 1895.

Churchill, Randolph S. *Youth, 1874–1900*. Vol. 1 of *Winston S. Churchill*. Hillsdale, Mich.: Hillsdale College Press, 1966.

Churchill, Sarah. *A Thread in the Tapestry*. New York: Dodd, Mead, 1966.

Churchill, Winston. *Ian Hamilton's March*. London: Longmans, Green, 1900.

———. *London to Ladysmith via Pretoria*. Wildside Press, 2005.

———. *Lord Randolph Churchill*. New York: Macmillan, 1906.

———. *Marlborough: His Life and Times*. Book One. Chicago: University of Chicago Press, 1933.

———. *My African Journey*. New York: W. W. Norton, 1989.

———. *My Early Life, 1874–1904*. New York: Touchstone, 1930.

———. *The River War*. London: Longmans, Green, and Co., 1902.

———. *Savrola*. London: Longmans, Green, 1899.

———. *The Story of the Malakand Field Force: An Episode of Frontier War*. London: Thomas Nelson & Sons, 1916.

———. *Thoughts and Adventures: Churchill Reflects on Spies, Cartoons, Flying, and the Future*. Edited by James W. Muller with Paul H. Courtenay and Alana L. Barton. Wilmington, Del.: ISI Books, 2009.

Churchill, Winston, and Martin Gilbert. *The Churchill Documents*, Vols. 1–3. Hillsdale, Mich.: Hillsdale College Press, 1967.

Clarke, Peter. *Mr. Churchill's Profession: The Statesman as Author and the Book That Defined the "Special Relationship."* New York: Bloomsbury Press, 2012.

Comaroff, John L., ed. *The Boer War Diary of Sol T. Plaatje: An African at Mafeking*. London: Macmillan, 1973.

Coote, Colin, and Denzil Batchelor, eds. *Maxims and Reflections of Winston Churchill*. Toronto: Collins Sons, 1947.

Cornwallis-West, Mrs. George. *The Reminiscences of Lady Randolph Churchill*. New York: The Century Co., 1908.

Coughlin, Con. *Churchill's First War: Young Winston and the Fight Against the Taliban*. London: Macmillan, 2013.

Cowles, Virginia. *Winston Churchill: The Era and the Man*. New York: Grosset & Dunlap, 1953.

Crossley, Alan, and C. R. Elrington, eds. *A History of the County of Oxford*. Vol. 12. London: Victoria County History, 1990.

Davenport, Jade. *Digging Deep: A History of Mining in South Africa*. Johannesburg: Jonathan Ball, 2013.

Davitt, Michael. *The Boer Fight for Freedom*. New York: Funk & Wagnalls, 1902.

Deacon, Janette, and Mike Wilson. "Peers Cave, 'the Cave the World Forgot.'" *Digging Stick* 9, no. 2 (Aug. 1992).

de Souza, C. W. L. *No Charge for Delivery*. Cape Town: Books of Africa, 1969.

deSouza, Francis. *A Question of Treason*. Hillcrest, South Africa: Kiaat Creations, 2004.

D'Este, Carlo. *Warlord: A Life of Winston Churchill at War, 1874–1945*. New York: HarperCollins, 2008.

Detailed History of the Railways in the South African War, 1899–1902. Chatham: Royal Engineers Institute, 1904.

Dickson, W. K.-L. *The Biograph in Battle: Its Story in the South African War*. London: T. Fisher Unwin, 1901.

Doyle, Arthur Conan. *The Great Boer War*. Lexington, Ky.: 2011.

———. *The War in South Africa: Its Cause and Conduct*. London: Smith, Elder, 1902.

Edgerton, Foster Hugh. *The History of the Boer War*. Vol. 1. London: Methuen, 1901.

Evans, A. J. *The Escaping Club*. Harmondsworth: Penguin Books, 1921.

Farrow, Edward Samuel. *A Dictionary of Military Terms*. New York: Thomas Y. Crowell, 1918.

Farwell, Byron. *Eminent Victorian Soldiers: Seekers of Glory*. New York: W. W. Norton, 1985.

———. *The Great Anglo-Boer War*. New York: W. W. Norton, 1976.

———. *Mr. Kipling's Army: All the Queen's Men*. New York: W. W. Norton, 1981.

———. *Queen Victoria's Little Wars*. New York: W. W. Norton, 1972.

Fincastle, Viscount, and P. C. Eliott-Lockhart. *A Frontier Campaign: A Narrative of the Operations of the Malakand and Buner Field Forces, 1897–1898*. London: Methuen, 1898.

Forster, John, and Jeri Bapasola. *Winston and Blenheim: Churchill's Destiny*. Woodstock: Blenheim Palace, 2005.

Forster, Margaret Elizabeth. *Churchill's Grandmama: Frances, 7th Duchess of Marlborough*. Stroud: History Press, 2010.

Fynn, Henry Francis. *The Diary of Henry Francis Fynn*. Edited by James Stuart and D. McK. Malcolm. Pietermaritzburg: Shuter and Shooter, 1950.

Gandhi, Mohandas K. *An Autobiography: The Story of My Experiments with Truth*. Boston: Beacon Press, 1957.

Gilbert, Martin. *Churchill: A Life*. New York: Henry Holt, 1991.

———. *Churchill: The Power of Words; His Remarkable Life Recounted Through His Writings and Speeches*. Boston: Da Capo Press, 2012.

———. *In Search of Churchill: A Historian's Journey*. New York: John Wiley & Sons, 1994.

Girouard, Édouard Percy Cranvill. *History of the Railways During the War in South Africa, 1899–1902*. London: Printed for His Majesty's Stationery Office, 1903.

Greaves, Adrian, and Xolani Mkhize. *The Zulus at War: The History, Rise, and Fall of the Tribe That Washed Its Spears*. New York: Skyhorse, 2013.

Griffith, Kenneth. *Thank God We Kept the Flag Flying: The Siege and Relief of Ladysmith, 1899–1900*. New York: Viking Press, 1974.

Gua, Ramachandra. *Gandhi Before India*. New York: Alfred A. Knopf, 2014.

Haldane, Sir James Aylmer Lowthrop. *How We Escaped from Pretoria.* Edinburgh: William Blackwood & Sons, 1900.

———. *A Soldier's Saga: The Autobiography of General Sir Aylmer Haldane.* Edinburgh: William Blackwood & Sons, 1948.

Hall, Darrell. *Halt! Action Front! With Colonel Long at Colenso.* Weltevreden Park: Covos-Day Books, 1999.

Haythornthwaite, Philip J. *The Colonial Wars Source Book.* London: Arms and Armour Press, 1995.

Herman, Arthur. *Gandhi and Churchill: The Epic Rivalry That Destroyed an Empire and Forged Our Age.* New York: Bantam Books, 2008.

Hillegas, Howard C. *Oom Paul's People.* New York: D. Appleton, 1900.

———. *With the Boer Forces.* London: Methuen, 1900.

Hofmeyr, Adrian. *The Story of My Captivity During the Transvaal War, 1899–1900.* London: Edward Arnold, 1900.

James, Lawrence. *Churchill and Empire: Portrait of an Imperialist.* London: Weidenfeld and Nicolson, 2013.

James, Robert Rhodes. *Lord Randolph Churchill.* London: Weidenfeld and Nicolson, 1959.

Jeal, Tim. *Baden-Powell: Founder of the Boy Scouts.* New Haven, Conn.: Yale University Press, 2001.

Jerrold, Walter. *Sir Redvers H. Buller, V.C.: The Story of His Life and Campaigns.* London: Edwin Dalton, 1908.

Keegan, John. *The Face of Battle.* New York: Penguin Books, 1976.

Kehoe, Elisabeth. *Fortune's Daughters.* London: Atlantic Books, 2004.

Kiley, Kevin F., and Digby Smith. *An Illustrated Encyclopedia of Military Uniforms of the 19th Century: An Expert Guide to the Crimean War, American Civil War, Boer War, Wars of German and Italian Unification, and Colonial Wars.* With Jeremy Black. Leicestershire: Lorenz Books, 2010.

Kipling, Rudyard. *Something of Myself.* Oxford: Benediction Classics, 2008.

Knight, Ian. *The Anatomy of the Zulu Army from Shaka to Cetshwayo, 1818–1879.* London: Greenhill Books, 1995.

Krige, Jan. *American Sympathy in the Boer War.* N.p.: Automatic Printing Press.

Kruger, Paul. *The Memoirs of Paul Kruger: Four Times President of the South African Republic, Told by Himself.* Capetown: Argus, 1902.

Kruger, Rayne. *Goodbye Dolly Gray: The Story of the Boer War.* London: Pimlico, 1996.

Laband, John. *The Rise and Fall of the Zulu Nation.* London: Arms and Armour Press, 1997.

Lang, John. *Power Base: Coal Mining in the Life of South Africa.* Johannesburg: Jonathan Ball, 1995.

Leakey, L. S. B., and Vanne Morris Goodall. *Unveiling Man's Origins: Ten Decades of Thought About Human Evolution.* Cambridge: Schenkman Publishing Co., 1969.

Lee, Celia, and John Lee. *The Churchills: A Family Portrait.* New York: Palgrave Macmillan, 2010.

Lee, Emanoel. *To the Bitter End: A Photographic History of the Boer War, 1899–1902.* Middlesex: Penguin Books, 1986.

Lelyveld, Joseph. *Great Soul: Mahatma Gandhi and His Struggle with India*. New York: Vintage Books, 2011.

———. *Move Your Shadow: South Africa, Black and White*. New York: Times Books, 1985.

Lovell, Mary S. *The Churchills: In Love and War*. New York: W. W. Norton, 2011.

Lukacs, John. *Churchill: Visionary, Statesman, Historian*. New Haven, Conn.: Yale University Press, 2002.

Mahan, Alfred Thayer. *Story of the War in South Africa, 1899–1900*. London: Sampson Low, Marston, 1900.

Manchester, William. *Visions of Glory, 1874–1932*. Vol. 1 of *The Last Lion, Winston Spencer Churchill*. Boston: Little, Brown, 1983.

Manchester, William, and Paul Reid. *Defender of the Realm, 1940–1965*. Vol. 3 of *The Last Lion, Winston Spencer Churchill*. New York: Little, Brown, 2012.

Marincowitz, Helena. *Prince Albert and the Anglo-Boer War, 1899–1902*. Cape Town: Gwynne-Plaka Press, 1999.

Maurice, Frederick. *History of the War in South Africa*. London: Hurst and Blackett Limited, 1906.

"Medical Aspects of the Boer War." *British Medical Journal: Reports and Analyses*, Dec. 2, 1899, 1556–57.

Meintjes, Johannes. *General Louis Botha: A Biography*. London: Cassell, 1970.

———. *President Paul Kruger*. London: Cassell, 1974.

Millin, Sarah Gertrude. *General Smuts*. London: Faber and Faber, 1936.

———. *General Smuts: The Second Volume*. London: Faber and Faber, 1936.

Morgan, Ted. *Churchill: Young Man in a Hurry, 1874–1915*. New York: Simon & Schuster, 1982.

Morris, Donald R. *The Washing of the Spears: The Rise and Fall of the Zulu Nation*. New York: Konecky & Konecky, 1965.

Muller, James W. *Churchill as Peacemaker*. Cambridge, U.K.: Cambridge University Press, 1997.

Mytum, Harold, and Gilly Carr, eds. *Prisoners of War: Archaeology, Memory, and Heritage of 19th- and 20th-Century Mass Internment*. New York: Springer Science+Business Media News, 2013.

Oliver, Roland. "The Problem of the Bantu Expansion." *Journal of African History* 7, no. 3 (1966): 361–76.

Pakenham, Thomas. *The Boer War*. London: The Folio Society, 1999.

———. *The Scramble for Africa: White Man's Conquest of the Dark Continent from 1876 to 1912*. New York: Perennial, 1991.

Pemberton, W. Baring. *Battles of the Boer War*. London: Pan Books, 1964.

Plaatje, Solomon Tshekisho. *Native Life in South Africa Before and Since the European War and the Boer Rebellion*. Whitefish, Mont.: Kessinger, 1998.

Pretorius, Fransjohan. *The Anglo-Boer War, 1899–1902*. Cape Town: Struik, 1998.

———. *Historical Dictionary of the Anglo-Boer War*. Lanham, Md.: Scarecrow Press, 2009.

Ratcliffe, Barrie M. *Great Britain and Her World, 1750–1914: Essays in Honour of W. O. Henderson*. Manchester: Manchester University Press, 1975.

Raugh, Harold E., Jr. *The Victorians at War, 1815–1914: An Encyclopedia of British Military History.* Oxford: ABC-CLIO, 2004.

Reitz, Deneys. *Commando: A Boer Journal of the Boer War.* London: Faber & Faber, 1929.

Reports from Commissioners, Inspectors, and Others: Forty-One Volumes. Sess. 2, Feb. 1904–15, Aug. 1904.

Riall, Nicolas, ed. *Boer War: The Letters, Diaries, and Photographs of Malcolm Riall from the War in South Africa, 1899–1902.* London: Brassey's, 2000.

Ridley, Jane. *Bertie: A Life of Edward VII.* London: Chatto & Windus, 2012.

Roberts, Brian. *Churchills in Africa.* London: Hamish Hamilton, 1970.

Robinson, Ronald, and John Gallagher. *Africa and the Victorians.* With Alice Denny. New York: St. Martin's Press, 1961.

Romer, C. F., and A. E. Mainwaring. *The Second Battalion Royal Dublin Fusiliers in the South African War.* London: A. L. Humphreys, 1908.

Rosslyn, James, 5th Earl of. *Twice Captured: A Record of Adventure During the Boer War.* Edinburgh: William Blackwood & Sons, 1900.

Roy, Andrew. *The Coal Mines: Containing a Description of the Various Systems of Working and Ventilating Mines.* Cleveland: Robison, Savage, 1876.

Russell, Douglas S. *The Orders, Decorations, and Medals of Sir Winston Churchill.* Hopkinton, N.H.: International Churchill Society of the United States, 1990.

———. *Winston Churchill, Soldier: The Military Life of a Gentleman at War.* London: Brassey's, 2005.

Sandys, Celia. *Churchill: Wanted Dead or Alive.* New York: Carroll & Graf, 1999.

———. *The Young Churchill: The Early Years of Winston Churchill.* New York: Dutton, 1994.

Scott, Alexander MacCallum. *Winston Spencer Churchill.* London: Methuen, 1905.

Sebba, Anne. *American Jennie: The Remarkable Life of Lady Randolph Churchill.* New York: W. W. Norton, 2007.

Seibold, Birgit Susanne. *Emily Hobhouse and the Reports on the Concentration Camps During the Boer War, 1899–1902: Two Different Perspectives.* Stuttgart: Ibidem, 2011.

Shelden, Michael. *Young Titan: The Making of Winston Churchill.* New York: Simon & Schuster, 2013.

Shirer, William L. *Gandhi: A Memoir.* New York: Washington Square Press, 1982.

Sibbald, Raymond. *The War Correspondents: The Boer War.* Dover: Alan Sutton, 1993.

Singer, André. *Lords of the Khyber: The Story of the North-West Frontier.* London: Faber and Faber, 1984.

Singer, Barry. *Churchill Style: The Art of Being Winston Churchill.* New York: Abrams, 2012.

Smuts, Jan. *Memoirs of the Boer War.* Edited by Gail Nattrass and S. B. Spies. Johannesburg: Jonathan Ball, 1994.

Soames, Mary. *A Daughter's Tale: The Memoir of Winston Churchill's Youngest Child.* New York: Random House, 2011.

Spencer-Churchill, Henrietta. *Blenheim and the Churchill Family: A Personal Portrait.* London: Cico Books, 2005.

Spender, Harold. *General Botha.* London: Constable, 1919.

Steevens, George Warrington. *From Capetown to Ladysmith: An Unfinished Record of the South African War.* London: William Blackwood and Sons, 1900.

Stevenson, Robert Louis. *Kidnapped.* New York: Modern Library, 2001.

Thomas, Antony. *Rhodes: The Race for Africa.* New York: St. Martin's Press, 1996.

Toye, Richard. *Churchill's Empire: The World That Made Him and the World He Made.* New York: St. Martin's Griffin, 2010.

Trew, Peter. *The Boer War Generals.* London: J. H. Haynes, 1999.

Warwick, Peter. *Black People and the South African War, 1899–1902.* Cambridge, U.K.: Cambridge University Press, 1983.

Wilson, Keith, ed. *The International Impact of the Boer War.* Chesham: Acumen, 2001.

Wilson, Lady Sarah. *South African Memories: Social, Warlike, and Sporting.* London: Edward Arnold, 1909.

Woods, Frederick. *A Bibliography of the Works of Sir Winston Churchill.* Dorking: Nicholas Vane, 1963.

———, ed. *Young Winston's Wars: The Original Dispatches of Winston S. Churchill, War Correspondent, 1897–1900.* London: Leo Cooper, 1972.

ILLUSTRATION CREDITS

INDEX

Page numbers beginning with 327 refer to notes.

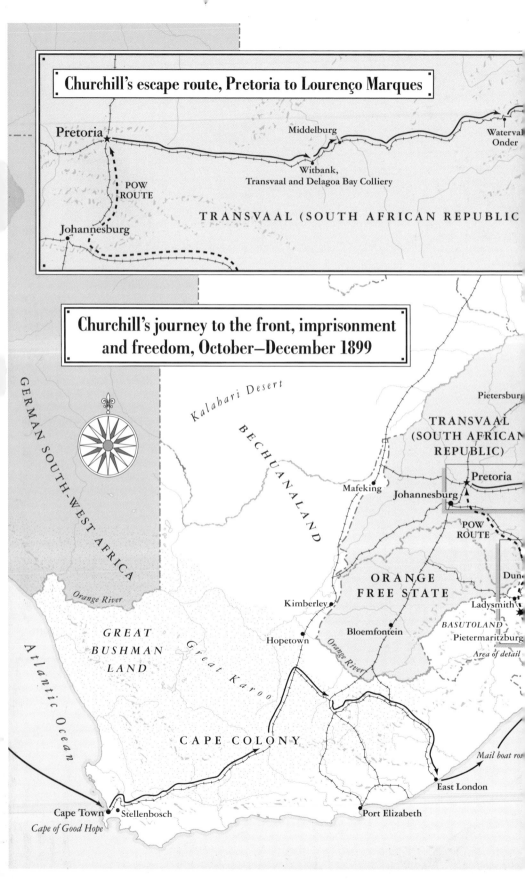

Churchill's escape route, Pretoria to Lourenço Marques

Pretoria

POW
ROUTE

Johannesburg

Middelburg

Witbank,
Transvaal and Delagoa Bay Colliery

Waterval
Onder

TRANSVAAL (SOUTH AFRICAN REPUBLIC

Churchill's journey to the front, imprisonment
and freedom, October–December 1899

GERMAN SOUTH-WEST AFRICA

Kalabari Desert

BECHUANALAND

Mafeking

Johannesburg

Pietersburg

TRANSVAAL
(SOUTH AFRICAN
REPUBLIC)

Pretoria

POW
ROUTE

Orange River

GREAT
BUSHMAN
LAND

Great Karoo

Kimberley

Hopetown

Orange River

ORANGE
FREE STATE

Bloemfontein

Dun

Ladysmith

BASUTOLAND
Pietermaritzburg

Area of detail

Atlantic Ocean

CAPE COLONY

Mail boat ro

East London

Cape Town • Stellenbosch

Port Elizabeth

Cape of Good Hope